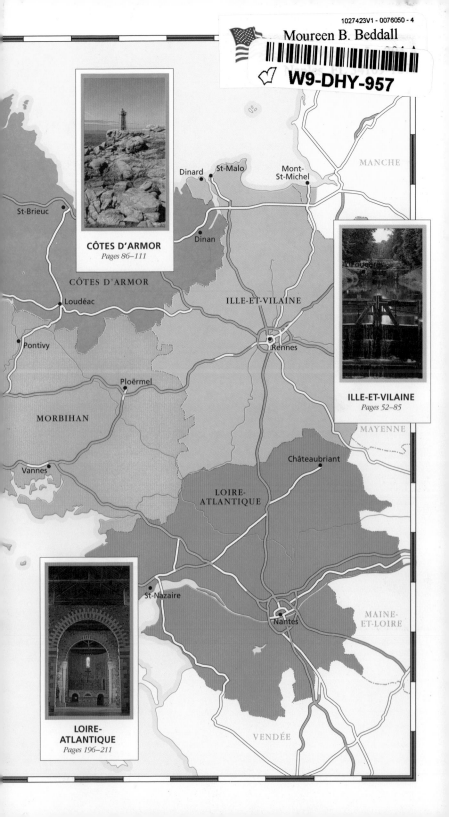

MANCHE

Dinard St-Malo Mont-
St-Michel

St-Brieuc

CÔTES D'ARMOR
Pages 86–111

Dinan

CÔTES D'ARMOR

ILLE-ET-VILAINE

Loudéac

Rennes

Pontivy

ILLE-ET-VILAINE
Pages 52–85

Ploërmel

MORBIHAN

MAYENNE

Châteaubriant

Vannes

LOIRE-
ATLANTIQUE

St-Nazaire

MAINE-
ET-LOIRE

Nantes

**LOIRE-
ATLANTIQUE**
Pages 196–211

VENDÉE

EYEWITNESS TRAVEL
BRITTANY

EYEWITNESS TRAVEL

BRITTANY

DK

LONDON, NEW YORK,
MELBOURNE, MUNICH AND DELHI
www.dk.com

PRODUCED BY Hachette Tourisme, Paris, France
EDITORIAL DIRECTOR Cécile Boyer
PROJECT EDITOR Catherine Laussucq
ART DIRECTOR JAD-Hersienne
DESIGNERS Maogani
CARTOGRAPHY Fabrice Le Goff

CONTRIBUTORS
Gaëtan du Chatenet, Jean-Philippe Follet,
Jean-Yves Gendillard, Éric Gibory, Renée Grimaud,
Georges Minois

Dorling Kindersley Limited
PUBLISHING MANAGERS Jane Ewart, Fay Franklin
ENGLISH TRANSLATION & EDITOR Lucilla Watson
DTP Jason Little, Conrad van Dyk
PRODUCTION Sarah Dodd

Reproduced in Singapore by Colourscan
Printed and bound in China by Toppan Printing Co. (Shenzhen Ltd).

First American Edition, 2003
09 10 9 8 7 6 5 4 3 2 1
Published in the United States by
DK Publishing, 375 Hudson Street,
New York, New York 10014

Reprinted with revisions 2005, 2007, 2009

Copyright © 2003, 2009 Dorling Kindersley Limited, London

PUBLISHED IN GREAT BRITAIN BY DORLING KINDERSLEY LIMITED

A CATALOG RECORD FOR THIS BOOK IS AVAILABLE
FROM THE LIBRARY OF CONGRESS.

ISSN 1542-1554
ISBN 978-0-75666-094-9

FLOORS ARE REFERRED TO THROUGHOUT IN ACCORDANCE WITH
EUROPEAN USAGE; IE THE "FIRST FLOOR" IS THE FLOOR ABOVE
GROUND LEVEL.

Front cover main image: boats moored in Roscoff harbour

We're trying to be cleaner and greener:

- we recycle waste and switch things off
- we use paper from responsibly managed forests whenever possible
- we ask our printers to actively reduce water and energy consumption
- we check out our suppliers' working conditions – they never use child labour

Find out more about our values and best practices at www.dk.com

---

**The information in every
DK Eyewitness Travel Guide is checked regularly.**

Every effort has been made to ensure that this book is as up-to-date as possible at the time of going to press. Some details, however, such as telephone numbers, opening hours, prices, gallery hanging arrangements and travel information are liable to change. The publishers cannot accept responsibility for any consequences arising from the use of this book, nor for any material on third party websites, and cannot guarantee that any website address in this book will be a suitable source of travel information. We value the views and suggestions of our readers very highly. Please write to: Publisher, DK Eyewitness Travel Guides, Dorling Kindersley, 80 Strand, London WC2R 0RL, Great Britain.

◁ **A beach at Brignogan, on the Pointe de Pontusval, Finistère**

CONTENTS

Santig Du, Cathédrale
St-Corentin, Quimper

INTRODUCING BRITTANY

Detail of traditional costume,
pardon of St-Anne-d'Auray

The impressive 13th-century Fort la Latte, on the Côtes d'Armor

BRITTANY REGION BY REGION

The Mer Blanche at Bénodet, a popular resort in Southern Finistère

TRAVELLERS' NEEDS

Detail of a stained-glass window, Cathédrale St-Corentin, Quimper

SURVIVAL GUIDE

A picturesque street in the fortified and well-preserved town of Vitré

Château de Josselin, in the Morbihan (pp192–3)

INTRODUCING
BRITTANY

DISCOVERING BRITTANY

his sea-buffeted peninsula jutting out from the corner of northwest France holds fast to its distinct personality. Mysterious prehistoric alignments, fascinating parish closes and medieval fortresses await discovery. It is the long jagged coastline which

Breton woman in costume

really distinguishes this "land of the sea", however. Sunbathe in sandy coves and marvel at pink granite cliffs. Explore modern, dynamic cities and bustling ports – sampling the fresh seafood – then escape to remote, flower-covered islands inhabited only by seabirds.

White, sheltered sands flanking the Pointe du Grouin promontory

ILLE-ET-VILAINE

• Mont-St-Michel and the northern coastline
• Lively capital Rennes
• Magical Paimpont forest

Ille-et-Vilaine's short northern coastline rewards beach-lovers and sightseers alike. Hiking along the **Sentiers des Douaniers** *(p76)* cliff path leads to the rocky promontory of the **Pointe du Grouin** *(p77)*, ablaze with wild flowers and surrounded by sheltered coves. Seafood-fans should make a detour to **Cancale** *(p77)*, for the fabulous oysters and mussels on offer. To the east, the romantic silhouette of the **Abbaye du Mont-St-Michel** *(pp74–5)* rises magestically from the water.

Must-see **St-Malo** *(pp78–83)* is a bustling port, famous for its walled citadel. Wander around the ramparts and absorb an atmosphere of pirates and swashbuckling corsairs. Nearby sits well-to-do **Dinard** *(p84)*, a chic resort town with aristocratic airs.

Rennes *(pp56–61)*, the Breton capital, lies inland and combines grand civic

architecture, medieval streets and a thriving nightlife.

At the western corner, stroll through the enchanted **Forêt de Paimpont** *(p62)*, haunted by tales of Merlin and Arthur.

Baskets of glistening oysters, fresh from the sea off Cancale

CÔTES D'ARMOR

• Côte de Granit Rose
• Colourful Île de Bréhat
• Medieval towns

This spectacular coastline, the **Côte de Granit Rose**, takes its name from the bizarrely shaped pink-hued rock formations found on the shore between **Paimpol**

(p99) and **Trébeurden** *(p94)*. Take the old coastguard's path that starts out from the candy-floss seaside world of **Perros-Guirec** *(p95)* to see the most curiously-shaped examples, or head to **Treguier** *(pp100–1)* Gothic cathedral to admire its rosy pink needle-like spire.

Nature-lovers are spoiled for choice with the **Cap Fréhel** *(p107)*, where guillemots and oystercatchers can be spyed from the gorse-covered headland, and the **Île de Bréhat** *(p98)*, an artists' retreat whose gentle micro-climate is a haven for an array of wild flowers. Bicycles can be hired on the island; no cars are allowed.

Inland, head for the medieval delights of pretty river-side **Dinan** *(pp108–11)* and **Moncontour** *(p104)*. Evoke a feudal atmosphere with a pre-dinner walk along the ramparts.

NORTHERN FINISTÈRE

• Fine coastline walks
• Fascinating parish closes
• Château de Kerjean

The landscape of Northern Finistère's coastal region is diverse and ideal for walking or touring by car. There are tempting sandy beaches, best avoided in peak season, at **Carantec** *(p120)* and **Plouescat** *(p122)* while the **Côte des Abers** *(pp126–7)* is scarred with creeks and estuaries waiting to be explored. Moving westwards, the landscape becomes wild and stormy with lighthouses guarding jagged reefs. At the weather-beaten westerly point, the "End of the Earth", lies the **Ouessant Archipelago** *(pp129–31)*, a series of largely uninhabited islands. Ouessant, the largest island, has a footpath circling the headland and an intriguing open-air museum.

Inland, the lush, sweeping countryside is scattered with **parish closes** *(pp138–9)*, the finest lying in the Elorn Valley. Be sure to inspect the ornately illustrated interiors and intricately carved calvaries of these remarkable 16th-century enclosures.

Historical treasures are also on offer at the charming **Château de Kerjean** *(pp124–5)*, one of Brittany's finest manor houses.

Seaward view of motorboats moored at Port-Tudy on the Île de Groix

Colourful timbered buildings in the old town quarter of Quimper.

SOUTHERN FINISTÈRE

- **Breton culture in Quimper**
- **Stormy cliffs, sandy beaches**
- **Walled town of Concarneau**

The capital of Cornouaille, **Quimper** *(pp158–9)* is the most Celtic of Brittany's towns. Look out for *bagadou* music, locally-made faience pottery, and stop to savour the most quintessential of Breton food, the *crêpe*. Enjoy the party with locals in costume during the Fête de Cornouaille in July.

This region contains myriad coastal delights, from the picturesque fishing ports and uncluttered sandy bays on the **Crozon peninsula** *(p146)* to the bleak craggy outcrops of the **Pointe du**

Raz *(p153)* and on to the sheltered sands of resorts such as **Bénodet** *(p165)* and the **Îles de Glénan** *(p157)* with its fantastic diving. Brittany's age-old marine industry still flourishes at the port town of **Concarneau** *(pp166–9)*, with its old town within ramparts. For the freshest fish, do not miss the Friday morning market.

MORBIHAN

- **Island-hopping from the Golfe du Morbihan**
- **Medieval Vannes**
- **Carnac megaliths**

The **Golfe du Morbihan** *(pp182-5)*, or "Little Sea" is a mud-rimmed tidal lagoon dotted with islands. All year round it draws countless nature-lovers to observe the varied bird species and vast range of marine and animal life. In summer, the waters become a mass of sailing boats and pleasure craft navigating between the multitude of verdant islands, including the lovely **Belle-Île-en-Mer** *(pp176–7)*, boasting sandy beaches and the **Île de Groix** *(p175)*, home to the only convex beach in Europe.

The other great attraction is the lively town of **Vannes** *(pp186–9)* with its pretty old-quarter and narrow medieval streets.

Morbihan oozes prehistory with the prime megalithic site being at **Carnac** *(pp178–9)*. This spine-tingling group of alignments, facing the sea, is best viewed at sunset.

LOIRE-ATLANTIQUE

- **Nantes, vibrant metropolis**
- **The Grande Brière park**
- **Châteaubriant & Ancenis**

Slicing through from east to west, the mighty Loire river gives this most southerly region its name. Upstream from the coast, city-slickers will love the dynamic atmosphere of **Nantes** *(pp204–9)*, once the historic capital of Brittany, and its wealth of top-class restaurants, shops and museums.

North from the river's mouth, the **Parc Régional de Grande Brière** *(pp202–3)* is a nature reserve of reed beds and canals and offers great walking, fishing and bird-watching. Upstream lie the border castles **Châteaubriant**, *(p211)*, which once defended Brittany from invading forces, and **Ancenis** *(p211)*, in the midst of fragrant vineyards.

Châteaubriant castle, peeking through the surrounding forest

Putting Brittany on the Map

Surrounded by 2,863 km (1,779 miles) of coastline, Brittany covers an area of 34,000 sq km (13,125 sq miles), or 6 per cent of French territory. It has over 4 million inhabitants (7 per cent of the French population) including Loire-Atlantique, and a population density of 119 per sq km (308 per sq mile). Over the last 25 years, Brittany's population has increased faster than the national average. The westernmost point of France, Brittany has become an economic hub of international importance. Its growing prosperity is paralleled by a strong cultural identity.

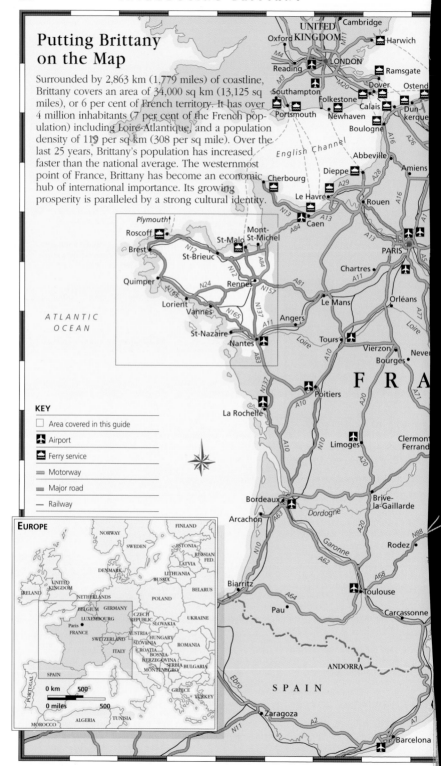

KEY

☐ Area covered in this guide

✈ Airport

⛴ Ferry service

▬ Motorway

▬ Major road

— Railway

EUROPE

0 km   500

0 miles   500

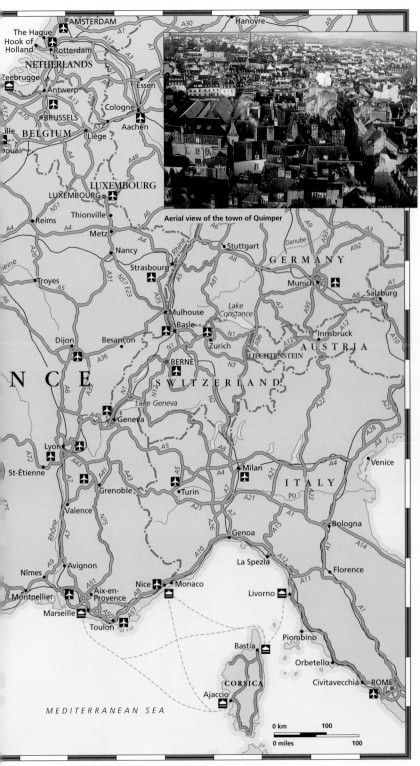

Aerial view of the town of Quimper

MEDITERRANEAN SEA

| 0 km | 100 |
| 0 miles | 100 |

A PORTRAIT OF BRITTANY

With its eventful history, contrasting landscapes, diverse economy and exceptionally rich cultural heritage, Brittany is a multifaceted region. While Breton traditions are very much alive, and while the region is famous for its menhirs, Brittany has also embraced the technological revolutions of the modern age. It is, for example, a major centre of the electronics industry.

Brittany consists of two distinct areas: a coastal region and an inland area. This is reflected in the Celtic names Armor, meaning "country by the sea", and Argoat, "wooded country". The coastline consists of a succession of cliffs, dunes, estuaries, mud flats and marsh land. The westernmost point of France, Brittany sinks beneath the sea, extended by a continental shelf. To the north, this shelf rises to form the British Isles. To the south, it extends along the coast of Brittany.

Since ancient times, this maritime region has provided rich fishing grounds. Today, the abundant fish stocks here are still a mainstay of the Breton economy. Another is the seaweed that grows along the coast and that is used by the food, pharmaceuticals and cosmetics industries.

Bordered by the English Channel and the Atlantic Ocean, Brittany is closely associated with seafaring. From the monks that sailed from Britain in their makeshift boats to evangelize Armorica (the old name for western Brittany), to the international yachtsmen of today, and including some great explorers and notorious privateers, Brittany's seamen have an illustrious place in the annals of European seafaring.

Young woman from Fouesnant

Stately ships at the Fête Internationale de la Mer et des Marins, a major event held in Brest every four years

◁ Procession, with parish banners and traditional costume, at the Grand Pardon in Quimper

Breton lace for sale at a market in Ste-Anne-d'Auray, in the Morbihan

It was shipbuilding and metalworking that stripped the Argoat region of most of its trees, which had already been heavily exploited since Roman times. Only 10 per cent of Brittany's primeval forest remains today.

A DIVERSE ECONOMY

Bretons have never been daunted by harsh natural elements. They went as far as Newfoundland and Iceland during the peak deep-sea fishing years of the 19th century, then, following the collapse of that trade, turned to factory ships, which concentrated on the Atlantic coastlines of Africa, Morocco,

Old advertising poster for Béghin-Say sugar

Mauritania, Senegal and South America. Local coastal fishing, by contrast, has proved more resistant to economic instability. However, while the industry still involves three-quarters of Breton fishing vessels, it has to contend with foreign imports, falling prices, dwindling fish stocks, industrial pollution, periodic oil spillages and competition from fish farming. The industry is now undergoing reorganization in order to strengthen its infrastructure.

While fishing has been under threat for some 50 years, agriculture, food crops and tourism underpin the region's economy. Brittany is the foremost milk producer in France. It also provides a quarter of the country's livestock and is a prime producer of fruit and vegetables. Breton produce is marketed under such well-known brand names as Saupiquet, Béghin-Say, Petit Navire, Paysans Bretons, Père Dodu and Hénaff (a famous pâté). Manufacturing and the service industry are also well developed. One Breton in five works in manufacturing or the building

Plage du Casino, one of the beautiful beaches at St-Quay-Portrieux, on the Côtes d'Armor

trade, while one in two works in retailing, the service industry or administration. High-tech industries have multiplied and many technological innovations have been developed in the region. Brittany is also one of the most popular tourist destinations in France.

A CULTURE REVIVED

Traditional Breton music underwent a major revival in the

Breton woman at the Festival Interceltique in Lorient

1960s thanks to Alan Stivell, Kristen Noguès, Gilles Servat and Tri Yann, who, with others, have been prominent among the *bagadou*, as Breton musical groups are known. For several years now, a second wave in the revival of Breton music has turned certain recordings into bestsellers. Denez Prigent, the pioneer of this generation, has also played a major role in the revival of traditional Breton dance and *festou-noz*, or popular Breton dance festivals.

However, the music scene in Brittany goes well

Street sign in Quimper

beyond traditional forms. In terms of their importance, rock festivals such as the Transmusicales in Rennes, the Route du Rock in St-Malo, and the Festival des Vieilles Charrues in Carhaix, are on a par with the great Festival Interceltique in Lorient.

In parallel with the Breton cultural revival of the 1960s and 1970s, the Breton language has also been re-invigorated, thanks most notably to the establishment of bilingual schools (known as Diwan). Although only a minority of Bretons support this revival, the whole population is aware of Armorica's great literary heritage.

The growth of high-tech establishments can seem incongruous in this land of menhirs, Romanesque chapels, Gothic churches, fortified castles, coastal forts and 18th-century manor houses. Since Neolithic times, when menhirs were raised, and cairns, megalithic monuments and other passage graves were built, religion has imbued local culture. Romanesque churches appeared in the 11th and 12th centuries, but the golden age of religious architecture came in the 13th century, with the Gothic period.

If religion has left its mark on the landscape of Brittany, so has secular life. Throughout the Middle Ages, local noblemen, engaged in wars with France and England, built fortresses and citadels. Indeed, Brittany is one of the regions of France with the greatest number of historic monuments. These, with the local traditions of furniture-making, textiles, gastronomy and painting, contribute to Brittany's fabulously rich cultural heritage.

The Roche aux Fées, one of Brittany's finest megalithic monuments, in the Ille-et-Vilaine

Landscape and Birds of Brittany

Montagu's harrier

Brittany attracts more sea birds than any other coastal region of France. At the end of the summer, birds that have nested in northern Europe begin to appear on the coast of Brittany. While some species continue on their southern migrations to spend the winter in warmer climates, many stay in Brittany until the early spring, when, together with birds newly returned from the south, they fly north once again to breed.

Male and female razorbills

FLAT, SANDY COASTLINE

Plants growing on beaches and dunes can withstand saline conditions. Sea rocket and several species of orach grow on the beaches. Among the grasses that take root on the dunes and prevent them from being eroded by wind, are spurge, sea holly, convolvulus and gillyflowers.

The ringed plover *patrols sandy beaches, where it feeds on marine worms, sandhoppers and small molluscs.*

The European bee-eater *is seen in Brittany from April to September. It overwinters south of the Sahara.*

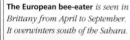

The sanderling, *which breeds in northern Europe, arrives in Brittany in August. It will either spend the winter there or fly south to Africa.*

BAYS AND MARSHY COASTS

Sandy, muddy coastal areas are covered with greyish, low-growing vegetation such as glasswort, salt-wort and obione, and sometimes with the purple-flowering sea lavender. These plants thrive in saline, waterlogged ground, which is washed by the tide twice a day.

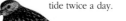

Sandpipers *move about in large flocks, constantly probing the mud with their beaks.*

Herring gulls *nest in northern Europe. At the end of August, they arrive in Brittany, where they spend the winter.*

The pied oystercatcher *can be seen in Brittany all year round. It feeds mostly on mussels, cockles and winkles.*

THE GUILLEMOT

This diving sea bird, with black and white plumage, a short neck and slender wings, spends the winter on the coasts of the English Channel and Atlantic Ocean. It nests in colonies on cliffs at Cap Fréhel and Cap Sizun, at Camaret and on the Sept-Îles, laying a single egg on a rocky ledge. It can also be seen on isolated rocks, often with penguins and kittiwakes. During the breeding season, its cry is a strident cawing. The young bird takes to the water 20 days after hatching, but begins to fly only at two months of age. It feeds mainly on fish, which it catches out at sea by diving to depths of more than 50 m (165 ft).

A colony of guillemots

CLIFFS AND ROCKY COASTS

Particular types of plants grow on the cliffs. They include sea pinks, the pink-flowering campion, golden rod and the yellow-flowering broom, as well as sea squill, small species of fern and many varieties of different-coloured lichen.

HEATHLANDS OF THE INTERIOR

For much of the year, various species of heathers cover Brittany's heathlands with a carpet of pink, which contrasts with the yellow flowers of the gorse and broom. The heathlands are also dotted with thickets of bramble and dog-rose.

The fulmar *spends most of its time at sea. It nests on the ledges of sheer cliffs.*

The puffin *feeds on fish that it catches far out at sea. In spring, it excavates deep burrows where the female lays a single white egg.*

The hen-harrier *preys on voles and small birds, which it finds in open land.*

The curlew *migrates from June onwards to the Atlantic coast, where large numbers spend the winter.*

The sheerwater's *only nesting grounds in France are in Brittany – on the Sept-Îles and in the archipelagos of Ouessant and Houat.*

The warbler *feeds all year round on small insects and spiders.*

Rural Architecture

Finial on gateway pillar

The scenic appeal of the Breton countryside owes much to its picturesque old houses, which seem to be fixed in time. Their appearance varies markedly according to topography, available materials and local traditions. In Upper Brittany, houses were built in rows, standing gable to gable so as to form rectangular groups *(longères)*. Typical of Lower Brittany is the *pennti*, a more compact house, with contiguous outbuildings, such as byres and coach houses surrounding the yard and providing shelter from the prevailing wind. Until the mid-19th century, these modest houses rarely had an upper floor. Thatched and asymmetrical, they blend harmoniously with the surrounding fields, heath and woodland.

Windows, *which are narrow and relatively few, are usually framed by dressed stones. They were once closed from within by wooden shutters.*

Chimneys are built into the gable wall.

The coping stone, sometimes decoratively carved, crowns the apex of the gable.

Lintels *above older windows are bevelled and sometimes have an ogee arch, a legacy of the Gothic style. Such windows are typical of manor houses.*

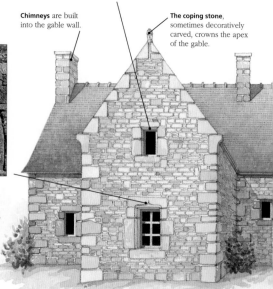

EXTERIOR STAIRWAYS

Several types of exterior staircase can be seen on Breton country houses. Many houses in the Léon and Vannes areas have a stairway parallel to the façade. The stairway, covered with an awning, led up to the loft, where hay and other provisions might be stored. The space beneath the steps was sometimes occupied by a pigsty. In plainer houses, the stairway, which often had no awning, was set in the angle of two buildings.

Steps parallel to the façade

Steps set between buildings, with no awning

AROUND THE HOUSE

Certain integral features of the rural Breton house are to be found not inside its walls but outside. One is the bread oven, the style of which has remained almost unchanged since the Middle Ages. Because of the danger of fire, the oven was often located away from the house. The granite trough, a traditional piece of equipment in Lower Brittany, served as a drinking trough for animals and was also used as a mortar in which fodder was ground before it was given to horses.

Granite drinking-trough or mortar

Bread oven with small recess

The ridge of the roof *was sometimes finished with a row of slates – known as* kribenn *in Breton. The slates may be carved into shapes such as cats or birds, or into dates or initials.*

HOUSES WITH EXTENSIONS

Many houses in Finistère have an extension – known as *apoteiz or kuz taol* in Breton – that protrudes 4 to 5 m (13 to 16 ft) from the façade. This additional space was used to store the table, benches and sometimes a box-bed, so as to create more space around the hearth.

Blocks of hewn stone were used as cornerstones in both houses and enclosure walls.

The granite doorway, *with a lintel consisting of three voussoirs (blocks of curved stone), is one of the most typical of Brittany.*

Dormer windows *are a relatively late feature of rural Breton houses. They did not appear until the 1870s.*

Religious Architecture

Detail of a choir stall

Brittany boasts several abbeys, nine cathedrals, some 20 large churches, about 100 parish closes and thousands of country chapels. This rich heritage is proof not only of the strength of religious faith but also of the skill of local builders. The golden age of religious architecture in Brittany occurred in the 16th and 17th centuries, when buildings were profusely decorated. Porches and rood screens sprouted motifs carved in oak, limestone or *kersanton*, a fine-grained granite that is almost impervious to the passage of time.

Calvary at Notre-Dame-de Tronoën (see p154)

PRE-ROMANESQUE AND ROMANESQUE (6TH–8TH C.)

The Romanesque style reached Brittany after it had become established in Anjou and Normandy, reaching its peak in about 1100 with the building of abbeys, priories and modest churches. A distinctive feature of these buildings is the stylized carvings on the capitals of columns.

Crypt of the Église St-Mélar in Lanmeur

Capital with carved leaf motif.

The cloister *of the Abbaye de Daoulas, restored in 1880, is one of the finest examples of Romanesque architecture in Brittany.*

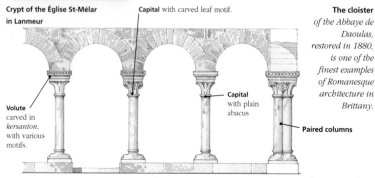

Volute carved in *kersanton*, with various motifs.

Capital with plain abacus

Paired columns

EARLY GOTHIC (13TH–14TH C.)

At a time when new buildings in the Romanesque style were still being constructed, the Gothic style and the art of the stained-glass window took root in Brittany. Buildings in this new, restrained style, shaped by Norman and English influences, were based on a rectangular or T-shaped plan, and had a tall steeple.

Statue of a bishop

North tower, left unfinished.

Buttresses

Foliate architrave

West front, built in the 12th century

Stained-glass, Cathédrale St-Samson, Dol-de-Bretagne

Dol's cathedral, *a fine example of Breton Gothic architecture, shares features in common with Coutances Cathedral in Normandy and with Salisbury Cathedral in England.*

FLAMBOYANT GOTHIC (14TH–15TH C.)

As an expression of their political power, the dukes and noblemen of Brittany funded the decoration of Gothic churches. These buildings thus acquired elegant chapels and finial belfries, carved doorways, wall paintings and beautiful rose windows.

Trefoil window

Rood screen in the Basilique du Folgoët

The Porche du Peuple of the Cathédrale St-Tugdual in Tréguier features some fine examples of 14th-century decorative carving.

Quatrefoil tracery framed by two trefoils.

Tierce-point arch divided into two trilobe arches.

BRETON RENAISSANCE (16TH C.)

The Flamboyant Gothic style was gradually superseded by a new, markedly purer style. Adopted by architects, metalworkers and sculptors, the Breton Renaissance style combined that of the Loire and that of Italy. In Lower Brittany, the fashion for parish closes and open belfries became established.

Figures of the 12 apostles.

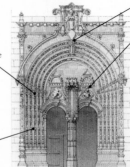

Arches decorated with secular motifs.

Bust of Francis I set within a scallop shell.

West door *of the Basilique Notre-Dame-du-Bon-Secours in Guingamp (1537–90).*

Pilaster with lozenge decoration.

Pediment, in the Baroque style, over the archway.

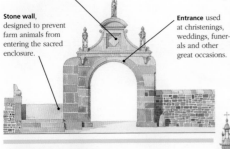

Stone wall, designed to prevent farm animals from entering the sacred enclosure.

Entrance used at christenings, weddings, funerals and other great occasions.

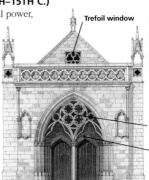

Detail of the rood screen of the church at La Roche Maurice

The ceremonial entrance *to the parish close of the Église St-Miliau in Guimiliau, one of the most important in northern Finistère.*

BAROQUE (17TH C.)

The Counter-Reformation brought out a taste for extravagant church decoration. This took the form of statues of apostles, dramatic depictions of the Pietà, highly ornate pulpits, Baroque altarpieces and garlanded columns. There are around 1,300 churches with such Baroque decoration in Brittany.

Finials

Broken pediment

Fluted columns

Statue of St Derrien flanked by the heads of two angels.

The great porch *(1645–55) of the church at Commana, whose interior furnishings are in an extravagant Baroque style, still has many Renaissance features.*

Breton Music

As it continues to grow in popularity, Breton music goes from strength to strength. In the 1990s, *L'Héritage des Celtes* and *Again*, two of Alan Stivell's albums, sold in their thousands, the instrumentalist Dan Ar Braz has twice been awarded the prestigious Victoire de la Musique, and the techno specialist Denez Prigent has won critical acclaim. In Brittany, music is a central aspect of popular culture. Almost 70 per cent of French traditional musicians are Bretons, and in Brittany new music venues open at a faster rate than anywhere else in France. Celtic heritage lives on.

BREST

FESTIVAL-CONCOURS NATIONAL DE MUSIQUE

4.5.6 JUIN 1932

Poster *advertising a music festival in Brest in 1932.*

TRADITIONAL INSTRUMENTS

The bagpipes and the bombard are the only two specifically Breton musical instruments. Although others are played by Breton musicians, the bagpipes and bombard, sometimes accompanied by a drum or tambourine, are the traditional combination.

Drum

The bombard, *a wind instrument similar to the oboe, is made of ebony or fruitwood.*

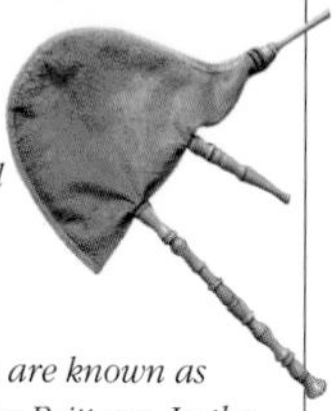

The Breton bagpipe *is increasingly neglected in favour of the larger Scottish bagpipes.*

Bagpipes *are known as biniou in Brittany. In the Guérande region and in the Breton fenlands of the Vendée they are known as veuze.*

Irish transverse flute

The Celtic harp, *sacred instrument of bards and Druids, captivated audiences throughout antiquity and the Middle Ages.*

The diatonic accordion, *known as bouëze in Brittany, has gradually replaced the old concertina that was once seen mostly in rural areas.*

Sonneurs *are players of Breton and Scottish bagpipes who traditionally perform together. In the early 20th century, some sonneurs learned to play the clarinet – popularly known as "tronc de choux" (cabbage stalk) – the accordion and later the saxophone. Sonneurs once made their living from music.*

Tri Yann, *a band that celebrated its 30th anniversary in 2001, practises the Breton musical tradition of extemporization. For the second time since the band came into existence, a woman has replaced one of its founders.*

Gilles Servat *gave a fresh boost to Breton music during the 1970s.*

Alan Stivell *has recorded over 20 albums since his* Reflets *was released in 1970.*

Scottish bagpipes

Dan Ar Braz, *from Quimper, has twice won the* Victoire de la Musique. *He has represented France at the Eurovision Song Contest and he now attracts a large audience. Describing the music that he plays, he prefers to call it the music of Brittany rather than traditional Breton music.*

BRETON ORCHESTRAS

Bagadou, or Breton orchestras, feature bombards, bagpipes and drums. It is these orchestras that are responsible for keeping alive Breton musical tradition. Among the most famous *bagadou* are those of Landerneau and Lann Bihoué.

THE CONTEMPORARY SCENE

The young generation understands that it is new kinds of music that will help Breton traditions survive. Erik Marchand, who was born in Paris, learned Breton songs and then went on to join forces with gipsy and Oriental musicians. Kristen Nikolas gives Breton music a techno flavour. His band, Angel IK, freely mixes wild guitar-playing with Breton songs. Yann-Fanch Kemener, who began his career as a singer of Breton songs, now performs with jazz musicians. One of the most outstanding young talents is Denez Prigent. After specializing in *gwerzou* (ballads) and *kan ha diskan* (songs with descant), he is now exploring techno.

Denez Prigent

Breton Literature

Emgann Kergidu

Perhaps because of its melancholy mists and secret woodlands, or because of the peculiar light that bathes its windswept coastline, Brittany is a strangely inspirational land. How else to account for the unique alchemy that encourages the imagination to take wing and that instills an innate penchant for the mystical, the mysterious and the marvellous? All those Bretons who figure in the history of regional as well as French literature, have this characteristic, the inevitable consequence of life lived on the edge of the world.

The Life of St Nonne, a popular Breton mystery play

LITERATURE IN BRETON

Relatively little is known about medieval Breton literature. Besides a few glimpses gained from the charters compiled in abbeys and a single page from an obscure treatise on medicine dating from the late 8th century, no single Breton text survives to this day.

There is every evidence, however, that Armorican poets enjoyed a certain prestige in courtly circles and that their lays – ballads or poems set to music and accompanied on the harp – played an important part in the development of the chivalrous epics of the Middle Ages. It was, indeed, this Breton tradition that provided French minstrels with tales of the valour of Lancelot, the adventures of Merlin and other wonders of the Forêt de Paimpont *(see p62)*, the legendary Forêt de Brocéliande.

Barzhaz Breizh

plays, religious scenes, such as *Buez Santez Nonn*, which tells the story of the life of a saint, were enacted. Performed in the open air, they were extremely popular, especially in the Trégor. The actors, who might be clogmakers or weavers by trade, knew by heart entire tracts of the most dramatic plays, such as *Ar pevar mab Hemon (The Four Sons of Aymon)*, which was still being performed in about 1880.

Contemporary with this popular repertoire, a handful of long, erudite poems with sophisticated internal rhyming has survived, as well as a considerable body of literature (such as missals and books of hours) written by clergymen in imperfect Breton. For hundreds of years, the latter was ordinary people's only reading matter.

STORIES AND LEGENDS

The literary genre in which Bretons excelled was that of stories and legends. During long winter evenings and at country gatherings, woodcutters, beggars and spinners would weave stories of make-believe filled with fairytale princesses and such legendary figures as giants in glass castles. It was by listening to these imaginative storytellers that Théodore Hersart de la Villemarqué (1815–95), whose Breton name was Kervarker, and François-Marie Luzel, or Fañch An Uhel, (1821–95) compiled collections of Breton literature. The stories are, however, too good to be true: it is now known that neither man set them down as he heard them but that they polished and rounded off the stories.

At the end of the 19th century, Lan Inizan (1826–91) published *Emgann Kergidu*, an historic

MYSTERY PLAYS

The earliest surviving evidence of a true literary tradition dates from the 15th century, in the manuscripts of mystery plays. In these

Théodore Hersart de la Villemarqué, a great 19th-century recorder of Breton tales and legends

Per-Jakez Hélias, author of the novel *Le Cheval d'Orgueil*

account of events that occurred in the Léon district during the Terror *(see p46)*. Anatole Le Braz (1859–1926), meanwhile, explored Breton legends that are concerned with death.

BRETON CLASSICS

During the 1930s, three accomplished novelists – Youenn Drezen, Yeun ar Gow and Jakez Riou – demonstrated that Breton literature was not limited to the description of life in the countryside in times gone by. While their novels had only a small readership, those of Tanguy Malmanche enjoyed wider renown. Two poets also emerged: Yann-Ber Kalloc'h (1888–1917), a native of Vannes, with his moving *Ar en deulin (Kneeling)*, and Anjela Duval (1905–81), of the Trégor.

The most widely read Breton writer is Per-Jakez Hélias, who came to the notice of the general public in 1975 with *Le Cheval d'Orgueil (Horse of Pride)*, later translated into 20 languages.

LITERATURE IN FRENCH

Although they did not belong to the canon of Breton writers, three of the greatest 19th-century French authors were, in fact, of

THE BRETON LANGUAGE

Brezoneg, an ancient Celtic language that is related to Welsh, is spoken west of a line running from Plouha to Vannes. Although this linguistic frontier has hardly changed since the 12th century, over recent generations Brezoneg has become much less widely spoken. In 1914, 90 per cent of the population of that part of Brittany spoke Brezoneg. After 1945, parents were encouraged to have their children speak French and, until 1951, Brezoneg was surpressed in schools. It was thus no longer passed down from parent to child. Today, although it is increasingly rare to hear Brezoneg spoken (only 240,000 Bretons over 60 know it well), it is attracting new interest. There are now bilingual schools (Diwan), an official Breton institute, and a Breton television channel (TV Breizh), all of which contribute to keeping Brezoneg alive.

Breton grammar books used in Diwan schools

Ernest Renan, noted for his writing on science and religion

Breton stock. Two were natives of St-Malo. One of these was the statesman, traveller and memoir-writer François René de Chateaubriand *(see p69)*, author of *Génie du Christianisme* and *Mémoires d'Outre-Tombe*. Describing his attachment to the region, he once said "It was in the woods near Combourg that I became what I am". The other was Félicité de Lamennais, whose social ideals included harnessing political liberalism to Roman Catholicism. At his manor house at St-Pierre-de-Plesguen, near Dinan, he

entertained a coterie of disciples. The third, Ernest Renan, author of *Vie de Jésus (Life of Jesus)*, often returned to his native Trégor, where, he said, "you can feel a strong opposition to all that is dull and flat".

In the 20th century, too, Breton soil spawned many writers of renown: they include the poets René-Guy Cadou, Eugène Guillevic and Xavier Grall, the essayist Jean Guéhenno, of Fougères, and the novelist Louis Guilloux, of St-Brieuc, whose *Le Sang Noir (Black Blood*, 1935) was hailed by critics as a work of major importance.

Louis Guilloux, author of *Le Sang Noir* and an active anarchist

Traditional Breton Costume

There were once 66 different types of traditional Breton costume and around 1,200 variations. Breton clothing differed from one small area to the next. In the 19th century, it was possible to tell at a glance the precise geographical origins of any Breton. Colours also indicated an individual's age and status: in Plougastel-Daoulas, young women wore a small flowery shawl, married women a shawl with squares, widows a white shawl, and, when they had lost a close relative, a winged headdress. Unmarried men wore green waistcoats, and married men, blue jackets.

Femmes de Plougastel au Pardon de Sainte-Anne by Charles Cottet (1903)

BIGOUDEN COSTUME

In the area of Pont-l'Abbé, capital of the Bigouden region, traditional costume is very uniform. Women were still wearing it as everyday dress in the early 20th century. According to their wealth, they either wore richly decorated, layered bodices or modest embroidered cuffs.

Shirt

Chupenn, a man's coat

Embroidered waistcoat

Embroidered sleeve

Lace gloves

Child's bonnet

Jewellery
In Cornouaille and western Brittany, the most popular pieces of jewellery were "pardon pins", brooches made of silver, copper or blown glass.

LACE AND EMBROIDERY

Aprons worn on feast days, women's bodices and men's waistcoats are richly embroidered with silk, metallic thread, and steel or glass beads. Executed in chain stitch, motifs include floral patterns featuring palmettes and fleur-de-lys, and stylized elements such as sun discs and concentric circles. They are always very bright, like the orange and yellow *plum paon* motifs that are typical of the Bigouden.

Lace-makers from Tréboul, in Finistère

Embroidery from Pont-l'Abbé

Embroidery from Quimper

Detail of a beaded costume

Newborn children, *represented here by dolls, were once all customarily dressed in a bonnet, gown and apron. Not until the age of five or six did boys swap their infant clothes for adult male clothing. Girls would start to wear a headdress from the time of their first communion.*

HEADWEAR

Traditional Breton headwear is extraordinarily diverse. This can be appreciated today only thanks to René-Yves Creston (1898–1964), an ethnologist who recorded its range before it ceased to be worn on a daily basis. Some headdresses had back-swept wings, others were tied at the chin with ribbons, and still others had "aircraft" or "lobster-tail" wings. Many women possessed two *koef*, or, in French, *coiffes* (headdresses), a small one made of lace netting that covered the hair, and a tall one, which was worn over the smaller one, though only on ceremonial occasions. The most spectacular headdresses are those of the Bigouden, which are almost 33 cm (13 in) high and which older women wear on Sundays. Men's hats are decorated with long velvet ribbons and sometimes with an oval buckle.

Small lace *coiffe*

Women's headdress

Apron

Brooch

Chain

Belt buckles, *like this heart-shaped example, were part of a man's costume. The waistcoat and trousers, which replaced the traditional baggy trousers in the mid-19th century, are tied at the waist by a belt.*

Men's waistcoats *were eye-catchingly sumptuous. In Plougastel, young men wore a green waistcoat under a purple jacket, and adult men a blue waistcoat, the hue being darker or paler according to their age. Men wore a purple waistcoat on their wedding day and at the christening of their first child.*

The back of the bodice *was decorated with flowers whose size indicated the wearer's status. A married woman's bodice featured gold thread, spangles and tinsel.*

Aprons, *worn to keep a woman's skirt clean, were originally plain rather than decorated. These voluminous working garments were made of ordinary fabric and were tied at the waist with a ribbon. Aprons were usually worn with a bib – a rectangular piece of fabric that covered the chest.*

BRITTANY THROUGH THE YEAR

In Brittany, every season has something to offer. In spring, towns and villages reawaken from their winter slumber: feast days in honour of patron saints and popular festivals mark this renewal. As the sun shines more brightly, heath and woodland come to life. Through the summer, the tourist season is in full swing,

Musician Festival Interceltique, Lorient

and every community holds its own *fest-noz* or pardon. The high point is the Festival Interceltique de Lorient, the greatest Celtic festival in France. By the autumn, the number of tourists begins to dwindle and festivals are fewer. Bretons ward off the rigours of winter by meeting in bistros or holding such events as the Transmusicales de Rennes.

SPRING

In Brittany, spring is a time of joyfulness. From March, watered by gentle showers, gorse blooms cover the landscape in a carpet of golden yellow. In May, broom comes into flower, with its lighter yellow blooms. Fruit and vegetables – including Brittany's famous artichokes – are piled high in the markets. The region is reborn, and welcomes the return of warm, sunny days.

APRIL

Salon du Livre *(mid-April)*, Bécherel, Ille-et-Vilaine. An antiquarian book festival held in a medieval town. Bookbinders, booksellers and second-hand dealers hold open house.

MAY

Festival En Arwen *(early May)*, Cléguérec, Morbihan. A festival of traditional Breton music, drawing many performers and enthusiasts.

Fields of gorse, thickly carpeted in flowers from March

SAINT-MALO
Étonnants Voyageurs
12ème festival international du livre

31 mai - 4 juin 2001

Advertisement for Étonnants Voyageurs, a festival held in St-Malo

Festival Étonnants Voyageurs *(first two weeks in May)*, St-Malo. The focus of this festival *(Amazing Explorers)*, held in the historic port of St-Malo, is travel writing and accounts of exploration. It features exhibitions, lectures and signing sessions. Organized by a group of enthusiasts, it has become a major cultural event, and is now taken to other countries.

SUMMER

As one of the most popular-tourist regions of France, Brittany receives a large number of visitors during the summer. Coastal resorts are busy, and bars and night-clubs are filled to capacity. Besides swimming in the sea or relaxing on the beach, going hiking or cycling, or taking a boat trip round the coast, there are many other activities for visitors to enjoy *(see pp256–9)*.

JUNE

Festival Art Rock *(mid-June)*, St-Brieuc, Côtes d'Armor. Concerts, exhibitions, shows and contemporary dance.

JULY

Festival Tombées de la Nuit *(early July)*, Rennes, Ille-et-Vilaine. Filled with musicians, comedians, mime artists and storytellers from all over the world, Rennes, the capital of Brittany, becomes a gigantic stage.

Contes et Légendes de Bretagne *(July–August)*, Carnac, Morbihan. Every Tuesday, against the backdrop of the menhir known as the Giant of Manio, a storyteller weaves beguiling Celtic tales.

Art dans les Chapelles *(early July to mid-September)*, Pontivy and environs, Morbihan. About 15 chapels in and around Pontivy, and dating from the 15th and 16th centuries, host

AVERAGE DAILY HOURS OF SUNSHINE

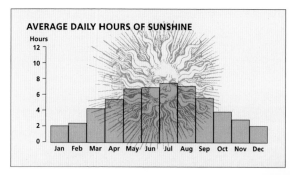

Hours
12
10
8
6
4
2
0

Jan Feb Mar Apr May Jun Jul Aug Sep Oct Nov Dec

Sunshine Chart
High pressure from the Azores gives southern Brittany more than 2,200 hours of sunshine per year. The north, by contrast, has only 1,700 hours per year. Coastal areas, where rainfall is lighter than in the interior, sometimes suffer from drought during the summer.

exhibitions of contemporary painting, sculpture and photography.

Troménie *(second Sunday in July)*, Locronan, southern Finistère. One of the largest and most elaborate pardons in Brittany.

Festival Médiéval *(14 July)*, Josselin, Morbihan. A day of medieval entertainment centred around the old market square, with troubadours and tumblers.

Festival des Vieilles Charrues *(mid-July)*, Carhaix-Plouguer, southern Finistère. Rock festival featuring both international stars and local bands. James Brown, Massive Attack and numerous others have performed in front of large audiences here.

Fête Internationale de la Mer et des Marins *(mid-July, every four years)*, Brest, northern Finistère. The largest tall ships regatta in the world, first held in 1992.

Fête de la Crèpe *(third week-end in July)*, Tronjoly-Gourin, southern Finistère. Pancake-tastings and lessons in how to made pancakes, held in the municipal park.

Fête des Remparts *(third weekend in July, every two years)*, Dinan, Côtes d'Armor. Historical reconstructions, theatrical farce, dancing, games, concerts, jousts and a procession in costume.

Grand Pardon *(26 July)*, Ste-Anne-d'Auray, Morbihan. The greatest Breton pilgrimage, with a following of a million.

Festival de Jazz *(last week of July)*, Vannes, Morbihan. Blues and jazz played by professional and amateur musicians are the festival's main attractions.

AUGUST

Fête des Fleurs d'Ajoncs *(first Sunday in August)*, Pont-Aven, southern Finistère. A picturesque procession in honour of flowering gorse, dating back to 1905.

Festival Interceltique *(first two weeks in August)*, Lorient, Morbihan. Musicians and other performers from Scotland, Ireland, the Isle of Man, Wales and Cornwall, Galicia and Asturia (in Spain), and, of course, Brittany gather for the largest Celtic festival in the world.

Fête internationale de la Mer et des Marins in Brest

Route du Rock *(mid-August)*, St-Malo, Ille-et-Vilaine. Held in the Fort de St-Père, a rock festival at the cutting edge of the genre.

Festival des Hortensias *(mid-August)*, Perros-Guirec, Côtes d'Armor. Accompanied by traditional music, festivities in honour of the hydrangea, whose deep blue flowers are prized and which thrives in Brittany's acid soil.

Fête des Filets Bleus *(mid-August)*, Concarneau, southern Finistère. Traditional Breton bands parade through the streets of the town, and a festival queen is chosen. The programme also includes concerts, shows and fishing competitions.

Fête de l'Andouille *(fourth Sunday in August)*, Guémené-sur-Scorff, Morbihan. The Confrérie des Goustiers de l'Andouille (sausage-makers' guild) celebrate this prized Breton delicacy.

Rock group at the Festival des Vieilles Charrues at Carhaix-Plouguer

AVERAGE RAINFALL

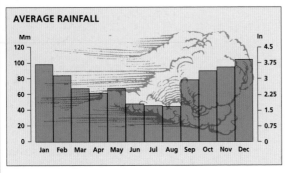

Rainfall
*The most elevated
regions of Brittany
receive up to
1,200 mm (47 in)
of rain, which falls
over an average of
200 days per year,
while the plateaux of
Lower Brittany
receive 800 mm
(31 in) of rainfall per
year. The heaviest
rainfall occurs in
autumn and winter.*

AUTUMN

Those of a romantic disposition who love open spaces will find this season particularly appealing. There are still many fine days. The equinox on 21/22 September marks the beginning of the great autumn tides, when large expanses of the sea bed are exposed. Rapidly changing weather and the dramatic ebb and flow of the sea also make for a landscape whose appearance alters by the hour. Inland, the leaves on the trees start to turn, catching the sunlight between scudding clouds. As tourists become fewer, Bretons return to their daily lives, anticipating winter.

SEPTEMBER

Championnat de Bretagne de Musique Traditionelle
(first weekend in September), Gourin, southern Finistère. The finest performers of tra-

ditional Breton music gather at the Domaine de Tronjoly to take part in marching, music and dancing competitions; these are held in two categories: *kozh* (with Breton pipes and bombards) and *bras* (with Scottish bagpipes and bombards). A *fest-noz* also takes place.

OCTOBER

Festival du Film Britannique *(early October)*, Dinard, Ille-et-Vilaine. The British film industry's producers and distributors come here to promote British cinema in France. The event attracts around 15,000 people.
Festival de Lanvallec *(second half of October)*, in the Trégor, Côtes d'Armor. The leading exponents of Baroque music perform in various churches in the region, particularly in Lanvallec, which has one of the oldest organs in Brittany.

Fête du Marron
(end of October), Redon, Ille-et-Vilaine. The town hosts a chestnut festival with a traditional fair, chestnut tastings and, most prominently, the largest *fest-noz* in Brittany. The Bogue d'Or, a musical contest in which the best traditional Breton musicians compete, takes place in the morning. In the evening, the winners give a performance, along with other traditional Breton music groups.
Quai des Bulles *(last week-end in October)*, St-Malo, Ille-et-Vilaine. An annual gathering attended by over 100 strip-cartoonists and animated cartoon producers, together with a following of enthusiasts. Showings of cartoon films and exhibitions also form part of the event. In the year 2000, when the festival marked its 20th year, the world's leading cartoonists and animators attended.

NOVEMBER

Festival des Chanteurs de Rue et Foire and St-Martin *(early November)*, Quintin, Côtes d'Armor. Since 1993, the St Martin's Fair, which dates back to the 15th century, has been held at the same time as this festival of street singers. Hawkers, entertainers and comedians re-enact historical scenes of daily life and singers perform time-honoured songs, with the audience joining in the chorus. Traditional Breton food is also on offer.

A signing session during the Quai des Bulles in St-Malo

AVERAGE MONTHLY TEMPERATURES

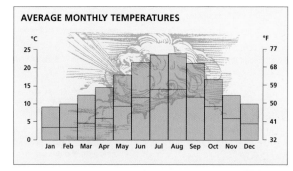

°C												°F
25												77
20												68
15												59
10												50
5												41
0	Jan	Feb	Mar	Apr	May	Jun	Jul	Aug	Sep	Oct	Nov	Dec	32

Temperatures
The chart shows the average minimum and maximum temperatures for each month. Average winter temperatures are between 6 and 8° C (43 and 46° F). Average summer temperatures are between 16 and 18° C (61 to 64° F).

WINTER

Winter brings periods of inclement weather, which become progressively more severe as the season advances. However, warm, moist air from the tropics can cause temperatures to rise to as much as 12° C (54° F), even in mid-January. Warm rainfall allows camellias to thrive, flowering in sheltered areas. In winter, the prevailing wind is from the northwest. Cold and strong, it batters the region in squally gusts. As an antidote to such tempestuous weather, Bretons hold rumbustious weekend festivals.

DECEMBER

Les Transmusicales *(early December)*, Rennes, Ille-et-Vilaine). The buzzing rock scene has spawned such artistes as Étienne Daho, Niagara, Marquis de Sade and a long list of bands that are well-known in France.

A still winter seascape in Brittany

For almost 25 years, this key festival has launched the careers of many British and American bands, as well as that of other musicians, such as the Icelandic singer Björk, who has performed in France since the start of her career. **Villages de Lumières** *(mid-December)*, Quessoy, Côtes d'Armor. A Christmas market, with such attractions as rides in horse-drawn carriages and displays of Christmas cribs, is held in the colourfully lit and decorated streets. Over

50,000 people come to enjoy this temporary fairyland.

FEBRUARY

Panoramas *(mid-February)*, Morlaix, northern Finistère. A festival introducing to the general public unknown singers and new talent in the field of rap and electronic music. Some established musicians also perform.

PUBLIC HOLIDAYS

New Year's Day
(1 January)

Easter Sunday and Easter Monday

Ascension (sixth Thursday after Easter)

Pentecost (second Monday after Ascension)

Labour Day (1 May)

Victory Day (8 May)

Bastille Day (14 July)

Assumption (15 August)

All Saints'Day (1 Nov)

Armistice Day (11 Nov)

Christmas Day (25 Dec)

A stall at the Christmas market in Brest

Pardons and Festou-noz

The term *pardon* dates from the Middle Ages, when popes granted indulgences (remissions of punishment for sin) to worshippers who came to church. The annual pardon later became a day of worship honouring a local patron saint, with a procession and pilgrimage. In rural areas, a large number of saints were venerated, and here, minor pardons have evolved into occasions when communities join together to celebrate. After mass, the confession of penitents and procession of banners, the secular *fest-noz*, with singing and dancing, begins.

Celtic cultural clubs, *which give displays at pardons, still perform dances that are specific to particular areas of Brittany.*

Gwenn ha du,
the Breton flag

The bagad
Playing bombards, bagpipes and drums, this group of musicians – the bagad – tours the streets. They provide dance music for the fest-noz.

Sonneurs, *bagpipe and bombard players, have always been an integral part of Breton festivities. Seated on a table or a large barrel, they took it in turns to play popular tunes both to accompany dancing and as entertainment during the outdoor banquet that traditionally followed a pardon.*

GOUEL AN EOST

In several parishes, pardons are also occasions when older people can relive the sights and sounds of a traditional harvest. Activities include threshing by traditional methods: threshers, truss-carriers and sheaf-binders set up the chaff-cutter and the winnowing machine, which separates the grain from the chaff, and harness horses to the circular enclosure where the grain is milled. A hearty buffet rounds off this *gouel an eost*.

Harvest festival

Traditional dancing *is not the exclusive preserve of Celtic cultural clubs. Far from sitting on the sidelines, local people and holiday-makers both eagerly join in, accompanied by the* sonneurs *and singers of* kan ha diskan *(songs with descant).*

Banners, *made of embroidered silk, are carried in procession during pardons. Each parish has its own banner, behind which the parishioners walk. This one belongs to the Chapelle Notre-Dame de Lambader, in Haut-Léon.*

A banner with the image of the patron saint of a parish.

The Troménie *at Locronan is not only a major pilgrimage but also a test of physical endurance for those who carry the banners. Dressed in traditional costume, for five hours they continuously circle a hill in the heat of July, holding aloft banners, statues and relics.*

TRO BREIZ

Held in honour of the seven saints – Samson, Malo, Brieuc, Paul Aurélien, Patern, Corentin and Tugdual – who established Christianity in Brittany, the *Tro Breiz* is not a modest parish pardon but a lengthy pilgrimage covering about 650 km (400 miles) and linking the towns of the seven saints. Pilgrims from all over the world have attended this event.

Modern banner, carried in honour of the well-known preacher Mikael an Nobletz *(see p127).*

The pardon of Ste-Anne-d'Auray *has become a spectacular event over the centuries, with a long procession of priests and pilgrims. After mass, they fervently sing Hail Marys and Breton hymns.*

Blessing the Sea
In villages around the coast of the Golfe du Morbihan, when a pardon takes place, the clergy boards a boat and blesses all the vessels in the harbour. This custom dates from the 19th century.

THE HISTORY OF BRITTANY

Brittany's long history, no less than its geography, has made it one of the most distinctive regions of France. It has a strong cultural identity, and, at the westernmost point of France, it has benefited from its location at the centre of Europe's Atlantic seaboard – between land and sea, and between Britain and France.

The borders of Brittany have altered often since ancient times. During the prehistoric period, the coastline was very different from what it is today. Many sites of human occupation, some of which date back 500,000 years, have been discovered in places that are now beneath the sea. During the glaciations of the early Quaternary period, the sea level was about 100 m (30 ft) lower than it is today.

Stone necklace, c. 4000-3500 BC

When the glaciers melted, about 10,000 years ago, the sea level rose dramatically. Large areas of land were flooded, creating the present coastline, which is indented by long narrow inlets – or rias – ancient river valleys flooded by the sea. It may be some remote memory of this cataclysmic event that gave rise to legends about submerged cities, like the town of Ys.

MEGALITH-BUILDERS

Traces of human occupation become more numerous at the beginning of the Neolithic period, around 5000 BC, when local populations adopted agriculture and a settled way of life. They made axes of polished granite, which were traded in the Rhône valley, in southeastern France, and in Britain. This was also a time of stable social organization, when impressive megalithic monuments were built. Skeletons and pottery were placed in megalithic tombs (menhirs), some in the form of burial chambers approached by a long corridor, consisting of huge blocks of stone covered by an earth mound. The oldest and most impressive of these megalithic monuments, the cairn at Barnenez (see p119), dates from 4600 BC. No less spectacular are the menhirs, standing stones that were probably connected to a religion involving astronomy. The most important dolmens are those at Carnac (see pp178–9). Some, like the Giant of Locmariaquer (see p180), are as much as 20 m (65 ft) high.

THE CELTS

In about 500 BC, the peninsula, which was then known as Armorica, or "country near the sea", was invaded by Celts. Five tribes settled there: the Osismes (in present-day Finistère), the Veneti (in the Morbihan), the Coriosolites (in the Côtes d'Armor), the Riedones (in the Ille-et-Vilaine),

TIMELINE

10,000 BC Sea levels begin to rise, flooding sites of human habitation

4000 BC–2000 BC Polished stone axes are made, at Plussulien and other sites

Polished jadeite axe

10,000 BC	5000 BC	4000 BC	3000 BC	2000 BC	1000 BC

5000 BC Start of the Neolithic period. The great megalithic tombs (dolmens) are built and menhirs erected

4600 BC The great burial mound at Barnenez is built

◁ **The mythical origins of the kingdom of Armorica, from Le Baud's *Chroniques de Bretagne* (1480–82)**

and the Namnetes (in the Loire-Atlantique). The Celts, who lived in villages and fortified settlements, were agriculturalists who also worked iron, minted coins and engaged in overseas trade. They were ruled by a warrior aristocracy and a priesthood, the Druids, at the head of a religion whose deities represented the forces of nature. Bards (poet-musicians) sang of the exploits of mythical heroes. Armorica gradually entered the annals of recorded history. Explorers from the Mediterranean, among them the Carthaginian Himilco (c. 500 BC) and the Greek merchant-explorer Pytheas (c. 320 BC), arrived on its shores.

Bronze figure of an ox, from a Roman villa at Carnac

of Romanization. Among them were Condate (now Rennes), Fanum Martis (Corseul), Condevincum (Nantes) and Darioritum (Vannes). While baths, amphitheatres and villas marked the influence of Roman civilization, Celtic and Roman gods were amalgamated. Rural areas, however, were less affected by the Roman presence. From AD 250–300, as the Roman Empire began to decline, instability set in. Raids by Frankish and Saxon pirates led to the desertion of towns. The coastline was ineffectually defended by forts, such as Alet (near St-Malo) and Le Yaudet (in Ploulec'h). As the 5th century dawned, Armorica was abandoned to its fate.

ROMAN ARMORICA

In 57 BC, the Romans occupied Armorica, as well as the rest of Gaul. However, in 56 BC, the Veneti rebelled and held the Romans at bay by taking refuge on the rocky promontories of the Atlantic coast. With difficulty, Julius Caesar routed them in a sea battle outside the Golfe du Morbihang.

For 400 years, Armorica, incorporated into the province of Lugdunensis, was under Roman domination. The province was divided into five areas *(pagi)*, corresponding to Celtic tribal territory. A network of roads was built and a few small towns established, which aided the process

Roman Venus from Crucuny, Carnac

ARRIVAL OF THE BRITONS

During the 6th century, large numbers of Britons from Wales and Cornwall crossed the English Channel to settle in Armorica, which they named "Little Britain", or "Brittany". This peaceful invasion continued for 200 years. Among the newcomers were many Christian monks, who introduced a Celtic variant of Christianity, distinct from Roman Christianity. Many isolated hermitages were built on small offshore islands, and monasteries were headed by an abbot who also acted as itinerant bishop. Among them were Brieuc, Malo, Tugdual (in Tréguier) and Samson (in Dol); with Gildas, Guénolé, Méen and Jacut, whose lives and miracles became the subject of hagiographies from the 8th century onwards, they inspired the religious traditions that survive today, marked by pilgrimages and pardons, such as the Troménie in Locronan *(see p153)*.

TIMELINE

500 BC	0	100	200	300
c. 500 BC The Celts reach Brittany	**57 BC** The Romans conquer Armorica	**1st and 2nd centuries** Armorica is Romanized	**3rd century** Saxon raids become more frequent	
	56 BC Julius Caesar defeats the Veneti in a naval battle			**4th century** The Romans withdraw from Armorica

Coins minted by the Veneti

St Corentin laying the foundation stone of Quimper Cathedral, before King Gradlon

It was these immigrants from Britain who introduced the typically Breton place names consisting of the prefix *plou*, or its derivatives *plo*, *plu*, *plé*, followed by a proper name or other word (as in Plougastel and Ploufragan). *Plou*, from the Latin *plebs* (the common people), refers to a community of Christians. *Lan* (as in Lannion and Lannilis) refers to a monastery. *Tré* (as in Trégastel), from the ancient British word *treb*, refers to a place of habitation. The concentration of these place names in western Brittany, and the frequency of those ending in *ac* in the eastern part of the region, from the Latin *acum* (as in Trignac and Sévignac), indicates a cultural duality. This is backed up by the coexistence of two languages: French, which is derived from Latin, east of a line running from La Baule to Plouha, and Breton to the west.

THE BRETON KINGDOM

From the 6th to the 10th century, the peninsula, now known as Britannia, fought off the attempts of Frankish kings who now controlled Gaul to dominate the region. Several times, Brittany was invaded by the Merovingians. Their influence was short-lived, however, and the Bretons kept their independence – ruled by warlike local chiefs or petty kings.

The powerful Carolingian dynasty could do no more than establish a buffer zone, the Marches, which extended from the Baie du Mont-St-Michel to the Loire estuary. From about 770, this was controlled by Roland, "nephew" of Charlemagne. In the 9th century, the Bretons established an independent kingdom, whose frontiers stretched to Angers in the east, Laval in the south and Cherbourg in the northwest. The kingdom was founded by Nominoë, who overcame Charles the Bald at the Battle of Ballon in 845. His son, Erispoë, succeeded him but was murdered in 857 by his cousin Salomon, whose reign, until 874, marked the peak of the short-lived Breton monarchy.

Brittany's political independence was strengthened by the clergy, who resisted the jurisdiction of the see of Tours. This was the great age of the Benedictine abbeys, rich centres of culture. Fine illuminated manuscripts were produced *(see p147)*, and the historic Cartulaire de Redon compiled.

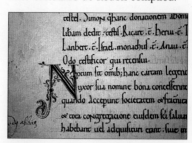

The Cartulaire de Redon, a charter in which statutes were recorded from the 9th century

c. 480 The first wave of Britons reaches Brittany	**630** Judicaël, the Breton leader, meets King Dagobert	**832** The monastery of Redon is founded	**843** The Normans sack Nantes
500	**600**	**700**	**800**	**900**

Altarpiece from St-Méliau

| **7th & 8th centuries** Armorica becomes Brittany | **753** Pepin the Short launches an expedition to Brittany | **845** King Nominoë is victorious at Ballon | **857–874** Reign of Salomon, king of Brittany |

William the Conqueror takes Dinan, a scene from the Bayeux Tapestry

THE NORMAN INVASIONS

From the end of the 8th century, the raids led by the Normans, from Scandinavia, became more frequent. Sailing up Brittany's coastal inlets and estuaries, they ransacked towns and monasteries, bringing terror to the land. Nantes was sacked in 843. Entire monastic communuties fled east, taking with them the relics of saints. After the murder of Salomon in 874, Brittany descended into chaos. From around 930–40, a semblance of order returned when King Alain Barbetorte regained Nantes in 937 and defeated the Normans at Trans in 939. Settling in neighbouring Normandy, the invaders gradually ceased their raiding activities, although they remained a dangerous presence.

FEUDAL BRITTANY

From the mid-10th century to the mid-14th, Brittany slowly evolved into a feudal state, maintaining a fragile independence from the

Henry II Plantagenet

kings of France and of England, both of whom had designs on Brittany.

In the 12th century, Brittany, now a county, narrowly avoided being absorbed into the Anglo-Angevin kingdom of the Plantagenets. Victorious at the Battle of Hastings in 1066, William the Conqueror had unified Normandy and England. His successor, Henry Plantagenet, was also Count of Anjou. In 1156, he took Conan IV, Count of Brittany, under his protection; Conan's daughter Constance was to marry Geoffrey, son of the king of England and brother of Richard the Lionheart and John Lackland. In 1203, the latter murdered Geoffrey's son, Arthur, and Brittany fell under the rule of the king of England. Philippe Auguste, king of France, then forced Alix, Arthur's half-sister, to marry a French prince, Pierre de Dreux, (Pierre Mauclerc). As a royal fiefdom, Brittany then came under the

TIMELINE

c. 900 The Norman invasion. Monks flee Brittany		c. 1000 The feudal system is established	1066 Led by William the Conqueror, many Bretons take part in the Norman Conquest of England	
900	**950**	**1000**	**1050**	
	937 Alain Barbetorte reconquers Brittany, expelling the Normans		11th century Many castles are built and small towns established	

Château de Vitré

direct control of the French Crown. The Count of Brittany paid obeisance to the king of France, pledging his loyalty and aid.

Despite these vicissitudes, a Breton state was forming. In 1297, Philip the Fair, king of France, made the fiefdom a vassal-duchy, and a ducal government was set up. Although tied to the king of France through his vassal status, by the 13th century the count (then the duke) of Brittany was in a sufficiently strong position to move towards independence. As Count of Richmond, in Yorkshire, he was also a vassal of the Plantagenet king, and was thus able to steer a political course between the two monarchs.

In Brittany, however, his authority was limited by the power of his vassals, who controlled extensive fiefdoms from the safety of impregnable castles. These included the barons of Vitré and Fougères, on the border with Normandy; the Viscount of Porhoët, who ruled over 140 parishes and 400,000 ha (990,000 acres) of land from the Château de Josselin; and the Viscount of Léon, who, with the Count of Penthièvre, controlled part of the northern coast around Lamballe.

The seven saints who founded the Breton sees

LIFE IN TOWN AND COUNTRY DURING THE MIDDLE AGES

Breton country-dwellers seem to have led more peaceful lives than those of their counterparts in France. In the west of the peninsula, there existed an unusual type of land tenure that persisted until the French Revolution. Every piece of farmland was owned by two people, one owning the land and the other the buildings and crops. Neither could be forced out without being paid for the value of what he owned. The towns, all of them small,

enjoyed no administrative autonomy. Almost all were fortified, and many stood at the head of an inlet. Town-dwellers lived from the linen trade.

Feudal Brittany was intensely religious. In areas of population growth, the number of parishes increased as new hamlets sprung up, their names prefixed with *loc* (as in Locmaria) or *ker* (as in Kermaria). Ancient pagan beliefs melded with the cult of old Breton saints, whose relics were the focus of pardons and pilgrimages. The best-known is the Tro Breiz, a tour of Brittany, about 650 km (400 miles) long, taking in shrines in St-Malo, Dol, Vannes, Quimper, St-Pol, Tréguier and St-Brieuc.

St Yves, between a rich and a poor man

ST YVES

Born at the Manoir de Kermartin, near Tréguier, in 1248, St Yves was a magistrate at the bishop's tribunal in Rennes, then in Tréguier. He was also the parish priest at Trédrez and then at Louannec, in the Trégor. He preached, led an ascetic life, and ensured justice for the poor, all of which brought him favourable renown. He died in 1303 and was canonized in 1347. He is the patron saint of Bretons and barristers. His skull is paraded in a procession at Tréguier that takes place on the third Sunday of May (see pp100–01).

1166 With Henry Plantagenet, Brittany is under English rule	1203 Arthur, Count of Brittany, is murdered by John Lackland	c. 1250 Dominican and Franciscan monasteries are founded	1297 Brittany becomes a vassal-duchy

William the Conqueror

1150	1200	1250	1300

12th century Cistercian abbeys are founded	1185 Geoffrey Plantagenet gives Brittany its own government	1203 With Pierre de Dreux, Brittany comes under the control of France	1270 John I sets off on a Crusade with St Louis	1303 Death of St Yves

St Louis

The Battle of Thirty, 1351, in which 30 Bretons, led by Beaumanoir, fought 30 Englishmen

WAR OF THE BRETON SUCCESSION

From 1341 to 1364, Brittany was ravaged by the warring of two families who claimed the dukedom. This conflict became part of the Hundred Years' War (1337–1453) fought between the kings of France and England. While the former supported Charles of Blois and his wife, Joan of Penthièvre, the latter aided John of Montfort and his wife, Joan of Flanders. This war, in which both women were closely involved, gave rise to such isolated incidents as the Battle of Thirty (1351).

The war ended in victory for the Montforts and their English allies: Charles of Blois was killed at the Battle of Auray (1364) and Bertrand du Guesclin was taken prisoner. John IV of Montfort's victory was ratified by the Treaty of Guérande and, for over a century, his dynasty held power in an almost independent Brittany, which could rely on English support to foil the ambitions of the king of France.

The Battle of Auray (1364), at which the Montforts and their English allies overcame the French

APOGEE OF THE BRETON STATE

The Breton state reached the peak of its power in the 15th century. The Duke of Brittany, who enjoyed the status of ruler and who was crowned in Rennes Cathedral, took up residence in Nantes. Surrounded by courtiers, he inaugurated a new age, patronizing artists and encouraging an interpretation of history that exalted Breton culture.

Government (the council, chancellery, court of exchequer, parliament and law court) was shared between Nantes, Vannes and Rennes. Every year, the States of Brittany held a meeting at which they voted on taxes. Complex and burdensome, these taxes were not sufficient to finance the duke's ever more extravagant tastes, nor to cover the upkeep of fortresses and the maintenance of an army. But, raising the necessary funds himself, the duke managed to keep his distance from the king of France.

From the reign of John V (1399–1442), Brittany remained relatively neutral in the Hundred Years' War. This allowed Bretons to enjoy a certain prosperity:

TIMELINE

1341 Start of the War of the Breton Succession	**1364** Death of Charles of Blois at the Battle of Auray	**1378** Charles V attempts to secure the dukedom of Brittany	**15th century** The duc of Brittany reaches its peak. Flowering of the Breton Gothic style
1340	**1360**	**1380**	**1400**	**1420**
1351 Battle of Thirty	**1365** Treaty of Guérande: the Montforts are victorious	**1380** Death of Bertrand du Guesclin	**1399–1442** Reign of John V. Shifting allegiance between France and England	

Equestrian statue of Olivier de Clisson

maritime trade developed, Breton seamen acting as middlemen between Bordeaux and England, and exporting salt from Guérande and linen cloth from Vitré, Locronan and Léon. The population of Brittany, less seriously affected by the great plagues than that of France, reached 800,000. Refugees from Normandy settled in the east, while many impoverished petty noblemen left to seek their fortune in France. During the Hundred Years' War, Breton mercenaries fighting on both sides won renown for their prowess. Three of them – Bertrand du Guesclin, Olivier de Clisson and Arthur de Richemont – became constables (chief military officers) of France.

Noblemen enlarged their castles, turning them into impressive residences. There was a lack of morality, however, and this reached its nadir in the depraved treatment of children and their cruel murder, in a satanic ritual, committed by Gilles de Rais, companion-at-arms of Joan of Arc, at the Château de Tiffauges, near Nantes.

In the 15th century, a typically Breton variant of the Gothic architectural style

BERTRAND DU GUESCLIN

A minor nobleman born in about 1320 near Broons, Bertrand du Guesclin showed his prowess as a warrior during the War of the Breton Succession.

Du Guesclin kneeling before Charles V

He was also victorious at some famous jousts and duels, such as the one he fought in Dinan with Sir Thomas Canterbury. In the service of Charles V, he retook part of France from the English, and defeated the king of Navarre at Cocherel in 1364. He led *compagnies* (bands of mercenaries) to Spain. He was taken prisoner by the Black Prince at Najera in 1367, but returned to the battlefield. He was made a constable of France, and died during a siege in 1380.

developed, combining the delicacy of the Flamboyant Gothic with the austerity of granite. The first texts in Breton appeared and, with the advent of printing in 1484, printed books were produced; one of the first was *Catholicon*, a Breton-French-Latin lexicon. A university was founded in Nantes in 1460.

THE END OF INDEPENDENCE

Francis II (1458–88), the incapable and debauched Duke of Brittany, was powerless to prevent the increasing use of royal power in France, where Louis XI abolished the last great vassals in 1477. The king then turned his attention to Brittany, the only major fiefdom that still remained to be subjugated. Forced into a war, Francis II was defeated in 1488. By the Treaty of Le Verger, the duke was forced to submit to the king if his successor was to rule Brittany. He died soon after. His daughter and successor, Anne of Brittany, was not yet 12 years old.

The execution of Gilles de Rais in 1440

Dance of Death (late 15th century)

1440 Execution of Gilles de Rais

1460 Foundation of the University of Nantes

1488 Battle of St-Aubin-du-Cormier. Treaty of Le Verger

1491 Anne of Brittany marries Charles VIII

1499 Anne of Brittany marries Louis XII

1514 Death of Anne of Brittany

1440	1460	1480	1500	1520

Anne of Brittany

Anne of Brittany

**Anne
of Brittany**

A central figure in the history of Brittany, Anne stood both for the duchy's independence and, through her marriage first to Charles VIII and then to Louis XII – both of them kings of France – for its integration with France. The vissicitudes of her short and eventful life also made her popular. She became a duchess at the age of 11, a queen at 13, a mother at 16, and a widow at 21. She died at the age of 37, having lost seven of her nine children. Even today, some Bretons revere her almost as a saint. A patron of the arts, she aided the development of Breton culture by supporting historians.

Anne of Brittany's coat of arms *feature a Franciscan nun, an ermine and the motto To my Life.*

Jean de Rely, bishop of Angers.

THE MARRIAGE OF CHARLES VIII AND ANNE OF BRITTANY

On the death of Francis II, Duke of Brittany, Charles VIII, the young king of France, resumed war with his successor Anne and forced her to marry him. The ceremony took place in Langeais on 6 December 1491. This early 19th-century painting shows the couple making their marriage vows.

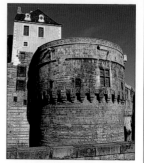

Pierre de Baud, *canon of Vitré, wrote a* History of Brittany *in 1505, at Anne's behest. The first account of its kind, it gave Breton identity a historical perspective.*

Anne of Brittany at the age of 15.

ANNE OF BRITTANY'S RESIDENCES

The castle in Nantes *(see pp208–9)* was Anne's main residence. She was born there, in the part known as the "old building", and she undertook the work that gives the castle its present appearance. As a young girl, she regularly stayed in Vannes, in the Château de l'Hermine and the Manoir de Plaisance, which now no longer exists, and in the Château de Suscinio, in the Morbihan, and the Château de Clisson, in the Loire-Atlantique. In Rennes, she lived in what is known as the Logis des Ducs, in the old town. During her tour of Brittany in 1505, she stayed in private houses, many of which are difficult to identify today. In Hennebont, Quimper, Locronan, Morlaix, Guingamp, St-Brieuc and Dinan, houses reverently known as "the Duchess Anne's houses" keep alive the memory of her visit. She also stayed for a few days in the castles at Hunaudaye, Vitré and Blain.

Château des Ducs de Bretagne, Nantes, Anne of Brittany's main residence

Louis XII, who succeeded Charles VIII, married Anne according to an agreement made at the time of her marriage to Charles.

Charles VIII

As patroness of the arts and a woman of the Renaissance, Anne supported artists and writers. Here, the Dominican friar Antoine Dufour presents to her his Lives of Illustrious Women.

Claude of Brittany, Anne's daughter, was born in 1499 and married Francis of Angoulême, the future Francis I. As king, he acquired through Claude the duchy of Brittany. Their son became Francis III, Duke of Brittany.

Burial of Anne of Brittany took place at the Château de Blois, on 9 January 1514. She was 37 years old.

This gold reliquary contains the heart of Anne of Brittany. According to her last wish, Anne's heart was brought from Blois to her native land, "the place that she loved more than any other in the world, so that it might be interred there". It was placed in the tomb that she had built for her parents in Nantes.

Map of Brittany in 1595, at the time of the wars of the Holy League

BRITTANY JOINS FRANCE

Brittany's integration into the kingdom of France made no fundamental difference to the lives of Bretons. The Treaty of Union of 1532 ensured that their "rights, freedoms and privileges" would be respected. The province was ruled on behalf of the king by a governor, who usually had connections with the great Breton families. The interests of the population were, in principle, defended by the States of Brittany, an assembly that was, however, unrepresentative, since the rural population had no delegate. The nobility and high clergy

played the most prominent role. Every year, the delegates agreed with the king the level of taxation to be levied on the province. Brittany paid lower taxes than the rest of the kingdom and was exempt from the salt tax.

Parliament, restored in 1554, was housed in a suitably imposing building in Rennes dating from 1618–55 *(see pp60–61)*. Parliament was the supreme court of Breton law and was also a court in which royal decrees became statute. Brittany was thus able to retain its own legal system.

In the 16th century, Brittany was largely unaffected by the Wars of Religion fought between Catholics and Protestants. Strongly Catholic, it contained only a small number of Calvinists. However, under Henry IV, king of France and governor of Brittany, was the ambitious Philippe-Emmanuel de Lorraine, Duke of Mercœur. One of the mainstays of the Holy League – a group of Catholic extremists – he attempted to harness the loyalty of Bretons to Rome so as to draw them into a war against the heretical king, and lured them with thoughts of independence. After ten years of conflict, from 1589 to 1598, Mercœur was forced to withdraw, and, in Nantes, Henry IV signed the Edict of Nantes, ending the Wars of Religion.

RESISTANCE TO THE MONARCHY

In the 17th century, royal power became absolute, and the monarchy in France developed centralized rule. Local autonomy was curtailed and taxes rose. New taxes on tobacco and

François d'Argouges, who became first Speaker of the Breton parliament, in 1669

TIMELINE

1532 Treaty of Union signed by Brittany and France

1534–1542 Jacques Cartier explores Canada

Jacques Cartier

1554 Creation of the Breton parliament

1589–1598 Wars of Religion

1598 Edict of Nantes

Parish close at La Martyre

c. 1600–1650 Parish closes are built

1530	1550	1570	1590	1610	1630	1650

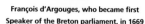

on printed paper used for legal documents caused a revolt in Lower Brittany in 1675. The harsh repression that followed was described by Madame de Sévigné *(see p67)*.

In 1689, so that his decisions might be more effectively implemented, Louis XIV placed the province under the control of an intendant, whose remit was to impose law and order and collect taxes. These measures caused a resurgence of Breton nationalism, most strongly among the petty nobility, that continued until the end of the Ancien Régime.

Henry IV on a military campaign against partisans of the Holy League, a group of Catholic extremists, in Brittany in 1598

Much more troublesome for royal rule was legal opposition mounted against the intendant and the governor led by the States of Brittany and the Breton parliament. While the States claimed to defend Breton autonomy, they in fact supported the interests of the nobility. From 1759 to 1770, tensions ran high, reaching a climax in the conflict between Louis-René de Caradeuc de La Chalotais, the Breton parliament's ambitious and popular procurator-general, and the Duke of Aiguillon, the authoritarian and effi-

cient commander-in-chief of Brittany. The "Breton question" enflamed the province and did not die down until the death of Louis XV, in 1774.

BRITTANY'S THRIVING PORTS

Under the Ancien Régime, Brittany experienced vigorous economic growth. Port activity prospered as a result both of Brittany's integration with France and of the opening of sea routes across the Atlantic. Brittany played its part in voyages of discovery with the expedition to Canada undertaken by Jacques Cartier, of St-Malo, (1534–42). The three busiest French seaports were St-Malo, Nantes and Lorient, built in 1666 as a base for the French East India Company. Conflict between France and England interfered with economic activity on the coasts, as the English launched attacks on St-Malo, Belle-Île and St-Cast. Naval warfare also led to Colbert's building an arsenal at Brest (c. 1680), while Vauban increased coastal defences.

St-Malo, France's major port at the end of the 17th century, used for trade and for fitting out the ships of privateers

1670	1690	1710	1730	1750	1770
1675 Revolt against taxes on tobacco and printed paper; the Bonnets Rouges		**1711** Rio de Janeiro taken by Duguay-Trouin	*René Duguay-Trouin*	**1758** The Duke of Aiguillon repulses an attempted English invasion at St-Cast	
1689 The administration of Brittany is set up	**1693** The English attack St-Malo	**1720** Pontcallec's conspiracy		**1764–74** The Breton Question (La Chalotais and the Duke d'Aiguillon)	

THE CHOUANS AND THE REVOLUTION

During the French Revolution, Brittany was divided between *"les bleus"*, who were in favour of new ideas, and *"les blancs"*, supporters of the Ancien Régime. *"Les bleus"* consisted of the liberal bourgeoisie and of country-dwellers of those cantons of Lower Brittany that were opposed to the clergy and nobility; *"les blancs"*, consisting mostly of nobility and unruly clergy, predominated in southern and eastern Brittany.

Jean Cottereau, known as Jean Chouan

In 1792, a few aristocrats led by La Rouërie hatched an unsuccessful counter-revolutionary plot, but in 1793, when the National Convention ordered that 300,000 men should be levied to fight in the war, the Loire-Atlantique, Morbihan and Ille- et-Vilaine rebelled. The Chouans, led by Cadoudal, Guillemot, Boishardy and Jean Chouan, fought a guerrilla war in the country-side. The Republicans responded by launching the Terror: in Nantes, 10,000 people were beheaded or drowned.

"Les blancs" had been dealt a blow. The army of Catholics and royalists was defeated at Savenay in 1793; attempts by émigré nobles to land in Brittany, with British aid, were quashed. At Quiberon, in June 1795, 6,000 of them were taken prisoner by Hoche's republican army and 750 executed.

Stability was not restored until the advent of Napoleon Bonaparte, who reconciled Church and State, appointed prefects, and ensured military control by building roads and establishing garrison towns, such as Napoléonville in Pontivy. Because of the Napoleonic Wars, during which the British ruled the seas, Brittany's fortunes were in decline, despite the exploits of privateers such as Robert Surcouf of St-Malo.

THE 19TH CENTURY

During the 19th century and until the 1950s, Brittany, isolated from the centres of the industrial revolution, became a rural backwater, although it supported a thriving canning industry. Fishing off Iceland and New-foundland was another key activity.

Awareness of Brittany's Celtic heritage gathered strength as poets, ethnologists and folklorists documented and recorded Breton traditions and ancient tales. The Breton language,

Mass drownings in the Loire at Nantes, ordered by Jean-Baptiste Carrier during the French Revolution

TIMELINE

Nantes is attacked by the Vendéens

1789 Riots in Rennes

1793–1802 Chouan uprising

1865 The Paris-Brest railway is completed

1886 Paul Gauguin arrives in Pont-Aven

1898 The URB is founded

1780	1800	1820	1840	1860	1880

1792 La Rouërie's plot

1795 The landing of royalist émigrés in Quiberon ends in failure

1839 La Villemarqué publishes *Barzaz Breiz*

1848 F. de Lamennais is elected people's delegate at the Constituent Assembly

De Lamennais

1896 La Borderie starts his *History of Brittany*

strongly discouraged in undenominational schools during the Third Republic (1870–1940), found ardent supporters among the clergy, while regional history became the object of renewed interest, culminating in La Borderie's monumental *History of Brittany*. Strong cultural regionalism asserted itself around 1900, with the Union Régionaliste Bretonne, followed by the formation of the Parti National Breton, which was supported by the occupying Germans in 1940–44.

In the 19th century, continuing high birth rates and the absence of industry caused large-scale rural emigration to Paris, where a vigorous Breton community became established. Bretons became prominent on the national stage. Among them were Chateaubriand, politician and writer of the Romantic age; René Pléven, a minister during the Fourth Republic; Félicité de Lamennais, a founder of social Catholicism; and the religious sceptic Ernest Renan. With the arrival of the railway in the mid-19th century, Brittany began to attract writers and artists, drawn by the wild beauty of its countryside and the exotic nature of its Celtic traditions.

Brittany suffered greatly during the two world wars: in 1914–18, the proportion of Breton soldiers killed was twice the national average. In 1939–45, the region was occupied, and several ports, including St-Nazaire, Lorient, Brest and St-Malo, were razed by fighting during the Liberation.

Poster for the inauguration of the Paris-Brest railway

BRITTANY IN THE MODERN WORLD

Brittany made a remarkable recovery after World War II. Since 1950, the Comité d'Étude et de Liaison des Intérê;ts Bretons has attracted investment and such decentralized operations as that of Citroën in Rennes and telecommunications in Lannion. Toll-free highways, high-speed train services and the installation of airports have ended Brittany's isolation. Cross-Channel links and a strong hotel industry make it the second-most popular tourist destination in France.

Brittany is also France's foremost producer of fruit and vegetables, and a leading producer of pigs and chickens. Such success has its price: farmers are crippled by the cost of modern equipment and soil is overloaded with nitrate. The region's problems are now being addressed: the need to preserve places of historic interest and natural beauty is seen as a priority, as is the importance of keeping alive Brittany's links with other Celtic regions in Europe.

Naval dockyards at St-Nazaire, where cruise liners are now built

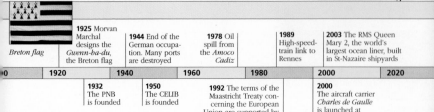

1925 Morvan Marchal designs the *Gwenn-ha-du*, the Breton flag	**1944** End of the German occupation. Many ports are destroyed	**1978** Oil spill from the *Amoco Cadiz*	**1989** High-speed-train link to Rennes	**2003** The RMS Queen Mary 2, the world's largest ocean liner, built in St-Nazaire shipyards

Breton flag

| 0 | 1920 | 1940 | 1960 | 1980 | 2000 | 2020 |

| **1932** The PNB is founded | **1950** The CELIB is founded | **1992** The terms of the Maastricht Treaty concerning the European Union are supported by 60 per cent of Bretons | **2000** The aircraft carrier *Charles de Gaulle* is launched at Brest naval arsenal |

BRITTANY REGION BY REGION

Brittany at a Glance

Brittany's beaches, like those on the Côte
d'Émeraude and Côte de Granit Rose, the
Golfe du Morbihan and Belle-Île, are very
popular with holiday-makers. Brittany is also
a land of history, with a rich heritage of ancient
monuments. The timber-framed houses in
Vannes and Dinan conjure up the Middle Ages,
while in Nantes and St-Malo the town houses
of shipowners reflect the fortunes that were
made in the 17th and 18th centuries. Coastal
forts such as that in St-Malo and castles in the
Breton marches have fiercely defended
Brittany from attack from
land and sea throughout
the centuries.

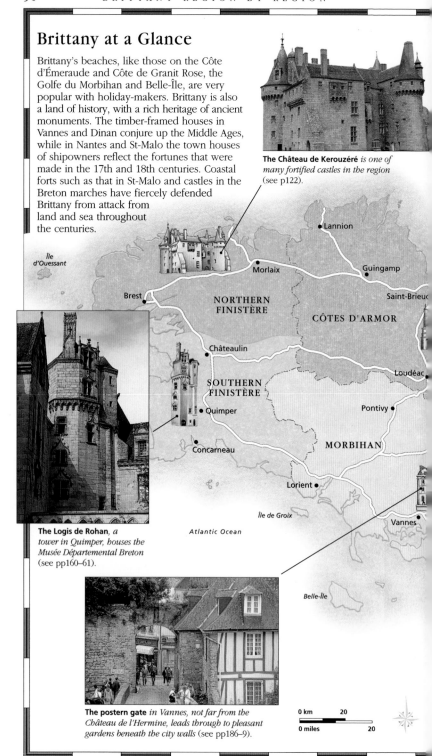

The Château de Kerouzéré *is one of
many fortified castles in the region*
(see p122).

Île
d'Ouessant

Lannion

Morlaix

Guingamp

Brest

Saint-Brieuc

**NORTHERN
FINISTÈRE**

CÔTES D'ARMOR

Châteaulin

Loudéac

**SOUTHERN
FINISTÈRE**

Quimper

Pontivy

Concarneau

MORBIHAN

Lorient

Île de Groix

Vannes

The Logis de Rohan, *a
tower in Quimper, houses the
Musée Départemental Breton*
(see pp160–61).

Atlantic Ocean

Belle-Île

The postern gate *in Vannes, not far from the
Château de l'Hermine, leads through to pleasant
gardens beneath the city walls* (see pp186–9).

0 km   20

0 miles   20

◁ **Vessels in the Passage du Toulinguet during Brest 2000, the annual tall ships festival**

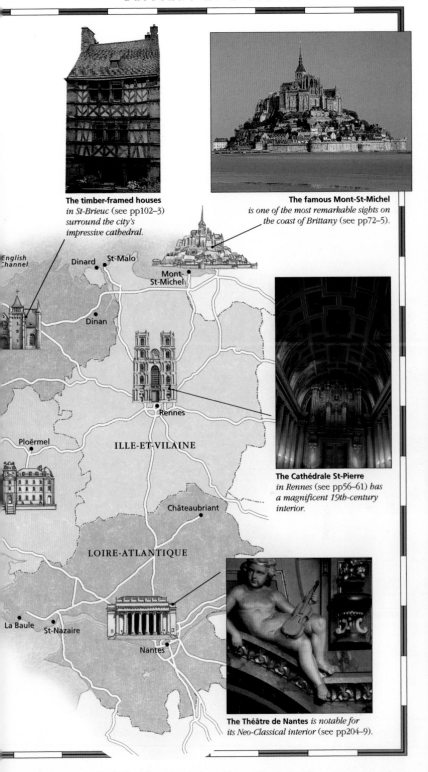

The timber-framed houses in St-Brieuc (see pp102–3) surround the city's impressive cathedral.

The famous Mont-St-Michel is one of the most remarkable sights on the coast of Brittany (see pp72–5).

English Channel

Dinard St-Malo

Mont-St-Michel

Dinan

Ploërmel

Rennes

ILLE-ET-VILAINE

Châteaubriant

LOIRE-ATLANTIQUE

La Baule St-Nazaire

Nantes

The Cathédrale St-Pierre in Rennes (see pp56–61) has a magnificent 19th-century interior.

The Théâtre de Nantes is notable for its Neo-Classical interior (see pp204–9).

ILLE-ET-VILAINE

In the north, the Côte d'Émeraude and Mont-St-Michel face onto the English Channel. Further south, at the confluence of the Ille and the Vilaine rivers, lies Rennes, the regional capital, which is famous for its elegant parliament building. To the east, the proud fortresses of the Breton marches, which once protected the duchy of Brittany, face neighbouring Normandy.

The beaches of the Côte d'Émeraude are lined by a succession of resorts. But well before this part of Brittany was discovered by tourists, Pierre-Auguste Renoir, Paul Signac and other artists had already been struck by its beauty when they came to paint in St-Briac.

Whether they are drawn to the megalithic Roche-aux-Fées or to the fortified castle in Fougères, lovers of ancient monuments will be spoiled for choice. On the coast, Mont-St-Michel stands as a jewel of Gothic religious architecture, while the citadel in St-Malo encloses within its ramparts several luxury hotels. Inland, noblemen built a multitude of manor houses, symbols of social standing, during the 16th and 17th centuries.

In the towns, a prosperous and influential middle class developed; the medieval houses in Vitré and Dol, as well as the town houses in Rennes, are proof of this opulence.

As acts of piety, tradesmen's guilds commissioned the artists of Laval to create rich altarpieces.

From Celtic mythology to French Romanticism, the *département* of the Ille-et-Vilaine also has two emblems of Breton literary heritage: one is the the Forêt de Paimpont, the legendary Forêt de Brocéliande where Merlin fell under the spell of the fairy Vivian; the other is the lugubrious Château de Combourg, haunted by the ghost of the 19th-century writer and statesman the Vicomte de Chateaubriand.

The Château de La Bourbansais, near Tinténiac

◁ The Promenade des Onze-Écluses, a path along a canal famous for its 11 locks, at Hédé

Exploring the Ille-et-Vilaine

This *département*, which covers an area of 6,758 sq km (2,608 sq miles), is named after the two rivers that flow through it: the Ille and the Vilaine. In the north, a hilly area culminating in Mont Dol overlooks the coast. East of Cancale, the marshlands of Dol have been converted into polders, sunken areas of land reclaimed from the sea. The coastline then descends to trace a bay out of which rises Mont-St-Michel. From the Pointe du Grouin, the Côte d'Émeraude (Emerald Coast) is marked by alternating jagged cliffs and soft sandy beaches. Rennes, in the centre of the *département*, is the administrative capital. On the eastern border of the Ille-et-Vilaine, the fortresses of Fougères and Vitré face neighbouring Normandy. Occupying a corner of the Morbihan and of the Ille-et-Vilaine, the Forêt de Paimpont is a vestige of Argoat, woodland that once covered the whole of inland Brittany.

THE REGION AT A GLANCE

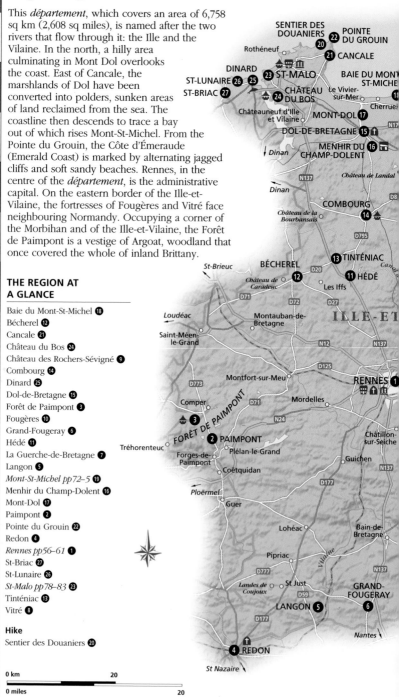

0 km   20

0 miles   20

For additional map symbols *see back flap*

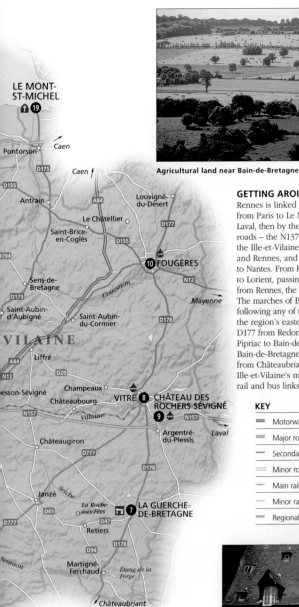

LE MONT-ST-MICHEL 🏛 ⑲

Pontorson   *Caen*

D175

D155   *Caen* ↑

Antrain   A84   Louvigné-du-Désert

Le Châtellier   D177

Saint-Brice-en-Coglès   D155

794

Sens-de-Bretagne   🏛 ⑩ **FOUGÈRES**

D175   N12

Saint-Aubin-d'Aubigné   Saint-Aubin-du-Cormier   *Couesnon*   *Mayenne*

VILAINE   D178

A84   Liffré

N12   D29

esson-Sévigné   Champeaux   VITRÉ ⑧   **CHÂTEAU DES ROCHERS-SÉVIGNÉ**

Châteaubourg   ⑨

N157   *Vilaine*   N157

Châteaugiron   Argentré-du-Plessis   *Laval*

D777

D178

Janzé   *Seiche*

D41   La Roche-aux-Fées   🏛 ⑦ **LA GUERCHE-DE-BRETAGNE**

D777   Retiers   D47

D94   D178

Semnon   Martigné-Ferchaud   *Étang de la Forge*

Châteaubriant

Agricultural land near Bain-de-Bretagne

GETTING AROUND
Rennes is linked to the A11 motorway from Paris to Le Mans, then the A81 to Laval, then by the N157-E50. Two major roads – the N137 and N24 – run through the Ille-et-Vilaine. The N137 links St-Malo and Rennes, and continues southwards to Nantes. From Rennes, the N24 runs west to Lorient, passing through Ploërmel. Also from Rennes, the N12-E50 runs to St-Brieuc. The marches of Brittany can be reached by following any of the minor roads leading to the region's eastern border: these are the D177 from Redon to Pipriac, the D772 from Pipriac to Bain-de-Bretagne, the D777 from Bain-de-Bretagne to Vitré, and the D178 from Châteaubriant to Fougères. The Ille-et-Vilaine's major towns are served by rail and bus links from Rennes.

KEY

▬	Motorway
▬	Major road
▬	Secondary road
═	Minor road
⁻⁻	Main railway
—	Minor railway
▬	Regional border

Timber-framed houses on the Place des Lices in Rennes

SEE ALSO

• *Where to Stay* pp218–20

• *Where to Eat* pp236–8

Street-by-Street: Rennes ❶

Around the cathedral, narrow streets wind between timber-framed houses that conceal courtyards. On Saturdays, the Place des Lices throngs with the colourful stalls of one of the liveliest markets in Brittany. During the week, the district's many bars and restaurants are filled with the animated babble of students. Neo-Classical buildings by the architect Jacques Gabriel (1698–1782) line Place de la Mairie. Rue Le Bastard, leading off the square, is a pedestrianized zone and the main link between the Vilaine and the northern part of the city.

★ **Rue du Champ-Jacquet**
Tall timber-framed houses dating from the 17th century back onto the old city walls.

★ **Hôtel de Blossac**
This is one of the finest mansions in Rennes. The building, in the Neo-Classical style, was designed by a follower of Jacques Gabriel.

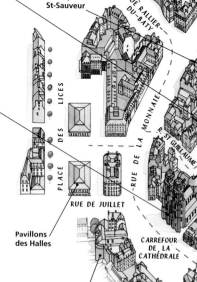

Hôtel de Robien

RUE LE BASTARD

RUE DU CHAMP JACQUET

Hôtel Hay de Tizé

Basilique St-Sauveur

RUE RALLIER DU-BATY

RUE DE TOULOUSE

RUE DE CLISSON

RUE ST SAUVEUR

PLACE DES LICES

RUE DE LA MONNAIE

R. ST GUILLAUME

R. DE LA PSALETTE

RUE DE JUILLET

CARREFOUR DE LA CATHÉDRALE

RUE DU GRIFFON

RUE DES

★ **Cathédrale St-Pierre**
The building stands on the site of an ancient place of worship. Although it retains its 16th-century façade, the cathedral was rebuilt from 1784.

Pavillons des Halles

Portes Mordelaises were the ceremonial gates used by dukes and bishops.

Rue de la Psalette is lined with medieval houses.

STAR SIGHTS

★ Cathédrale St-Pierre

★ Hôtel de Blossac

★ Rue du Champ-Jacquet

KEY

– – – Suggested route

0 m   100
0 yards   100

For hotels and restaurants in this region see pp218–20 and pp236–8

Parlement de Bretagne
Now housing the law courts, this building's sumptuous decoration and paintings have been restored to their original splendour following a fire in 1994 (see pp60–61).

Église St-Germain reflects the opulence of the haberdashers' parish in the 16th century.

TIPS FOR VISITORS

Road map E3. 🔍 *212,500.*
🚉 🚌 ✈ *Rennes Metropolitan.*
🛒 *Sat am; Place des Lices.*
ℹ *11 Rue St-Yves,*
(02) 99 67 11 11. 🎭 *Les Tombées de la Nuit (theatre & concerts; Jul), Transmusicales (rock and electro; first week in Dec), Film Festival (Feb).*
www.ville-rennes.fr

Theatre
In designing the theatre, which consists of a rotunda with arcades and covered alleyways, the architect Millardet wished to create a meeting place and centre of trade. He also designed the neighbouring residential buildings.

Hôtel de Ville
Built by Jacques Gabriel after the great fire of 1720, the town hall consists of two wings framing the clock tower, with a belfry in the Italian style. Sculptures by Jacques Verberckt decorate the main entrance.

Chapelle St-Yves
houses the tourist office.

***Head of an Angel** by Botticelli, in the Robien Collection*

ROBIEN'S CABINET OF CURIOSITIES

Built at the beginning of the 17th century, the mansion known as the Hôtel de Robien was acquired in 1699 by Christophe Paul de Robien. Filled not only with paintings and statues but also with plants and minerals, it became a true cabinet of curiosities. Robien bequeathed the collection to his son in 1756, but it was confiscated by the Revolutionaries in 1792. It was stored in the Church of the Visitation, then in the Carmelite convent in Rennes. The Robien Collection now forms part of the city's Musée des Beaux Arts.

Exploring Rennes

Despite the fire that devastated the city centre in 1720, Rennes still has some fine medieval houses. It also has many delightful mansions and a remarkable 17th-century palace. The city has stood at a strategic crossroads since Roman times. In the 10th century, it withstood Norman invaders and became a symbol of Breton resistance. In the 15th century, new fortifications were built to strengthen the existing Gallo-Roman ramparts. When Brittany became part of France in 1532 and the parliament of Brittany was created *(see pp60–61)*, Rennes became the regional capital. After the fire of 1720, a Neo-Classical city centre with rigidly straight streets was built. This layout, and the buildings dating from the same period, give Rennes a somewhat austere appearance. A university town, Rennes has a conspicuously lively population of students.

Timber-framed houses around Place des Lices

🏠 Old Town

Between the Vilaine in the south and Place des Lices in the north, the medieval centre of Rennes is full of timber-framed houses. **Place des Lices** (Square of the Lists) takes its name from the lists where jousting tournaments where once held. It was here that Bertrand du Guesclin *(see p41)* first entered the lists. Around the square, three mansions – the Hôtel du Molant, Hôtel de la Noue and Hôtel Racapée de la Feuillée – all built before the fire of 1720 – stand as symbols of the power of the Breton parliamentary nobility.

The **Portes Mordelaises**, at the end of Rue de la Monnaie, were the main gateway through which dukes and bishops entered the city. Behind the **Cathédrale St-Pierre**, in Rue du Chapitre, the Hôtel de Brie and **Hôtel de Blossac**, with a monumental stairway, are among the finest residences.

Place de la Mairie is a large Neo-Classical square designed by Jacques Gabriel. The most prominent feature of the **Hôtel de Ville**, overlooking the square, is the clocktower, which replaced the old belfry. The sculptures on the doors are by Jacques Verberckt, who worked on the decoration of Versailles for Louis XV. The **theatre** and arcaded residential buildings opposite were designed by Millardet in 1836.

The 17th–18th century **Basilique St-Sauveur**, in Rue de Clisson, is associated with the composer Gabriel Fauré, who was organist there. Rue St-Georges, lined with old houses, leads to the **Église St-Germain**, whose transept is a fine example of Breton Romanesque architecture. Behind the Église Notre-Dame is the **Jardin du Thabor**, a masterpiece by the Bühler brothers *(see p59)*.

Wooden statue in Impasse de la Psalette

🔒 Cathédrale St-Pierre

Between the Portes Mordelaises and Rue de la Psalette.
The cathedral stands on the site of an ancient shrine in front of which a trove of Gallo-Roman artifacts was discovered. Work on the building began in the 16th century, and the façade was completed in the 17th century. The rest was built from 1784 to plans by the architect Crucy. The 19th-century stuccowork and gilding within give the interior an opulence worthy of Roman basilicas. The gilt wood altarpiece, dating from 1520 and by the Flemish School, is of particular note.

Marine Bleue, by G. Lacombe, in the Musée des Beaux-Arts, Rennes

THE BUHLER BROTHERS

Although little-known today, Denis (1811–90) and Eugène (1822–1907) Bühler revolutionized the art of garden design. Giving imagination free reign, they rejected the strictures of the classic formal gardens in the French style. The Bühler brothers designed some 100 gardens. About 20 of these are in Brittany, and

The Jardin du Thabor, laid out by the Bühler brothers

they include the gardens of the Château de Kervenez in St-Pol-de-Léon and of the Château de la Briantais in St-Malo. But it was in Rennes that they designed their finest garden, the Jardin du Thabor. Laid out in the style of a 19th-century park, the garden follows the contours of the land and incorporates greenhouses, pavilions and an aviary. Exotic and indigenous trees frame the garden's perspectives.

🏛 Musée des Beaux-Arts

20 Quai Émile-Zola. **Tel** (02) 99 28 55 85. 🔵 closed for extensive renovations in 2009. 📷

The Robien Collection (see p57) contains drawings by Leonardo da Vinci, Botticelli, Donatello and Dürer. Besides early Italian painting, the most interesting part of the museum is devoted to the

17th century, with works by Le Brun and Philippe de Champaigne, Rubens' *Tiger Hunt* and *Nouveau-né* by Georges de La Tour, the museum's star painting. Modern art is represented by such painters as Lacombe, Corot, Gauguin, Sisley, Denis and Caillebotte. The contemporary collection

includes works by Poliakoff, Nicolas de Staël, Raymond Hains and Dufrêne.

🏛 Les Champs Libres

10 Cours des Alliés. **Tel** (02) 23 40 66 00. 🔵 Tue–Sun pm only. 🔵 2 weeks in Jul. 📷

This cultural centre has a museum on Brittany, a science centre, a public library and a conference hall. Exhibitions address subjects such as literature, history, physics and astronomy.

🏛 Écomusée de la Bintinais

On the road to Châtillon-sur-Seiche, via the D82, 4 km (3 miles) south of Rennes. **Tel** (02) 99 51 38 15. 🔵 Mon and public holidays. 📷

La Bintinais is one of the largest old farms in the countryside around Rennes. Converted into a living museum, it illustrates the history of rural life.

Fields have been planted to show various farming practices of the past, and a conservation orchard has been created to preserve varieties of cider apples that have become rare.

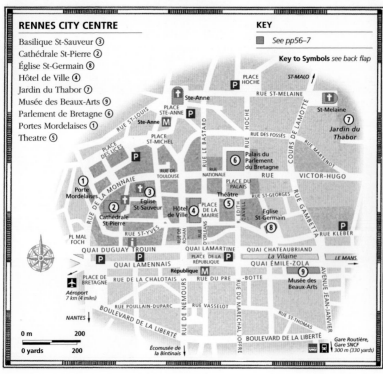

RENNES CITY CENTRE

Basilique St-Sauveur ③
Cathédrale St-Pierre ②
Église St-Germain ⑧
Hôtel de Ville ④
Jardin du Thabor ⑦
Musée des Beaux-Arts ⑨
Parlement de Bretagne ⑥
Portes Mordelaises ①
Theatre ⑤

KEY

⬛ See pp56–7

Key to Symbols see back flap

Parlement de Bretagne

The Breton parliament, dating from 1618–55, is a major landmark in the city of Rennes. Salomon de Brosse, the architect of the Palais du Luxembourg in Paris, designed the façade in the Italian style. The interior courtyard, by contrast, is built in brick and stone in the French style. The interior decoration of the building emphasizes the hallowed importance of Brittany's independent political power: the sumptuous Salle des Pas-Perdus, with the coat of arms of Brittany and France, and the ceiling of the Grand'Chambre, designed by Louis XIV's foremost painter, amply express this. Gutted by fire in February 1994, the building took ten years to restore.

★ Court of Assises
The tables and benches in the audience chambers are made of oak. The room is lit by antique and modern chandeliers.

Former Court of Criminal Justice

★ Salle des Pas-Perdus
The door to the Salle des Pas-Perdus (the lobby) features windows decorated with metalwork. The room has an ornate wooden coffered ceiling.

Salle Jobbé-Duval
The allegories painted by Félix Jobbé-Duval in 1866 were the last decorative elements to be added. The allegory seen here is Eloquence.

Pediment

Salle des Piliers
This is the grand entrance hall to the parliament building. Like the rest of the interior, it is built of stone, a traditionally French construction that contrasts with Jacques Gabriel's classical façade.

STAR FEATURES

★ Court of Assises

★ Grand'Chambre

★ Salle des Pas-Perdus

Upper Gallery
The audience chambers on the upper level are arranged in a gallery running around the court.

VISITORS' CHECKLIST

Place du Parlement-de-Bretagne.
📷 *Compulsory. Information from the tourist office;* (02) 99 67 11 66.
www.tourisme-rennes.com

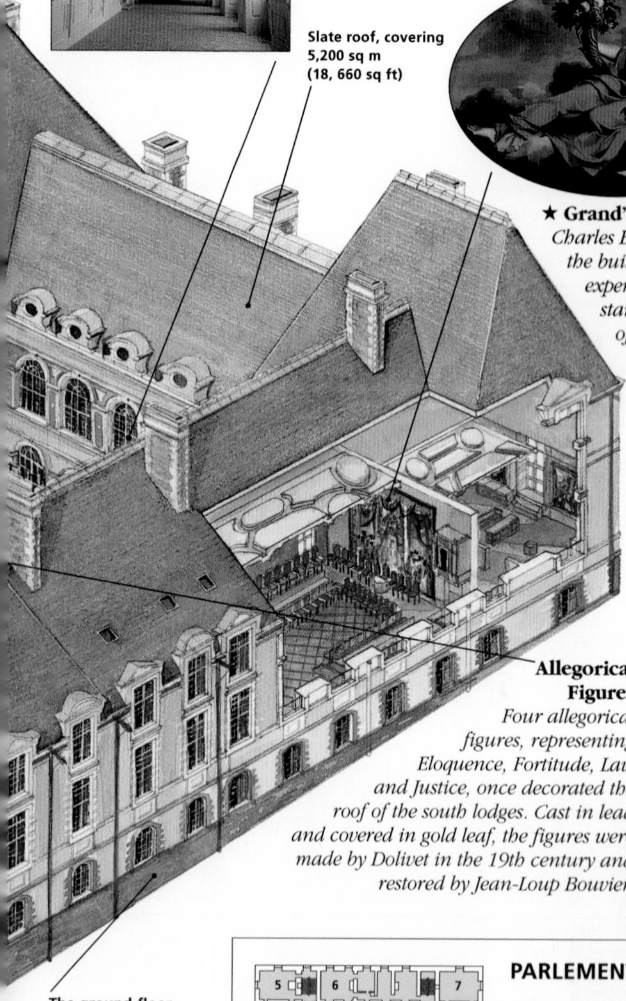

Slate roof, covering 5,200 sq m (18, 660 sq ft)

★ Grand'Chambre
Charles Errard, in charge of the building's decoration, experimented here before starting the decoration of Versailles. For the Grand'Chambre, he called on his pupil Noël Coypel, and, for the First Chamber, on Jean-Baptiste Jouvenet. Both decorated the rooms with allegorical paintings.

Allegorical Figures
Four allegorical figures, representing Eloquence, Fortitude, Law and Justice, once decorated the roof of the south lodges. Cast in lead and covered in gold leaf, the figures were made by Dolivet in the 19th century and restored by Jean-Loup Bouvier.

The ground-floor rooms were used for religious and official ceremonies.

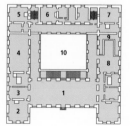

PARLEMENT DE BRETAGNE

1 Salle des Pas-Perdus (lobby)
2 Salle Jobbé-Duval
3 Chapel
4 Court of Assises
5 Salle Nicolas Gosse
6 Salle Ferdinand Elle
7 Salle Jean Jouvenet
8 Grand'Chambre (upper house)
9 Library
10 Courtyard and galleries

The Château de Trécesson, built in the late 14th century and surrounded by a moat

Paimpont ❷

Road map E3. 30 km (18.5 miles) south of Rennes via the N24 then the D38. 🚊 *Rennes*. 🏘 *1,385.* 🅸 *Paimpont (02) 99 07 84 23; Pays de Brocéliande, 37 Avenue de la Libération, Plélan-le-Grand (02) 99 06 86 07.* 🎭 *Pardon (Whitsun).*

The village grew up around an abbey founded in the 7th century. Of this, only the 13th-century abbey church and a 17th-century building, now the village hall, survive. The abbey church features Romanesque elements, a Gothic rose window and some 17th-century woodcarvings. The village is the starting point for hikes in the Forêt de Brocéliande.

Environs
Industrial buildings at **Forges-de-Paimpont**, 6 km (4 miles)

Forêt de Paimpont, vestige of the legendary Forêt de Brocéliande

southeast of Paimpont on the D773, are vestiges of the village's former iron and steel industry, which began in 1663. The metal foundries declined after the rise of the iron and steel industry in northern and eastern France.

Forêt de Paimpont ❸

Road map E3. Around Paimpont. 🅸 *Pays de Brocéliande, 1 Rue des Korrigans, Plélan-le-Grand; (02) 99 06 86 07.*

This woodland, the Forêt de Brocéliande of Celtic legend, was originally the extensive forest that once covered almost all of inland Brittany. Today, the woodland around Paimpont is all that remains and it is peppered with sites that have kept Arthurian legends alive. The Château de Comper, where the fairy Vivian is supposed to have lived, houses the **Centre de l'Imaginaire Arthurien**, where exhibitions and shows take place, and from which walks are organized. Rebuilt in the 18th century in Renaissance style, the building features three 14th-century towers.

The D31 leads northeast to Merlin's Tomb and the Fountain of Youth. The tree above the tomb is filled with strange offerings. From the hamlet of Folle Pensée, a short walk leads to the Fontaine de Barenton, into

which young women once cast pins in order to find a husband. Here, druids are supposed to have nursed people suffering from foolish thoughts *(folles pensées).*

Environs
At Coëtquidan is the École de St-Cyr, a military academy. The **Musée des Souvenirs des Écoles** here displays gifts from prominent alumni, such as the statesman General de Gaulle (1890– 1970). It is at Coëtquidan that Merlin is said to have met the fairy Vivian. The unusual Chapelle de Tréhorenteuc, 14 km (9 miles) west of Paimpont, contains mosaics and stained-glass windows on the theme of the Round Table. This is the starting point for the Promenade du Val-sans-Retour (Valley of No Return), dwelling place of Morgan le Fay, Arthur's half-sister, who trapped unfaithful men here. Passing the lake known as the Étang du Miroir-aux-Fées, the path leads up onto moorland and then on through the valley. Further south is the 14th-century red schist **Château de Trécesson.**

♣ **Centre de l'Imaginaire Arthurien**
Château de Comper. **Tel** *(02) 97 22 79 96.* ⬜ *Apr–Jun, Sep–Oct: Thu–Mon; Jul–Aug: Thu–Tue.*

♣ **Château de Trécesson**
⬛ to visitors.

🏛 **Musée des Souvenirs des Écoles** Coëtquidan. **Tel** *(02) 97 70 77 49.* ⬜ *Tue–Sun.* ⬛ *Thu pm.*

Romances of the Round Table

A large number of romances (medieval vernacular tales) make up the cycle of Arthurian literature. From that of Chrétien de Troyes, writing in the 12th century, to that of Sir Thomas Malory, in the 15th, there are almost 100 separate accounts. While the earliest are in verse, later ones are in prose, and they are written either in French, English or German. They tell of the adventures of Gawain, of the love of Tristan and Iseult (the queen with the milk-white hands), of Arthur's unstoppable rise, of Merlin's tragic fate, of the creation of the Round

The knight Tristan carries away Queen Iseult

Table, of magic and sorcery in Brittany, of the quest for the Holy Grail and of the epic Battle of Salesbières. A conflation of several different ideologies, Arthurian literature contains pagan Celtic and Indo-European elements, and Christian dialectic, giving an insight into the multifaceted culture of the late Middle Ages. Long neglected, Arthurian literature was rediscovered at the beginning of the 20th century. It has inspired not only literature but also music (Wagner's *Parsifal*, for example), and film (John Borman's *Excalibur*, for instance).

The conception of Merlin
the wizard took place between the Devil and a pious mortal.

Angels support the Holy Grail, an aspect of Christianity incorporated into Arthurian legend.

The Holy Grail, symbol of the mystery of the Eucharist.

Sir Galahad, destined to find the Holy Grail.

THE HOLY GRAIL
The vessel used by Christ and his disciples at the Last Supper appeared before the Knights of the Round Table. In *The Quest of the Holy Grail*, it is said to have floated in mid-air, giving the knights divine sustenance while a heavenly voice invited them to go in search of it.

King Arthur and the Knights of the Round Table are *shown in this fresco by Eugène Viollet-le-Duc. The knights are dressed in their familiar colours.*

Merlin's passion for Vivian led the *wizard to reveal to his pupil the secrets that were to lead him to his unhappy fate. He was imprisoned forever in a tree.*

The cloister of the Eglise de St-Sauveur in Redon, dating from the 17th century

Redon ❹

Road map E3. 🏙 10,500.
🚉 🛈 Place de la République,
(02) 99 71 06 04. 🖴 Mon, Fri & Sat.
🎭 Mois du Marron, Oct.
www.tourisme-pays-redon.com

This town is located on the borders of three *départements*: the Ille-et-Vilaine, the Loire-Atlantique and the Morbihan. From the 9th century, it was renowned for its Benedictine abbey, which was the most important in Brittany. The Cartulaire de Redon *(see p37)*, the earliest document in the history of Brittany, was written here. At the hub of roads and railways, and near the con-

fluence of two rivers, Redon developed a diverse economy and has become an industrial centre. In the 20th century, several important companies chose it as their base.

In the historic centre, timber-framed houses dating from the 15th, 16th and 17th centuries can be seen around Grande-Rue. In the harbour, houses with over-hanging upper storeys alternate with 17th- and 18th-century shipowners' mansions. In Rue du Port, three 17th-century salt ware-houses, now restored, can be seen at Nos. 32, 36 and 40. The **Musée de la Batellerie**, on Quai Jean-Bart, illustrates the history of river navigation in Brittany through models and documents.

The **Eglise de St-Sauveur**, the most important abbey in Brittany during the Middle Ages, is a monument to the power of the Benedictine order. Its Romanesque belfry, built in limestone and granite and set apart from the abbey itself, rises in three open tiers. It is unique in Brittany. The Romanesque nave with wooden ceiling contrasts with the choir, which has quatrefoil columns and Gothic chapels. The cloister was rebuilt in the 17th century. In 1622, Richelieu was an abbot here.

Environs
Some 10 km (6 miles) north of Redon, the perfume manufacturer Yves Rocher and the Muséum National d'Histoire Naturelle have joined forces to create the **Végétarium de La Gacilly**, Here, over 1,000 species of plants are grown in their appropriate habitat and their uses explained.

St Just, 20 km (12 miles) north of Redon, is at the centre of an area rich in megaliths, including the galleried grave at **Tréal** and the **Landes de Coujoux**, a long narrow ridge with many megaliths. At Lohéac, 15 km (9 miles) north of St Just, the **Manoir de l'Automobile** contains a display of over 200 collectors' cars, including Rolls-Royces, Ferraris, Lamborghinis, Cadillacs and pre-war models. There is also a go-karting circuit.

Exhibits at the Manoir de l'Automobile in Lohéac

🏛 **Musée de la Batellerie**
Quai Jean-Bart. **Tel** (02) 99 72 30 95. 🕐 times vary, phone ahead. 🖾

⛪ **Eglise de St-Sauveur**
Place St-Sauveur. **Tel** (02) 99 71 06 04. 🖼 Jul–Aug; Mon & Fri.

🌺 **Végétarium de La Gacilly**
La Croix-des-Archers
Tel (02) 99 08 35 84. 🕐 end Apr–mid-Jun & mid-Sep–mid-Oct: Sat–Sun & public holidays; mid-Jun– end Sep: daily. ● Oct–Apr. 🖾

🗿 **Tréal Archaeological Site and Landes de Coujoux**
🕐 all year. **Tel** (02) 99 72 69 25. 🖼 end-Jun–mid-Sep. 🖾

🏛 **Manoir de l'Automobile**
Lohéac, on the D177.
Tel (02) 99 34 02 32. 🕐 Jul–Aug: Tue–Sun. ● Sep–Jun.

CHURCH ALTARPIECES

Reacting against Protestant austerity, the Counter-Reformation in Brittany extolled the Catholic faith through magnificent church ornament. Altarpieces carved in wood or stone in an extravagant Baroque style graced the region's churches. The town of La Guerche-de-Bretagne is located in the heart of a region in which artists from Laval excelled in this field. Working with marble from Laval and Le Mans, and with tufa from the Loire, the sculptors Houdault, Corbineau and Langlois created consoles, pyramids, putti, foliate scrolls and garlands of fruit.

Detail of altarpiece at Domalain

The Chapelle Ste-Agathe, dedicated to Venus, in Langon

Langon ❺

Road map E3. 20 km (13 miles) northeast of Redon via the D177 then the D55. 🏠 *1,300.*

This small town is separated from the Vilaine river by marshland known as the Marais de l'Étier. The **Chapelle Ste-Agathe** is a rare survival from the Gallo-Roman period. It is dedicated to Venus and, behind the altar, there is a fresco depicting Venus rising from the waves and Eros astride a dolphin. The **Église St-Pierre** is worth a visit for its unusual bell tower, which features 12 bell-turrets.

On the Lande du Moulin stands an alignment of menhirs known as the Demoiselles de Langon. According to legend, young girls who chose to dance on the heath rather than attend vespers were punished by being turned to stone.

Grand-Fougeray ❻

Road map E3. 30 km (18.5 miles) northeast of Redon, via the D177 then the D54. 🏠 *4,125.*

The Tour du Guesclin is all that remains of the medieval castle that once stood in Grand-Fougeray. The fortress belonged to the Rieux family, allies of John IV, Duke of Brittany, against the constable (chief military officer) Olivier de Clisson. In 1350, an English sea captain took the castle. Bertrand du Guesclin (*see p41*) and his men later recaptured it for France and ever since it has borne his name.

La Guerche-de-Bretagne ❼

Road map F3. 20 km (12.5 miles) south of Vitré via the D178. 🏠 *4,090.* 🛈 *Maison du Chapitre, 2 Rue du Cheval Blanc; (02) 99 96 30 78.* 🚗 *Tue.*

On the border with Normandy, La Guerche-de-Bretagne is one of the fortified towns that once defended the borders of Brittany. Its geographical location also made it a centre of commerce, and it was especially renowned for its linen trade (*see p104*). The market that takes place here was first held in 1121 and is one of the oldest in France.

Half-timbered houses dating from the 16th and 17th centuries line the main square. The many gables on the **Collégiale Notre-Dame** are fine examples of the Flamboyant Gothic style of Upper Brittany (*see p21*).

The church, built in the 15th and 16th centuries, has unusual Renaissance choir stalls (1525) with carvings depicting the Seven Deadly Sins. The dark blue barrel-vaulted ceiling and 15th-century stained-glass windows are also notable.

Environs
La Roche-aux-Fées stands 15 km (9 miles) west of La Guerche-de-Bretagne. It was built during the third millenium BC and is one of the most important dolmens in France. It consists of 41 stones, some of which weigh 45 tonnes, and is 19.5 m (64 ft) long and 4 m (13 ft) high. The interior contains four chambers. How and why it was built has still not been determined.

The ponds and wood around Martigné-Ferchaud, 15 km (9 miles) south of La Roche-aux-Fées, have become a sanctuary for migratory birds. The Étang de la Forge is a haven for ducks, coots and small waders. The pond is named after the ironworks, dating from 1672, that are to be found nearby.

🔒 **Collégiale Notre-Dame**
Place Charles-de-Gaulle. *Tel* (02) 99 96 30 78. ☐ *daily.* 🎵 *by request, phone the tourist office.*

🗼 **La Roche-aux-Fées**
From La Guerche-de-Bretagne, take the D178 towards Chateaubriant then the D47 towards Retiers and the D41 towards Janzé. The site is 2 km (1 mile) from Retiers. ☐ *daily. Open access.*

La Roche-aux-Fées, one of Brittany's mysterious megalithic monuments

Vitré ⑧

Road map F3. 🏘 *15,910.* 🚉
ℹ️ *Place St-Yves; (02) 99 75 04 46.*
🛒 *Mon & Sat.* **www**.ot-vitre.fr

Unusually well preserved, this fortified town has a wealth of picturesque houses. Until the end of the 17th century, it owed its prosperity to the trade in linen cloth, which was exported all over Europe and as far away as South America. In 1472, the Brotherhood of the Annunciation became the organizational force behind this international trade.

A succession of powerful lords – Laval, Montmorency and Montfort – were prominent in the region's history. In the 16th century, Guy XVI established what amounted to a court in Vitré. The **Château**, perched on a rocky outcrop, is one of the great fortresses that defended the marches of Brittany. It was enlarged from the 13th century onwards. The entrance is defended by a small castle flanked by machicolated towers. A triangular wall set with towers encloses the complex.

The museum within the castle contains a remarkable 16th-century triptych decorated with 32 Limoges enamels. Also on display are medieval and Renaissance sculpture, 16th- and 17th-century tapestries, and

Breton paintings. The top of the Tour Montafilant commands a superb panorama over the town.

The **Église Notre-Dame**, in Rue Montafilant, was rebuilt from 1420 to 1550, and is in the Flamboyant Gothic style; this can be seen clearly on its southern side, which bristles with finials. Inside are altarpieces *(see p64)* and a beautiful Renaissance stained-glass window. A plaque commemorates Field-marshal Gilles de Rais *(see p41)*, lord of Vitré and companion-at-arms of Joan of Arc. He was, however, executed for having murdered children.

Around the church, in Rue d'Embas, Rue Baudrairie, Rue St-Louis and Rue de Paris, the finest medieval and Renaissance houses in Vitré can be seen.

Environs

The 15th-century **Collégiale de Champeaux**, 9 km (6 miles) west of Vitré, recalls the former power of the lords of Espinay. It contains canopied Renaissance choir stalls with notable carvings, as well as 16th-century stained glass by the Fleming Jehan Adrian.

⚜ **Château de Vitré**
Place du Château. **Tel** *(02) 99 75 04 54.* ◯ *May–Sep: Wed–Mon; Oct–Apr: Wed–Mon.* ⬤ *Sun am.* 🎟

⛪ **Collégiale de Champeaux**
On the D29. **Tel** *(02) 99 49 82 99* (information from the mairie). ◯ *daily.*

The Breton coat of arms in the Eglise Notre-Dame in Vitré

Château des Rochers-Sévigné ⑨

Road map F3. 8 km (5 miles) southeast of Vitré via the D88. **Tel** *(02) 99 75 04 54.* ◯ *May–Sep: Wed–Mon; Oct–Apr: Wed–Sat, Sun pm.* 🎟

This castle, located 8 km (5 miles) southeast of Vitré, was built in the 15th century and later remodelled. It consists of two wings set at right angles. At the intersection is a polygonal turret, which contains a staircase. The circular tower on the opposite side predates the 15th century. The 17th-century chapel has a hull-shaped roof and is crowned by a lantern.

On the ground floor of the north tower, visitors can see a plan of the castle as it was in 1763, and, on the first floor, a portrait of Madame de Sévigné *(see p67)*. The castle overlooks an elegant garden, laid out in the 17th century by Charles de Sévigné, son of the *marquise.*

The Château de Vitré, once defending the marches of Brittany and now containing a museum

Timber-framed houses in the Marchix quarter of Fougères

Fougères

Road map F2. 22,800.
Place de la République.
2 Rue Nationale; (02) 99 94 12
20. Sat; cattle market 5–9am Fri.
Voix des Pays; Jul). Fêtes des
Angevines (early Sep).
www.ot-fougeres.fr

A major town in the marches
of Brittany, Fougères has had
a chequered history over the
centuries. The French
invasion of 1488 (see p41)
began here, and the defeat
of the Bretons at the Battle of
St-Aubin-du-Cormier sounded
the death-knell for their
independence.

The imposing **Château
de Fougères** is a superb
example of medieval military
architecture. It was built
between the 12th and 15th
centuries, and its ramparts, set
with 13 towers, enclose an
area of 2 ha (5 acres).

It is built to a concentric plan
that is typical of 12th-century
fortresses. In the 15th century,
with the development of
artillery, the walls were
strengthened and the
embrasures widened so as to
accommodate the barrels of
canons. The five towers that
defend the walls – the
Châtelet de l'Avancée, de
Coëtlogon, du Cadran, de
Guibé and de Coigny – also
date from this period. The
rampart walk offers a fine
view over the town.

The Église St-Sulpice,
with a slender spire, was built
between the 15th and 18th
centuries in the Flamboyant
Gothic style. The two 15th-
century granite altarpieces in
the transept contrast with the
monumental 18th-century
altarpiece in the choir. Also
of note is a fine 14th-century
Virgin and Child in painted
limestone.

The old town (Bourg Vieil), at
the foot of the castle, is filled
with old timber-framed
houses, particularly in **Place
du Marchix** and Rue de
Lusignan. The new town
(Bourg Neuf) overlooks the
castle. Gutted by fire on
several occasions, it was rebuilt in the 18th century.

A timber-framed building in
Rue Nationale, with a porch
and corbelling typical of
15th–16th-century houses in
Upper Brittany, contains the
**Musée Emmanuel-de-La-
Villéon**. As well as 70 paintings
dating from the 17th and 18th
centuries, the museum contains
18 works by Emmanuel de La
Villéon (1858–1944), an
Impressionist who was born
in Fougères, and whose work
depicts Breton landscapes
and scenes of daily life.

Château de Fougères, a masterpiece
of military architecture

Environs
The **Parc Floral de Haute-
Bretagne**, 20 km (13 miles)
northwest of Fougères was
laid out in the 19th-century as
an English landscaped park.

⚜ Château de Fougères
Place Pierre-Symon. *Tel* (02) 99 99
79 59. ☐ daily. ● Jan.

**🏛 Musée Emmanuel-
de-La-Villéon**
Rue Nationale. ☐ mid-Jun–mid-
Sep: daily.

**♣ Parc Floral
de Haute-Bretagne**
La Foltière, Le Châtellier. *Tel* (02) 99
95 48 32. ☐ Mar–Nov: daily.

LETTERS OF THE MARQUISE DE SÉVIGNÉ

The walls of the Château des Rochers-
Sévigné seem still to breathe the finely
honed prose of Madame de Sévigné.
In 1644, Marie de Rabutin-Chantal
married the Marquis Henri de
Sévigné, a spendthrift and liber-
tine. After his death in a duel, the
marquise withdrew to the
chateau. She filled her days by
writing long and frequent letters to
her daughter – to whom she addressed
almost 300 – as well as to the
Countess of Grignan, who was living
in the Drôme, in southern France.
The immediacy of this correspon-
dence is still compelling today.

Marie de Rabutin-
Chantal, Marquise
de Sévigné

The locks at Hédé, still manually operated

Hédé ⓫

Road map E2. 14 km (9 miles) south of Combourg on the D795. ⚒ *1,930.* ℹ Town Hall; (02) 99 45 46 18. ⊟ Tue & Sun.

Gustave Flaubert described the valley in which Hédé is located as "wide, beautiful and fertile, broad vista of greenery and trees". Of Hédé's castle, only a part of the walls and one side of the keep remain. The church, built in the 11th century, is in the early Romanesque style.

La Madeleine, 1 km (0.5 mile) north of Hédé, is the starting point of the **Promenade des Onze-Écluses**, a delectably bucolic walk along the Ille-et-Rance canal, which has a flight of 11 locks with a 27-m (88-ft) rise.

Bécherel ⓬

Road map E2. 17 km (10.5 miles) north of Monfort via the D72, D70 and D20. ⚒ *670.* ℹ 9 Place Alexandre-Jehanin; (02) 99 66 75 23. ⚑ Fête du Livre Ancien (Easter weekend). **www**.becherel.com

With a wealth of antiquarian booksellers, second-hand book dealers, bookbinders and bookshops, Bécherel has both a literary and a medieval atmosphere. The castle, built in 1124 and now in ruins, was wrested from the English by Bertrand du Guesclin in 1374 after a 15-month siege. In the 17th and 18th centuries, the town prospered from the

linen and hemp trade, exporting cloth throughout Europe. This former wealth can be seen in the houses of the town's historical middle class – handsome granite buildings of uniform design.

Environs
The **Château de Caradeuc**, 1 km (0.5 mile) west of Bécherel, once belonged to L. R. de Caradeuc La Chalotais (1701–85), Attorney-General of the Breton parliament and a heroic figure in Breton resistance to centralized French government. Built in the 18th century, the chateau has an elegant Regency façade and is set in a lovely park.

Les Iffs, 6 km (4 miles) east of Bécherel, is named after the 100-year-old yew trees *(ifs)* in its parish close. The church here, built in Flamboyant Gothic style, has nine beautiful stained-glass windows. The Fontaine St-Fiacre, just outside Les Iffs on its northern side, is a spring that was enclosed in the 15th century. In time of drought, pilgrims would come here to pray for rain.

The **Château de Montmuran**, on the road to Tinténiac, has associations with Bertrand du Guesclin, who was knighted in its chapel in 1354. The gatehouse, with original portcullis, is 14th-century, while the main building is mostly 18th-century, with 13th-century towers.

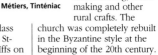

Clogs, Musée de l'Outil et des Métiers, Tinténiac

🏰 **Château de Caradeuc**
Tel (02) 99 66 77 76. 🕐 Park only: Jul–Aug: daily; Sep–Jun: Sat–Sun pm. 📷

🏰 **Château de Montmuran**
Tel (02) 99 45 88 88. 🕐 daily for groups by prior arrangement. 📷 Jun–Sep: Sun–Fri pm. 📷

Tinténiac ⓭

Road map E2. 30 km (19 miles) north of Rennes via the N137 then the D20. ⚒ *2,500.* ⊟ Wed.

This small town is associated with the Chevalier de Tinténiac, who fought alongside the Chouans *(see p46)*. The **Musée de l'Outil et des Métiers**, located on the canalside, contains collections of tools used for rope-making, harness-making, blacksmithing, barrel-making and other rural crafts. The church was completely rebuilt in the Byzantine style at the beginning of the 20th century.

Environs
The Château de La Motte-Beaumanoir, 12 km (8 miles) north of Tinténiac, has been rebuilt many times and is now a hotel. The façade gives an idea of its appearance in the 15th century: the main part of the castle is a two-storey building with a corner tower containing a staircase. In 1776, the naval captain Jean Thomas de Lorgeril, who had prospered as a privateer,

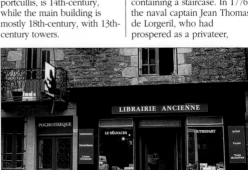

Le Seanachi, one of many antiquarian bookshops in Bécherel

The Château de Combourg, now inhabited by a descendant of Chateaubriand's elder brother

acquired the manor, adding two wings to it.

About 12 km (8 miles) north of Tinténiac, in the direction of Dinan, is the **Château de la Bourbansais**, built in the 16th century and enlarged in the 18th. On the ground floor are 18th-century furniture, Aubusson tapestries and Oriental porcelain imported by the French East India Company. The park now contains a zoo.

🏛 **Musée de l'Outil et des Métiers**
Magasin à Grain, Quai de la Donac. **Tel** (02) 99 23 09 30. ⬜ Jul–Sep: daily except Sun am & Mon. 🖼

🏰 **Château de la Bourbansais and Zoo**
Pleugueneuc. **Tel** (02) 99 69 40 07.

Chateau 🖼 Apr–Sep: daily; Oct–Mar: Sat–Sun & public holidays. 🖼 **Zoo** ⬜ Apr–Sep: daily; Oct–Mar: daily, pm. 🖼 🚻

Combourg ⓮

Road map E2. 🏘 4,843. 🚉 ℹ
Maison de la Lanterne, 23 Place Albert-Parent; (02) 99 73 13 93. 🖼 Mon. 🖼 Foire de l'Angevine, first Mon in Sep.

This town is closely associated with the French Romantic writer François René de Chateaubriand, who lived in the **Château de Combourg**, an imposing building with pepperpot towers. The castle, whose origins go back to the 11th century, was rebuilt in the late Gothic style in the 14th and 15th centuries.

In 1761, it was acquired by Chateaubriand's father, a rich shipowner from St-Malo. As a child, Chateaubriand spent much time here, as described in *Mémoires d'Outre-Tombe*.

Inside the castle, the writer's desk, armchair and deathbed, and a bust of him by David d'Angers, can be seen in the archive room. The rest of the interior was entirely restored in 1875. The landscaped park was designed by the Bülher brothers (*see p59*).

Environs
The **Château de Landal**, 15 km (9 miles) northeast of Combourg, has an impressive location, within ramparts. Before it was acquired by Joseph de France, in 1696, it belonged to some of the greatest Breton families. Two of its corner towers date from the 15th century. Falconry displays take place outside.

🏰 **Château de Combourg**
Tel (02) 99 73 22 95. **Park** ⬜ Apr–Jun, Sep: Sun–Fri; Jul–Aug: daily. **Chateau** ⬜ as above but pm only. ⬤ Nov–Mar. 🖼 obligatory. 🖼

🏰 **Château de Landal**
3 km (2 miles) north of Broualan, on the Aigles de Bretagne route. **Tel** (02) 99 80 10 15. ⬜ Apr–Nov: Wed–Mon.

FRANÇOIS RENÉ DE CHATEAUBRIAND

"It was in the woods around Combourg that I became what I am," stated Chateaubriand (1768–1848) in his *Mémoires d'Outre-Tombe* (*Memoirs from Beyond the Grave*; 1830-41). Born in St-Malo, this great Romantic writer spent periods of time in the family castle. He later studied in Dol-de-Bretagne, Rennes, then Dinan, and regularly stayed with his sisters in Fougères until 1791. He came to fame with *Atala* (1801). *Le Génie du Christianisme* (*The Genius of Christianity*; 1802) established his reputation. The biographical *Mémoires* are considered to be his masterpiece.

François René de Chateaubriand

Dol-de-Bretagne ⓯

Road map E2. 🏛 5,020. 🚉
ℹ 5 Place de la Cathédrale;
(02) 99 48 15 37). 🚌 Sat.
🎪 Folk festival (last Sun in Jul);
Christmas market.

The religious capital of
Nominoë, king of Brittany
during the 9th century, Dol
owes its prestige and
prosperity to its cathedral,
which is one of the finest
examples of Gothic
architecture in Brittany.

In about 548, St Samson,
one of the seven monks who
established Christianity in
Brittany, arrived from England
and founded a monastery. A
town grew up around it and,
despite suffering repeated
attacks by English-controlled
Normandy and from the kings
of France, it flourished and
enjoyed great prestige until
the abolition of its see in
1801. In 1793, it was the
scene of bloody conflict
between Chouan royalists and
Republicans *(see p46)*.

The **Cathédrale St-Samson**
stands on the site of a
Romanesque church that was
burned down by Jean sans
Terre in 1203. The great 14th-
century doorway on the south
side is finely decorated. The
north side, by contrast, faces
the open countryside and has
the appearance of a fortified
wall. The interior is
impressive through its sheer
size. In the nave, 93 m (305
ft) long, seven spans of
arches rise through three tiers
(an arcade, triforium arches
and a clerestory), and the
crossing is crowned by a 20-
m (65-ft) high dome. The
columns, arches and
stylized motifs with
which they are

decorated are in the Anglo-
Norman Gothic style, and are
similar to those in Salisbury
Cathedral.

A very expressive
Scourging of Christ can be
seen in the north aisle, and in
the north transept lies the
splendid tomb of Thomas
James, bishop of Dol from
1482 to 1504. Dating from the
16th century, with figures of
classical inspiration, this tomb
is one of the earliest signs of
the Renaissance in Brittany. It
was carved in the workshop
of the Florentine sculptor Jean
Juste, who also made the
tomb of Louis XII in St-Denis,
near Paris. The 77 choir stalls
are lit by an outstanding 13th-
century stained-glass window
with medallion-shaped
panels. Some of the stained-
glass windows here are
among the oldest in Brittany.

By means of modern tech-
niques, **Medièvalys**, in the
former bishop's palace on
Place de la Cathédrale, tells
the history of cathedral-
building, from methods of
construction and the various
crafts involved, to the
symbolism of the decoration
on the façade and the making
of stained-glass windows.

The Promenade des Douves
(Moat Walk), which passes
behind the cathedral's apse,
follows the ramparts on the
northern side of the town,
from where there is a view of
the marshes and of Mont Dol.
Grande-Rue-des-Stuart, with
houses with pillared porches,
offers a glimpse of Dol as it
appeared in the Middle Ages.
At No. 17, the Maison des
Petits-Palets, with carved
Romanesque arcades, is a
rare example of
French 12th-

century town architecture.
Opposite, a porch leads to
the Cour aux Chartiers, a
15th-century courtyard.

The Logis de la Croix Verte,
at No. 18, also dating from
the 12th century, was once
an inn run by the Knights
Templar. The Maison de
la Guillotière, at No. 27,
has a porch supported on
polygonal columns with
carved capitals.

🏛 **Cathédrale St-Samson**
Place de la Cathédrale.
🔲 Jul–Aug: daily.
Concerts Thu eve in Jul–Aug.

🏛 **Medièvalys**
Place de la Cathédrale.
Tel (02) 99 48 35 30. 🔲 daily.
🔲 Jan. 🈹

**The Menhir du Champ-Dolent,
in the "Field of Sorrow"**

Menhir du Champ-Dolent ⓰

Road map E2. About 2 km (1 mile)
south of Dol-de-Bretagne on the
D795. 🔲 daily. Open access.

Consisting of a single block of
granite 9.5 m (31 ft) high, the
Menhir du Champ-Dolent is
the tallest – and some would
say also the finest – of
Brittany's standing stones.
According to legend, it fell
from the sky, separating two
warring brothers who were
locked in deadly battle. It is
this legend that accounts for
the name "Champ Dolent",
meaning "Field of Sorrow".

Arch of the porch of the Cathédrale St-Samson in Dol-de-Bretagne

Sand yachts on wide, flat beaches near Cherrueix

Mont Dol ⑰

Road map E2. 2 km (1 mile) north of Dol-de-Bretagne on the D155.

This outcrop of granite, 65 m (213 ft) high, commands a breathtaking view over an expanse of polders (reclaimed land). Like neighbouring Mont-St-Michel and Mont Tombelaine, Mont Dol was once an island. During the Palaeolithic period, the region was covered in steppe and fenland. Finds of animal bones and stone tools prove that hunter-gatherers lived on the meat of reindeer, mammoth, lion, woolly rhino, horse, aurochs, bear and wolf. Much later, Mont Dol became a sacred place where druids worshipped.

A legend tells how St Michael and the Devil fought a battle on Mont Dol. Supposed traces of this can be seen on the rock: the Devil's claw marks, a hole for the Devil dug by St Michael, and footprints left by the Archangel Michael when he leaped across to Mont-St-Michel.

South of Mont Dol lies the small town of the same name. Frescoes dating from the 12th and 14th centuries, depicting scenes from the life of Christ, have been discovered in the nave of the church here.

Baie du Mont St-Michel ⑱

Road map E-F1. ⓘ *Dol-de-Bretagne; (02) 99 48 15 37.* 🎪 *Fête des Moules (Jul); Pardon de Ste-Anne in Roz-sur-Couesnon (Aug).*

The coastline here flattens out into a wide expanse of sand from which, almost magically, Mont-St-Michel rises. The appearance of its silhouette subtly changes with atmospheric conditions. It is, apparently, possible to predict the weather accordingly, and every bit as accurately as the official forecast.

Oak stakes, known as *bouchots*, can be seen all along the bay. Driven into the sea bed, they are used for mussel-breeding, a practice that goes back as far as the 13th century. A quarter of all mussels farmed in France are raised in this bay, where the yield reaches 10,000 tonnes per year.

Windmills and low thatched houses line the coast as far as Cancale. At Le Vivier-sur-Mer, the **Maison de la Baie** houses a exhibition on mussel-farming and on the area's plants and animals. Visits to the *bouchots*, which are reachable on foot or by tractor-drawn transport, also start from here. Beware of fast-rising tides and quicksand. At Cherrueix, there is a sand-yachting centre, where this sport (*see p259*) is taught on the beaches.

🍴 **Maison de la Baie**
Le Vivier-sur-Mer. **Tel** *(02) 99 48 84 38.* ⬜ *Mon–Sat (Jul–Aug: daily).* 📷 *for exhibitions.*

POLDERS – LAND RECLAIMED FROM THE SEA

As glaciers began to melt at the end of the Ice Age, 10,000 years ago, the sea level rose, flooding coastal Brittany. The marshland around Mont Dol was eventually invaded by the sea. Work to reclaim the land began in the Middle Ages, when dykes were built. Crops were grown on these areas of fertile land, known as polders. However, since a dyke was built between Mont Dol and the mainland, sediment is no longer flushed out to sea on the ebbing tides, so that the bay is silting up. A solution under consideration is to remove part of the dyke, allowing Mont Dol to become an island again.

Cultivation on the polders in Baie du Mont-St-Michel

Mont-St-Michel ⑲

The abbey in the 10th century

Wreathed in mist and surrounded by the sea, Mont-St-Michel is one of the most extraordinary sights on the coast of France. Rising proudly from the bright waters of the bay, it stands at the Couesnon estuary, between Brittany and Normandy. It was known originally as Mont-Tombe, and a small oratory was built here in the 8th century. Work on the abbey began in the 10th century; by the 16th century, it increased the height of the mount almost two-fold. A place of pilgrimage, particularly during the 12th and 13th centuries, the mount drew many pilgrims, some travelling great distances. "Mont-Michel", as it was known in the anti-religious climate of the French Revolution, became a prison. In 1874, its upkeep was entrusted to the Service des Monuments Historiques. Major roadworks are underway as eventually a bridge will replace the causeway that links it to the mainland.

St Michael

The abbey in the 11th century

The abbey in the mid-17th century

Chapelle St-Aubert
Built on the rock in the 15th century, the chapel is dedicated to St Aubert, who founded Mont-St-Michel in AD 708.

Tour Gabriel

★ Ramparts
The town was fortified during the Hundred Years' War, to protect it from attack by the English.

Entrance

TIMELINE

966 A Benedictine abbey is founded	**1211–1228** Gothic buildings of La Merveille are completed	**1434** Final attack by the English. Ramparts are built	**1877–1879** The dyke is built **1789** During the Revolution, the mount is used as a prison for political dissidents	**1895–1897** The tower, spire and statue of St Michael Archangel are added **1922** Church services resume	
700	**1000**	**1300**	**1600**	**1900**	
1017 Work starts on the building of the abbey **708** St Aubert builds an oratory on Mont-Tombe	**1516** The abbey declines **1067-1070** Mont-St-Michel is depicted in the Bayeux Tapestry *Detail of the Bayeux Tapestry*	**1874** Upkeep of the mount is entrusted to Monuments Historiques	**1969** Benedictine monks return to the mount **2007** The monks leave the abbey once more		

Tides in Baie de Mont St-Michel
The bay is washed by unusually long tides, which flow unimpeded over the smooth quicksand. The strong spring tides can move at speeds of up to 10 kmh (6 mph).

VISITORS' CHECKLIST

🚉 *as far as Pontorson, then by bus.* 🛈 *Corps de Garde des Bourgeois, at entrance to Mont St Michel (02) 33 60 14 30.*
Abbey Tel *(02) 33 89 80 00.*
🕐 *May–Aug: 9am–7pm daily; Sep–Apr: 9:30am– 6pm daily.*
⬤ *1 Jan, 1 May, 1 Nov, 25 Dec.*
🎟 *free 1st Sun of month from Nov–Mar.* ✝ *12:15 pm Tue–Sat, 11:30am Sun.* 📷 ⚟
www.abbaye-montsaintmichel.com
www.ot-montsaintmichel.com

★ Abbey
Enclosed within high walls, the abbey and its church occupy an impregnable position.

Saut Gauthier
This vantage point at the top of the Grand Degré commands a magnificent view over the south side of the bay.

Église St-Pierre

Tour de la Liberté

Tour de l'Arcade,
where the guards were
accommodated

Tour du Roy

STAR FEATURES

★ Abbey

★ Grande-Rue

★ Ramparts

★ Grande-Rue
The route once taken by pilgrims as they made their way to the abbey, but now filled with tourists and souvenir shops, passes the Église St-Pierre.

Abbaye du Mont-St-Michel

The history of Mont-St-Michel can be read in its architecture. The abbey, the most prominent building, has served several different purposes; once attached to the Benedictine monastery, it later became a prison for political dissidents. The original abbey church was built in 1017, on the site of a 10th-century, pre-Romanesque building, Notre-Dame-Sous-Terre. In the early 13th century, La Merveille, an imposing three-storey building, was added to the north side of the church, built directly onto the rockface.

Cross in the choir

★ Abbey Church
Only four of the original seven bays in the nave survive. The other three collapsed in 1776.

★ La Merveille
This masterpiece of Gothic architecture took 16 years to complete.

Monks' Refectory
This large room is bathed in soft light entering through windows in the end wall and through high, narrow niches.

Salle des Chevaliers
The vaulting and capitals in the Knight's Hall are in a pure Gothic style.

UPPER LEVEL (CHURCH)

INTERMEDIATE LEVEL

LOWER LEVEL

Crypte Notre-Dame-des-Trente-Cierges (Our Lady of the Thirty Candles) is one of two crypts beneath the transept.

★ Cloisters
With slender pudding-stone columns in an off-set alignment, the cloister is a perfect example of Anglo-Norman Gothic.

ABBEY GUIDE

The three levels on which the abbey is built reflect the hierarchy of the monastery. The monks' cells were on the upper level, where the church, cloister and refectory were also located. Important guests were entertained by the abbot on the intermediate level. On the lower level was accommodation for the guards, as well as for humbler pilgrims. The customary route for pilgrims was from the almshouse (which is now a shop), where the poor were given alms, to the church via the grand gothic staircase.

CHURCH

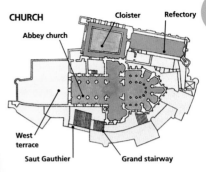

Cloister · Refectory · Abbey church · West terrace · Saut Gauthier · Grand stairway

INTERMEDIATE LEVEL

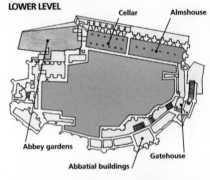

Salle des Chevaliers · Crypte Notre-Dame-des-Trente-Cierges · Salle des Hôtes · Notre-Dame-sous-Terre · Chapelle St-Étienne · Crypte St-Martin · Abbatial buildings

LOWER LEVEL

Cellar · Almshouse · Abbey gardens · Abbatial buildings · Gatehouse

Interior of the Church
The choir, in the Flamboyant Gothic style and supported by flying buttresses, was built between 1446 and 1521.

Crypte St-Martin, a barrel-vaulted chapel, gives an idea of the austere appearance of the original abbey church.

The abbatial buildings, near the square in front of the church, allowed the abbot to entertain important visitors in suitable comfort. Lesser pilgrims were received at the almshouse.

Benedictines
The small community of Benedictine monks left the abbey in 2007. Now the Fraternité de Jérusalem inhabit the abbey instead.

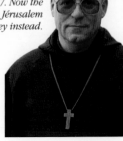

STAR SIGHTS

★ Abbey Church
★ Cloisters
★ La Merveille

Sentier des Douaniers ⑳

This stretch of the GR34 (a *grande randonnée*, or long-distance path) starts at Cancale, follows the Pointe du Grouin along the edge of cliffs 40 m (130 ft) high, and ends at Les Daules. On one side is the English Channel and on the other a residential area with well-designed modern houses.

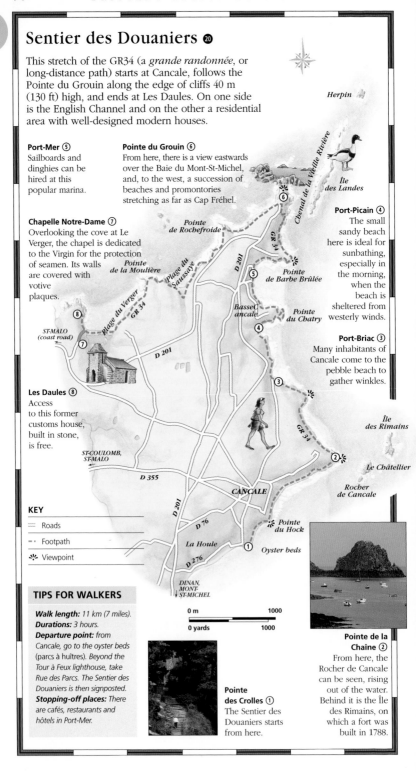

Port-Mer ⑤
Sailboards and dinghies can be hired at this popular marina.

Pointe du Grouin ⑥
From here, there is a view eastwards over the Baie du Mont-St-Michel, and, to the west, a succession of beaches and promontories stretching as far as Cap Fréhel.

Chapelle Notre-Dame ⑦
Overlooking the cove at Le Verger, the chapel is dedicated to the Virgin for the protection of seamen. Its walls are covered with votive plaques.

Port-Picain ④
The small sandy beach here is ideal for sunbathing, especially in the morning, when the beach is sheltered from westerly winds.

Port-Briac ③
Many inhabitants of Cancale come to the pebble beach to gather winkles.

Les Daules ⑧
Access to this former customs house, built in stone, is free.

Herpin

Île des Landes

Chenal de la Vieille Rivière

Pointe de Rochefroide

Pointe de la Moulière

Plage du Saussaye

Pointe de Barbe Brûlée

Basse Cancale

Pointe du Chatry

Plage du Verger

ST-MALO (coast road)

D 201

Île des Rimains

Le Châtellier

Rocher de Cancale

CANCALE

ST-COULOMB, ST-MALO

D 355

D 201

Pointe du Hock

La Houle

D 76

Oyster beds

D 276

DINAN, MONT-ST-MICHEL

KEY

= Roads
-•- Footpath
🌿 Viewpoint

TIPS FOR WALKERS

Walk length: 11 km (7 miles).
Durations: 3 hours.
Departure point: from Cancale, go to the oyster beds (parcs à huîtres). Beyond the Tour à Feux lighthouse, take Rue des Parcs. The Sentier des Douaniers is then signposted.
Stopping-off places: There are cafés, restaurants and hôtels in Port-Mer.

```
0 m                    1000
0 yards                1000
```

Pointe des Crolles ①
The Sentier des Douaniers starts from here.

Pointe de la Chaîne ②
From here, the Rocher de Cancale can be seen, rising out of the water. Behind it is the Île des Rimains, on which a fort was built in 1788.

Cancale ㉑

Road map E1. 🏘 *5,350.* 🚌
ℹ *44 Rue du Port; (02) 99 89 63 72.*
🎭 *Fêtes des Reposoirs (15 Aug); Fêtes de la Confrérie des Huîtres (third Sat in Sep).* 🗓 *Sun.* www.cancale-tourisme.fr

This centre of oyster-farming has kept its distinctive identity. The flat oysters *(belons)* that are farmed here today are famed for their large size. Along the harbour at La Houle, fishermen's houses have been converted into restaurants, cafés and shops.

When the cod-fishing industry collapsed in the 19th century, Cancale's fishermen turned to oyster-farming, using their boats – the *bisquines* – to harvest the oysters in the bay. Visitors can take a trip out to sea in one of them, **La Cancalaise**.

The **Musée des Arts et Traditions Populaires de Cancale et sa règion**, laid out in a deconsecrated church, the 18th-century Église St-Méen, describes the history of oyster-farming. It also looks at the lives of the seamen who once sailed to Newfoundland to fish for cod and those of their wives, whose legendary outspokenness goes back to the time when they would hawk fish on the quayside.

Port-Mer, Cancale's residential quarter, has an excellent sailing school. The terraces above the beach are an inviting place to stop and rest before walking around the Pointe du Grouin on the coast path, the Sentier des Douaniers.

🏛 **Musée des Arts et Traditions Populaires de Cancale et sa règion**
Place St-Méen. **Tel** *(02) 99 89 79 32.*
◻ *Jul–Aug: daily except Mon am; Jun & Sep: Sat & Sun, pm only.* 🖼

🚢 **La Cancalaise**
Boat trips. **Tel** *(02) 99 89 77 87.*
◻ *Apr–Oct: daily.* 🖼

ÎLE DES LANDES BIRD SANCTUARY

Declared a bird sanctuary in 1961, the Île des Landes is separated from the Pointe du Grouin by a narrow channel, the Chenal de la Vieille Rivière. The island attracts the largest colony of cormorants in Brittany. Other species include the crested cormorant, herring gull and various other species of gull, and pied oystercatchers as well as the Belon sheldrake, the only sea duck native to Brittany. From August through to October, puffins, gannets and other sea birds flock to the island. Visitors can watch the birds through a fixed telescope and, every day throughout the summer, Bretagne Vivante (Living Brittany) organizes interesting nature walks on the island.

Pied oystercatchers on the Île des Landes

Pointe du Grouin, halfway along the Sentier des Douaniers

Pointe du Grouin ㉒

Road map E1. ℹ *(02) 99 89 63 72 (Cancale); (02) 98 49 07 18 (Bretagne Vivante).*

The longest promontory in the Ille-et-Vilaine, Pointe du Grouin is covered with heath and coastal grassland that are typical of Brittany's rocky coast.

Having suffered degradation caused by excessive numbers of visitors, the area, which covers 21 ha (52 acres), is now under environmental protection. Soil erosion, the degradation of the chalky grassland and damage to protected species of plants by walkers have led the local council to lay out official paths and close off areas in order to allow grasses and wildflowers to recover. This plan of action has borne fruit, although the area is still vulnerable.

During World War II, German forces built *blockhausen* (blockhouses, or fortified gun positions) here to defend the strategically important headland. Most have survived intact, and one has been converted into a visitor centre. The greater horseshoe bat, one of the most endangered animals in France, nests in the abandoned blockhouses.

The lighthouse west of the promontory, built in 1861 and modernized in 1972, was decommissioned in 1999.

Environs
The Chapelle du Verger, which has been rebuilt on several occasions, nestles in an inlet known as the Cul-du-Chien (Dog's Bottom Cove). The belfry, at the foot of which many votive offerings have been laid, overlooks Cancale's largest sandy beach.

Flat-bottomed boats like these are used to harvest the oysters in the bay at Cancale

For hotels and restaurants in this region see pp218–20 and pp236–8

Street-by-Street: St-Malo's Walled City ㉓

At the end of the 17th century, St-Malo was France's foremost port, and shipowners who held a monopoly over trade with the East Indies amassed huge fortunes. Following attacks by the English in 1693 and 1695, plans were made to build a new fortified town, and the architect was Siméon de Garangeau. From 1708 to 1742, St-Malo grew rapidly, expanding by over one third. Tragically, during fighting at the end of World War II, in August 1944, 80 per cent of the port city was destroyed. It was, however, rebuilt in a style in keeping with its historic character, using granite-clad concrete. Immediately after the war, some buildings were reconstructed using their original stones.

The best view of St-Malo, from Dinard

Porte St-Vincent
The main entrance to the city is through a gateway in the walls, which are 7 m (23 ft) thick. From the gateway, a stairway leads up to the rampart walk.

Grande Porte
A niche inside the gate contains a 15th-century statue of Notre-Dame-de-Bon-Secours.

Cathédrale St-Vincent

QUAI SAINT VINCENT

SAINT QUAI VINCENT

ESPLANADE SAINT VINCENT

The castle's four towers were built by Francis II and Anne of Brittany.

PLACE DU POIDS DU ROI

GRANDE RUE

RUE DE

PORCON DE LA BARBINA

RUE SAINT VINCENT

PLACE CHÂTEAUBRIAND

RUE SAINT THOMAS

CORNE DU CERF

RUE DU PÉLICOT

RUE SAINTE BARBE

RUE DU COLLÈGE

PLACE J. CHÂTILL

RUE CHATEAUBRIAND

PLACE VAUBAN

L'ÉVENTAIL

RUE TOUILLER

R. DE LA VICTOIRE

RUE DES CH

RUE DU CHATEAU GAILLARD

PLAGE MALO

Rue du Pélicot

★ Château
Built by John V, Duke of Brittany, and enlarged by Anne of Brittany, the castle now houses the local council offices and the Musée d'Histoire de St-Malo. The museum is in the castle's keep.

Église St-Benoît
The doorway of the former Église St-Benoît was built by the architect Jean Poulier in 1705, to a design by Garangeau. It consists of a pair of granite columns supporting a curved pediment.

★ Hôtel Magon-d'Asfeld

This mansion, once the residence of Auguste Magon de La Lande, head of the French East India Company in 1715, is fronted by a courtyard and a gateway. It was used as a prison during the Revolution. Chateaubriand's mother was incarcerated here.

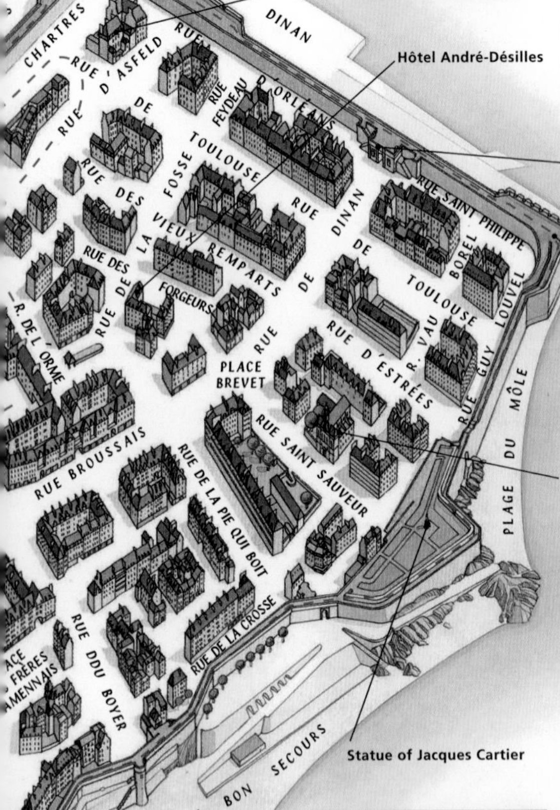

VISITORS' CHECKLIST

Road map E1. 🚗 48,057.
✈ Dinard-Pleurtuit-St-Malo.
🚢 (02) 23 18 15 15.
🚉 Avenue M. Marville.
ℹ Esplanade St-Vincent; 0825 135 200.
🛒 Tue & Fri in the old town.
🎭 Étonnants Voyageurs (Book Fair, Whitsun); Folklore du Monde (Jul); Festival de Musique Sacrée (Jul–mid-Aug); Route du Rock (mid-Aug), Quai des Bulles (Nov), Route du Rhum (transatlantic race; Nov, every four years from 2006).
www.saint-malo-tourisme.com

Hôtel André-Désilles

Porte de Dinan

Bastion St-Philippe

Église St-Sauveur

Completed in 1743 by the architect Michel Marion to plans by Garangeau, the church is now used as a venue for temporary exhibitions. The west front, which faces the street, is plain to the point of being austere.

Statue of Jacques Cartier

```
0 m                    100
0 yards                100
```

KEY

– – – Suggested route

STAR SIGHTS

★ Château

★ Hôtel d'Asfeld

★ Ramparts

★ Ramparts

Many stages of the city's history can be seen from the rampart walk. Among the oldest parts are the Cavalier des Champs-Vauverts and the Tour Bidouane, built around the late 16th-century arsenal that predates the 17th-century fortified town.

Exploring St-Malo

Throughout its history, this port city, sheltered from battering winds by its ramparts, has maintained a fierce spirit of independence. This is reflected in the motto "Foremost a native of St-Malo, a Breton perhaps, and a Frenchman last". Its indomitable seamen have sailed the high seas in search of undiscovered lands and of exotic goods that could be traded for a high return in Europe. Both privateers and shipowners made their fortunes here, and, in the 17th and 18th centuries, the kings of France as well as St-Malo itself also profited handsomely. The private residences and *malouinières* (grand country residences) that can be seen today are proof of this fabulous success.

An eventful history

As early as 1308, the inhabitants of St-Malo showed their mettle by establishing the first free town in Brittany, and, in 1395, rebelling against the Duke of Brittany, they obtained leave to answer only to Charles VI, king of France. St-Malo was then granted the status of an independent port, and for the next 300 years its economic success was assured. In 1415, John V, Duke of Brittany, attempted to regain authority over St-Malo and began to build the castle here. In 1436, the English described the seamen of St-Malo in these terms: "The people of St-Malo are the greatest thieves …that ever sailed the seas… These pilferers who sail under false colours … have no respect for their dukes." Neither did they have respect for France, as, in 1590, they formed an independent, albeit shortlived, republic in defiance of Henry IV's royal authority. By the end of the 15th century, having grown prosperous through trade and from fishing off Newfoundland, St-Malo had become a port of international renown. From 1698 to 1720, cargo ships sailing from St-Malo exported linen cloth, lace and other everyday goods to America, returning laden with gold and precious stones. The immensely rich shipowners were "invited" to lend the king half of the cargo brought back by their ships, thus saving France from bankruptcy.

Cathedral gargoyle

St-Malo's Walled City

The main entrance into the walled city of St-Malo is **Porte St-Vincent**, built in 1709 and standing on its northeastern side. Inside the pedestrians' entrance is a map of the city showing the main stages in its construction and identifying the most important buildings.

GARANGEAU

The civil and naval architect Siméon de Garangeau (1647–1741) had worked in Marseille and in Brest before he took charge of building St-Malo's fortifications. The great military engineer Vauban considered that the coastal fort of La Conchée, which Garangeau built, was the best building in France. As a civil architect, Garangeau was also responsible for much of St-Malo's unique architectural character.

Fortifications of St-Malo

A stairway leads up to the rampart walk, which offers a wide view of the city. Further north, in front of Place du Poids-du-Roi, is **Grande Porte**, a 15th-century gateway with machicolated towers.

Cathédrale St-Vincent, on Place de Châtillon, was begun in the 12th century and completed in the 18th. Grimacing gargoyles stare down from the heights of the outer walls. Inside, the high, delicate Gothic choir contrasts with the nave, in the Angevin

The Quai St-Louis and Quai St-Vincent, on the western side of St-Malo

For hotels and restaurants in this region see pp218–20 and pp236–8

Romanesque style. It is an example of the influence of Anglo-Norman architecture on the design of churches in northern Brittany. The great rose window is filled with modern, brightly coloured glass. The tomb of Jacques Cartier, the 16th-century explorer from St-Malo, can be seen in the north chapel.

At No. 3 Cour de la Houssaye, near Rue Chateaubriand, is the **Maison de la Duchesse Anne** *(see p42)*. With its outer tower, it is a typical example of a late Medieval urban manor house. Destroyed during World War II, it was rebuilt on the basis of old engravings.

Rue du Pélicot, which runs across Rue Chateaubriand, has some unusual "glass houses" – early 16th-century wooden houses with glazed galleries. At the end of Rue Mac-Law stands the Chapelle St-Aaron (1621), perched on the summit of the rock and

facing the law courts. The evangelizing monk Aaron, St-Malo's original inhabitant, chose this spot for his hermitage.

The rampart walk on the eastern side of the walled city, near Porte de Dinan, offers a bird's-eye view of several 18th-century shipowners' houses that either escaped war damage or were reconstructed. Built in a restrained and uniform style, they have an aristocratic elegance, and reflect both the personal wealth and social standing of their owners, who used them as a base for trading activities. The ramparts also afford fine views as far as Dinard and the Côte d'Emeraude.

🏠 Hôtel Magon-d'Asfeld
Demeure de Corsaire

5 Rue d'Asfeld. *Tel (02) 99 56 09 40.* 🗓️ *Jul–Aug: daily; Feb–Jun & Sep–Nov: Tue–Sun.* ⚫ *Dec–Jan.* 🎫
This fine building was once the residence of Auguste

Maison de la Duchesse Anne, a typical urban manor house

Magon de La Lande, one of the wealthiest shipowners in St-Malo and the head of the French East India Company in 1715.

Open to visitors, it offers the opportunity to see inside one of these aristocratic houses, with their vaulted cellars.

ST-MALO CITY CENTRE

0 m   400
0 yards   400

KEY

■ See pp78–9

Key to Symbols *see back flap*

♣ Château

Place Chateaubriand, in the Citadel.
Built in the 15th and 16th
centuries, the castle was used
by Jean V, Duke of Brittany
(1399–1442) mainly as a base
from which to keep watch
over the infamously rebellious
people of St-Malo. John's
daughter Anne *(see pp42–3)*,
who became queen of France
through her marriage to
Charles VIII, enlarged the castle,
with the same purpose in
mind. Knowing the dissenting
character of the townspeople,
she had these words engraved
in the wall of a tower in the
castle's east wing: *"Quic en
groigne, ainsi sera, car tel est
mon plaisir"* (Thus will it be,
whoever complains, for this
is my will.) The people of
St-Malo defiantly christened
the castle Quic-en-Groigne.

⛪ Musée d'Histoire de St-Malo

In the castle keep. *Tel* (02) 99 40 71
57. ⬭ Apr–Sep: daily. ⬤ Nov–Mar:
Mon and public holidays. ⬭
This museum, dedicated to
the history of St-Malo, occupies
the keep, which stands at the
entrance to the castle. With
granite walls and high chimneypieces, it provides a sumptuous
setting for the exhibits.

The collection consists of
paintings, sculpture, figure-
heads, models of ships and
topographical models illustrating the city's history and its
seafaring traditions. Prominent
citizens of St-Malo, such as
Robert Surcouf and Jacques
Cartier, Chateaubriand *(see
p69)* and Lamennais *(see p25)*
are also honoured.

LEE MILLER'S WARTIME SCOOP

In October 1944, an eight-page report on the siege of
St-Malo appeared in the pages of American *Vogue*. The
report and accompanying photographs were by-lined
Lee Miller, Man Ray's companion, a friend of Paul Éluard
and Pablo Picasso, and a model and fashion
photographer. The only journalist in the city during the
bombings, she recorded the destruction of St-Malo. "My
heel sank into a disembodied hand, and I cursed the

Germans for the horrible
destruction that they had
inflicted on this once-
splendid city," she wrote
at the time. Antony
Penrose, Lee Miller's son
and the author of her
biography, relates that
the photographs taken by
his mother were such a
scoop that they were
confiscated by the British
censors: it was during
the liberation of St-Malo
that napalm had first
been used.

Place Chateaubriand in 1944

♣ Fort du Petit-Bé

Tel 06 08 27 51 20. ⬭ depends on
the weather; phone ahead. ⬭ ⬭
Facing the Bidouane Tower
and Champs-Verte gate, this
fort, which was designed by
Vauban *(see p167)* in the 17th
century, is accessible either by
foot at low tide or by boat. It
was owned by the French
army until 1885, then decommissioned and restored to the
city of Saint-Malo. It was classified as a historic monument in
1921. Reproductions of 17th-
and 18th-century military plans
illustrate the history of the
defence of St-Malo. An ancient
mareographe, used to calcu-
late the tides, is also on display.

♣ Fort National

Northeast of the castle. *Tel* (02) 99
85 34 33. Accessible on foot at low
tide. When the French flag flies over
the fort, it is open to the public.
⬭ Jun–Sep: daily. ⬭
In the 18th century, five
coastal forts – La Varde,
Le Petit-Bé, La Conchée,
Harbourg and the Fort
National – defended the Baie
de St-Malo. The Fort National
was designed by the military
engineer Vauban in 1689. It
was built by Garangeau *(see
p80)* on the Rocher de l'Islet,
where criminals were once
executed. From here, there is
a splendid view of the
ramparts, the Rance estuary
and the Îles Chausey.

⛪ St-Servan

This residential district to the
south of the walled city of
St-Malo contains some fine
houses. Numerous sailing
ships are berthed in the Les
Bas-Sablons harbour. From
here, a road leads to Alet.

⛪ Musée du Long Cours Cap-Hornier

In the Tour Solidor. *Tel* (02) 99 40 71
58. ⬭ Apr–Sep: daily. ⬤ Nov–Mar:
Mon & public holidays. ⬭
The tower now houses a
museum devoted to those
who, following trade routes,

The Fort National, designed by Vauban and built by Garangeau

Notre-Dame-des-Flots, an oratory on the cliffs near Rothéneuf

sailed round Cape Horn in the 19th and 20th centuries. Items on display include navigational instruments, models of ships, sails, sperm whales' teeth and canoe paddles from New Caledonia. The tower, which is some 30 m (33 ft) high, was built on the orders of John IV, Duke of Brittany, between 1364 and 1382. It commands a fine view of the estuary.

Corniche d'Alet

Alet, inhabited by Celts in 80–70 BC, was settled before St-Malo was founded. Around 270, the peninsula was enclosed by walls and then, in about 350, a *castellum* (small fort) was built here, on a site now covered by the gardens of the Château de Solidor. In about 380, Alet became the capital of the Coriosolites, a Gaulish tribe inhabiting what is now the Côtes d'Armor. In the mid-12th century, the see of St-Malo was transferred to Alet, causing the city to decline. The walls, cathedral and castle were razed on the orders of St Louis, although a few ruins can still be seen.

The coast walk offers a breathtaking view of the walled city, the Île du Petit-Bé and Île du Grand-Bé, where Chateaubriand was laid to rest.

Paramé

On the road north out of St-Malo. Paramé and Rothéneuf have formed part of St-Malo since 1967. The coastal resort of Paramé was established at the end of the 19th century, when developers built the dyke and the eclectic-style holiday villas here. Two beaches, the Plage du Casino and Plage Rochebonne, stretch for 4 km (2 miles).

Rothéneuf

Northeast of Paramé, via the D201. A long-distance footpath (GR34) follows the coast to Rothéneuf from Pointe de la Varde, from where the view stretches from the Baie de St-Malo right round to Cap Fréhel *(see p107)*. This is a quiet village with two beaches, one of which lines a cove.

🐟 Grand Aquarium

La Ville-Jouan, Avenue du Général-Patton. *Tel (02) 99 21 19 00.* ☐ *daily.* This fascinating modern aquarium offers the opportunity to view almost 500 different species of cold-water and warm-water marine life. The route through the aquarium corresponds to that taken by the great navigators, from the North Atlantic to the Caribbean Sea. With a circular tank containing sharks, a tropical room, tanks where visitors can touch the fish, and the reconstruction of the wreck of a galleon, the aquarium has much to interest people of all ages.

Havre du Lupin

On the road north out of Rothéneuf. Also known as Havre de Rothéneuf, this cove is a saltwater lake at high tide and an expanse of sand at low tide. It is connected to the sea by a 300-m (985-ft) wide channel running between the coast and a peninsula, the Presqu'île Benard.

Carved Rocks

Chemin des Rochers-Sculptés. *From the walled city of St-Malo, take the track in the direction of Rothéneuf.* *Tel (02) 99 56 23 95.* ☐ *daily.*

Between 1870 and 1895, the Abbé Fourré, a partly paralysed country priest, produced a masterpiece of naive art. He carved about 300 figures – a fantastic assemblage of grimacing monsters, animals and humans – out of the granite rockface.

From here, a path leads to the **Oratoire Notre-Dame-des-Flots**, in a converted coastguard's house. The simplicity of this chapel, on the cliff edge, gives the spot a special atmosphere.

One of the figures carved out of the living rock by the Abbé Fourré

🏛 Manoir Jacques-Cartier

Manoir du Limoëlou. *Accessible via Rue David-Mac-Donald-Stewart.* *Tel (02) 99 40 97 73.* ☐ *Jun–Oct.* The museum is housed in a farmstead built in the 15th and 16th centuries and enlarged in the 19th century. It is devoted mainly to the explorer Jacques Cartier, who discovered Canada in 1534 and lived here between 1541 and 1557. There is also an excellent section illustrating daily life in the region during the 16th century.

The Manoir de Limoëlou, housing the Manoir Jacques-Cartier

The Château du Bos, country residence of the Magons, built in 1717

Château du Bos **24**

Road map E1-2. 5 km (3 miles) south of St-Malo via the N137, turning off to the right onto the road to La Passagère, Quelmer. **Tel** (02) 99 81 40 11. ● *closed to the public.*

This is a fine example of the fully-fledged *malouinière*, a residence characteristic of the environs of St-Malo. It was built in 1717 for the Magons, an important shipowning family, whose prominence is reflected in a local saying of the time: "In Paris, the Bourbons, in St-Malo the Magons".

Through its sheer size, this chateau is similar to the type of grand country house where a shipowner would stay only occasionally, living for most of the time in his town house in St-Malo. The architect was

Bulet de Chamblain, who worked for the French and Swedish royal courts, and who also designed the Château de Champ-sur-Marne and the Château de la Chipaudière.

The formal garden, decorated with white marble busts in the Italian style, slopes down towards the River Rance. The façade overlooking the garden features a semicircular bay, built in Chausey granite, that contains the main reception room.

The oval drawing room, the *boiseries* (decorative woodwork) and the interior decoration are in the style that was fashionable during the reign of Louis XVI. The Regency *boiseries* in the dining room are similar to those in private residences in the walled city of St-Malo *(see pp78–81).*

MALOUINIÈRES

Part of the façade of a *malouinière* in Puits-Sauvage

Second residences of the wealthy shipowners of St-Malo, *malouinières* were built in the 17th and 18th centuries, a time when this port city of privateers was expanding. Their design being influenced by military architecture, *malouinières* typically have simple outlines, harmonious proportions and a certain austerity. Further characteristics are a steeply pitched roof and high chimneys with lead or terracotta stacks, emblems of the new élite. Bands of dressed Chausey granite surround window frames and mark the angles of the walls. The emphasis on symmetry and ordered perspective is in keeping with the Neo-Classical style of the period.

Dinard **25**

Road map E1. 🏠 *11,000.* ✈ *Dinard-Pleurtuit-St-Malo; (02) 99 46 18 46.* ⛴ *Emeraude Lines; (02) 99 46 10 45.* 🚌 🚍 ℹ *2 Boulevard Féart; (02) 99 46 94 12.* 🕒 *Tue, Fri & Sat.* 🎭 *Festival de Musique Classique (Aug); Festival du Film Britannique (end Sep–beginning Oct).* **www**.ot-dinard.com

At the beginning of the 19th century, Dinard was no more than a small fishing village. This was before a small group of British and Americans created the fashion for comfortable mansions in coastal resorts. Dinard remains a high-class resort with a certain old-world appeal.

In 1873, the Lebanese aristocrat Joseph Rochaïd Dahda purchased land on which to build. English-style manor houses then appeared, along with Louis XIII-style chateaux, colonial houses and mock-Breton villas. British and European aristocrats flocked to Dinard's palatial residences. The attraction, albeit slightly antiquated, is still alive today, and the smart young set continues to come here.

Dinard, a fashionable and elegant resort since the 19th century

Walks in either direction along the coastal promenade pass various ostentatious villas typical of Dinard in its fashionable heyday. While the **Promenade de la Malouine**, leads westwards, the **Promenade Robert-Surcouf** leads eastwards to the Pointe du Moulinet, from where there is a spectacular view.

While the **Aquarium**, on Avenue Georges-V, is devoted to the marine plants and animals of the region, the **Musée de la Mer**, next door, documents the polar expeditions undertaken by Jean-Baptiste Charcot in the early 20th century. The **Musée du Site Balnéaire**, not far from Plage du Prieuré, is housed in a villa built for Empress Eugénie in 1867. It documents upper-class life in the resort at the height of its popularity with the British, a time when over 400 stately villas were built. As well as photographs and models, the exhibits include swimming costumes and sculpture.

Environs

A **tidal power station** *(usine marémotrice)* is located on the bridge over the Rance estuary, on the Dinard side. Harnessing the energy of the tides, which are among the strongest in the world here, the power station generates enough electricity to supply a town of 250,000 inhabitants for a year, or a quarter of what a nuclear power station would produce. It has no negative environmental impact. Built on the principle of tidal mills, it was inaugurated in 1966, after 25 years' research and six years' building work. It consists of a dam, a lock and an embankment, which contains the power station.

Aquarium and Musée de la Mer
7 Avenue Georges-V. **Tel** (02) 99 46 13 90. ● for rebuilding.

Musée du Site Balnéaire
Villa Eugénie, 12 Rue des Français-Libres. **Tel** (02) 99 46 81 05. ● currently closed.

The harbour at St-Briac, depicted by many 19th-century painters

St-Lunaire ㉖

Road map E1. 2 km (1 mile) west of Dinard, via the D786. ㊟ *2,200.* 🚉 🖺 *Blvd Générale de Gaulle; (02) 99 46 31 09.*

This small resort, which, like Dinard, came into being at the end of the 19th century, is named after an Irish monk who settled here in the 6th century. The 11th-century **church** is one of the oldest in Brittany. It contains the tomb of St Lunaire, with a 14th-century recumbent figure.

Pointe du Décollé, north of St-Lunaire, is worth the detour for the panorama of the Côte d'Émeraude that it commands. The point is connected to the mainland by a natural bridge spanning a chasm known as the Trou du Chat (Cat's Hole).

St-Briac ㉗

Road map E1. 5 km (3 miles) southwest of Dinard, via the D786. ㊟ *1,825.* 🖺 🚉 *49 Grande-Rue; (02) 99 88 32 47.* **www**.tourisme-saint-briac.fr

Like Pont-Aven, in Finistère, this former fishing village, located on the right bank of the Frémur, attracted many painters at the end of the 19th century, among them Auguste Renoir, Henri Rivière, Émile Bernard and Paul Signac. The **Chemin des Peintres**, a former customs' officers' path that leads out of the village, has been especially arranged for art-lovers. The walk is lined with reproductions of paintings placed at spots where various artists set up their easels to paint the landscape.

The stained-glass windows in the 19th-century church show scenes from the life of St Briac, who, it is said, looked after the insane. Certain members of the Habsburg and Hohenzollern families used to visit the resort. The Grand Duke of Russia himself, pretender to the Russian throne, would come to stay in the family residence here.

The pleasingly simple 11th-century church in St-Lunaire

CÔTES D'ARMOR

*I*t is on the Côtes d'Armor that the most timeless aspects of Brittany are preserved. While jewel-like churches and chapels hidden in remote hamlets express a profound piety, a wealth of fine buildings stands as ample proof of material riches derived from the linen trade. Here, also, are gentle landscapes and thriving crops, as well as fishing harbours and pirates' nests that are now picturesque holiday resorts.

Majestic Cap Fréhel, on the Côte d'Émeraude, marks the eastern boundary of the Côtes d'Armor, where the coast is lined with beaches and where pink limestone cliffs and windswept heathland create an impressive landscape.

The hinterland south of St-Brieuc is the border between the Celtic, western part of Brittany and Lower Brittany. Lamballe, east of St-Brieuc, marks a later boundary. It was once the capital of the duchy of Penthièvre, enemy of the house of Brittany, and several fortresses were built near here.

While the historic towns of Quintin and Moncontour owe their rich heritage to the manufacture of linen cloth in the 17th and 18th centuries, Paimpol, on the Côte du Goëlo, looks back to an illustrious past, when courageous seamen left from here to sail for Iceland: 2,000 of Paimpol's fishermen never returned.

For nature-lovers, the Île de Bréhat, which has an almost Mediterranean microclimate, offers the opportunity to enjoy scenic walks, while the Sept-Îles archipelago is home to 15 species of sea birds. On the Côte de Granit Rose, outcrops of warm-toned granite eroded by wind and rain create a striking sight.

With their attractive settings and many beaches, resorts such as Perros-Guirec and Trégastel throng with holiday-makers during the summer. Inland, the heaths of the Trégor give way to the fields and wooded valleys of ancient Argoat. Churches and calvaries here reflect centuries of religious faith. Tréguier, with a delicately ornamented Gothic cathedral, is one of the finest cities in Brittany.

The Léguer estuary, winding for almost 6 km (4 miles) between Lannion and the English Channel

◁ Pink granite boulders at the Pointe de Squewel, near the resort of Ploumanac'h

Exploring the Côtes d'Armor

The name "Côtes d'Armor", meaning "coasts of the sea country", comes from the area's deeply indented coastline formed by rias (ancient river valleys flooded by the sea). Jutting headlands, like the Trégor, alternate with wide inlets, such as the Baie de St-Brieuc. The highest point of the Côtes d'Armor are the Monts d'Arrée and the heathland of Le Méné, in the south. Coastal resorts such as Val-André, St-Cast and Perros-Guirec are the region's main tourist spots, and fishing harbours and islands, particularly the Sept-Îles archipelago and Île de Bréhat, are popular with holiday-makers. Inland are such picturesque medieval towns as Dinan, Quintin and Moncontour, and many impressive religious buildings, such as Tréguier's great Gothic cathedral.

Cloister of the Cathédrale St-Tugdual, Tréguier

SEE ALSO

- *Where to Stay* pp220–22

- *Where to Eat* pp238–41

THE REGION AT A GLANCE

GETTING AROUND

The N12, a major road, runs through the heart of the Côtes d'Armor. St-Brieuc is the hub of the region's road network. From here, the D786 runs along the Côte de Granit Rose to Plestin, and, heading southwards, the D790 and D700 link St-Brieuc with the heart of the region. From Rennes, the N12 leads to Montauban and the N164 to Loudéac, Mûr-de-Bretagne, Gouarec and Rostrenen. There is a bus service from St-Brieuc to Vannes every two hours. From Guingamp, a train service runs five times a day both to Carhaix and to Paimpol.

The coast path between Perros-Guirec and Ploumanac'h

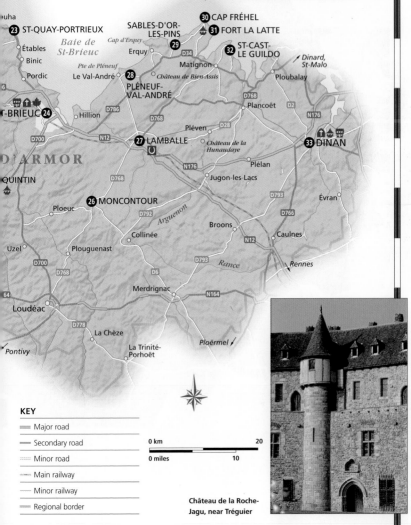

'uha

23 ST-QUAY-PORTRIEUX

Étables
Binic
Pordic

Baie de St-Brieuc

Cap d'Erquy

SABLES-D'OR-LES-PINS
29
Erquy
D34
Matignon

Pte de Pléneuf

Le Val-André
28
Château de Bien-Assis

PLÉNEUF-VAL-ANDRÉ

30 CAP FRÉHEL
31 FORT LA LATTE

32 ST-CAST-LE GUILDO

Dinard, St-Malo

Ploubalay

-BRIEUC 24
Hillion
D786
D768
Plancoët
D768
D2
N176

Pléven
D28

27 LAMBALLE
Château de la Hunaudaye

33 DINAN

D'ARMOR

QUINTIN
Ploeuc

26 MONCONTOUR
D792
Arguenon

Plélan

Jugon-les-Lacs

D768

N176

D793
Évran

Collinée
Broons
D766

Uzel
Plouguenast
N12
Caulnes

D700
D768
D793
Rance

64

Merdrignac
N164

Loudéac

D778
La Chèze

D6

Rennes

Pontivy
La Trinité-Porhoët

Ploërmel

KEY

═══ Major road

─── Secondary road

┅┅┅ Minor road

╍╍╍ Main railway

──── Minor railway

═══ Regional border

0 km   20

0 miles   10

Château de la Roche-Jagu, near Tréguier

Mûr-de-Bretagne ❶

Road map D2. 17 km (11 miles) west of Loudéac via the N164. 👥 *2,140.* 🄸 *Place de l'Église; (02) 96 28 51 41 or (02) 96 26 31 37.* 🄰 *Jul–Aug: Fri.* 🄰 *Festival des Arts Traditionnels (Jul).*

The town of Mûr marks the linguistic boundary between the Celtic, western part of Brittany and the eastern part.

The menhirs in the vicinity, especially the Neolithic **Menhir de Botrain** and **Menhir de Boconnaire**, as well as the numerous burial mounds, show that the region was quite densely populated in prehistoric times.

The **Chapelle Ste-Suzanne**, north of Mûr, in a stand of oak trees, was painted by Corot (1796–1875). It was built in 1496, although the choir (1694) and belfry (1752–64) are later.

Lac de Guerlédan and Forêt de Quénécan ❷

Road map D2. 22 km (14 miles) west of Loudéac via the N164. **Watersports centre** *Tel (02) 96 67 12 22.* **Holiday village** *Tel (02) 96 28 50 01.* 🄸 *(02) 96 28 51 41.* 🄰 *Fête du Lac (15 Aug).*

Filling a valley that was flooded when a hydroelectric dam was built in 1930, the Lac de Guerlédan, just west of Mûr-de-Bretagne, stretches for 12 km (8 miles). A water-sports centre, a camp site and a holiday village, it attracts lovers of the great outdoors. From the banks

of the Blavet, there is a stunning view of the Barrage de Guerlédan, which is not open to the public. The power station is open to visitors however. The **Musée de l'Électricité** nearby illustrates the history of electricity production, and the ways in which electricity is used.

Southwest of the lake is the 3,000-ha (7,400-acre) Forêt de Quénécan, with beech, spruce and pine. Like the Forêt de Paimpont, it is a vestige of the Forêt de Brocéliande *(see p62).*

🏛 **Musée de l'Électricité**
St-Aignan. *Tel (02) 97 27 51 39.* ◯ *Jun–mid-Sep: daily; for other times phone ahead.* 🄰

Gorges de Daoulas ❸

Road map C2. 30 km (18.5 miles) west of Loudéac via the N164.

The high escarpments and the plant life of the Gorges de Daoulas give this gorge the appearance of an Alpine defile. The river here has eroded the schist, and the water flows swiftly between high cliffs that have a wild beauty.

The partially ruined **Abbaye Cistercienne de Bon-Repos**, just off the N164, was built in the 12th century. The monastic buildings and cloister both date from the 18th century. An exhibition hall has a biannual contemporary art exhibition.

Abbaye Cistercienne de Bon-Repos, founded in the 12th century and now partly in ruins

🄰 **Abbaye Cistercienne de Bon-Repos**
St-Gelven. Via the N164. *Tel (02) 96 24 82 20.* ◯ *for exhibitions mid-May–Jun, daily pm.* 🄰

Guingamp ❹

Road map C2. 👥 *8,830.* 🄸 *2 Place au Champ-au-Roy; (02) 96 43 73 89.* 🄰 🄰 *St-Brieuc.* 🄰 *Fri.* 🄰 *Bugale Vreizh (Breton dancing and Pardon de Notre-Dame, early Jul); Fête de la St-Loup (mid-Aug).*

Standing at a crossroads and once fortified, Guingamp is an attractive town with fine timber-framed houses, particularly on Place du Centre.

The **Basilique Notre-Dame**, in Rue Notre-Dame, was built in several stages between the 13th and 16th centuries, and therefore exhibits several different styles. While the columns at the crossing, which are decorated with grotesque figures, are typically Romanesque, both the west door and the triforium are in an accomplished Renaissance style. The apse, by contrast, is Gothic.

The **Hôtel de Ville**, on Place Verdun, occupies the former Monastère des Hospitalières, dating from the early 17th century. The Baroque chapel here contains paintings by the Pont-Aven group *(see p169)* . Ramparts on Place du Petit-Vally are all that remains of the 15th-century castle, which was demolished in 1626.

Environs
10 km (6 miles) west of Guingamp is the holy mountain of **Menez-Bré**. From the summit, there are spectacular views of the Trégor. The 17th-century chapel here is dedicated to St

The Lac de Guerlédan, offering many watersports activities

Hervé, healer, exorcist and patron of bards. The fountain 300 m (330 yds) from the chapel is said to have sprung at his command. Sick children were dipped in its miraculous waters in the hope of curing them.

Châtelaudren, 13 km (8 miles) east of Guingamp via the N12-E50 then the D7, is well worth the detour for the Chapelle Notre-Dame-du-Tertre, which contains 132 remarkable 15th-century frescoes on biblical themes.

The nave of the Basilique Notre-Dame in Guingamp

Bulat-Pestivien ❺

Road map C2. 18 km (11 miles) southwest of Guingamp via the D787 then the D31. ⛪ *440.* ☛ *Pardon (early Sep).*

This small village (famous, rather quirkily, as a centre for the breeding of the Breton spaniel) boasts a magnificent 14th-century **church**. Its tower is the earliest example of Renaissance architecture in Brittany. Like those of the church at Loc-Envel *(see below)*, the exterior walls are covered in gargoyles, monsters and grimacing *ankous* (skeletons). Both the porch and the main entrance dazzle with their elaborate decoration. According to legend, this church was built by a lord in thanks to the Virgin Mary, who restored his son to him when the child was snatched by a monkey. This

strange scene is depicted in the sacristy.

Environs
One km (0.5 mile) to the north is a charming **parish close** with a calvary dating from 1550. The **Gorges du Corong**, 10 km (6 miles) south of Bulat-Pestivien, are wreathed in ferns and have a wild and dramatic beauty. According to legend, the great rocks beneath which the river flows are the stones that a giant shook out of his clogs.

Belle-Isle-en-Terre ❻

Road map C2. 18 km (11 miles) west of Guingamp via the N12. ⛪ *1,110.* ℹ *15 Rue de Crec'h-Ugen; (02) 96 43 01 71.* 🚉 *Guingamp.* 🛒 *Wed.* ☛ *Pardon (third weekend of Jul).*

This town lies between the rivers Guer and Guic, which join to form the Léguer, the river that flows into the Baie de Lannion. It is a popular area for fishing, and the meadows and woods round about are ideal walking country.

Tradition dictates that the origins of Belle-Isle-en-Terre go back to the 9th century and its name is probably from the monks of Belle-Isle, an island off the western coast of Brittany, who founded a monastery in nearby Locmaria.

Just north of the village is the Chapelle de Locmaria, which has a 15th-century rood screen.

The castle here houses the **Centre Régional d'Initiation à la Rivière**, which is dedicated to environmental protection.

The church at Bulat-Pestivien, in the Renaissance style

Environs
The village of **Loc-Envel**, 4 km (3 miles) southwest of Belle-Isle via the D33, stands on the edge of the **Forêt de Coat-an-Noz**.

Loc-Envel is well worth a visit for its 16th-century church. The belfry, with gargoyles, is in the Gothic style, but it is the interior that is particularly fascinating. The rood screen, richly decorated in the Flamboyant Gothic style, and the vaulting of the nave, from which hosts of carved monsters stare down, are remarkable.

The forest, with age-old trees whose branches are covered with moss, lichen and ferns, is a magical place in which to stroll. The forest's undulating terrain, and the paths that wind between clumps of box-tree dating from Roman times, make it interesting walking country.

The Flamboyant Gothic rood screen in the church at Loc-Envel

The Château de Rosanbo, owned by the same family for 600 years

Plestin-les-Grèves ❼

Road map C1. 15 km (9 miles) southwest of Lannion via the D786. 🚶 *3,300.* 🚉 *Morlaix, Lannion and Plouaret.* 🛈 *Place de la Mairie; (02) 96 35 61 93.* 🚌 *Sun.*

The jewel in the area around Plestin (*Plistin* in Breton) is a wide, soft sandy beach known as **Lieue de Grève**. This beach, which stretches for miles when the tide is out, has held a strong appeal for holiday-makers since the 1930s. Several holiday residences, including the Villa Trenkler (House of the Eagle) and Villa Lady Mond (*see p91*) at the coastal village of St-Efflam, date from this period.

Unfortunately, since 1970, the water on this small stretch of coastline has been regularly infested with prolific, foul-smelling green algae. However, if taking the sea air is out of the question, it is possible to climb up to the Grand Rocher, which, 80 m (262 ft) high, overlooks the beach, or to follow the coast road, the Corniche de l'Armorique (D42), for a view of the Baie de Locquirec (*see p119*). Several species of birds, including sheldrake and sandpiper, can also be seen here.

Environs
The **Château de Rosanbo**, which has been in the same family for 600 years, is located just 6 km (4 miles) from Plestin-les-Grèves. This fine residence was restored in the Neo-Gothic style in 1895. The chateau's formal garden, with hedgerows and bowers, was designed by Duchêne, the landscape gardener who laid out the gardens at Vaux-le-Vicomte. The architect Lafargue designed the library for the 8,000-book collection of Claude Le Pelletier, who was to succeed Colbert as Louis XIV's finance minister. The dining room was reconstructed on the basis of 18th-century inventories.

The church in the village of **Lanvellec** is also worth a visit. It contains a fine organ built by Robert Dallam in 1653.

⚜ **Château de Rosanbo**
Lanvellec (D22). **Tel** (02) 96 35 18 77. ⏲ *times vary, phone ahead.* 🖼 🈲

Ploubezre ❽

Road map C1. 3 km (2 miles) south of Lannion via the D11. 🚶 *2,700.* 🛈 *Mairie; (02) 96 47 15 51.*

To discover so fine a chapel in a remote location such as this is always a pleasant surprise. **Notre-Dame de Kerfons**, in Ploubezre, is one of the finest examples of religious architecture in Brittany.

The chapel was built in the Flamboyant Gothic style, probably under the aegis of a powerful local lord. When it was remodelled in the Renaissance style, its builders took the trouble to use stones from the same quarry, the better to blend the new style with the old.

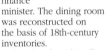

Altarpiece in the Chapelle de Notre-Dame de Kerfons

The detailed and elaborate decoration of the interior culminates in the rood screen, a tracery of painted and gilt wood, with reliefs depicting Christ, the 12 Apostles, St Barbara and St Mary Magdalen.

The **Château de Kergrist**, built in 1537 by Jean de Kergrist and remodelled in the 17th and 18th centuries, is characteristic of the great Renaissance residences built by the Breton aristocracy. The Huon de Penanster family, which has owned the castle since 1860, has opened to visitors the gardens and one of the three blocks that frame the main courtyard. The interior, which is only open for guided tours of 20 or more people, is filled with interesting traditional Breton furniture, including a decorated wardrobe, and tapestry door screens.

🛈 **Notre-Dame de Kerfons**
Kerfons (D31b). ⏲ *Mid-Jun–mid-Sep: Wed–Mon.* 🖼

⚜ **Château de Kergrist**
Ploubezre (D11). **Tel** (02) 96 38 91 44. ⏲ *Easter–May: Sat & Sun; Jun–Sep: daily.* 🖼 🅰 *Garden & ground floor only.*

Lieue de Grève, a wide sandy beach north of Plestin-les-Grèves

The ruined 13th-century Château de Tonquédec

Environs

About 2 km (1 mile) from the Château de Kergist stands the impressive ruins of the **Château de Tonquédec**, built in the 13th century by the lords of Tonquédec. During the Wars of the Holy League, the castle had become a Huguenot stronghold. Because of this, it was partly demolished in 1626 on the orders of Cardinal Richelieu, principal minister to Louis XIII. The fortifications consist of 11 towers and a courtyard in which attackers could easily be trapped. From the rampart walk there is a panoramic view of the wooded valley of the Léguer.

♣ **Château de Tonquédec**
Tonquédec (D31b). **Tel** (02) 96 54 60 70. ◻ check times. 🖼

Lannion ❾

Road map C1. 🏰 19,400.
🚉 🚌 🛈 Quai d'Aiguillon; (02) 96 46 41 00. 🎷 Festival de Musique (Jul–Aug); Estivales de la Photographie (Jul–Sep). 🛍 Thu.
www.ot-lannion.fr

This bustling town has profited handsomely from the installation of the Centre National d'Études des Télécommunications here in 1960, and from the new TGV (high-speed-train) link. The nexus between the telecommunications centre at Pleumeur-Bodou (see p94) and newly installed optical industries, Lannion (Lannuon in Breton) has attracted thousands of researchers and students of engineering specializing in state-of-the-art technology.

Such dynamism might have altered the town's identity and picturesque character. Far from it: Breton is still spoken in the busy market square. The heart of the old town has ancient paved alleyways and some charming timber-framed, granite and cob houses, such as those at Nos. 1–3 Rue des Chapeliers, which escaped destruction during the Wars of Religion (1591), and Nos. 29–31 Place du Général-Leclerc, which were rebuilt after 1630. These houses are clad in slate and decorated with human figures, animals, crosses and lozenges. Some have overhanging windows.

Of all the religious buildings in Lannion, the most appealing is the **Église de Brélévenez**. It is reached via a flight of steps lined with small, attractive houses decorated with statues of patron saints or ceramic friezes. The church was founded in the 12th century by a branch of the order of the Knights Templar, the Trinitarians of St John. The choice of materials used in its construction reflects the importance of this church: pink and yellow granite for the south porch, large ashlars for the apse, black marble and tufa for the high altar, and painted wood for the altarpiece (1630) in the north transept – a slightly macabre reminder of the Day of Judgment.

🔒 **Église de Brélévenez**
🛈 (02) 96 46 41 00. ◻ daily. 🖼 Jul–Aug: Mon–Fri, Sun pm, by arrangement at the tourist office.

Le Yaudet, in a beautiful setting on the Léguer estuary

Environs

About 3 km (2 miles) west of Lannion, on the left bank of the Léguer, is **Loguivy-lès-Lannion** (Logivi in Breton), whose parish close has a notable portal and a Renaissance fountain. The oak altarpiece inside features a wealth of carvings.

The coast road leads on to the scenic hamlet of **Le Yaudet** (Ar Yeoded in Breton), whose granite houses cling to the hillside. Uniquely in Brittany, the village chapel contains a depiction of a recumbent Virgin next to the figure of Christ.

Set on a promontory, with a stunning view of the Léguer estuary, Le Yaudet has one of the most beautiful natural settings in the Trégor. Excavations led by archaeologists from Brest and Oxford have uncovered a Gallo-Roman fishing village on the promontory.

🏕 **Le Yaudet**
Le Yaudet (D88). **Tel** (02) 96 46 41 00. 🖼 Mon & Fri. 🖼

Half-timbered houses in the historic centre of Lannion

A beach at the popular coastal resort of Trébeurden

Trébeurden ⑩

Road map C1. 7 km (4 miles) northwest of Lannion via the D65. 🚉 *Lannion*. 🏠 *3,540*. ℹ️ *Place de Crec'h-Héry; (02) 96 23 51 64.* 🚌 *Tue.* 🎭 *Fest-noz (Jul); concerts (Wed in summer).* **www**.trebeurden.fr

A popular coastal resort, Trébeurden has several beautiful beaches either side of Le Castel, a rugged peninsula with pink granite rocks. The **Île Milliau**, opposite the peninsula, is accessible at low tide. More than 270 species of plants grow there. The island was inhabited 7,000 years ago; evidence of human habitation is a Neolithic passage grave, the **Allée Couverte de Prajou-Menhir**, 14 m (46ft) long and with carvings on its stones. The **Marais du Kellen**, behind Plage de Goas-Trez, attracts snipe, teal grebe and other birds.

Pleumeur-Bodou ⑪

Road map C1. 6 km (4 miles) northwest of Lannion via the D65 then the D21. 🚉 *Lannion*. 🏠 *4,000*. ℹ️ *11 Rue des Chardons; (02) 96 23 91 47.* 🚌 *Sat.* **www**.pleumeur-bodou.com

Bristling with giant antennae that provide worldwide communication, Pleumeur-Bodou is well known as the site of the telecommunications centre where the first satellite link between the United States and Europe was made, in 1962. The radar dome, a gigantic sphere 50 m (160 ft) high, is open to visitors.

There is also a **Museum**, tracing the 150-year history of telecommunications from their earliest days to the age of digital communications, and a **Planetarium**, with a screen measuring 600 sq m (6,460 sq ft).

Opposite the planetarium is the reconstruction of a Gaulish settlement, the **Village de Meem le Gaulois**. This whole complex goes under the name **Cosmopolis**.

🏛 **Cité des Télécoms**
Tel (02) 96 46 63 80. ⏰ *Apr–Sep: daily; Oct–Mar: during school holidays.*

🏛 **Planetarium**
Tel (02) 96 15 80 32. ⏰ *school holidays: daily; phone ahead for other times.* 🌙 *Jan.*

🏛 **Le Village Gaulois**
Tel (02) 96 91 83 95.
www.levillagegaulois.asso.org
⏰ *Jul–Aug: daily; Easter–Jun & Sep: Sun–Fri, pm only.*
♿

Environs
The **Île Grande**, north of Trébeurden, is accessible via a bridge on the D788. As well as beaches and footpaths, the island has an ornithological centre. The **Maison LPO**, a centre set up by an organization for the protection of birds, highlights the rich flora and fauna of the Sept-Îles archipelago. Tours are also organized from here. The **Menhir de St-Uzec**, 2 km (1 mile) from Penvern, is a standing stone 8 m (26 ft)

Board for Aquarium Marin, Trégastel

high, one of the finest in Brittany. In the 17th century, a cross and a depiction of the Passion of Christ were carved on it to convert it into a Christian monument.

🦅 **Maison LPO**
Île Grande. Tel (02) 96 91 91 40. ⏰ *Jun–Aug: daily; school holidays: daily pm; other times: Sat–Sun pm.*

Trégastel-Plage ⑫

Road map C1. 6 km (4 miles) west of Perros-Guirec via the D788. 🚉 *Lannion*. 🏠 *2,290*. ℹ️ *Place Ste-Anne; (02) 96 15 38 38.* 🚌 *Mon.* 🎭 *Fest-noz (Jun); 24 Heures de la Voile (mid-Aug).*

This resort is famous for the blocks of pink granite that rise up behind its beaches, Plage du Coz-Pors and Plage de Grève-Blanche. The orientation table between these two beaches offers a splendid panorama of the coast and of the countryside inland.

At the **Aquarium Marin**, housed in a cave, visitors can see fish and other marine life of the waters around Brittany.

Kerguntuil, 2 km (1 mile) south, on the D788 towards Trebeurden, is of interest for its Neolithic passage grave and dolmen.

🐟 **Aquarium Marin**
Boulevard de Coz-Pors. Tel (02) 96 23 48 58. ⏰ *Apr–mid-Nov: daily; mid-Nov–Mar: school holidays.*

Meem le Gaulois, the reconstruction of Gaulish village, Pleumeur-Bodou

Ploumanac'h ⑬

On account of its spectacular rocks, this former fishing village, now a district of Perros-Guirec, is one of the greatest tourist attractions in Brittany. **Pointe de Squewel**, one hour's walk along the coast path from Plage St-Guirec, north of Ploumanac'h, is a promontory with gigantic piles of rocks that suggest such incongruous shapes as tortoises, rabbits and tricorn hats. The **Maison du Littoral**, level with the lighthouse, contains displays explaining how the rocks were formed, and describing local flora and fauna.

The **Chapelle Notre-Dame-de-la-Clarté** (1445), midway between Ploumanac'h and Perros-Guirec, is the focus of a very lively annual pardon. The chapel has an interesting porch with relief decoration, and, inside, a stoup (1931) decorated with heads of Moors and the Stations of the Cross. It was made by Maurice Denis, a founder of the group of

Granite rocks at Pointe de Squewel, a major tourist attraction

painters known as the Nabis. The **Vallée des Traouïéros**, between Ploumanac'h and Trégastel, runs between blocks of granite and lush vegetation. The restored tidal mill here dates from the 14th century.

🍽 Maison du Littoral
Opposite the lighthouse.
Tel (02) 96 91 62 77. ☐ Mid-Jun–mid-Sep: Mon–Sat; school holidays: Mon–Fri pm.

Plage de Trestraou, one of several beaches at Perros-Guirec

Perros-Guirec ⑭

Road map C1. 🚊 Lannion.
🏘 7,890. 🛈 21 Place de l'Hôtel-de-Ville; (02) 96 23 21 15; in season: Fri & Sun. 🎭 Festival de la Bande Dessinée (Apr); Fête des Hortensias (Aug); Ploumanac'h Regatta (Aug); Pardon de Notre-Dame-de-la-Clarté (15 Aug).

With about a dozen beaches and many hotels, this coastal resort attracts large numbers of visitors in summer. As at Ploumanac'h, the coast here has extraordinary rock formations shaped by the erosion of wind and rain.

The coast path, running the 6 km (4 miles) between Plage de Trestraou and the famous rocks at Ploumanac'h, offers stunning views.

Environs

From Perros-Guirec there is a boat service to the **Sept-Îles Archipelago**, one of the best places to see sea birds. One of the islands, the **Île aux Moines**, is named after the Franciscan friars who settled there in the Middle Ages. Also on the island is a lighthouse and a small fort built by Garangeau, the architect responsible for St-Malo's fortifications (see pp78–83).

⛴ Embarcadère des Sept-Îles
(boarding point for boat service), Plage de Trestraou. **Tel** (02) 96 91 10 00. ☐ Feb–Nov & school holidays: daily; rest of the year: by arrangement.

SEPT-ÎLES BIRD SANCTUARY

Although the islands' best-known inhabitant is the puffin, the Sept-Îles archipelago, a protected area, is also home to fulmars, kittiwakes, pied oystercatchers, gulls, crested cormorants and other sea birds. Twenty thousand pairs breed in this protected area. Only one island, the Île aux Moines, is accessible to the public, although the birds on the other islands can be observed from motorboats. On the Île de Roizic, 15,130 pairs of gannets and 248 pairs of puffins nest in the craggy rocks. Grey seals can sometimes be seen at the foot of the cliffs in the islands' secluded creeks.

The puffin, emblematic inhabitant of the Sept-Îles

Stained-glass window in the Église Ste-Catherine in La Roche-Derrien

La Roche-Derrien ⑮

Road map C1. 15 km (9 miles) northeast of Lannion via the D786 then the D6. 🚉 Guingamp or Lannion. 👥 1,100. 🚏 Pays du Trégor-Goëlo, 9 Place de l'Église; (02) 96 91 50 22. 🏛 Fri.

In the middle ages, La Roche Derrien (*Ker Roc'h* in Breton, meaning Town of the Rock), was a fortified town over which many battles were fought. The castle, over-looking the Jaudy valley, was besieged during the War of the Breton Succession, a conflict between the English, the French and the Bretons *(see p40)*. In the 14th century, the castle passed into the hands of Bertrand du Guesclin *(see p41)*. He is said to have planted the yew tree still standing in the close of the 18th-century Chapelle de Notre-Dame-de-la-Pitié, on the road to Kermezen.

Altarpiece in the chapel at Confort

Today, La Roche-Derrien offers pleasant walks on the banks of the Jaudy. In the town, several timber-framed houses line Place du Martray. The Église Ste-Catherine, built in the 12th and 15th centuries, contains an elaborate 17th-century altarpiece. The modern stained-glass window in the transept depicts the battle between supporters of Charles of Blois and the English.

Environs
The 16th-century chapel at **Confort**, 13 km (8 miles) southwest of La Roche-Derrien on the D33, is built in a combination of the Flamboyant Gothic and Renaissance styles. The belltower, in the style of Lannion belfries, incorporates a stair turret. The chapel contains an altar-piece in which the Virgin is depicted in the likeness of Anne of Brittany and the Angel Gabriel in that of Louis XII, king of France *(see pp42–3)*.

About 6 km (4 miles) southeast of La Roche-Derrien on the D8, the church at **Runan**, dating from the 14th–16th centuries, was once owned by the Knights Templar, then by the Knights of St John of Jerusalem. It has a richly decorated façade and the south porch, with a pointed arch, has some notable reliefs. While the lintel is carved with a scene of the Annunciation and with a Pietà, the side panels feature a host of carved figures, four of whom stick out their tongues at the viewer. In front of the church is a rare 15th-century outdoor pulpit.

Port-Blanc ⑯

Road map C1. 8 km (5 miles) northwest of Tréguier via the D70a, the D70 then the D74. 🚉 Lannion. 👥 2,500. 🚏 12 Place. de l'Église, Penvenan; (02) 96 92 81 09. 🏛 Sat. 🎉 Pardons (Whitsun & 15 Aug).

Lying west of Plougrescant and sheltered by a barrier of dunes, the coastal village of Port-Blanc is a pleasant holiday resort. The highly picturesque 16th-century **chapel**, which nestles among rocks, is the focal point of the village. The chapel's roof is unusual in that it reaches almost to the ground. The 17th-century calvary in the close depicts St Yves, St Joachim, St Peter and St Francis. The chapel contains several old statues, including the traditional group depicting St Yves between a rich and a poor man.

From the harbour, trips out to sea are offered in an old sardine boat, the *Ausquémé*. The coast path from Port-Blanc to Buguélès commands some magnificent views.

🚤 **Ausquémé**
Tel 06 07 59 04 03. ⏱ Jul–Aug: daily; Sep–Jun: by arrangement.

The 16th-century chapel at Port-Blanc

The Sillon de Talbert, a natural spit of land with the Héaux lighthouse in the distance

Plougrescant 🕖

Road map C1. 6 km (4 miles) north of Tréguier on the D8. 🚉 *Guingamp or Lannion.* 🚍 *1,430.* 🛈 *Pays du Trégor-Goëlo, 9 Place de l'Église, La Roche-Derrien; (02) 96 91 50 22.* **www**.plougrescant.fr

The most prominent feature of Plougrescant is its chapel, the **Chapelle St-Gonery**, which has an eyecatchingly crooked belfry. The church consists of two sections, the first of which is Romanesque, dating from the 10th century. From this section rises the belfry, built in 1612. The other part is the nave, which was built in the 15th century.

The chapel is of interest chiefly for its remarkable 15th-century frescoes. Covering the barrel-vaulted ceiling, they loosely depict scenes from the Old and New Testaments. These scenes, which are depicted on an ochre background dotted with stars, are in a naive style. The contrasting colours, and areas of black and white, emphasize outlines and accentuate perspective.

The strikingly fine monuments inside the chapel include the tomb of Guillaume du Halgouët, bishop of Tréguier, and an alabaster statue of the Virgin, both dating from the 16th century, and a reliquary with finely carved panels.

During the summer, trips out to sea in an old sailing boat, the *Marie-Georgette*, depart from the harbour.

🚢 *Marie-Georgette*
Tel *(02) 96 92 09 15/ 58 83.*
🕐 *Apr–Sep.*

FAMOUS NAMES IN PORT-BLANC

Théodore Botrel

Port-Blanc has appealed to a variety of different people, from authors and songwriters to scientists and pioneers of aviation. In 1898, the writer Anatole Le Braz bought the property known as Kerstellic. He recorded Breton stories and legends that he heard told by the inhabitants of the Trégor. *La Légende de la Mort* (1893), is considered by Armorican Bretons to be his best work. Le Braz's friend and neighbour was the writer Ernest Renan (*see p101*), who lived at Rosmapamon. The songwriter Théodore Botrel, who wrote *La Paimpolaise*, bought land at Port-Blanc on which he built a house that he named *Ty Chansonniou* (House of Songs). He later left to live in Pont-Aven. In 1922, Alexis Carrel, winner of the Nobel Prize for Medicine, purchased the Île St-Gildas, where he was buried in 1944. His friend Charles Lindbergh was a frequent visitor. In 1938, after his pioneering flight across the Atlantic, Lindbergh acquired the Île d'Illiec, where he briefly lived before returning to the United States.

Sillon de Talbert 🕗

This natural spit of land extends for 3 km (2 miles) from the tip of the Presqu'île Sauvage, the peninsula between Tréguier and Paimpol. Made up of sand and pebbles, the spit was created by the opposing currents of two rivers, the Trieux and the Jaudy. It is now a protected site, as, were it to disappear, the two inlets on each side of the peninsula would be at the mercy of tidal currents. A kite festival takes place on the spit in July each year. The Héaux lighthouse can also be seen from here.

Île de Bréhat ⓳

Because of the luxuriant vegetation that thrives in its gentle climate, the Île de Bréhat is also known as the Island of Flowers. Bréhat, a paradise for walkers and a haven for artists, actually consists of two large islands linked by a bridge. In the north, heathland predominates and the indented coastline is reminiscent of Ireland. In the south, the landscape is softer, with pine trees, pink pebble beaches and Mediterranean plants. There is no motorized transport, but it is easy to walk or cycle along the island's sunken paths.

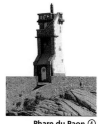

Phare du Paon ④
Destroyed by German forces during World War II, the lighthouse was rebuilt in red porphyry in 1947. Stairs lead up to the platform, from which there is a view of the open sea.

Chapelle St-Michel ⑥
Perched on a rise 26 m (85 ft) high, the Chapelle St-Michel overlooks the whole island. It was rebuilt in 1852, and has long served as a landmark for shipping. The path leads straight down to an old tidal mill.

Phare du Rosédo ⑤
The 19th-century lighthouse overlooks the heathland of the northwest of the island. Ernest Renan *(see p101)* came here to enjoy the beauty of the surroundings.

Le Goareva ⑦
This fort is a fine example of 18th-century military architecture.

Port-Clos ①
In 1770, Charles Cornic built this harbour, a port of call for ships from the mainland.

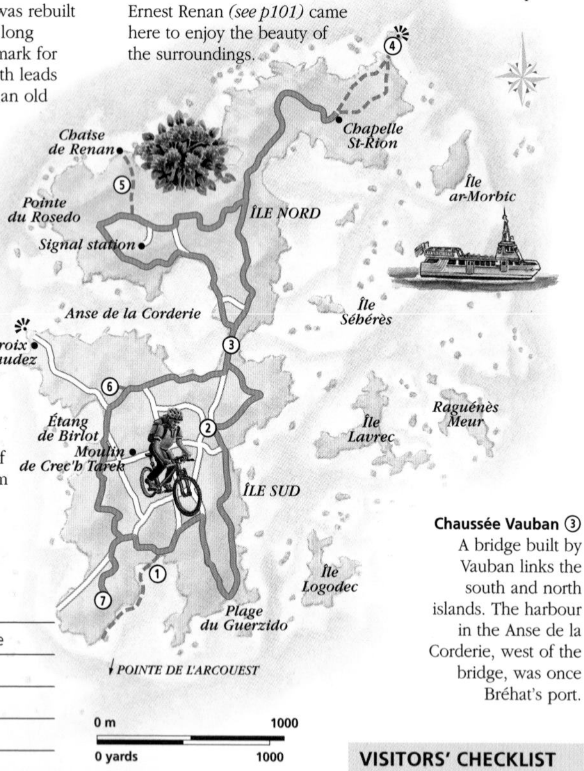

Chaise de Renan
Pointe du Rosedo
Signal station
ÎLE NORD
Chapelle St-Rion
Île ar-Morbic
Anse de la Corderie
Île Sébérès
la Croix de Maudez
Étang de Birlot
Moulin de Crec'h Tarek
Île Lavrec
Raguénès Meur
ÎLE SUD
Île Logodec
Plage du Guerzido
POINTE DE L'ARCOUEST
0 m
1000
0 yards
1000

Chaussée Vauban ③
A bridge built by Vauban links the south and north islands. The harbour in the Anse de la Corderie, west of the bridge, was once Bréhat's port.

KEY

- Suggested route
- Footpaths
- Other routes
- Viewpoint

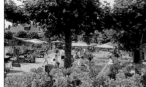

Bréhat, the island's flower-filled town

The town ②
Bréhat consists of houses clustered around a 12th-century church with 17th–19th-century alterations.

VISITORS' CHECKLIST

Tour: *about 9 km (5.5 miles).*
Access: *10 minutes from Pointe de l'Arcouest; information*
Tel *(02) 96 20 04 15. Bicycles can be hired in Port-Clos.*
Stopping-off places: *La Potinière, on Plage du Guerzido offers oysters and mussels; Le Paradis Rose, in the north, serves crêpes.*

Paimpol

Road map D1. 🏛 *8,420.*
🚌 *Avenue Général-de-Gaulle.* 🚂
ℹ️ *Place de la République; (02) 96 20 83 16.* 🛒 *Tue.* 🎭 *Fête des Terre-Neuvas et des Islandais (third Sun in Jul); songs of the sea (every 2 years in Aug from 2009); Fest-noz (14 Jul).*
www.paimpol-goelo.com

Although pleasure boats have now replaced the schooners that once filled the harbour, this is still the heart of Paimpol, with coasters and trawlers tied up alongside the quais. As Pierre Loti, in his novel *Pêcheurs d'Islande (An Iceland Fisherman)*, so eloquently described, the sea has exacted a heavy price from Paimpol: 100 schooners and 2,000 men were lost in the fishing expeditions that left Paimpol for Iceland.

The first left in 1852 and, in 1895, 82 schooners of 400 tonnes burden set sail for the North Sea. Each was crewed by about 20 seamen, who for six months endured not only cold and great physical strain, but also separation from their families. Their wives, the famous *Paimpolaises* immortalized by Théodore Botrel, would scour the horizon for their return at the Croix des Veuves-en-Ploubazlanec, north of the town. When the ships came in, there were either joyful reunions or scenes of mourning. The last expedition to Iceland left Paimpol in 1935.

The Place du Martray, in the town centre, is lined with 16th-century houses. On the corner of Rue de l'Église is a shipowner's house in the Renaissance style, with a turret. The house was used as

The 13th-century Abbaye de Beauport, in Paimpol, now in ruins

a hunting lodge by the Rohans, a powerful Breton dynasty. The **Musée du Costume**, in Rue Pellier, contains displays of *coiffes* and costumes from the Trégor and Goëlo. Through photographs, models, ships' logs, nautical equipment and votive offerings, the **Musée de la Mer**, in a building once used for drying cod, describes the fishing expeditions to Newfoundland and Iceland.

From Paimpol, visitors may take a **boat trip** out to sea in an old sailing boat, or a ride on a **steam train** up the Trieux valley to Pontrieux.

🏛 **Musée du Costume**
Rue Pellier. **Tel** *(02) 96 53 31 70.*
🔲 *Jul–Aug: daily.* 🔲

🏛 **Musée de la Mer**
Rue Labenne. **Tel** *(02) 96 22 02 19.* 🔲 *mid-Jun–Aug: daily; Sep–Jun: pm.* 🔲

📷 **Boat Trips**
Tel *(02) 96 55 44 33.*
www.voilestraditions.fr
Sardine Boat Trips Tel *(02) 96 55 99 99.* 🔲 *Apr–Nov.*
www.eulalie-paimpol.com
Steam Train Tel *08 92 39 14 27.* 🔲 *May–Sep: daily.*

Environs

The ruined Romanesque **Abbaye de Beauport**, 2 km (1 mile) south of Paimpol via the D786, is one of the most beautiful abbeys in Brittany. Built in the Anglo-Norman style in the early 13th century, it was an important centre of religion. Visitors can see the chapterhouse, cloisters, refectory and storerooms. From the abbey, a road leads to the **Chapelle Ste-Barbe**, the starting point of a coastal path.

The **Pointe de l'Arcouest**, reached via the D789 from Paimpol, is the main boarding point for the Île de Bréhat.

Loguivy-de-la-Mer, 4 km (2.5 miles) north of Paimpol, is one of the oldest harbours in Brittany. It is a busy fishing port and is renowned for the sea crayfish, lobsters and crabs that are landed here.

🏛 **Abbaye de Beauport**
On the D786. **Tel** *(02) 96 55 18 58.* 🔲 *daily.* 🔲

📷 **Pointe de l'Arcouest**
Les Vedettes de Bréhat. **Tel** *(02) 96 55 79 50.*

ARTISTS ON BRÉHAT

Between the late 19th and early 20th centuries, many writers and artists came to Bréhat. Writers included Ernest Renan, the Goncourt brothers, Pierre Loti and Théodore Botrel, and the artists Henri Rivière, Paul Gauguin, Henry Matisse, Tsugouharu Foujita, Henri Dabadie and many others. All found inspiration in the island's landscapes, but they also frequented the town's cafés. Mme Guéré, the fearsome landlady of a certain café, once threatened to behead a customer if he failed to settle his slate. Taking her at her word, the miscreant painted his face on the side of his glass. Ever since, artists have customarily painted their portraits on glasses at the Café des Pêcheurs, which now has a collection of 200 such glasses.

Une Rue à Bréhat, a painting by Henri Dabadie

Steam train in the station at Pontrieux

Tréguier ㉑

Creatures from Tréguier cathedral

The capital of the Trégor and an ancient bishopric, Tréguier is today a quiet city. The narrow streets around the splendid cathedral are lined with timber-framed houses and grander granite residences. The 16th-century timber-framed house in Rue Renan that is the birthplace of the writer Ernest Renan is now a museum, and visitors can see the nursery, Renan's studio and various other exhibits relating to his life and work. The Flamboyant Gothic Cathédrale St-Tugdual, one of the finest examples of Breton religious architecture, dominates Tréguier. The Pardon de St-Yves, in May, honours the cathedral's patron saint, who is also that of lawyers.

VISITORS' CHECKLIST

Road map C1. 🚌 *Paimpol or Lannion.* 🚶 *2,950.* 🛈 *13 Place de l'Église, Penvénan; (02) 96 92 81 09.* 🗓 *Wed.* 🎉 *Pardon de St-Yves (third Sun in May); Festival en Trégor (concerts; Jul–Aug).*

🔒 **Cathédrale St-Tugdual**
Place du Martray. ◯ *Jun–Sep: 9am–7pm daily; Oct–May: 9am–noon & 2–6pm daily.* ⬤ *to visitors during services.* 🎫 📷 *(Easter–Sep only).*
The cathedral was built on the site of a 12th-century Romanesque church, the only vestige of which is the Tour Hastings. The Porche des Cloches, in the south side, features a Flamboyant Gothic stained-glass window, and from the tower rises an 18th-century spire. The outer wall on the south side is covered in Gothic tracery.

CATHÉDRALE ST-TUGDUAL
A masterpiece of Breton Gothic religious architecture, the cathedral was built in the 14th–15th centuries.

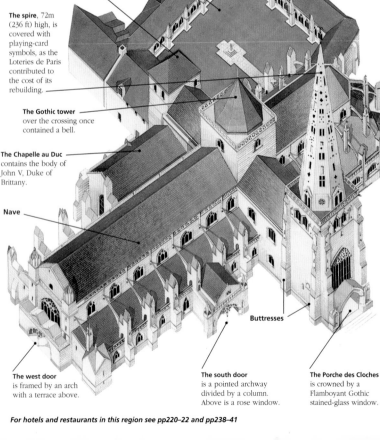

The Tour Hastings, with Romanesque arches, is the cathedral's oldest tower.

The courtyard was hired out to traders during the city's fair.

The spire, 72m (236 ft) high, is covered with playing-card symbols, as the Loteries de Paris contributed to the cost of its rebuilding.

The Gothic tower over the crossing once contained a bell.

The Chapelle au Duc contains the body of John V, Duke of Brittany.

Nave

Buttresses

The west door is framed by an arch with a terrace above.

The south door is a pointed archway divided by a column. Above is a rose window.

The Porche des Cloches is crowned by a Flamboyant Gothic stained-glass window.

The arches inside rise in three tiers to a height of 18 m (59 ft) above the nave, and grotesques stare down from the base of some of the arches. The choir, in the Anglo-Norman style, has 46 Renaissance stalls with strikingly realistic decoration. The cathedral also contains the tomb of John V, Duke of Brittany, the tomb of St Yves (1890), and the saint's reliquary. The 15th-century cloisters north of the choir are the best-preserved in Brittany. The ambulatory is filled with sculptures of recumbent figures.

🏛 Maison Natale d'Ernest-Renan
20 Rue Ernest-Renan. *Tel (02) 96 92 45 63.* ⬜ *Apr–Jun: Wed–Sun; Jul–Aug: daily; Sep: Wed–Sun.* ⬤ *Oct–Mar.* 🅿 *Aug–Sep: book ahead.* 📷

Environs
The village of **Minihy-Tréguier**, 1 km (0.5 mile) south of Tréguier, is famously associated

ERNEST RENAN

Ernest Renan, a native of Tréguier

Born in Tréguier, Ernest Renan (1823–92) intended to join the priesthood, but his reading of the philosopher Hegel turned him against this vocation. A philologist who specialized in Semitic languages, he published writings that were thought to be scandalous because they proposed a rational, analytical approach to Christianity. Renan's *Vie de Jésus* (Life of Jesus) had particularly dramatic repercussions. When his statue was unveiled in 1903, the police were forced to act to prevent its desecration.

with Yves Helory de Kermartin, who was canonized in 1347. A member of the local nobility, he became a protector of the poor, and turned the village into a refuge *(minihy)*. An annual pardon *(third Sun in May)* is held in his honour. The 15th-century church contains painted wooden statues of St Yves, shown, as usual, between a rich and a poor man.

The **Château de La Roche-Jagu**, 14 km (9 miles) south-east of Tréguier, was built in the 15th century, on the site of one of the ten forts that, from the 11th century, defended the Trieux valley.

♣ Château de La Roche-Jagu
Tel (02) 96 95 62 35. ⬜ *all year: daily.* 📷 *Jul–Aug: fêtes and music.* 📷

Fresco of the Dance of Death in the Chapelle de Kermaria-an-Iskuit

Chapelle de Kermaria-an-Iskuit ㉒

Road map D1. 11 km (7 miles) north-west of St-Quay-Portrieux via the D786 then D21. 📷 *Pardon (third Sun in Sep).*

About 3 km (2 miles) from Plouha, via the D21, stands the Chapelle Kermaria-an-Iskuit, "Chapel of Mary Restorer of Health". Founded in the 13th century by a former Crusader, it contains some extremely rare frescoes. One of them (1501) depicts the Dance of Death, which expresses the

fear of death that was widespread in late medieval Europe. Regardless of their rank, the *Ankou* (skeletal figure) leads men, from pope and king to knight and peasant, in a macabre dance.

St-Quay-Portrieux ㉓

Road map D1. 🚊 *St-Brieuc.* 🚶 *3,430.* ⛴ *Motorboat service to Île de Bréhat Apr–mid-Sep.* ℹ *17 bis Rue Jeanne-d'Arc; (02) 96 70 40 64.* 📅 *Mon & Fri.*

The pleasant coastal resort of St-Quay-Portrieux, north of St-Brieuc, once relied for its livelihood on fishing off

Newfoundland. Uniquely for a town of this size, the deep-water harbour here can berth 1,000 boats. A coast path leads to a signal station.

Environs
The resort of **Binic**, 7 km (4 miles) south of St-Quay-Portrieux, was a large port in the 19th century. The **Musée d'Arts et Traditions Populaires** is devoted to local history, especially the Newfoundland fishing industry. Breton headdresses are on display.

🏛 Musée d'Arts et Traditions Populaires
Avenue du Général-de-Gaulle, Binic. *Tel (02) 96 73 60 12.* ⬜ *Jul–Aug: daily pm; Apr–Sep: Wed–Mon.* 📷

The bay at St-Quay-Portrieux, a coastal resort with beautiful beaches

St-Brieuc ㉔

Carved figures in a panel in Rue Fardel

The history of St-Brieuc is closely linked to its evolution as a centre of religion. In the 5th century, Brieuc, a Gaulish monk, founded an oratory on the site of the present Fontaine St-Brieuc, in Rue Notre-Dame. The city was sacked in the late 16th century, during the Wars of the Holy League (*see p44*), although stability returned in the 17th and 18th centuries. Lying between the valleys of the Gouédic and the Gouët, St-Brieuc, capital of the Côtes d'Armor, is a pleasant city. Also a dynamic centre of culture, it has spawned cultural organizations and hosts events such as Art Rock (*see p28*). It also has associations with several great French writers.

Timber-framed house in Rue Fardel, in the old town of St-Brieuc

One of the towers on the fortified Cathédrale St-Étienne

🏛 Old Town

Built in the 14th and 15th centuries, the **Cathédrale St-Étienne**, located on Place du Général de Gaulle, has the appearance of a fortress. Its central porch is flanked by two sturdy towers: the 14th-century Tour Brieuc, 28 m (92 ft) high, and the 15th-century Tour Marie, 33 m (108 ft) high. Both are pierced with openings that allowed defensive weapons of many kinds to be used.

The large Chapelle de l'Annonciation, dating from the 15th century, has a notable altarpiece made by Yves Corlaix in 1745. With rocaille decoration, gilt polychrome and curves and counter-curves, it is a masterpiece of Baroque art. In the choir, some of the capitals are carved with grotesques or foliage. The organ was built by Cavaillé-Coll, who also built the organ in St-Sulpice in Paris.

Rue Pohel, Rue Fardel and Rue Quinquaine, in the vicinity of the cathedral, are lined with many timber-framed houses dating from the 15th and 16th centuries.

The 15th-century house in Rue Fardel known as **Maison Ribault** is the oldest house in St-Brieuc. In Rue Quinquaine, the Hôtel des Ducs de Bretagne, the ducal residence built in 1572, is also of interest for its elegant Renaissance façade with grotesque masks and figures carved in relief. On Place du Chai, modern buildings stand alongside restored wine warehouses. A covered passageway links the square with Rue Houvenagle, which is lined with ancient timber-framed houses faced with pilasters and featuring overhanging upper storeys. Three pedestrianized streets, Rue St-Gouéno, Rue Charbonnerie and Rue-Guillaume, the city's main shopping area, are also worth seeing.

🏛 Musée d'Art et d'Histoire

Cours Francis-Renaud.
Tel (02) 96 62 55 20. ⬤ Oct–Apr: Wed–Sat, Sun pm; May–Sep: Tue–Sat, Sun pm.
Through models, paintings, objects from everyday life, films and dioramas, this museum presents the history of the *département* of the Côtes d'Armor from its origins in the 18th century up until the 20th century. The displays illustrate several themes, including fishing, shipbuilding, the cloth and linen trade, agriculture and land reclamation, as well as popular traditions.

LITERARY LIFE IN ST-BRIEUC

Jean Grenier

Growing up in St-Brieuc in the early 20th century, Jean Grenier and Louis Guilloux formed a strong friendship. While the latter spent his life in St-Brieuc, Grenier left in 1930 to teach at the *lycée* in Algiers, where one of his pupils was the young Albert Camus. As a teacher, Grenier influenced Camus' later work. Camus, the author of *L'homme Révolté* and winner of the Nobel Prize for Literature in 1957, is steeped in the writings of both Grenier and Guilloux, and of Georges Palante, another philosopher who was a native of St-Brieuc. Guilloux came to the attention of the publisher Gaston Gallimard, winning the Prix Renaudot with *Le Jeu de Patience* (1949). Gide and Malraux judged his novel *Le Sang Noir* (1935) to be a work of major importance.

Anse d'Yffiniac, seen from the Maison de la Baie

❦ **Parc des Promenades**
These walks circle the law courts. East of Rue St-Guillaume, the municipal garden, decorated with sculptures, follows the outline of the old city walls. On the right of the law courts stands a bust of the writer Villiers de l'Isle-Adam, who was born in St-Brieuc, by Elie Le Goff, and a sculpture entitled *La Forme se Dégageant de la Matière* (Form Emerging from Matter) by Paul Le Goff. There is a also a monument dedicated to Paul Le Goff on Boulevard de La Chalotais.

Environs
Lying some 3 km (2 miles) inland, St-Brieuc is linked to the sea by the port of **Légué**, on the Gouët estuary. Here, shipowners' houses evoke the great age of the 19th-century Newfoundland cod-fishing industry, which has been replaced by the scallop industry. A footpath runs around the Pointe du Roselier. From the point, there is a view of the whole bay, from Cap d'Erquy in the east to the Île de Bréhat in the northwest. After passing an 18th-century cannon-ball foundry, the long-distance footpath GR34 leads to Martin-Plage. The Anse d'Yffiniac, an inlet behind the bay, is a seabird sanctuary: 50,000 birds of various species nest in this protected site. They arrive from northern Europe at the end of summer. Most spend the winter here. The **Maison de la Baie**, north of Hillion, has displays documenting the bay's flora and fauna and describing its seafaring economy.

Near Hillion, long paths leading far into the Dunes de Bon-Abri allow walkers to have a closer look at the plant life of the protected site.

🏛 **Maison de la Baie**
Rue de l'Etoile. *Tel* (02) 96 32 27 98. ⬜ Oct–May: Wed, Fri, Sun pm; Jun, Sep: Wed–Fri, Sun; Jul–Aug: Mon–Fri daily, Sat–Sun pm.

VISITORS' CHECKLIST

Road map D2. 🚊 *Boulevard Charner.* 🚌 *6 Rue du Combat-des-Trente.* 🏠 *48,900.* ℹ️ *7 Rue St-Guéno; 08 25 00 22 22; Comité Départemental, 7 Rue St-Benoit; (02) 96 62 72 00.* 🛒 *Wed &Sat.* 🎭 *Art Rock (Whitsun); L'Été en Fête (theatre, dance & concerts, first weekend in Jun).* **www**.baiedesaintbrieuc.com

ST-BRIEUC CITY CENTRE

Cathédrale St-Étienne ①
Parc des Promenades ④
Maison Ribault ②
Musée d'Art et d'Histoire ③

0 m 200
0 yards 200

Key to Symbols *see back flap*

The elegant Château de Quintin, built in the 17th century

Quintin **25**

Road map C2. 18 km (11 miles)
southwest of St-Brieuc via the D700,
the D790 and the D7. 🚊 St-Brieuc.
🏠 2,930. 🚌 6 Place 1830; (02) 96
74 01 51. 🕐 Jul–Aug: Thu pm.
🚗 Tue. 🚩 Pardon de Notre-Dame
(second Sun in May); St-Jean (son et
lumière, Jun); Fête des Tisserands
(early Aug).

During the 17th and 18th
centuries, Quintin was an
important centre of the linen
cloth industry. This age of
prosperity gave the town its
chateau as well as the timber-
framed houses and fine
granite-built residences that
line Place 1830, Place du
Martray and Grande Rue. The
Musée-Atelier des Toiles, in
Rue des Degrés, documents
this period of the town's history.

The 19th-century Neo-Gothic
Basilique Notre-Dame, in Rue
de la Basilique, is dedicated
to the patroness of spinners.
A relic reputed to be a piece
of the Virgin's girdle is kept in
the basilica. It is particularly
venerated by pregnant women.

Opposite the tourist office,
the chateau, built in the
17th–18th centuries, houses
a Musée de la Porcelaine
(porcelain museum).

♣ **Château de Quintin**
Entrance on Place 1830. **Tel** (02) 96
74 94 79. 🕐 Jul–Aug: daily; Apr &
May: Sun & school holidays pm; Jun
& Sep: daily pm.

🏛 **Musée-Atelier
des Toiles de Quintin**
Rue des Degrés. 🕐 Jun–Sep: Tue–
Sun.

Moncontour **26**

Road map D2. 15 km (9 miles)
southwest of Lamballe via the D768.
🚊 Lamballe. 🏠 900. 🚌 4 Place de
la Carrière; (02) 96 73 49 57.
🚩 Fête Médiévale (every 2 years;
3 weeks Jul–Aug); Festival de Musique
(Sep).

This medieval walled town
stands on a promontory at the
point where two valleys
meet. Fine 16th- and 18th-
century residences and
half-timbered houses line
Rue des Dames and
Place de Penthièvre,
where a linen market
was once held. The
Église St-Mathurin,
dating from the 16th–
18th centuries, is well
worth a visit for its
16th-century stained-
glass windows. Those
showing scenes from the
life of St Yves, on the left of
the nave, show Flemish
influence.

Pietà in the Église
St-Mathurin

Lamballe **27**

Road map D2. 🚌 Boulevard Jobert.
🚊 🏠 11,200. 🚌 Place du Champ
du Foire; (02) 96 31 05 38. 🚗 Thu.
🚩 Foire des Potiers (Jun); traditional
threshing (mid-Aug); Pardon de
Notre-Dame (Sep).
www.lamballe-tourisme.com

Founded in the sixth century,
Lamballe began to develop in
the 11th century, when it
became the capital of the
duchy of Penthièvre. Until the
18th century, the latter was in
repeated conflict with its rival,
the house of Brittany.

The **Musée d'Art Populaire
du Pays de Lamballe**, on
Place du Martray, is laid out
in a charming half-timbered
house that also contains the
tourist office. With exhibits
dating from prehistory, as
well as local costumes,
headdresses and tools, the
collections illustrate the daily
life in Lamballe and its
environs in historical times.

The **Musée Mathurin-
Méheut**, on the first floor,
has a large collection
relating to this local
painter, who was also
a leading exponent of
Art Nouveau. About
4,000 of his works
are exhibited in
rotation, illustrating
a different theme
each year.

The **Collégiale
Notre-Dame-de-
Grande-Puissance** in Rue
Notre-Dame, has the
appearance of a fortified
church. It is built in a
combination of Romanesque

LINEN CLOTH

A loom on which linen
cloth was once woven

The linen cloth industry brought
prosperity to Brittany in the 17th
and 18th centuries. St-Brieuc,
Quintin, Uzel, Loudéac and
Moncontour – which, between
them, had more than 8,000
weavers – were the main centres
of production. In 1676, a statute
was passed regulating the standards
of quality of the linen cloth woven
in western Europe. That produced
in Brittany was then acknowledged
to be the best in France. Loaded
onto ships in St-Malo and Nantes,
it was exported worldwide.

MATHURIN MÉHEUT

Painter, interior decorator, illustrator, designer of jewellery and wallpaper, Mathurin Méheut (1888–1958) was a multi-talented artist. One of the earliest exponents of Art Nouveau, Méhuet was commissioned to design the interior decoration of 27 liners. This included producing four oil paintings for the *Normandie*. After World War II, he was appointed painter to the French Navy and produced many fishing scenes. In 1923, a retrospective exhibition of his work was held in San Francisco.

Mathurin Méheut, a pioneering exponent of Art Nouveau

and Gothic styles. The north door, dating from the 12th century, has capitals carved with foliage. The thick columns and floral motifs in the nave show Norman influence, while the Flamboyant Gothic rood screen (1415) is perfectly counterbalanced by the

Louis XIII organ loft of 1741. Near the church, a walk has been made on the site of a castle that was destroyed in 1626.

The **Haras National**, in Place du Champ-de-Foire, in the west of Lamballe, is the second-largest national stud in France. Set up in 1825, it was well regarded in the early 20th century, and is still important today. It has capacity for 400 animals, and the horses bred here include Breton post-horses, thoroughbreds and Connemaras, thus helping to preserve these breeds.

The Maison du Bourreau, in Lamballe, which houses a museum

🔘 Haras National
Place du Champ-de-Foire.
***Tel** (02) 96 50 06 98.*
Mid-Jun–mid-Sep: daily; other times: Tue–Sun pm.

Environs
Northeast of Lamballe, not far from Pléven, are the ruins of the restored **Château de La Hunaudaye**. In summer, for the benefit of visitors, actors in costume populate the castle. Of particular interest is the 15th-century keep, pierced by loopholes, the seigneurial quarters, with a fine Renaissance staircase, and two 13th-century towers.

⚓ Château de La Hunaudaye
On the D28. ***Tel** (02) 96 34 82 10.*
Apr–Jun & Sep: Sun & public holidays, pm; Jul–Aug: Mon–Sat; Sun pm.

🏛 Musée d'Art Populaire du Pays de Lamballe
Hosté du Pilori. ***Tel** (02) 96 34 77 63.* Sat; Jun–Sep: Tue–Sat.

🏛 Musée Mathurin-Méheut
Maison du Bourreau. ***Tel** (02) 96 31 19 99.* Apr–Sep: Mon–Sat pm; May, Oct–Dec: Wed, Fri & Sat pm. Jan–Apr.

⛪ Collégiale Notre-Dame-de-Grande-Puissance
Rue Notre-Dame. call tourist office for information. early Jul–late Aug: Mon–Sat.

The charming medieval village of Moncontour, perched on a promontory

The Château de Bien-Assis, near Pléneuf-Val-André

Pléneuf-Val-André ⑳

Road map D2. 🚗 🚉 *Lamballe.*
🏃 *3,770.* ℹ️ *Cours Winston-Churchill; (02) 96 72 20 55.* 🚢 *Tue in Pléneuf; Fri in Val-André.* 🎪 *Fête du Nautisme & regatta (May); jazz (Jul–Aug: every Tue); Pardon de Notre-Dame-de-la-Garde (Aug); Fête de la Mer (mid-Aug).*

Originally no more than a quiet fishing harbour, Pléneuf Val-André was transformed in the late 19th century, when developers turned it into one of Brittany's most sophisticated holiday resorts. With a beautiful sandy beach 2 km (1 mile) long, it soon became very popular.

From the 16th century, fishermen from the neighbouring village of Dahouët came to Pléneuf Val-André to prepare for cod-fishing expeditions off Newfoundland. In those days, ships' captains would call at local inns to enlist sailors, whose drunkenness would guarantee that they signed up without protest.

From Pléneuf Val-André, two walks, to Pointe de la Guette and to Pointe de Pléneuf, offer spectacular views. The **Îlot du Verdelet**, opposite Pointe de Pléneuf, is a bird sanctuary, and it is accessible at low tide. Trips out to sea on the sailing boat *Pauline* are organized during the holiday season.

🚢 Pauline

Port de Dahouët. *Tel (02) 96 63 10 99.* 🕐 *Jun–Sep: daily; Oct–May: by arrangement.*

Environs
The **Château de Bien-Assis**, 4 km (3 miles) east of Pléneuf-Val-André, was built in 1400 and has been remodelled several times since. The only surviving original part is a tower behind the chateau. Destroyed during the Wars of the Holy League (*see p44*), the chateau was rebuilt in the 17th century: the part framed by towers dates from this phase. The interior contains Breton Renaissance furniture and a monumental stairway. There is also a formal garden.

🏰 Château de Bien-Assis
Sur la D786. *Tel (02) 96 72 22 03.* 🕐 *Mid-Jun–mid-Sep: Mon-Sat, Sun pm: mid-Sep–mid-Jun: by arrangement.* 🎟️

The fishing port of Erquy, base of many deep-sea trawlers

Sables-d'Or-les-Pins ㉙

Road map E1. 8 km (5 miles) southwest of Cap Fréhel via the D34a.
🏃 *2,100.* 🚗 🚉 *Lamballe.* ℹ️ *Plurien; (02) 96 72 18 52 all year. Erquy; (02) 96 72 30 12.* 🚢 *Tue.* **www**.plurien-tourisme.com

This coastal resort with smart villas in the neo-Norman style was created in the early 1920s as a rival to Deauville. With a 3-km (2-mile) long sandy beach and pine trees, it is very popular with holidaymakers.

Environs
Erquy, on the D786 west of Sables-d'Or, is renowned for its clams and scallops. It is also the base for a large fleet of deep-sea trawlers. Of all the beaches nearby, the Plage de Caroual is the best. In summer, the tourist office organizes boat trips to the Île de Bréhat (*see p98*) and the Baie de St-Brieuc (*see p103*).

Cap d'Erquy is less well known than Cap Fréhel, yet it is one of the most beautiful headlands in Brittany. Many marked footpaths cross the flower-covered heath here and run along the indented cliffs, beneath which are shingle beaches. The views from the headland are stunning; to the west, there is a panorama across the Baie de St-Brieuc and to Pointe de Pléneuf beyond.

One of the paths on the promontory passes an *oppidum* popularly known as Caesar's Camp; it was, in fact, a fortified Gaulish settlement and its Iron Age earthworks are still visible. Classified in 1978, the site was bought by the local authority in 1982 so as to protect it from erosion caused by motorcyclists using it as a rough circuit. In summer, daily walks on Cap d'Erquy are organized by the **Syndicat des Caps** (*02 96 41 50 83*).

Fort La Latte, built in the 13th century, with a commanding view of the sea

Cap Fréhel ❸⓪

Road map E1.
i Frehel; (02) 96 41 53 81.
🚢 Boat trips with Campagnie
Corsaire; 0825 138 035 (St-Malo);
0825 138 130 (Dinard).
Summer walks with Syndicats des
Cap; (02) 96 41 50 83.

Located 8.5km (5 miles) from
the town centre of Fréhel, the
spectacular headland of Cap
Fréhel is one of the most
beautiful landscapes in
Brittany. Heathland covered
with heather and gorse
stretches to infinity, and sheer
pink limestone cliffs rise
vertically from the sea to
heights of 70 m (230 ft).

The view from here stretches
from Pointe du Groin in the
east to the Île de Bréhat in the
west. In clear weather, it is
even possible to see the
Channel Islands. Sea birds,
such as fulmars, kittiwakes,
cormorants, guillemots and
pied oystercatchers, nest in
nooks in the cliffs and on the
neighbouring small islands.

There are two lighthouses
on the promontory: one built
by Vauban in the 17th century
and the other dating from
1950. The latter used to be
open to the public but has
now closed.

In summer, the Syndicat des
Caps organizes walks on the
promontory every day, and
there are numerous picnic
spots. Trips by motor-boat
from Dinard and St-Malo
allow visitors to admire the
cliffs from the sea.

Fort La Latte ❸①

Road map E1. 4 km (3 miles)
southwest of Cap Fréhel via the D16.
Tel (02) 96 41 57 11. 🗓 Apr–Sep: daily;
Oct–Mar: Sat–Sun pm.
🚢 Boat trips with Campagnie
Corsaire; 0825 138 035 (St-Malo);
0825 138 130 (Dinard).

This impressive fortress
overlooking the sea was built
in the 13th century by the
powerful Goyon-Matignon
family. It was captured
by Bertrand du Guesclin
(see p41) in 1379 and was
besieged by the English in
1490, then by the Holy
League in 1597. On Vauban's
orders, Garangeau (see p80)
restored it in the 17th century.
The keep and the cannon-ball
foundry are of particular
interest to visitors.

From the rampart walk, there
is a sublime view of the Côte
d'Émeraude. Abandoned in
the 19th century, the fort
passed into private ownership
in 1892, and was classified as
a historic monument in 1931.

**The spectacular headland at Cap
Fréhel, with sheer limestone cliffs**

St-Cast-
Le Guildo ❸②

Road map E1. 🚌 🚉 Lamballe.
🏠 3,290. **i** Place Charles-de-Gaulle;
(02) 96 41 81 52. 🛒 Fri: in season:
Mon & Fri. 🎵 Concerts (Jul–Aug).

Now a popular coastal resort,
St-Cast-Le Guildo has no less
than seven beaches, and in
summer its population
increases ten-fold. Its
expansion began at the end
of the 19th century, when the
painter Marinier purchased
the headland and set about
developing it.

The ruins of the **Château du
Guildo**, in the parish of
Créhen, recall the fratricidal
conflict between Giles of
Brittany, son of John V, Duke
of Brittany, whose allegiance
was to the English crown, and
his brother Francis I of
Brittany, a supporter of the
king of France. Francis
murdered Giles, but the latter
had prayed to God that his
brother might outlive him by
just 40 days; Francis indeed
died exactly 40 days later. It
was not until 1758 that the
English, who suffered defeat
at St-Cast, finally relinquished
their intentions of invading
the coast of Brittany.

From here, visitors may
enjoy two walks along part
of the GR34 long-distance
footpath. One goes south to
Pointe de la Garde, which
offers a beautiful panorama
of the Ebihens archipelago
and Presqu'île St-Jacut; the
other goes north, to the
Pointe de St-Cast, which
commands a fine view of
Fort La Latte and Cap Fréhel.

The fort and Cap Fréhel can
also be admired from the sea
by taking a trip in the **Dragous**,
an old sailing boat, which
leaves from St-Cast-Le-Guildo.

The town's **church**
contains a 12th-century
Romanesque stoup decorated
with grotesques and a statue
of St Cast, the monk who
established a hermitage here
in the 6th century.

🚢 **Dragous**
Port de St-Cast. **Tel** (02) 96 41 86
42. ⬜ Apr–Sep: daily; Oct–Nov: by
arrangement.

Street-by-Street: Dinan ⦿

In the words of Victor Hugo, Dinan perches "on an overhanging precipice...like a swallow's nest". From the 14th to the 18th centuries, a flourishing trade in linen cloth, leather, wood and cereals – cargoes that left Dinan from its harbour on the Rance – led to the creation of an exceptionally rich architectural heritage: the old town has some extremely fine half-timbered houses. The town is enclosed by 3 km (2 miles) of walls that are both the most massive and the oldest in Brittany. The 14th-century machicolated keep, as well as the Basilique St-Sauveur, with a magnificent Romanesque porch, are some of the other attractions of this medieval town.

★ Basilique St-Sauveur
This is built in a style combining Gothic and Romanesque influences.

Tour Ste-Catherine
The oldest tower in the town's 13th-century walls commands a splendid panorama of the harbour and the Rance valley.

★ Rue de Jerzual
Until 1783, when the viaduct was built, travellers entering Dinan would follow this street, which was once a steep track.

Tour du
Gouverneur

Porte de
St-Malo

Franciscan Monastery
Built in the 13th century, this former Franciscan monastery now houses a private school.

★ Castle and Town Walls

The castle consists of a keep, the Tour de Coëtquen and the Porte du Guichet. The 14th-century keep houses a museum of local history.

Benedictine monastery

STAR SIGHTS

★ Basilique St-Sauveur

★ Castle and Town Walls

★ Place des Merciers

★ Rue du Jerzual

KEY

– – – Suggested route

0 m ———— 100
0 yards ———— 100

Tour de l'Horloge

Porch of the Hôtel Beaumanoir

The street entrance of this residence is framed by a stone archway decorated with carved dolphins.

★ Place des Merciers

In the heart of the old town, the Place des Merciers (Haberdashers' Square) is lined with medieval timber-framed houses. The Restaurant de la Mère Pourcel, a 15th-century timber-framed building with overhanging upper storey, also lines the square.

Exploring Dinan

The history of Dinan is closely linked to events in Breton political history. In about 1000, noblemen from a family called Dinan took possession of the town and, in 1283, it came under the control of the duchy of Brittany. Dinan enjoyed an initial period of prosperity thanks to its maritime trading links with Flanders and England, and to the trade in linen sheets and cloth. In the 14th century, the Wars of the Breton Succession, during which Dinan supported the king of France, curtailed the town's development. However, from the 16th century, Dinan was again prosperous and it enjoyed a second golden age in the 17th and 18th centuries. This can be seen from the fine timber-framed houses that line the town's streets. At this time, religious orders also established several large convents and founded new churches in Dinan.

The old town of Dinan, on the banks of the Rance

🏦 Old Town and Harbour
In the harbour, the commercial activity that once brought Dinan such riches has been replaced by a flotilla of pleasure boats. The leafy banks of the Rance offer the opportunity of scenic walks.

Rue du Quai leads to **Rue du Petit-Fort**. At No. 24 is the **Maison du Gouverneur**, a fine 15th-century residence. Before the viaduct was built in 1852, travellers would enter Dinan via **Porte du Jerzual**, a 14th-century gate with Gothic arcades. They would then follow **Rue du Jerzual**, which is lined with timber-framed houses dating from the 15th and 16th centuries. Once filled with traders, the street has been taken over by cabinet-makers and gilders.

Rue de l'Apport has several well-restored houses. This street leads to **Place des Merciers**, which also contains attractive houses with wooden porches and overhanging upper storeys. The **Hôtel de Keratry**, a 16th-century mansion with granite columns, is housed at no 6 **Rue de l'Horloge**.

🏦 Town Walls
These were built in the 13th century and strengthened in the 15th century by Francis I, Duke of Brittany. They were renovated in the 17th century by Garangeau (*see p80*) on the orders of Vauban. The walls are set with eight towers, the most impressive of which is the Tour Beaumanoir.

Two walks along the walls, the Promenade de la Duchesse Anne and the Promenade des Grands Fossés, offer views of the town and of the Rance.

🏦 Franciscan Monastery
Place des Cordeliers. ◯ *Mon–Fri.*
This former monastery was established in the 13th century by a Crusader who became a Franciscan friar. Several 15th-century buildings survive. Among them are the Gothic cloisters, the main courtyard and the chapter-house, which is used as a refectory by the school that now occupies the monastery.

🔔 Église St-Malo
Grande-Rue ◯ *daily, 9am–4pm.* ● *to visitors during services.*
The church, with a slate-covered bell-turret, was begun in the 15th century and completed 400 years later. The exterior has a remarkable Renaissance doorway. Pillaged during the Revolution, the interior is somewhat bare, apart from more recent additions such as the high altar (1955) in granite carved by Gallé and a series of stained-glass windows (1927) by Merklen, depicting various quarters of Dinan, such as the Jerzual and Place des Cordeliers.

🔔 Basilique St-Sauveur
Place St-Sauveur. ◯ *daily, 9am–4pm.* ● *to visitors during services.*
Built in a combination of Romanesque and Gothic styles, the basilica is unique in Brittany. It was founded by a knight who had safely re-turned from a crusade against the Saracens. Begun in the 12th century, it was not completed until the 16th century.

The façade has a remarkable Romanesque doorway carved with depictions of the vices and with such monstrosities

Rue du Petit-Fort, lined with fine 15th-century houses

BIRTH OF A LEGEND

In 850, some monks dressed in rags met King Nominoë *(see p37)* and asked him to help them. The king agreed on condition that he be given some relics in return. To fulfil this obligation, the monks set sail for Sark, in the Channel Islands, where they found the body of St Magloire (525-605), Bishop of Dol. On their return, the king fell to his knees before the relic and founded the Prieuré de St-Magloire-de-Lehon.

**Relic of
St Magloire**

VISITORS' CHECKLIST

Road map E2. 🏠 *15,000.*
🛈 *9 Rue du Château;
(02) 96 87 69 76.* 🚌 *Apr–Jun
& Sep: Sat; Jul–Aug: daily.*
🚉 🚌 *Place du 11-Novembre-
1918.* 🛒 *Thu.* 🎭 *Festival de
Harpe Celtique (second week in
Jul); Fête des Remparts (every 2
years from 2006; third weekend
in Jul); Fête de la Pomme (first
weekend in Nov).*

as sirens, human-headed serpents and a toad at a woman's breast. The interior combines the Romanesque and Flamboyant Gothic styles. The heart of Bertrand du Guesclin *(see p41)* is entombed in one of the chapels. There are also some fine stained-glass windows, both ancient and modern.

The former cemetery is now a terraced garden with a view of the Rance valley. In the garden are busts of the explorer Auguste Pavie and of Néel de la Vigne, mayor of Dinan during the Revolution.

⌚ Tour de l'Horloge

Rue de l'Horloge.
◌ *Apr–Sep: daily.*
The top of the tower commands an extensive view over Dinan. The bell was a gift to the town made in 1507 by Anne of Brittany.

⛪ Benedictine Monastery

Rue de Léhon. ◌ *Mon–Fri.*
Built in the 17th and 18th centuries, the monastery now houses a private school where Chateaubriand *(see p69)* was once a pupil.

♜ Castle & Museum

Rue du Château. *Tel (02) 96 39 45
20.* ◌ *daily.* ● *Jan.*
The castle consists of a 14th-century keep, the 13th-century Porte du Guichet and the Tour de Coëtquen. Strengthened by Mercœur, leader of the Holy League *(see p44)*, the castle withstood attack by Protestant soldiers but, with the help of the people of Dinan, Henry IV

**Statue from
the castle**

managed to break through the Porte de St-Malo.

The keep, built in 1380, must have served both as a fortress and as living quarters, as it features spy-holes and look-outs as well as mullioned windows and monumental chimneys. A platform at the top of the keep offers a magnificent view of Dinan and its environs.

Tour Coëtquen, with tomb effigies, was built in the 15th century, nearly a hundred years after its keep was built.

The **museum** of local history, which is located in the keep, displays interesting archaeological artifacts, paintings and sculpture.

🏛 Maison d'Artiste de la Grande-Vigne

103 Rue du Quai. *Tel (02) 96 87 90
80.* ◌ *Jul–Sep: 10am–6:30pm daily;
Oct–Jun 2–6:30pm daily.*
This house was the home of Yvonne Jean-Haffen

**The Tour de l'Horloge, offering a
wide view over Dinan**

(1895–1993), an artist who was a pupil and friend of Mathurin Méheut *(see p105)*. Among the 4,000 works that Jean-Haffen bequeathed to the town are engravings, ceramics and watercolours depicting scenes of Brittany.

Exhibited in rotation, these works illustrate a variety of themes.

Tour de Coëtquen, built by the architect Estienne Le Fur

NORTHERN FINISTÈRE

Two very distinct geographical and historical entities make up northern Finistère. West of the Morlaix river lies the territory of the former diocese of the Léon, whose religious and economical capital was St-Pol. East of Morlaix is a small section of the Trégor, the neighbouring diocese that became part of Finistère after the Revolution.

The Trégor Finistérien, that part of the Trégor annexed to Finistère, is a charming part of Brittany, a patchwork of valleys and sunken lanes. The Léon, by contrast, is a large plateau that in the 1960s was stripped of its trees to maximize intensive agriculture. This is especially true of the Haut-Léon, a prime producer of artichokes and cauliflowers. Its commercial dynamism even led to the creation of Brittany Ferries, founded to export the Léon's prized local produce.

Commercially successful, the Haut-Léon is also deeply religious. Not for nothing is it known as "the land of priests", and it boasts some of Brittany's architectural jewels: the parish closes, built with funds provided by local rural inhabitants who, from the 13th century, had grown rich through the thriving linen cloth trade.

The Bas-Léon, surrounded on three sides by the sea (the Abers, the Mer d'Iroise and the Rade de Brest), has a quite different landscape. Here are wide deserted beaches and narrow secret creeks, wooded estuaries and cliffs topped by lighthouses, banks of dunes and windswept promontories. In the extreme west, battered by the Atlantic Ocean, lies Ouessant, the end of the known world in ancient times, and the low-lying islands of the Molène archipelago, which, like the Monts d'Arrée and the magical forest of Huelgoat, form part of the Parc Régional d'Armorique.

Each of these different environments offers wonderful walking country, providing unlimited peace, fresh air and unspoiled landscapes.

Halyards and stays coiled and hung to dry on belaying pins after fishing

◁ The Parc du Menez Meur in the Monts d'Arrée

Exploring Northern Finistère

The northern part of Finistère, meaning "Land's End", consists of several protected environments. Among these are the Baie de Morlaix, the heathland of the Monts d'Arrée *(see pp140–41)*, the dunes of Keremma, the deeply indented Côte des Abers *(see pp126–7)* and the Ouessant archipelago, battered by wind and spray. As the distances between these areas are small, it is easy to explore them while also stopping off to visit the chateaux, manor houses and parish closes that make up the rich architectural heritage of the area, once the diocese of Léon. Alternating between coastal and inland areas, particularly around Landerneau and Landivisiau, visitors will appreciate the many facets of this rugged region, which is bathed in a pearly light.

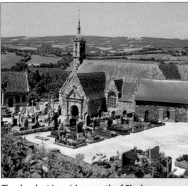

The church at Lannédern, north of Pleyben

SEE ALSO

0 km   20

0 miles   10

NORTHERN FINISTÈRE AT A GLANCE

KEY

═══ Major road

─── Secondary road

═══ Minor road

┄┄┄ Main railway

─── Minor railway

─── Regional border

The small town on the Île de Batz

ÎLE DE BATZ
⬧ **5**

4 ROSCOFF

Plougasnou   St-Jean-
du-Doigt   Locquirec

Sibiril   Térénez   **D64**

ler   **3**   Guimaec

ST-POL-   **2** CARANTEC
LOUESCAT   DE-LÉON

Château de   **D46**   **D786**   Lannion
Kergournadeac'h   Plouézoc'h

D58   **D73**

Taulé

D788   **D69**

CHÂTEAU DE KERJEAN   **1** MORLAIX   **N12**

D30   Plouigneau   Guingamp,
St-Brieuc

22 BODILIS   **N12**   **25** ST-THÉGONNEC   **D9**

divisiau   Pleyber-Christ   Plougonven

LAMPAUL-   **D785**
23 GUIMILIAU   **D9**

24 GUIMILIAU   **D769**

LA MARTYRE   FINISTÈRE

Sizun   **D764**   Commana

MONTS   D'ARRÉE   Berrien

St-Rivoal   Brennilis   **26** HUELGOAT

D18   **27**   **D36**
Montagne
St-Michel   **D764**

D785   St-Herbot

D14

Quimper   Pleyben   Carhaix-Plouguer

Wooded countryside around St-Rivoal, southeast of Sizun

GETTING AROUND

Morlaix and Brest, the two major towns in northern Finistère, are linked by a motorway, the N12, and by the TGV (high-speed train) service. The TGV journey time between these two towns is 45 minutes. The port of Roscoff, a ferry terminal for services to and from Britain and Ireland, is served by buses and TER trains run by the French state railway company, SNCF. Several coach companies (such as Bihan, CAT, St-Mathieu, Douguet, Kreisker and Le Roux) provide regular links between the towns of the Léon. Particularly scenic routes are the coast roads D73 (Morlaix to Carantec), D76 (Plouézoc'h to Térénez) and D127 (Portsall to Argenton), as well as those that follow the estuaries of the Côte des Abers and along the banks of the Élorn (D712 and D30) and Queffleuth rivers (D769).

Street-by-Street: Morlaix ●

On the border of the Léon to the west and the Trégor to the east, and with the sea to the north and the Monts d'Arrée to the south, Morlaix (*Montroulez* in Breton) was once one of the largest ports on the English Channel. From early times, ship-owners, privateers and merchants exploited to the full the town's favourable geographical location. Its focal point were the docks, from which ships bound for Spain were laden with delicate linen cloth woven inland, and those bound for Holland with salt from Guérande, lead from the mines of Huelgoat, leather and wine from the vine-yards of Bordeaux. In the 19th century, ships could still sail up the estuary to a point level with Morlaix's town hall. Lined with arcades and warehouses, the quays were as busy as any modern stock exchange.

The Morlaix viaduct, with a pedestrian bridge on the lower of its two levels

★ Place des Otages
The square is lined with 17th-century mansions, such as that at No. 15, built for a member of the Breton parliament, and with charming timber-framed houses, like that at No. 35, shown here. It contains the bookshop La Nuit Bleu Marine.

Église St-Melaine and Viaduct
The impressive viaduct that bestrides Morlaix's old town was built by the engineer Victor Fenoux in 1861 to carry a stretch of the Paris–Brest railway. The church is dedicated to Melaine (462–530), a priest who was chancellor to Hoel II, a Breton king, and counsellor to Clovis, king of France.

PLACE ÉMILE SOUVESTRE

The town hall was built in 1841.

STAR SIGHTS

★ No. 9 Grand'Rue

★ Place des Otages

0 m   100

0 yards   100

The old town walls are vestiges of medieval Morlaix.

Rue Ange-de-Guernisac is lined by houses with slate-clad façades.

For hotels and restaurants in this region see pp223–5 and pp241–3

★ No. 9 Grand'Rue

This was the street where the linen cloth market was once held. The house at No. 9 has a pondalez, a staircase that is typical of residences in Morlaix. The building also features windows with sliding shutters and 17th-century painted beams.

VISITORS' CHECKLIST

Road map C1. 🏃 17,300.
🚉 Rue Armand-Rousseau.
🛈 Place des Otages;
(02) 98 62 14 94.
🗓 Sat.
🎭 Festival des Arts (street festival; mid-Jul–mid-Aug).
www.morlaix.fr

Maison de la Duchesse Anne

This is one of the fine town houses built in the 15th and 16th centuries for the nobility of Morlaix and for rich merchants in the linen cloth trade.

Musée de Morlaix
Together with the nearby Maison à Pondalez, this Jacobin convent houses part of the museum's collection. Art exhibitions are held in the gallery space.

Église St-Mathieu

The tower (1548) was once crowned by a dome. Inside the church is a rare "vierge ouvrante", a statue of the Virgin and Child that opens to reveal the Holy Trinity.

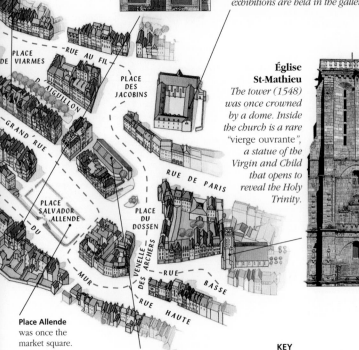

PLACE DE VIARMES
RUE AU FIL
D'AIGUILLON
PLACE DES JACOBINS
GRAND'RUE
DU
PLACE SALVADOR ALLENDE
PLACE DU DOSSEN
RUE DE PARIS
MUR
VENELLE DES ARCHERS
RUE BASSE
RUE HAUTE

Place Allende
was once the market square.

New market

KEY

– – – Suggested route

Exploring Morlaix

Morlaix sadly lost much of its character when, in 1897, its docks were filled in and covered by two squares, the Place des Otages and Place Cornic. Efforts are now being made to make the town more vibrant and to renovate the historic quayside buildings – mansions with dormer windows and houses with *pondalez* (spiral staircases) – that merchants built in a more prosperous age. Pleasure boats are the only vessels that now tie up in the harbour, as, with the closure of the tobacco-processing plant, it is now devoid of the ships that once serviced that industry. The resulting loss of 2,000 jobs has forced Morlaix, the third-largest town in the Finistère, to seek prosperity in other industries.

Stained-glass window in the Église St-Mathieu

Timber-framed and slate-clad houses in Morlaix

⌂ Église St-Melaine
Rue Ange-de-Guernisac.
***Tel** (02) 98 88 4519.*
Built in the Flamboyant Gothic style by the Beaumanoirs and completed in 1489, St-Melaine is the oldest church in Morlaix. As well as an organ built by Thomas Dallam in 1682, it contains painted wooden statues of saints and has fine 16th-century beams carved with plant motifs, angels, animals, including ermines (emblem of Anne of Brittany) and, amusingly, caricatures of prominent people of the time.

🏛 Les Jacobins
Place des Jacobins. ***Tel** (02) 98 88 68 88.* ⬜ *varies.* 📷 ✔
The main collection of the Musée de Morlaix is housed at La Maison à Pondalez, but here, in a former convent founded in the 13th century, is a small collection with several themes: local history,

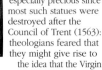

Furniture detail, Musée de Morlaix

painting inspired by Brittany and contemporary art. Of particular interest are the 15th- to 17th-century religious statuary, including an *Ankou* (skeletal figure in the Dance of Death), and some Breton antique furniture.

⌂ Église St-Mathieu
East of the Rue de Paris.
***Tel** (02) 98 88 4519.*
This church, rebuilt in 1824, is notable for its tower, one of the earliest examples of the Renaissance style in Brittany, and for the curious statue that it contains. Made in about 1390 in a workshop in Westphalia, it depicts the Virgin and Child but opens to reveal the Holy Trinity. It is especially precious since most such statues were destroyed after the Council of Trent (1563): theologians feared that they might give rise to the idea that the Virgin could have engendered the Holy Trinity.

♛ Maison de la Duchesse Anne
33 Rue du Mur. ***Tel** (02) 98 88 23 26.*
⬜ *Jun–Sep: Mon–Sat.* ⬤ *Sun & public holidays, am.* 📷
This house, one of several in the region where Anne of Brittany is reputed to have stayed, consists of three sections, the central part with a monumental chimneypiece rising the full height of the building.
The house also has a staircase known as a *pondalez*. This is a spiral staircase that, by means of a walkway, allows access to the rooms in the different parts of the house.

Windows of the Maison de la Duchesse Anne

♛ No. 9 Grand'Rue
⬜ *Oct–Mar & Jun: Mon, Wed–Sat; Apr, May & Sep: Sun pm, Mon, Wed–Sat; Jul & Aug: daily.* 📷 ✔
Restored in 1997, the house at No.9 Grand'Rue is another 16th-century residence with a *pondalez* staircase, which is profusely carved. The windows of the house were designed to allow merchants to display their wares.
The main collection of the Musée de Morlaix is found here (the other is at Les Jacobins). On four levels, the collection details the history and architecture of the town.

CAPLAN & CO

This café and bookshop, which opened in 1933, is one of the most atmospheric places in Finistère Nord. It is housed in a former grocer's shop overlooking the beach at Poul-Rodou, on the coast road between Locquirec and Guimaëc. Outside, there is a terrace with tables. Inside, where the décor replicates a school classroom, is an excellent selection of books by an international range of authors.

Caplan & Co, one of the region's most famous cafés

Environs

The **Trégor Finistérien**, the small region of heath and woodland between Morlaix and Locquirec, is worth exploring, not least for its archaeological sites and beautiful coastal landscapes. From Morlaix, take the D76 that runs along the estuary to Dourduff-en-Mer.

🪨 Cairn de Barnenez

Presqu'île de Barnenez, Plouézoc'h. **Tel** *(02) 98 67 24 73.* ◯ *Apr–Sep: daily.* ◑ *winter: Mon.*
This megalithic monument crowns the Presqu'île de Barnenez. Built in about 4,500 BC, it is the largest and oldest cairn in Europe. It contains 11 dolmens, and excavations have uncovered pottery, bones and engraved motifs. From the tip of the peninsula, there is a superb view of the Château du Taureau *(see p120)*, the Île Stérec and the small fishing harbour of Térénez.

🏖 Plages de Plougasnou

The beaches tucked away along the coast between Térénez and St-Jean-du-Doigt are the most beautiful in the Trégor

Finistérien. They are at Samson, Guerzit and Port-Blanc (reached via the D46A2) and Primel-Trégastel (via the D46).

Walkers will enjoy the coast path that runs round the Pointe du Diben. The headland bristles with rocks in strange zoomorphic shapes, such as those of a dromedary and a sphinx. The Pointe de Trégastel offers a wide panorama of the English Channel, the Île de Batz and the Île Grande.

St-Jean-du-Doigt

6 km (4 miles) northeast of Morlaix via the D46. 🚌 *from Morlaix.*
In the late 19th century, the pardon held in this small town (*Sant Yann ar Biz* in Breton) would attract up to 12,000 faithful. It is named after a famous relic, the finger of St John the Baptist, that is kept in the church here.

The relic reputedly has the power to restore sight, and, in the 16th century, Anne of Brittany came to seek a cure for a troublesome left eye. Duly healed, she funded the building of the church, whose spire and three bell-turrets

were struck by lightning in 1925. The town also has an elegant fountain decorated with lead statues.

🏛 Musée des Vieux Outils

Le Prajou, Guimaec, 13 km (8 miles) northeast of Morlaix. **Tel** *(02) 98 67 54 77.* ◯ *summer: daily pm.*
The museum is housed in a barn on the road running between the small town of Guimaec and the wild coast around Beg an Fry. It contains almost 2,500 traditional tools and implements of the Trégor, including flails, gorse-crushing hammers, combs for carding linen, cream separators and old stills.

Fountain in St-Jean-du-Doigt, decorated with lead statues

Locquirec

Road map *C1. 19 km (12 miles) northwest of Morlaix on the D786 then the D64.* 🏘 *1,242.* 🚉 & 🚌 *from Morlaix.* 🛈 *Place du Port; (02) 98 67 40 83.* 🛒 *Wed am.*
It was in this small fishing village on the border between the Trégor and the Côtes d'Armor that the thick, heavy Locquirec slate – with which almost all local buildings are roofed – was once mined. Locquirec (*Lokireg* in Breton) is now a coastal resort, with nine beaches, a large hotel and a coast path that offers a fine view of the bay. The church, with a belfry built by Beaumanoir in 1634, is as dainty and intimate as the village itself. It has a painted wooden ceiling and a charming statue of Our Lady of Succour. The **Chapelle Notre-Dame-des-Joies**, 5 km (3 miles) further south, has a 16th-century oak chancel decorated with fruits, flowers and chimeras, and a *Virgin and Child*.

Cairn de Barnenez, one of the most remarkable burial mounds in Europe

The beach at the elegant coastal resort of Carantec

Carantec ❷

Road map B1. 🏚 *2,800.*
🚉 from Morlaix. 🚌 *4 Rue Pasteur;
(02) 98 67 00 43.* 🅰 *Thu am.*
📅 *Pardon de Notre-Dame-de-Callot
(Sun after 15 Aug).*

With the arrival of the first
foreign visitors, between the
1870s and the 1900s, the
history of Carantec (*Karanteg*
in Breton) took a decisive
turn. One of these visitors
found the location
enchanting, and largely
thanks to him, a fashionable
coastal resort was created. Its
smart hotels and elegant villas
no longer exist, however.

The magical views here can
be enjoyed by following a
marked footpath running
from Grève Blanche to the
pine wood at Penn al Lann.
The two-hour walk takes in
Porspol beach, a rocky
platform known as the
Chaise du Curé (Parson's
Chair) and another beach,
Le Cosmeur. There are also
views of the **Île Callot**, with
sandy inlets, and the Île Louët,
a small island with a lighthouse
and a keeper's cottage, as well
as the recently renovated
Château du Taureau. The
castle was built by the
inhabitants of Morlaix as a
defence against the incursions
of English pirates. Strengthened
by Vauban, it became a
prison. Guided tours of the
château include not just the
garrison but also a boat trip.

In Carantec itself, the small
Musée Maritime contains
some vintage sailing boats,
including a boat in which 193
British pilots and members of
the Résistance crossed the
Channel during World War II.

🏰 **Château du Taureau**
⭕ *Guided tours, which include a
boat trip, available from Mar–Nov.*
Tel *(02) 98 62 29 63.* 📷
www.chateaudutaureau.com.

⛴ **Île Callot**
*Accessible from Grève Blanche at low
tide. Check with the tourist office.*

🏛 **Musée Maritime**
8 Rue Albert-Louppe. **Tel** *(02) 98 67
00 43.* ⭕ *varies, phone ahead.* 📷

St-Pol-de-Léon ❸

Road map B1. 🏚 *7,400.* 🚉 🚌
Place de l'Évêché; (02) 98 69 05 69.
🅰 *Tue.*

This city is the capital of
Brittany's artichoke- and
cauliflower-growing region.
St-Pol (*Kastell Paol* in Breton)
is named after Pol-Aurélien, a
Welsh evangelizer who founded
a monastery here in the 6th
century. Soon after, it became
the see of the diocese of Léon.
The clergy's powerful influence
here is evident both from the
number of religious institutions
– monastic communities and
seminaries – and from its

religious buildings. The 12th-
century **cathedral**, which
towers over the market square,
is one of the very few
churches in Brittany still to have
its original ciborium (canopy).
This one takes the form of a
palm tree, its spreading
branches covered in putti,
vine leaves and ears of corn.
According to an ancient tradition, the ciborium is suspended
over the altar. Other notable
features are a 16-petal rose
window (1431), trompe-l'œil
decoration on the organ, built
by Robert Dallam, 16th-
century choir stalls with carvings
of fabulous animals, and
reliquaries containing skulls.

The most notable build-
ing in St-Pol is, however, the
**Chapelle Notre-Dame-du-
Kreisker**, whose belfry is the
tallest in Brittany; the climb
up its 170-step spiral staircase
is rewarded by a breathtaking
view of the bay, the fields
forming the Ceinture Dorée
(the "golden belt" that is a
prime producer of early
vegetables), and, below, the
old town of St-Pol. From this
vantage point there is a
bird's-eye view of other
jewels of St-Pol's Renaissance
architecture, such as the
Maison Prébendale (canons'
house) on Place du 4-Août-
1944, the Hôtel de Keroulas
in Rue du Collège, and the
Manoir de Kersaliou, on the
road to Roscoff, a charming
16th-century manor house.

🏰 **Chapelle Notre-Dame-du-
Kreisker**
Town centre. **Tel** *(02) 98 69 01 15.* ⭕
Apr–Oct: daily. 📷 *Belfry.*

View of St-Pol-de-Léon from the belfry of Notre-Dame-du-Kreisker

THE STORY OF THE JOHNNIES

When Henri Olivier, an inhabitant of Roscoff, sailed for Plymouth in a ship loaded with onions, he was unwittingly establishing a tradition. Hundreds of agricultural workers, many of whom were very young, followed Olivier's example, going from from port to port in Wales, Scotland and England selling strings of onions to housewives, who nick-named them Johnnies. Until the 1930s, this seasonal migration was an essential opportunity for trade, and many families who lived on the coast of Brittany began to adopt such British habits as drinking tea and playing darts. They also began to speak Breton interspersed with various English words and expressions.

Johnnies with their strings of onions

Roscoff ❹

Road map B1. 🚶 *3,720.* 🚉
📧 *from Morlaix.* ⛴ 🛈 *Quai d'Auxerre; (02) 98 61 12 13.* ⬛ *Wed am.* 🎭 *Pardon de Ste-Barbe (mid-Jul).*

From the fish farms at Ste-Barbe to the seaweed boats in the old harbour, most of Roscoff is focused on the sea. The **Église Notre-Dame-de-Kroaz-Baz** (1515), built with funds from merchants and privateers, has caravels carved on its exterior walls. Inside are alabaster reliefs from an English workshop.

Roscoff (*Rosk o Gozen* in Breton), whose port handles ferry links with Plymouth, has longstanding, if sometimes stormy, connections with Britain. Not only did Roscovites fight naval battles with the British and suffer their raids, they were also accomplices in smuggling. In the 18th century, enormous quantities of contra-band tea, brandy and other liquor left Roscoff to be landed in Britain. Shipowners grew prosperous, as the fine houses that they built in Rue Armand-Rousseau, Rue Amiral-Réveillère and Place Lacaze-Duthiers clearly show.

A small museum presents the history of the Johnnies, which was the name given to the Roscoff producers who went to Great Britain to sell their distinctive pink onions.

🏛 **Maison des Johnnies et L'Oignon Rose**
48 Rue Brizeau. **Tel** *(02) 98 61 25 48.*
⬤ *varies, phone ahead.* ⬤ *Jan.* 📷
📷 *obligatory.*

Île de Batz ❺

Road map B1. 🚶 *740.*
🛥 *4 motorboats run by CFTM (02 98 61 78 87) & ARMEIN (02 98 61 74 04) from Roscoff.* 🛈 *(02) 98 61 75 70.*
🎭 *Pardon de Ste-Anne (late Jul).*

Separated from Roscoff by a narrow channel, the Île de Batz (*Enez Vaz* in Breton) is a small island just 4 km (3 miles) long and 2 km (1 mile) wide. It has about 20 sandy beaches and creeks.

As the crossing from Roscoff's old harbour or from the groyne takes only 20 min-utes, the island attracts crowds of visitors, up to 4,000 a day over certain summer week-ends. Outside the high season, however, Batz is a haven of tranquility, with far fewer visitors than continue to flock to the Île de Bréhat (*see p98).*

Most of the islanders are market gardeners. The seaweed that they spread on their small plots of land helps produce the best fruit and vegetables in the region.

From the landing stage, an alley to the right leads to the ruined Romanesque Chapelle

Jardin Exotique Georges-Delaselle, the colonial garden on the Île de Batz

de Ste-Anne and the a **Jardin Exotique George-Delaselle**, in the southeast of the island, created in 1897. Some 1,500 plants from southern Africa, California and New Zealand thrive in the island's gentle microclimate.

♣ **Jardin Exotique Georges-Delaselle**
Porzan Iliz. **Tel** *(02) 98 61 75 65.*
⬤ *Apr–Jun, Sep–Oct: Wed–Mon pm; Jul–Aug: daily pm.* 📷 📷

Île de Batz, a small treeless island with sandy beaches, off Roscoff

The 16th-century covered market in Plouescat, a rare sight in Brittany

Plouescat **❻**

Road map B1. 14 km (9 miles) west
of St-Pol-de-Léon via the D10.
🏘 *3,780*. 🚌 *Brest then change at
Lesneven*. 🛈 *8 Rue de la Mairie; (02)
98 69 62 18*. 🛒 *Sat am*. 🎫 *Horse
racing in the Baie du Kernic (Aug)*.

The two most memorable
features of Plouescat
(*Ploueskad* in Breton), a major
coastal resort and centre of
vegetable production, are its
beach, the Plage du Pors
Meur, and the 16th-century
covered market, one the few
remaining in Brittany.

Environs

Further inland are several
interesting chateaux. Among
them is the **Château de
Traonjoly**, an attractive
Renaissance manor 4 km
(3 miles) northeast of Plouescat.
The main building is flanked
by wings set at right angles to
it. A balustraded terrace closes

The Château de Traonjoly, a
charming Renaissance manor

the fourth side, thus forming
the main courtyard. The more
austere **Château de Kerouzéré**,
9 km (5 miles) east of
Plouescat, is a fortified castle
with a machicolated rampart
walk and thick granite walls.
Built between 1425 and 1458
by Jehan de Kerouzéré, it was
twice besieged during the Wars
of the Holy League (*see p44*).

The **Château de Maillé**,
3 km (2 miles) south of
Plouescat, is different again.
Remodelled in about 1560 in
the late Renaissance style by
the Carman-Goulaine family,
it has an elegant pavilion.

The most romantic of all
these castles is the **Château
de Kergournadeac'h**, 6 km (4
miles) south of Plouescat,
although it is gutted. Built in
the 17th century by the
Kerc'hoënt and Rosmadec-
Molac families, it was
destroyed a century later on
the orders of its owner, the
Marchioness of Granville; it
is said that she feared that
so beautiful a residence
would keep her son away
from the royal court.

⚜ **Château de Traonjoly**
Cléder. *Tel (02) 98 69 40 01.*
🎫 *by arrangement*.

⚜ **Château de Kerouzéré**
Sibiril. *Tel (02) 98 29 96 05.*
🎫 *mid-Jul–Aug: 2:30–5pm daily.*

⚜ **Château de Maillé**
Plounévez-Lochrist. *Tel (02) 98 61
44 68.* 🎫 *by arrangement.*

⚜ **Château de
Kergounadeac'h**
5 km (3 miles) south of Plouescat
on the D30. 🎫 *Jul–Aug: by
arrangement; contact the tourist
office in Cléder (02) 98 69 43 01.*

Environs

In the countryside around
Plouescat are two jewels of
religious architecture: the
parish close of Notre-Dame
de Berven, 5 km (3 miles)
northeast of Plouescat, and
the Chapelle Notre-Dame-de-
Lambader, 9 km (5 miles) to the
east of the town.

In the **Église Notre-Dame-
de-Berven**, the Virgin is
traditionally invoked to help
young children learn to walk
at an early age. The church
has a stone chancel and a
wooden rood screen with
reliefs showing the four scenes
from the Passion of Christ. A
superb late 16th-century
Virgin of Jesse of Flemish or
Rhenish inspiration stands in
a shuttered niche.

Notre-Dame-de-Lambader
has a balustraded belfry with
four corner-towers like that of
Notre-Dame-du-Kreisker in St-
Pol-de-Léon (*see p120*). The
Flamboyant Gothic rood
screen (1481) is flanked by a
spiral staircase and a 16th-
century statue of the Virgin
that is carried in procession at
the Whitsun pardon.

Château
de Kerjean **❼**

See pp124–5.

Goulven **❽**

Road map B1. 23 km (14 miles) west
of St-Pol-de-Léon via the D10. 🏘 *460*.
🛈 *Plounéour-Trez; (02) 98 83 45 03.*

The 16th-century church in
Goulven has an interesting
interior. It contains a small altar
with reliefs of the six miracles
performed by St Goulven,
and painted wooden panels
depicting the saint with
Count Even de Charruel, who
fought at the Battle of Thirty
(*see p40*). The belfry, built on
the model of that of Notre-
Dame-du Kreisker in St-Pol-
de-Léon (*see p120*), overlooks
a wide bay. At low tide the
sea retreats 5 km (3 miles),
making the bay a favourite
spot for sand yachting. It also
attracts many different species
of birds, including curlew,
teal and sandpiper.

The Pontusval lighthouse,
near Brignogan

Environs

Keremma, 3 km (2 miles) east of Goulven, is one of the most scenic places on the coast of the Léon. It has a long string of dunes created in 1823 by one Louis Rousseau (1787–1856). With his wife Emma, Rousseau purchased the marshy Plaine de Tréflez. Having installed a dyke and drained the land, he built over 80 farms and villas. This newly created polder *(see p71)* increased the agricultural land of the parish by a quarter.

Louis Rousseau's descendants, who still come to spend the summer here, have entrusted the dunes to the Conservatoire du Littoral, a conservation body.

The coastal resort of **Brignogan**, 5 km (3 miles) further north, has a beautiful white sandy beach (below the Pontusval lighthouse) and a *men marz*, 8.50 m (28 ft) high, one of a small number of Christianized menhirs.

Lesneven ⑨

Road map B2. 22 km (13.5 miles) north of Brest on the D788. 🚌 *6,920*. 🚆 *Brest or Landerneau.* ℹ️ *14 Place du Général-Le-Flô; (02) 98 83 01 47.* 🗓️ *Mon.* **www**.lesneven-tourisme.com

Apart from some old houses – at No. 21 Place du Général-Le-Flô and No. 1 Rue du Comte-Even – the main focus of interest in Lesneven is the **Musée du Léon**, which is housed in a wing of a former Ursuline convent.

The exhibits trace the history of the parish, which, until the Revolution, was the seat of the seneschalsy (stewardship) of the Léon. The museum documents the frightful scenes of terror that occurred in the

town in 1793, when many local peasants resisted conscription to the revolutionary cause and were massacred by Republican soldiers.

The museum also has an attractive display of costumes of the 1830s. They include a red silk skirt, an embroidered apron and a gold-embroidered bodice *(see pp26–7)*, a feast-day outfit that would be worn, with a square *coiffe*, by the women of Kerlouan.

🏛 **Musée du Léon**
12 Rue de la Marne. *Tel* (02) 98 21 17 18. 🔘 *for restoration. Due to re-open Spring 2009, phone ahead.* 🖼️

Le Folgoët ⑩

Road map B2. 20 km (13 miles) north of Brest via the D788. 🚌 *3,094*. 🚆 *Brest.* 🎪 *Grand Pardon (first weekend in Sep).*

The name of this small town means "Fool's Wood", and its origins lie in a strange story.

There was once a simpleton named Salaün who lived near a spring on the edge of the wood near Lesneven, and who tirelessly repeated the words "Ave Maria". The villagers nicknamed him *fol goad* (madman of the woods). One day, in 1358, Salaün was found dead near the fountain. Some time afterwards, a lily sprouted on his neglected grave; it bore two words in golden letters: Ave Maria.

The story of this miracle was broadcast throughout the duchy. John V, Duke of Brittany, and the duchy's noble families then financed the building of a collegiate chapel in Le Folgoët. This is the imposing **Basilique Notre-Dame** (1422–60). One of the most illustrious places of pilgrimage in Brittany, it has a delicate *kersanton* (granite) rood screen.

🔒 **Basilique Notre-Dame**
Tel (02) 98 83 09 78. 🗝️ *Jul–Aug.*

Basilique Notre-Dame, in Folgoët

Château de Kerjean ❼

Christ, in the chapel

In 1618, Louis XIII described this stately residence as "one of the most beautiful in the kingdom". It was built between 1566 and 1595 by Louis Barbier, with the fortune that his uncle Hamon, a rich canon of St-Pol-de-Léon, had amassed. It has the characteristics both of a traditional Breton manor and of a French chateau. The architect in charge of the project was clearly familiar with the architectural treatises of the period and also with Renaissance decorative motifs. He remains anonymous, but his style was to influence future buildings in the Léon, including the churches at Berven and Bodilis and the parish close at St-Thégonnec. Ransacked in 1793, Kerjean was sold to the state in 1911. It now contains a fine collection of 17th- and 18th-century furniture of the Léon.

Dormer Windows
The richly decorated dormer windows relieve the plainness of the façades.

The Kitchen
This large, 6-m (20-ft) high room has two hearths and a bread oven.

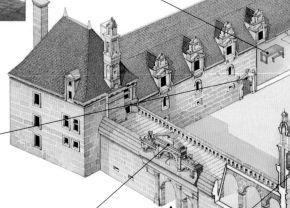

Pediment over the Central Doorways
The doorways of the stable wing are topped by pediments set with urns.

Main entrance

The wooden beams of the chapel ceiling are decorated with representations of the Four Evangelists and Mary Magdalen.

A museum of stonework is housed in one of the guardrooms.

★ Main Entrance
Elaborate ornamentation, with caryatids and volutes, crowns the main entrance.

STAR FEATURES

★ Chapel

★ Main Entrance

For hotels and restaurants in this region see pp223–5 and pp241–3

General view of the chateau from the grounds

VISITORS' CHECKLIST

Road map B1.
St-Vougay. 32 km (20 miles) west of Morlaix via the N12 then the D30. **Tel** *(02) 98 69 93 69.* ⬤ *Jan–Mar & Nov–Dec: Wed & Sun pm; Apr–Jun & Sep–Oct: Wed–Mon pm; Jul–Aug: daily. Theatre and live music: phone for details.*

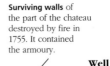

Surviving walls of the part of the chateau destroyed by fire in 1755. It contained the armoury.

Well
The elegant canopy is based on a design provided by the architect Androuet du Cerceau in 1561.

In the projection room, a film traces the chateau's history.

★ Chapel
The chapel has interesting vaulting and contains some fine carved reclining figures. It is located above a room that was used as a guardroom.

BRETON FURNITURE AT KERJEAN

Linen press

As well as grain bins and chests that double as seats, Kerjean contains a few pieces of furniture that are typical of the Léon. These are *gwele kloz* (box beds), some of which are decorated with the monograms of Christ and of the Virgin, and *pres lin* (linen presses), in which cloth was kept before it was taken for sale. These presses are valuable items associated with the weaving industry that brought prosperity to the region.

Box bed

Côte des Abers ⓫

Three long, fjord-like indentations
scar the coastline between Brignogan
and Le Conquet. These are known as
abers – a Celtic word meaning
"estuary". They were formed as
glaciers began to melt at the end of
the Ice Age, 10,000 years ago. As the
sea level rose, sea water flowed up
the valleys far inland, where it met
the fresh water of the streams. These
estuaries are very characteristic of this
part of Brittany, and they are
strikingly different from the coastline
itself. There are no gleaming mud
flats along the *abers* but piles of
rocks and white, sandy dunes where
the local inhabitants once spread
seaweed out to dry.

Aber Wrac'h, a popular sailing and diving centre

KEY

▬ Suggested route

═ Other roads

༖ Viewpoint

0 km   5

0 miles   3

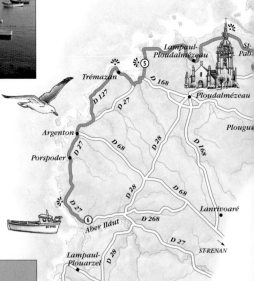

Portsall ⑤
It was on the rocks of Portsall
that the Liberian oil tanker
Amoco Cadiz foundered in 1978.
The whole area has still not
forgotten this ecological disaster.
Tragic for wildlife, the oil spill
was doubly unfortunate as the
stretch of coastline between
St-Pabu and Argenton is one
of the most beautiful and least
developed in the Léon.

Lanildut ⑥
The village (*Lannildud* in Breton) is the largest
seaweed-processing port in France, handling almost
50 per cent of the national harvest. The coastline
is riddled with the ovens in which laminaria, a
green seaweed, was once burned to produce
soda, from which iodine was in turn extracted.

MISSION PICTURES

In 1613, Michel Le Nobletz, a native of Plouguerneau and a zealous missionary, developed an ingenious method of teaching Christian doctrine and backing up the teachings of the Church. On his evangelizing missions, he showed the inhabitants of local coastal parishes pictures of biblical scenes and parables annotated in Breton. These moralizing paintings *(taolennou)* were highly successful. Used until 1950 by missionaries in other countries, they have been translated into 256 languages.

Le Miroir du Monde,
by Michel Le Nobletz

TIPS FOR DRIVERS

Tour length: 56 km (35 miles).
Stopping-off places: The coast has many crêperies where you can enjoy a pancake and local cider. There is also the Auberge de Vieux Puits in Lampaul-Plouarzel (see p242). Alternatively, the oyster farms and bakeries in Lannilis will provide all you need for a picnic on one of the small islands along the abers (but take care not to become marooned by rising tides). For a night stop, there is the Hôtel de la Baie des Anges, 350 Route des Anges, Aber Wrac'h village.

Lilia ①
At 82.5 m (270 ft) high, the Île Vierge lighthouse, opposite Lilia, is the tallest manned lighthouse in Europe. It was built in 1902 to protect shipping from treacherous rocks along a stretch of the coast known as Bro Bagan, "pagan country".

Plouguerneau ②
The Écomusée des Goémoniers de Plouguerneau is an open-air museum devoted to the local seaweed-gathering industry. Also of interest is Iliz Koz, where ruins of a church engulfed by sand in the 18th century have been uncovered.

Seaweed being carried from the coast on an *ar gravazh*, a wooden stretcher

Aber Benoît ④
A footpath runs along the south bank of the *aber*. The walk from the coast to the end of the *aber* takes three to four hours, and reveals every aspect of the estuary.

Aber Wrac'h Harbour ③
This small fishing harbour is now a very popular stopping-place for pleasure boats, and has a diving centre. It is also an ideal base for exploring Aber Wrac'h, the longest and least developed of the three *abers* that indent this stretch of the coast of Brittany.

St-Renan ⑫

Road map B2. 9 km (6 miles) northwest of Brest via the D5. 🏠 *7,900.* 🚌 *from Brest or Landerneau.* ℹ️ *Place du Vieux Marché; (02) 98 84 23 78.* 🛒 *Sat.*

Until the early 17th century, St-Renan (*Lokournan* in Breton) was an important town with a court of justice that served 37 parishes, including Brest. The town's few surviving granite or timber-framed houses, the finest of which are around the Église Notre-Dame-de-Liesse and on Place de la Mairie, date from this period. The weekly market held on this square is widely renowned for the local produce sold there.

The history of these markets and of the horse fairs for which St-Renan was also famous is illustrated in a small museum, the **Musée du Patrimoine**. Breton head-dresses, furniture, domestic objects and exhibits relating to the rich tin mines of the parish are also displayed.

The **Menhir de Kerloas** stands 4 km (2.5 miles) west of St-Renan. Erected on a crest, it is one of the tallest megaliths in Brittany. Newly married couples who wanted children would come to rub their abdomens against the stone.

🏛 Musée du Patrimoine
16 Rue St-Mathieu. **Tel** (02) 98 32 44 94. ◯ *Sep–Jun: Sat am; Jul–Aug: daily pm; groups by arrangement.*

Timber-framed houses on Place du Marché in St-Renan

The fishing harbour at Le Conquet, seen from Pointe de Kermorvan

Le Conquet ⑬

Road map A2. 20 km (12 miles) southwest of Brest via the D789. 🏠 *2,400.* 🚌 *from Brest or Plougonvelin.* ⛴️ *Île Molène & Île d'Ouessant.* ℹ️ *Parc de Beauséjour; (02) 98 89 11 31.* 🛒 *Tue am.* 🎉 *Blessing the sea (mid-Aug).*

For many Bretons, the name of this small, busy fishing port is associated with the radio station on Pointe des Renards that, from 1948 to 2000, broadcast shipping forecasts.

Le Conquet (*Konk Leon* in Breton) has few old buildings besides those known as the *maisons anglaises* (English houses), which the English spared when they attacked the port in 1558, and the Chapelle Notre-Dame-de-Bon-Secours, which contains mission pictures invented by Michel Le Nobletz (*see p127*).

By contrast, the coast between Le Conquet and Lampaul-Plouarzel has some splendid and varied landscapes for walkers. Beyond the Presqu'île de Kermorvan, a peninsula that offers a fine view of the Île Molène and Île d'Ouessant, the long-distance footpath GR34 runs along the dunes of Blancs-Sablons, the beach at Porsmoguer and the cliffs of Le Corsen, 12 km (7.5 miles) to the north. On this rocky headland, the most westerly point in France, stands CROSS, the centre that coordinates rescue operations and monitors maritime traffic in the approaches to Ouessant.

The **Trézien lighthouse**, 2 km (1 mile) northeast, is open to visitors. It is part of the navigation aids (17 light-houses on land and 13 at sea, 85 lightships and 204 buoys)

installed in the 19th century to alert seamen to the hidden dangers of the Mer d'Iroise.

🔦 Phare de Trézien
Trézien en Plouarzel. **Tel** (02) 98 89 69 46. 📷 *Jul–Aug: daily pm.*

Lobster pots stacked on the quay at Le Conquet

Pointe St-Mathieu ⑭

Road map A2. 22 km (14 miles) southwest of Brest via the D789 then the D85. 🚌 *from Brest, changing at Plougonvelin.* ℹ️ *Trez Hir in Plougonvelin, Boulevard de la Mer.* **Tel** (02) 98 48 30 18.

The lighthouse on Pointe St-Mathieu, built in 1835, is open to visitors. Its beams project 60 km (37 miles) across the Mer d'Iroise and its many reefs, including those known as Les Vieux-Moines and La Chaussée des Pierres-Noires.

At the foot of the lighthouse are the ruins of a monastery that was probably founded in the 6th century. At nightfall, the Benedictine monks who settled in this windswept abbey in 1656 would light a fire at the top of the church tower in order to guide ships.

Ouessant Archipelago ⓯

Road map *A1.* 🚶 *1,207.*
🚤 *Motorboats run by Penn Ar Bed
(02 98 80 80 80). Flights from
Finist'Air, (02) 98 80 54 87.* ℹ️ *7 Rue
de la Mairie, in Lampaul (02) 98 84
04 74; in Ouessant (02) 98 48 85 83.*

Battered by strong westerly
winds and lashed by the sea,
the seven islands and dozen
islets that make up the
Ouessant archipelago lie
some 20 km (13 miles) off
the mainland. Only two of
the islands – Ouessant (*Eussa*
in Breton*)* and Molène
(*Molenez*) are inhabited. Each
of these islands preserves its
identity and rich natural
environment and wildlife.

Pointe St-Mathieu, where Benedictine monks once settled

With heathland lapped by
the waves, piles of lichen-
covered rocks and an
exceptionally varied plant
life that thrives in the
moist salt air, the
fascinating
Ouessant archi-
pelago is a world like
no other. In 1989
Unesco declared it a World
Biosphere Reserve.

**Shelduck on the
Ile d'Ouessant**

Just 1.2 km (0.75 mile) long
and 800 m (875 yds) wide,
the **Île Molène** can be walked
around in half an hour. At
first sight, the tiny bare, low-
lying island's only interesting
feature is a small town of 277
inhabitants huddled behind a
breakwater.

But Molène deserves a
closer look: it is a welcoming
place in which to linger.
Quirkily, it keeps English
time. It offers one great
advantage – no cars – and

three specialities: lobster,
seaweed-smoked sausage and
sea rescue. A small museum
pays tribute to the courage of
the islanders who, in 1896,
came to the rescue of
passengers on the wrecked
*Drummond
Castle.*

From the top of
the former signal
station there is a
view of the islands
of the archipelago:
Beniget, with a
population of wild
rabbits, and Banneg,
Balaneg and Trielen, which
were inhabited until the 1950s
and which are today classified
nature reserves. They are
home to a small colony of
otters, shelducks and gulls,
and 120 species of plants,
including the curiously named
Sabot du Petit Jésus (Baby
Jesus's Slipper) and Cierge de
Marie (Mary's Candle).

The largest and highest
island in the archipelago,
the **Île d'Ouessant** is a wild
granite plateau. With its
rugged landscapes, the
island has been the subject

of the most fanciful legends.
In ancient times, the Celts
considered it to be the final
gateway to the Otherworld.

A striking feature of
Ouessant is that it is divided
into extremely small parcels
of land, of which there are
about 55,000. The population
is widely spread over 92
hamlets and a small main
town, Lampaul.

The parish church of
St-Pol-Aurélien, in Lampaul,
has a spire that was built with
funds provided by the British
crown. Queen Victoria
wished to thank the islanders
for their valiant actions after
the *Drummond Castle* was
shipwrecked off the coast of
Ouessant in 1896.

Walkers who do not have
time to explore the whole
island should make for the
northwestern part, starting
with a visit to the open-air
museum in Le Niou Huella
and the Musée des Phares et
Balises (*see pp130–1*).

🏛 **Musée Drummond Castle**
Mairie, Île Molène. ***Tel*** *(02) 98 84
28 65.* ⏲ *Jul–Aug: daily pm.* ♿

The Ile d'Ouessant, the largest and highest island in the Ouessant archipelago, seen from Corz

Exploring Ouessant

With its 45km (28 miles) of coastal paths and its
breathtakingly beautiful landscape, Ouessant attracts
some 120,000 visitors – walkers and city-dwellers in
search of fresh air – every year. The island's wildness is
accentuated by its location. At the point where the
Atlantic Ocean and English Channel meet, Ouessant is
ceaselessly washed by waves and salt spray.

The Phare du Stiff, and to the right, a radar station, on Ouessant

Lampaul, 4km (2.5 miles)
from the landing stage, is
Ouessant's main town. A good
place to start out from on an
exploration of the island is the
hamlet of Niou Huella, where
the **Écomusée d'Ouessant**
opened in 1968.

This open-air museum has
two traditional houses which
themselves make a perfect
introduction to the island's
history and traditions. One of
the houses contains pieces of

furniture made with *peñse an
aod* (wood from wrecks
washed up on the shore) and
painted in blue, white and
other bright colours, the
remains of the paint used to
decorate the hulls of ships.
The other house contains a
display of tools, costumes,
souvenirs of shipwrecks and
objects relating to the ritual of
the *proëlla*, a small wax
candle symbolizing the body
of a sailor lost at sea.

The **Phare de Créac'h**, which
towers over the surrounding
heathland, is one of the most
powerful lighthouses in the
world, with a beam that
carries for 80 nautical miles
(150 km/93 miles). Since it
was inaugurated in 1863, its
xenon lamps (which emit two
white flashes every 10
seconds) have guided more
than 100,000 vessels through
one of the busiest and most
hazardous shipping lanes –
the infamous Ouessant strait
linking the Atlantic Ocean and
the English Channel.

The **Musée des Phares et
Balises**, on the subject of
lighthouses and buoys, has
opened in the lighthouse's
former generator room.

**Exhibits in the Musée des Phares
et Balises, in the Phare de Créac'h**

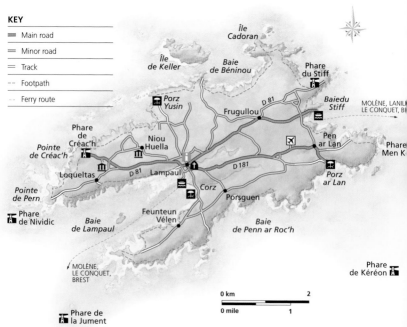

OUESSANT'S SHEEP

Out of the high season, Ouessant's sheep graze freely on the island's salty pastures. Then, on the first Wednesday in February, the day of Porzgwenn's traditional fair, they are collected by their owners. Although sheep-rearing has always been an important activity on Ouessant, the local breed, which is related to the ancient wild sheep of Asia Minor, has almost disappeared from the island. This small, hardy black sheep is being rivalled by the white-fleeced merino.

One of Ouessant's black sheep

The Phare du Stiff, built by Vauban in 1695

From the Musée des Phares et Balises, a coast path runs between pebble ridges and low dry-stone walls, leading to the **Pointe de Pern**, the island's most westerly point. Beyond the tip of this spectacular promontory, with rocks eroded into strange and fantastic shapes, rises the Phare de Nividic, bathed in spray.

The island's northern coast has been colonized by sea birds, including herring gulls, common gulls, puffins, pied oystercatchers and kittiwakes. Further east, grey seals can be seen in the narrow inlets of the Presqu'île de Cadoran. They can also sometimes be seen basking in the sun on rocks at Toull Auroz and Beninou.

The path continues towards the **Phare du Stiff**, which stands on the island's highest point (65m/213 ft). Built by

Vauban in 1695, it is one of the oldest lighthouses in France. From here, in clear conditions, it is possible to see the whole archipelago, the west coast of the Léon and the Île de Sein. Below nestles Stiff harbour, where the *Enez Eussa*, the *Fromveur* and other vessels from the mainland tie up each day.

The **Presqu'île de Pen ar Lan**, southeast of Stiff, is worth a visit primarily for its small sandy inlet, which attracts fewer visitors than Corz, the beach at Lampaul, and for its cromlech, dating from 2,000 BC. This is an elliptical arrangement of menhirs that probably served astronomical purposes.

These are not the only signs of prehistoric habitation on Ouessant. At the foot of the Colline St-Michel, in Mez Notariou, archaeologists have

discovered fragments of pottery and pieces of amphora that show that Ouessant was an early and important centre of trade.

Out at sea opposite Porz ar Lan is the Phare de Kéréon, built in 1907 in extremely difficult conditions. Another lighthouse, the Phare de la Jument, dating from 1904, protects shipping from the dangerous rocks that extend the **Presqu'île de Feunteun Velen**, to the southwest.

🏛 **Écomusée d'Ouessant**
Niou Huella. *Tel* (02) 98 48 86 37.
⏰ daily (Nov–Apr: Tue–Sun pm only).

🏛 **Musée des Phares et Balises**
Créac'h. *Tel* (02) 98 48 80 70.
⏰ daily, winter season pm only.

The rocky Pointe du Créac'h, on the southwest side of Ouessant

For hotels and restaurants in this region see pp223–5 and pp241–3

Brest ⑯

The second-largest town in Brittany after Rennes, Brest has always played a leading military role. From the early days of the Roman Empire, legionnaires had seen the advantage of establishing a secure base on the rocky spur here, overlooking a river, the Penfeld, and perfectly protected by a peninsula, the Presqu'île de Crozon. At the instigation of Richelieu, Colbert and Vauban, who throughout the 17th century worked to transform this natural harbour into the kingdom's foremost naval base, life in the city revolved around the naval dockyard. Brest remained a major shipyard until World War II. After 165 bombing raids and 43 days of siege, the conflict reduced Brest to rubble.

Navy vessel and pleasure craft in the roadstead at Brest

Exploring Brest

A city of rigidly straight streets, regimented residential blocks and lifeless districts, Brest, which was entirely rebuilt after World War II, cannot be described as a prime tourist destination. Yet, visitors who take the trouble to explore it will be rewarded.

Although there are no old buildings here, the town has a pervading and stimulating naval atmosphere. There are dry docks, warships in the naval dockyard, vessels in the roadstead (sheltered anchorage), where there is a viewing platform, and

everywhere the cry of seagulls. Of special interest are the opportunity to experience the undersea world at Océanopolis (*see p135*) and, every four years, the great international gathering of tall ships in the harbour.

🏢 Rue de Siam

The name of this lively commercial thoroughfare commemorates the arrival in Brest of ambassadors sent by the king of Siam to the court of Louis XIV in 1686.

More prosaically, Rue de Siam is a perfect example of 1950s town planning. It has a very uniform appearance. Here, as in the entire district between the Pont de Recouvrance and the town hall, large four-storey residential buildings are arranged symmetrically on a strictly rectilinear axis. However, the recent installation of seven black fountains by the Hungarian sculptor Marta Pan has given the Rue de Siam a noticeable lift.

Rue de Siam, Brest's lively commercial thoroughfare

🏛 Église St-Louis

Place St-Louis, Rue de Lyon.
◻ *daily.* 📷 &.
Built between 1953 and 1958 on the site of the original church of St-Louis, which was destroyed in 1944, this place of worship is the largest of all those built in France in the post-war period.

The materials used – yellow stone from Logonna-Daoulas and reinforced concrete – are a clear departure from Breton architectural traditions, and they produce an admirable effect. The bold lines and restrained decoration of the interior are no less impressive.

The church has two notable features: stained-glass windows on the west front, by Paul Bony, and a lectern in the shape of an eagle, one of the very few pieces that were salvaged from the original church.

🏢 Quartier St-Martin

The former outlying district of St-Martin, which became part of Brest in 1861, is one of the few surviving quarters of the old town. It is also one of the most convivial, judging by the cafés and Irish pubs here, which attract many students from the Université de Bretagne Occidentale.

Retired people and idle onlookers also gather here, to stroll in the market or play boules on Place Guérin, between the school and the Église St-Martin (1875), two buildings that survived the wartime bombings.

The Neo-Romanesque-Gothic church in the Quartier St-Martin

For hotels and restaurants in this region see pp223–5 and pp241–3

La Mer Jaune, by Georges Lacombe, Musée des Beaux-Arts

VISITORS' CHECKLIST

Road map B2. 🏠 *156,200.* ✈ *Brest-Guipavas, 9 km (5.5 miles) from the town centre.* 🚉 *Place du 19e-R-I.* 🚌 *Place du 19e-R-I.* ℹ *Place de la Liberté; (02) 98 44 24 96.* 🛒 *Mon–Sat in Halles St-Martin.* 🎭 *Fête Internationale de la Mer et des Marins (mid-Jul; every four years); Jeudis du Port Jul–Aug; Festival International du Film Court (Nov); Festival du Conte (Dec).* **www.**brest-metropole-tourisme.fr

🏛 Musée des Beaux-Arts

24 Rue Traverse. **Tel** (02) 98 00 87 96. ☐ *Tue–Sat, Sun pm.* ⬤ *Public holidays.* 🎫 *Oct–May.* 📷

The original collection held by this museum was quite literally annihilated by bombing in 1941. However, thanks to the efforts of the curator, the collection has been rebuilt, now consisting of around 300 works of art.

There is a fine collection of Baroque paintings on the first floor, where Guerchin's *Judith and Holophernes* is the centrepiece, and an interesting assemblage of paintings by members of the Pont-Aven School *(see p169)* on the ground floor. Among the most notable works in the collection are *Vue du Port de Brest* by Louis-Nicolas Van Blarenberghe, a Dutch artist who painted siege and battle scenes for Louis XV. Although the artist took liberties with his depiction of the course of the Penfeld river, this painting is of great documentary value as it shows in minute detail the work carried out by convicts and carpenters in the naval dockyards of Brest in 1774.

BREST CITY CENTRE

Cours Dajot ④
Église St-Louis ②
Musée de la Marine ⑥
Musée des Beaux-Arts ③
Musée de la Tour Tanguy ⑨
Naval Dockyard ⑦
Quartier de Recouvrance ⑧
Quartier St-Martin ⑤
Rue de Siam ①

0 m 200
0 yards 200

Key to Symbols *see back flap*

🎠 Cours Dajot

This promenade on the southern part of the town walls was built by convicts in 1769, to a plan by Dajot, a pupil of Vauban. It offers a panoramic view of the commercial port, built in 1860, and of Brest's famous roadstead, which has long given it a strategic and military advantage. Like a huge marine amphitheatre, the roadstead covers 150 sq km (60 sq miles) between the Elorn estuary and the Pointe des Espagnols, with the Île Longue, where there is a nuclear submarine base, in the background.

Of passing interest is the 1900s-style Maison Crosnier, on the corner of Rue Traverse. This is the only house on Cours Dajot that was not destroyed during the war.

Forteresse de Brest, built in the 15th and 16th centuries

🏛 Musée de la Marine

Château de Brest. *Tel (02) 98 22 12 39.* ◯ Apr–Sep: daily; Oct–Nov, Feb–Mar: daily pm. ◯ Jan. ◯ Apr–Sep. ◱

This great fortress on the Penfeld estuary was built in the 15th and 16th centuries. It was a lynchpin in the duchy of Brittany's defences and, for many years, the English had designs on it. It withstood many assaults by the Holy League in 1592 and the Bonnets Rouges in 1675, and was later used as barracks and as a prison. The castle now houses

the naval prefecture as well as a small naval museum. The keep, built by Vauban in 1683, contains the oldest exhibits, which include ship models, lanterns, pieces salvaged from wrecks and wooden figure-heads carved in the work-shops of the naval dockyard. The modern collections, with navigational instruments, a German mini-submarine, and other exhibits, are displayed in the gatehouse towers.

From the top of the keep there is a fine view of the Quartier de Recouvrance and the Penfeld river.

🎠 Quartier de Recouvrance

The Penfeld river, like a fjord, separates the town centre from the Quartier de Recouvrance. The river is spanned by the Pont de Recouvrance, a vertical-lift bridge built in 1954. Its 525-tonne roadway can be raised 26 m (85 ft) in less than three minutes.

The Quartier de Recouvrance used to be a run-down district, as can be seen from the derelict houses in Rue de St-Malo. Before World War II, it was populated by the families of fishermen and of naval dock-yard workers. Though slightly insalubrious, with illegal bars and inebriated sailors, the quarter inspired the writers Mac Orlan and Jean Genet (in *Querelle de Brest*).

The 18th-century Maison de la Fontaine, at No. 18 Rue de l'Église, is one of the oldest houses in Brest. It has a fountain dating from 1761 and a 15th-century medieval granite cross.

Crew hoisting sails in the rigging of a tallship

🏛 Musée du Vieux Brest

Tour Tanguy. *Tel (02) 98 00 88 60.* ◯ Jun–Sep: daily; winter: Wed–Thu & Sat–Sun pm. ◱ Groups only, by arrangement.

A fuller picture of the Quartier de Recouvrance as it was in the past, with its dives and its shady streets, can be gained through a visit to the Musée du Vieux Brest, in the Tour Tanguy.

Built in the 14th century, the Tour de la Motte-Tanguy was once owned by the powerful Chastel family. In 1964, the tower was converted into a museum devoted to historic Brest.

By means of dioramas, documents and other exhibits, the museum illustrates such major events in the town's history as the naval battle fought by Hervé de Portzmoguer in 1512, the arrival of ambassadors from Siam in 1686, and a visit by Napoleon III in 1858.

The Pont de Recouvrance, a vertical-lift bridge across the Penfeld river

For hotels and restaurants in this region see pp223–5 and pp241–3

The bar Le Tour du Monde

LE TOUR DU MONDE

The regular haunt of the famous yachtsman Olivier de Kersauson, this bar is located above the port authority building. Le Tour du Monde (Round the World) was opened in 1997, the year that Kersauson won the Jules Verne round-the-world yachting trophy in his trimaran *Port-Elec*. The yacht is moored near the bar. When he is not at sea, the Admiral, as Kersauson is affectionately known, can often be seen in this wood-panelled bar, which is filled with all manner of souvenirs of his yachting exploits.

⚙ Naval Dockyard

Porte de la Grande-Rivière, Route de la Corniche. *Tel* (02) 98 22 11 78.
☐ *Easter, 15 Jun–15 Sep: daily pm.*
🚫 *Admission restricted to nationals of countries that are accessors to the Schengen Convention (the UK is not). Identification compulsory.* 📷 *obligatory.*

Brest's naval dockyard (Arsenal) was established at the instigation of Cardinal Richelieu. Work began in 1631, and workshops, dry docks and rope-works

Rope-works on the banks of the Penfeld

appeared on the banks of the Penfeld. It was here also that workmen and convicts fitted out ocean-going vessels and provided the labour for further installations. Between 1749 and 1858, 70,000 convicts worked here. Replaced by the penal settlement in Cayenne, French Guiana, the convict centre in Brest closed in 1858.

The guided tour of the naval dockyard takes in the installations that were built at the mouth of the estuary after 1889. They include the naval college,

the former submarine base and the quays, where the most advanced vessels of the French navy are tied up. The reorganization of the French navy and of its dockyards threatens the future of Brest, which is focused on naval defence.

🌿 Conservatoire Botanique

52 Allée du Bot. *Tel* (02) 98 41 88 95. **Park:** ☐ *daily.* **Greenhouses:** ☐ *Jul–mid-Sep: Sun–Thu, pm; mid-Sep–Oct: Wed & Sun pm.* 📷 📷 *for groups, by arrangement.*

This, one of eight similar institutes established in France, is the first to have seriously addressed the issue of saving endangered species of plants from extinction.

Specializing in the plants of the Armorican massif and of the former French colonies (including Madagascar, Martinique and Mauritius), the institute has four greenhouses, in each of which different climatactic zones have been re-created.

A Noah's Ark of the plant kingdom, the institute has been able to reintroduce certain species into their original environment. One such is loosestrife, which became extinct in Spain's Balearic Islands in about 1925.

The park, covering 22 ha (54 acres), is laid out in the little valley of the Stangalar, just north of the greenhouses. It is a paradise for both nature-lovers and joggers.

Part of the tropical pavilion at Océanopolis

🐟 Océanopolis

Moulin-Blanc Marina. *Tel* (02) 98 34 40 40. ☐ *daily.* ⬤ *two weeks in Jan.* 📷 ♿ 📷

A day is hardly long enough to explore Océanopolis. Three pavilions re-create polar, temperate and tropical marine conditions. With a spectacular presentation and state-of-the-art technology, the centre is simultaneously educational, fascinating and entertaining.

Visitors can ride in a glass-sided lift that descends through a pod of sharks, or step into a bathyscaph (submersible vessel) to float through leathery fronds of seaweed. In environments ranging from from ice floes to coral reefs, 1,000 species of sea creatures can be observed in elaborate aquariums with viewing tunnels running through them. There is also a colony of penguins.

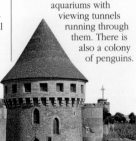

The Tour Tanguy, home to the Musée du Vieux Brest

Plougastel-Daoulas ⑰

Road map B2. 🏠 *12,000*. 🚌 *from Brest.* 🛈 *Place du Calvaire; (02) 98 40 34 98.* 🗓 *Thu am.* 🎭 *Fête des Fraises (second Sun in Jun); Pardon de la Fontaine-Blanche (15 Aug).*

Lying between the Elorn and Daoulas rivers, the Plougastel peninsula is a world apart. Plougastel-Daoulas (*Plougastell-Daoulaz* in Breton) itself only came under the administration of Brest in 1930.

The special character of this part of Brittany is well illustrated by the collections in the **Musée de la Fraise et du Patrimoine**. These focus on local culture (furniture, ceremonial dress and the tradition of *pain des âmes*, special loaves eaten on All Soul's Day) and on the history of strawberry-growing in the area, from the time that the first plants were brought back from Chile by Amédée-François Frézier in 1712 to the conquest of the British market in the early 20th century.

In 1602, the inhabitants built an elaborate calvary to thank God for the passing of an epidemic of the plague. Similar to that at Guimiliau *(see p138)*, it has 180 figures depicting scenes from the life of Christ.

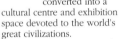

Poster, Musée de la Fraise

🏛 Musée de la Fraise et du Patrimoine
Rue Louis-Nicolle. **Tel** *(02) 98 40 21 18.* ☐ *Jun–Sep: Tue–Fri, Sat–Sun pm; Oct–May: Wed–Fri pm, Sun pm.* 🎟 *All year, by arrangement.* 📷 ♿

The Abbaye de Daoulas, founded in 1167 by Augustinians

Daoulas ⑱

Road map B2. 🏠 *1,866.* 🚌 *From Brest.* 🛈 *Landerneau; (02) 98 85 13 09.* 🗓 *Sun am.*

The town of Daoulas (*Daoulaz* in Breton) developed thanks to the linen-weaving and kaolin-extraction industries.

The **abbey** here was founded in 1167 by Augustinian canons. When they left, in 1984, the *département* of the Finistère purchased the buildings, which had been abandoned in the 19th century. They have been converted into a cultural centre and exhibition space devoted to the world's great civilizations.

Of particular interest are the remains of the cloisters, with 32 arcades and a monolithic fountain, decorated with masks and geometric motifs such as stars, guilloche patterns, wheels and crosses.

The monastic tradition of growing medicinal herbs continues in a garden near the cloisters that contains 300 species native to Brittany, Asia, Africa and Oceania. At the far end of the abbey grounds is Notre-Dame-des-Fontaines, a charming oratory of 1550.

♫ Abbaye de Daoulas
21Rue de l'Église. **Tel** *(02) 98 25 84 39.* ☐ *May–Jan: daily.* 📷 🎟

Landerneau ⑲

Road map B2. 🏠 *15,035.* 🛈 *Pont de Rohan; (02) 98 85 13 09.* 🚌 *Place François-Mitterrand.* 🚂 *Quai Barthélemy-Kerros.* 🗓 *Tue & Fri, am, Sat.* 🎭 *Festival Kann al Loar (Jul); Festival Lunatic (mid-Aug).*

One of the most striking features of Landerneau (*Landerne* in Breton) is the **Pont de Rohan**, built in 1510 and one of the few surviving habitable bridges in Europe.

The historic Pont de Rohan in Landerneau, a bridge all but hidden by the buildings on it

For hotels and restaurants in this region see pp223–5 and pp241–3

The houses and shops of metalworkers, millers and cloth merchants were built on piles or, like the superb house of the magistrate Gillart (1639), built directly on the riverbed.

Although the Elorn, which flows through the town, now carries hardly any river traffic, Landerneau was for centuries a busy port. All kinds of goods bound for the naval dockyard in Brest, as well as linen cloth, passed through Landerneau.

Rood screen figure, La Roche-Maurice

Most of the old houses beside the river date from this age of prosperity (1660–1720). Built in yellow stone from Logonna, they have dormer windows, pepperpot roofs and ornate cornices. Every Wednesday throughout the summer, the tourist office here organizes an architectural walk through the town.

Of particular interest on the south bank are the old Auberge de Notre-Dame-de-Rumengol, at No. 5 Rue St-Thomas, and the houses at Nos. 11, 13 and 15 Rue Rolland. On the north bank is the Maison de la Sénéchaussée at No. 9 Place du Général-de-Gaulle, with one façade of dressed stone and another clad in slates; the residence of the ship-owner Mazurié de Keroualin at No. 26 Quai de Léon; the Ostaleri an Dihuner (Inn of the Alarm Clock) at No. 18 Rue du Chanoine-Kerbrat; and the house of the merchant Arnaud Duthoya, at Nos. 3–5 Rue du Commerce.

La Roche-Maurice ⓴

Road map B2. 4 km (3 miles) northeast of Landerneau via the D712. ▓ 1,740. ▣ Landerneau. ⓘ Mairie; (02) 98 20 43 57. ▨ Pardon de Pont-Christ (15 Aug).

As in many other small towns and villages in the Léon, the **church** here is an architectural gem. The belfry, which has two superimposed bell chambers, is decorated with Gothic spires, gargoyles and Renaissance lanterns.

Inside, the wooden ceiling features angels on a blue background, while the rood screen is striking for its skilled craftsmanship and decoration of fauns and gorgons, apostles and saints. Other notable features are the stained-glass window of the Passion of Christ (1539) by Laurent Sodec, of Quimper, and, above the stoup at the ossuary (1639), an *Ankou* (skeletal figure) with his spear and his motto "Je vous tue tous" ("I kill you all").

The **castle** above the town was one of the main residences of the viscounts of Léon. It passed into the ownership of the dukes of Rohan, who bequeathed it to the parish in 1985. It is currently closed to the public due to archaeological digs.

La Martyre ㉑

Road map B2. 7 km (4 miles) east of Landerneau via the D35. ▓ 610. ⓘ Town Hall; (02) 98 25 13 19. ▣ Landerneau.

This fortified close was begun in the 9th century.The house on the left of the entrance was once the look-out post from which the borders of the medieval kingdom, then duchy, of Cornouaille were watched.

The annual fair that was held here would draw crowds of merchants from England, Holland and Touraine, who came to deal in linen cloth,

livestock and horses. As it levied taxes on every trans-action that took place, the parish grew rich and could thus afford to commission the best workshops to decorate the close and the church.

Everything about the church, dedicated to St Salomon, is, indeed, remarkable: from the 16th-century door and rampart walk, to the tympanum over the south porch, the beams over the north aisle and the stained-glass window of the Crucifixion. Over the ossuary, two angels hold banners that are inscribed in Breton with words that, loosely translated, read: "Death, judgment, freezing hell. Think on that and fear it. Foolish is he who does not know that he must die."

Bodilis ㉒

Road map B2. 21 km (13 miles) northeast of Landerneau via the D770, the N12 and the D30. ▓ 1,400. ⓘ Town Hall; (02) 98 68 07 01.

The 16th-century church in Bodilis (in Breton) is another jewel of religious architecture in Haut-Léon. It has a superb Renaissance porch (1585–1601), which the stoneworkers of Kerjean decorated with statues of the 12 apostles. The interior has a painted wooden ceiling, a Baroque high altar and beams richly decorated with scenes of labour and, somewhat unexpectedly, of drunkenness: a man is shown drinking from a barrel while worms infest a skull.

The fortified close of La Martyre, built by Hervé VII of Léon

The church in St-Thégonnec, once one of the richest in Léon

Lampaul-Guimiliau ❷

Road map B2. 3 km (2 miles) west of Guimiliau. 🏠 *2,037.* 🚌 *Landivisiau.* 🛈 *14 Avenue Foch, Landivisiau; (02) 98 68 33 33.*

The parish close at Lampaul (*Lambaol* in Breton) was built in stages, starting with the porch in 1533 and ending with the sacristy in 1679. Masterpieces here are six stunning altarpieces and an *Entombment of Christ* by Antoine Chavagnac, a sculptor to the French Navy in Brest.

Guimiliau ❷

Road map B2. 🏠 *850.* 🚌 *Landivisiau.* 🛈 *14 Avenue Foch, Landivisiau; (02) 98 68 33 33.*

The calvary in the parish close at Guimiliau (*Gwimilio* in Breton) dates from 1588. Almost 200

figures in amusing or pathetic attitudes make up an earthy and unusual depiction of the life of Christ.

Inside the church is an organ built by Thomas Dallam, and an altarpiece of St Joseph in the Laval style. The baptismal fonts, dating from 1675, are graced by elegant spiral columns.

St-Thégonnec ❷

Road map C2. 13 km (8 miles) south of Morlaix via the D769. 🏠 *2,310.* 🚌 *Morlaix.* 🛈 *Town Hall; (02) 98 79 70 36.*

The porch of the **parish close** here is in a triumphal and ostentatious style that perfectly reflects the opulence that St-Thégonnec (*Sant Tegoneg* in Breton) enjoyed during the Renaissance, when it was one of the richest parishes in the Léon.

Although the church was severely damaged by fire in 1988, some 16th- and 17th-century masterpieces survive. Among them is a priest's chair decorated with medallions and putti, and with armrests in the shape of dolphins' heads. There is also a Rosary altarpiece; a shuttered niche with the Tree of Jesse; a pulpit, which was originally gilded; and an organ built by Thomas Dallam.

The ossuary contains a beautiful painted wood *Emtombment of Christ* dating from 1702. Like the triumphal porch, the architecture of the ossuary is exuberant, with bell-turrets, windows and slender columns.

The altarpiece, *set at the back of the altar, provides a focal point for prayer. This one depicts St Joseph.*

GUIMILIAU PARISH CLOSE

This is a typical parish close, with three essential features: an entrance framed by an arch or a monumental gateway, a calvary with figures depicting biblical scenes, and an ossuary attached to the church.

The cemetery, where members of the small parish community were buried.

Calvaries *were built for the elevation of the souls of believers towards God, but they also provide an insight into daily life in the past.*

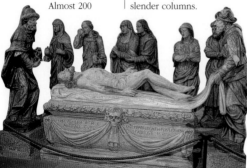

The Entombment of Christ, part of the calvary at Lampaul-Guimiliau

Parish Closes

The phenomenon of Brittany's parish closes *(enclos paroissiaux)*, of which there are almost 70 in Lower Brittany, is closely connected to the rise of the linen industry in the 16th and 17th centuries. The most numerous and elaborate parish closes are those in the Élorn valley. Here, encouraged by evangelizing missions, the religious fervour of the faithful and the generosity of the rich *juloded* (local linen merchants), parishes would virtually rival one another in their efforts to build the finest close. Centred around cemeteries, these remarkable religious complexes consist of a church, an ossuary, a calvary and a triumphal entrance, with Baroque altarpieces and sculptures carved in lacelike detail.

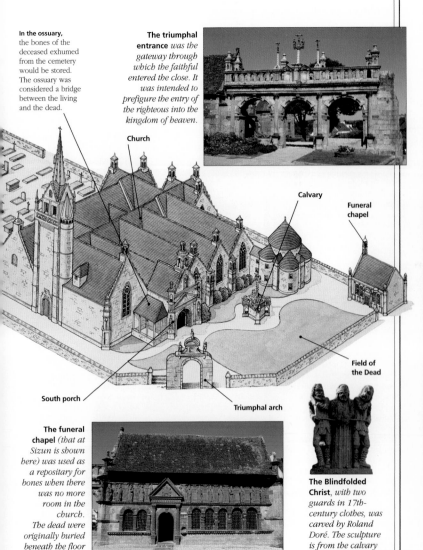

In the ossuary, the bones of the deceased exhumed from the cemetery would be stored. The ossuary was considered a bridge between the living and the dead.

The triumphal entrance *was the gateway through which the faithful entered the close. It was intended to prefigure the entry of the righteous into the kingdom of heaven.*

Church

Calvary

Funeral chapel

Field of the Dead

South porch

Triumphal arch

The funeral chapel *(that at Sizun is shown here) was used as a repository for bones when there was no more room in the church. The dead were originally buried beneath the floor of the church.*

The Blindfolded Christ, *with two guards in 17th-century clothes, was carved by Roland Doré. The sculpture is from the calvary at St-Thégonnec.*

The Moulin du Chaos, at the start of Huelgoat's impressive rocks

Huelgoat 26

Road map C2. Morlaix.
1,748. Moulin du Chaos,
(winter at Rue de Dr Jacques); (02) 98
99 72 32. Thu.

A shining river, a mass of strangely shaped fallen rocks, great moss-covered trees and menhirs make Huelgoat (High Wood) a mysterious and atmospheric place around which popular imagination has woven many legends.

From the Moulin du Chaos, marked footpaths link various places of interest in the area around Huelgoat, which is now part of the Parc Naturel Régional d'Armorique (see right). The river, which from 1750 to 1867 worked the wheels of a lead mine, winds between the Grotte du Diable (Devil's Cave), the first stop on the Chemin de l'Enfer (Path to Hell) of legend, and the famous Roche Tremblante (Shaking Rock), a 100-tonne stone that can be made to rock back and forth simply by applying pressure to it in the right place.

Keen walkers will want to continue to the Mare aux Sangliers (Wild Boars' Pond) and the Camp d'Artus, a Gaulish *oppidum* (fortified settlement), where the fabulous treasure of King Arthur (see p63), is said to lie.

The **Jardin de l'Argoat** and the **Arboretum du Poërop** contain various plants and trees in danger of extinction, including 128 species of magnolia and orchards with ancient varieties of fruit trees.

❀ **Arboretum du Poërop and Jardin de l'Argoat**
55 Rue des Cieux. *Tel* (02) 98 99 95 90. ☐ Sun pm.

Tour of the Monts d'Arrée 27

The hilly area between Léon and Cornouaille can hardly be described as mountainous, as nowhere does it exceed an altitude of 384 m (1,260 ft). Nevertheless, the Monts d'Arrée, covering 60,000 ha (148, 000 acres), are the spine of Finistère. With fewer than 40 inhabitants per square kilometre (103 per square mile), it is sparsely populated. It contains spectacular landscapes, with huge areas of heath, hilly crests and peat bogs, level expanses of granite, ubiquitous lichens and rare species of ferns. Rich in legends and tales of sorcery, this arid region becomes even more extraordinary when the marshy Yeun Elez depression is shrouded in mist. Threatened by forest fires, encroaching wasteland and desertification, it is a fragile environment. The Parc Naturel Régional d'Armorique is working to protect its plant life and to ensure that the local economy remains viable.

KEY

▬▬ Suggested route

═ Other roads

☆ Viewpoint

LANDIVISIAU, LANDERNEAU ⑤
D 18
④ *D 764*
Élorn *Barrage du Drenr*
D 30
LE FAOU
St-Cadou
D 342
D 42
LE FAOU *D 21*
D 121
PONT-DE-BUIS-LÈS-QUIMERCH

Sizun
Renowned for its salmon-rich rivers, Sizun is also worth a visit for its church, with a fine organ case by Thomas Dallam and a 17th-century high altar with dramatic décor. The triumphal entrance leads to the ossuary, which is decorated with apostles and which contains a small museum of religious art.

Maison Cornec ③
This historic farm just outside the small town of St-Rivoal is a prime example of rural architecture. It also offers an excellent insight into country life in Brittany in the 18th century.

Moulin de Kerhouat ⑤
Built in 1610 and in use until 1942, the Moulin de Kerhouat (High Mill) has been converted into an open-air museum of the daily life and work of local millers.

Commana ⑥
The parish church here contains two painted wooden altarpieces, one depicting St Anne and the other, of 1682, Christ displaying his wounds.

Brennilis ⑦
A village strongly associated with legends, Brennilis is located near a strange peat bog – the Yeun Elez – which reputedly marks the entrance to Hell. The church has two 16th-century altars.

St-Herbot ①
The chapel, dedicated to St Herbot, patron saint of livestock, has a chancel and two stone tables on which people placed offerings when requesting his aid.

Montagne St-Michel ②
A stony track leads to the summit of this bare mountain, 380 m (1,247 ft) high, from which there is a panoramic view of one of the wildest areas of Brittany.

SOUTHERN FINISTÈRE

*T*his part of Brittany has wild and rugged coastline but also some very sheltered beaches, and is swept by strong winds while also enjoying a temperate climate. The outstanding cultural heritage of southern Finistère is amply evident in Quimper, the capital city, and during the Festival de Cornouaille that is held here.

Corresponding to the historic kingdom of Cornouaille, southern Finistère is bordered to the north by the Monts d'Arrée and the Presqu'île de Crozon, and to the east by the Montagnes Noires. Like northern Finistère, to the north, and the Morbihan, to the southeast, the region has an indented coastline with impressive promontories, wide bays and sheltered coves.

The Pointe du Van and Pointe du Raz, two promontories at the western extremity of southern Finistère, are among the region's wildest and most beautiful places. It is here, on the edge of the Atlantic, that the four of the largest inshore and deep-sea fishing ports in Brittany – Concarneau, Douarnenez, Le Guilvinec and Camaret – have developed.

Inland, southern Finistère is an area of unspoiled countryside, with lush woods and narrow rivers running through deep valleys where unexpectedly splendid chapels, many with splendid altarpieces and calvaries, can be discovered.

It is also in southern Finistère, together with the Morbihan, that the spirit of ancient, mythical, pre-Christian Brittany most tangibly lives on. The Breton spirit is suffused with the otherworldy, with ancient pagan ideas and rituals that have given birth to legends surrounding countless saints. Armorica is also the land of the Knights of the Round Table and the companions of King Arthur, whose legends enliven a part of this region's enthralling and romantic history.

Picnicking at the foot of a rock on the Île de Sein

◁ The triumphal entrance to the parish close at Argol, built in 1659

Exploring Southern Finistère

The northwestern part of this region is made up of the Parc Naturel Régional d'Armorique, which consists of a small section of the Montagnes Noires and the whole Presqu'île de Crozon, with its long sandy beaches, forests and moors. The Châteaulin basin, in the centre of Finistère Sud, is drained by the Aulne river. Further south, at the confluence of the Steir and the Odet, is the historic city of Quimper, Cornouaille's administrative and cultural capital. The region has two major towns: Douarnenez, in the west, a seafaring town built around an extensive bay, and the fortified town of Concarneau in the south. With a mainly southern orientation, southern Finistère encourages a relaxed way of life. Sheltered coastal resorts, like Morgat, contrast strongly with the rugged Ménez-Hom and the dramatic Pointe du Raz. Never far away are nature reserves that are of particular interest to bird-watchers. The Glénan archipelago, the Île Tristan and Île de Sein each offer superb ports of call for yachtsmen and much that will appeal to divers.

POINTE DES ESPAGNOLS **3**

LANDÉVENNE

Alignements de Lagatjar

CAMARET **4**

POINTE DE PEN-HIR **5**

CROZON **2**

MORGAT **6**

St-Hernot

Cap de la Chèvre

Baie de Douarnenez

RÉSERVE DU CAP SIZUN

DOUARNENEZ **11**

POINTE DU VAN **13**

12

Pont-Croix

D765

D7

POINTE DU RAZ **14**

ÎLE DE SEIN **15**

Primelin

D784

Goyen

D143

16

AUDIERNE

Plozévet

Baie d'Audierne

Plonéo Lanve

D2

SEE ALSO

- **Where to Stay** pp225–7
- **Where to Eat** pp243–5

0 km · · · · · · · · · 10
0 miles · · · · · · · · · 10

NOTRE-DAME DE-TRONOËN **17**

St-Guénolé

PENMARC'H **18**

LE GUILVIN

The wide Plage de Veryach at Camaret

GETTING AROUND

From Paris, Quimper can be reached in four hours by TGV (high-speed train). The principal roads linking Quimper and Nantes and Quimper and Rennes are, respectively, the N165 motorway in the south and the N24. The N165 heading north leads to Châteaulin and goes onto Brest, and the Presqu'île de Crozon via the D791. Quimper-Cornouaille, the regional airport, is located at Pluguffan, 10 km (6 miles) from Quimper via the D785.

SIGHTS AT A GLANCE

Audierne 16
Bénodet 25
Camaret 4
Châteaulin 8
Concarneau pp166–8 27
Crozon 2
Douarnenez 11
Fouesnant 26
Le Guilvinec 19
Île de Sein 15
Îles Glénan 23

Landévennec 1
Locronan 10
Loctudy 20
Manoir de Kérazan 21
Ménez-Hom 7
Morgat 6
Notre-Dame-de-
  Tronöen 17
Penmarc'h 18
Pleyben 9
Pointe de Pen-Hir 5

Pointe des Espagnols 3
Pointe du Raz 14
Pointe du Van 13
Pont-Aven 29
Pont-l'Abbé 22
Quimper pp158–65 24
Quimperlé 30
Réserve du Cap Sizun 12
Rosporden 28

Huelgoat

Brest
Le Faou
égarvan
Morlaix
Carhaix-Plouguer

N165
D785
D764
D36
N164
Loudeac,
Rennes

MÉNEZ-HOM
Port
Launay
9 PLEYBEN
-Marie-du-
enez-Hom
8 CHÂTEAULIN
Châteauneuf-
du-Faou
Montágnes Noires

Cast
D107
Aulne
D785
D72
D15

FINISTÈRE
LOCRONAN
St-Venec
Quilinen
N165
Briec
Odet
Coray
D36
D15
Scaër
D6
D4
Touch

Gorges de
Stangala
Ploneis
D39

24 QUIMPER

28 ROSPORDEN
Bannalec
D70
Isole
D765
Arzano

D34
D783
N165

La Fôret-
Foueснant
26 FOUESNANT
BÉNODET
25
30 QUIMPERLÉ
N165
D44

2 PONT-L'ABBÉ
21 MANOIR DE KERAZAN
20 LOCTUDY
27 CONCARNEAU
Pointe du
Cabellou
29 PONT-AVEN
D783
Moëlan-s-Mer
D24
Lórient,
Vannes

onil
Port-Manec'h

D785

The picturesque mill at Pont Aven

ÎLES DE GLÉNAN
23

KEY

▬	Major road
─	Secondary road
═	Minor road
▬	Main railway
┄	Minor railway
▬	Regional border

The Pointe du Van, where the cliffs are 65 m (210 ft) high

Ruins of the Abbaye de Landévennec, founded in the 5th century

wooden altarpiece of the Ten Thousand Martyrs *(see pp148–9)*, also dating from the 16th century.

Pointe des Espagnols ❸

This promontory on the north side of the Presqu'île de Crozon encloses Brest's roadstead *(see p134)* and also offers a view of Île Longue, where there is a nuclear submarine base.

The promontory (Spaniards' Point) is named after a fort that the Spaniards, allies of the Holy League, built in 1594 during their war with Henry IV. It was, however, captured and destroyed by the king's soldiers.

Landévennec ❶

Road map B2. 18 km (11 miles) south of Crozon via the D791 and the D60. 🚶 370. 🚍 Brest or Quimper, then taxi or bus. 🚌 ℹ️ (02) 98 27 78 46 (summer); (02) 98 27 72 65 (winter).

In the fifth century, where Landévennec (*Landevenneg* in Breton) now stands, St Guénolé founded an abbey . Destroyed by the Normans in 913, rebuilt in the 13th century, pillaged by the English in the 16th and dissolved during the Revolution, the abbey remained an important centre of Christianity despite these vissicitudes.

Among the ruins of this fine example of Romanesque architecture are a 16th-century statue of St Guénolé and a tomb that is said to be that of Gradlon, legendary king of Cornouaille. The capitals and the bases of the abbey's columns are well preserved, and they bear Celtic patterns and animal motifs.

The **Musée de l'Ancienne Abbaye** presents the history of this religious centre in the context of Christianity in Brittany. Artifacts, such as manuscripts and statues, that were discovered during archaeological excavations here, are also on display.

The **Corniche de Térénez**, leading towards Le Faou, follows the Aulne estuary and leads to a viewpoint offering a splendid panorama of the meandering river and a view of the French navy's scrapyard.

🏛 **Musée de l'Ancienne Abbaye**
Tel (02) 98 27 35 90. ⬜ varies (groups by arrangement). 🈺 🄿

Crozon ❷

Road map B2. 🚶 7,800. 🚍 Brest or Quimper. 🚤 🚆 to Brest (summer only). ℹ️ Boulevard de Pralognan-la-Vanoise; (02) 98 27 07 92. 🗓 Tue–Sun.

In summer the coast here becomes a paradise of beautiful turquoise lagoons and white sandy creeks.

According to the Cartulaire de Landévennec, King Gradlon gave a third of the land around Crauthon (the old name of Crozon) and its church to St Guénolé. Because of its strategic location, Crozon (*Kraozon* in Breton) was invaded by Normans in the 10th century, by English allies of the Montforts in the 14th century, by the English again in the 15th and 16th centuries and later by the Spanish. It also suffered bombing during World War II.

Although the Église St-Pierre has been damaged by vandals and the ravages of time, it still has its 16th-century porch and a magnificent painted

Camaret ❹

Road map A2. 9 km (6 miles) west of Crozon via the D8. 🚶 2,735. 🚍 🚤 Brest-Guipavas or Quimper-Cornouaille. ℹ️ Quai Kléber; (02) 98 27 93 60. 🎪 Pardon de Notre-Dame de Rocamadour (first Sun in Sep). 🗓 third Tue in the month (daily in summer).

Once a sardine port, Camaret (*Kameled* in Breton) turned to the crayfish industry at the beginning of the 20th century. Ships take on cargoes of crayfish from the farms located all along the coast of Brittany. Foreign competition has, however, somewhat curtailed this industry.

The **Tour Vauban**, begun in 1689 and rendered in orange, is the focal point of the fortifications that Vauban *(see p167)* built around

Pointe du Tourlinguet, between Pointe de Pen-Hir and Camaret

One of the beaches at the small coastal resort of Morgat

Camaret. It was these fortifications that made possible the destruction of the Anglo-Dutch fleet when it made an attempted landing here in 1694.

The **Chapelle de Notre-Dame-de-Rocamadour** was built on a shingly spit, the Sillon de Camaret, in the 16th century. It is named for the pilgrims who stopped there on their way to the Église de Notre-Dame in Rocamadour, southwestern France. The top of the belfry was destroyed by a cannon ball fired by the English in 1694. In stormy weather, the church bells are rung to guide seamen.

Environs
Just off the road from Camaret to Pointe du Tourlinguet are the **Alignements de Lagatjar**, 142 menhirs that stand facing the sea. Opposite are the ruins of the Manoir de Coecilian, where St-Pol Roux, a poet and pioneer of Surrealism, lived from 1905.

🏛 **Tour Vauban**
⬜ mid-Jun–mid-Sep: daily.

🔲 **Alignements de Lagatjar**
D8, towards the Pointe du Tourlinguet.

Pointe de Pen-Hir ❺

Road map A2. 5 km (3 miles) west of Crozon via the D8, or 6 km (4 miles) via the D355.

Rising to a height of 63 m (207 ft), Pointe de Pen-Hir offers one of the most breathtaking panoramas in Brittany. Breaking the waves just below the point is a cluster of rocks, the Tas de Pois (Pile of Peas). On the left is Pointe de Dinan (from which there is a fine view of a rock known as the Château) and on the right Pointe du Tourlinguet and Pointe de St-Mathieu.

The **Musée Memorial de la Bataille de l'Atlantique**, on the road running round Pointe de Pen-Hir, describes the German occupation here, and is a memorial to the Bretons who died in World War II.

Cormorant on Pen-Hir

🏛 **Musée Memorial de la Bataille de l'Atlantique**
Kerbonn, commune of Camaret.
Tel (02) 98 27 92 58. ⬜ May–Oct: daily. 🖼

Morgat ❻

Road map A2. 4 km (3 miles) south of Crozon via the D887. 🏠 7,880. 🔳
ℹ *Place d'Ys;* (02) 98 27 29 49. 🚌 Jul–Aug: first & third Wed in the month.
🎪 *Fête du Thon* (15 Aug).

The small coastal resort of Morgat (*Morgad* in Breton) developed at the beginning of the 20th century, thanks to the publicity that it gained from its association with the Peugeot family, who built hotels here. The villas in the resort date from this era. Morgat is now administratively part of Crozon, and this has contributed to the latter's development.

Although Morgat has pleasant beaches, today it is the large nature reserves nearby, such as the Marais de l'Aber, that draw visitors. With its population of birds and otters, the Étang de Kerloc'h, covering 110 ha (270 acres) between Camaret and Crozon, is of particular interest to lovers of wildlife. A fascinating feature here are the sea caves carved out of the schist cliffs by the waves.

Environs
The **Maison des Minéraux** in St-Hernot, on the road to Cap de la Chèvre, contains a splendid collection of local minerals and a rare display of fluorescent rocks.

🏛 **Maison des Minéraux**
St-Hernot, Crozon. **Tel** (02) 98 27 19 73. ⬜ Jul–Aug: daily; Sep–Jun: Mon–Fri, Sun pm. 🖼 ♿

CARTULAIRE DE LANDÈVENNEC

This ninth-century book of gospels demonstrates Landévennec's importance in the production of religious texts. Written in Latin, in Carolingian minuscule – the clear calligraphic style introduced by Charlemagne – it contains more than 300 parchment pages. The Four Evangelists are symbolized by animals. St Mark is associated with the horse (*marc'h* means "horse" in Breton), an animal that, in Armorican tradition, replaces the lion. The two feast days honouring St Guénolé, held on 3 March and 28 April, are mentioned. This rare manuscript was presented to the New York Public Library by an American collector in 1929.

Cartulaire de Landévennec, the oldest manuscript created in Finistère

Crozon: Altarpiece of the Ten Thousand Martyrs

The Église St-Pierre in Crozon (*see p146*) contains an altarpiece that gives a magnificent visual account of the story of the Ten Thousand Martyrs. It tells the story of the 10,000 soldiers of the Theban Legion who, as punishment for their Christian faith, were put to death on Mount Ararat by Emperor Hadrian during his Armenian campaign in the second century. The soldiers' crucifixion and their composure in the face of death were intended to reflect the Passion of Christ. The altarpiece, made in 1602, is certainly the work of several artists, and it is one of many depictions of the theme that were created during the Renaissance. The story also appears in Anne of Brittany's *Book of Hours*.

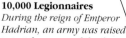

Acace Garcère and his troops

The legionnaires, under the command of the orator Acace Garcère, choose death rather than denial of their Christian faith. The Roman soldiers, meanwhile, show their determination as they prepare for war and execute an ostentatious military parade.

10,000 Legionnaires

During the reign of Emperor Hadrian, an army was raised to put down a revolt by the inhabitants of Armenia.

Angel

On the eve of battle, the angel invites the martyrs to embrace their faith.

Confusion of Battle

The future martyrs throw themselves into battle. Despite their entreaties to the gods, fear spreads among the pagan ranks.

Hadrian's soldiers gather stones to throw at those who profess their faith in Christ, but the stones fly back to hit them.

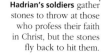

Pagan Soldiers
Hadrian's pagan troops are depicted kneeling before an idol, while the newly converted Christians are shown turning their backs on it.

VISITORS' CHECKLIST

Road map B2.
Église St-Pierre **Tel** (02) 98 27 05 55 (local caretaker). 🚌 Brest or Quimper, then by bus.
⬤ 9am–6pm daily. 📷 ♿

Grotesque Figure
Kneeling in front of the martyrs, this figure acts out a parody of the Scourging of Christ.

The upper triptych depicts the martyrs receiving communion.

The Crown of Thorns, which was suffered by Christ, is inflicted on the martyrs.

Way to Mount Ararat
The blood that flows from the martyrs' chests is used for their baptism into the Christian faith. They then make their way up to Mount Ararat.

The condemned reassert their faith after they have been led by the angel to the place of their execution.

The Martyrs' Death
The martyrs die on Mount Ararat, at the same hour as Christ died on the Cross.

View from the summit of Ménez-Hom, with the Aulne river below

Port-Launay, on a bend in the Aulne 2 km (1 mile) north-east of Châteaulin, was once the town's port. With low houses lining the riverbank, it offers a timeless picture of Brittany.

In the 16th century, when the plague was taking a heavy toll, a chapel dedicated to St Sebastian, patron saint of healing, was built in St-Ségal, 3 km (2 miles) northwest of Port-Launay. The calvary, monumental entrance and altarpiece are among the finest in southern Finistère.

◼ Notre-Dame-de-Rumengol
Châteaulin. **Tel** (02) 98 86 02 11.

Ménez-Hom 🟑

Road map B2. West of Châteaulin via the D887.

A peak on the western edge of the Montagnes Noires, Ménez-Hom (*Menez-C'hom* in Breton) rises to a height of 330 m (1,083 ft). It overlooks the Baie de Douarnenez and, in clear weather, Pointe du Van and Cap de la Chèvre can be seen from the summit.

This mountain, which the Celts held to be sacred, is also the land of the *korrigans* (evil spirits) and of the elves of Armorican popular belief and literature. Wildlife here includes Montagu's harrier and warblers, and the marshes of the Aulne estuary at the foot of the mountain are home to herons and ducks, as well as many species of plants. On 15 August each year, during the Festival du Ménez-Hom, the sound of bombards and Breton bagpipes (*see pp22–3*) fills the air.

The chapel in the hamlet of Ste-Marie-du-Ménez-Hom contains a beautiful altarpiece. There is also a parish close and a 16th-century calvary here. In Trégarvan, about 12 km (8 miles) away, an early 20th-century school has been converted into the **Musée de l'École Rurale en Bretagne**.

🏛 Musée de l'École Rurale en Bretagne
Trégarvan. **Tel** (02) 98 26 04 72.
⬭ varies, call ahead. 🖼

Châteaulin 🟖

Road map B2. 🏘 *5,700*. 🚊
🚉 *Quimper-Cornouaille.*
🛈 *Quai Cosmao; (02) 98 86 02 11 (Apr–Sep).* 🛒 *Thu.* 🎉 *Boucles de l'Aulne (27 Aug).*

The Grand Prix des Boucles de l'Aulne that is held here has made this town the Breton capital of cycle racing. The Aulne is the most salmon-rich river in France, so that Châteaulin (*Castellin* in Breton) also attracts large numbers of anglers. Trips along the Aulne on a restored riverboat, the **Notre-Dame-de-Rumengol**, leave from here (Jul–Aug).

A short walk upriver leads to the Chapelle Notre-Dame, on a wooded hill on the left bank of the Aulne. The church has a 15th-century calvary with a depiction of the Last Judgment.

Port-Launay, where the salmon-rich river attracts many anglers

Pleyben 🟙

Road map B2. 🏘 *3,800*. 🛈 *Place Charles-de-Gaulle; (02) 98 26 71 05.* 🎉 *Pardon (1 Aug).* 🛒 *Sat.*

The parish of Pleyben (*Pleiben* in Breton) is mentioned in the 12th-century Cartulaire de Landévennec (*see p147*). Pleyben – a conflation of "Iben", the name of a Breton saint, and the prefix "ple" (*see pp36–7*) – was one of the parishes established when immigrants from Britain arrived in the fifth to seventh centuries.

The **parish close** consists of a calvary – one of the finest in Brittany – an ossuary, a monumental entrance and a church. The latter, dedicated to St Germain of Auxerre, has two belfries. The one on the right is a Renaissance tower, and the one on the left a Gothic spire. Between them is a stair turret with pinnacles and an ornate spire. The nave has a 16th-century painted ceiling with beams carved and painted with sacred and secular scenes. The high altar, dating from 1667, is lit by 16th- and 17th-century stained-glass windows.

The 16th-century ossuary has been converted into a museum of the history of Pleyben. The triumphal entrance, or *porz ar maro* (gate of the dead), through which every deceased member of the parish used to be carried, was built in 1725.

The Pleyben Calvary

This gospel in stone, designed for the edification of illiterate worshippers, was constructed in 1555 and completed in 1650 with the addition of sculptures by Julien Ozanne, of Brest. These, carved in *kersanton*, the dark Breton granite, are on the first tier of the east side of the calvary. They depict The Last Supper, The Entry into Jerusalem, and Christ Washing the Feet of his Disciples. In 1738, the calvary was given the monumental appearance that it has today. There are two curious depictions. One, on the northeastern spur, shows the Devil disguised as a monk who tempts Christ. The other, on the western side, is of Peter weeping for his denial of Christ before a cockerel, of which only the feet survive. The scenes are arranged in sequence, starting with The Visitation, in which the angel appears to Mary. The next scene is The Nativity.

THE PASSION OF CHRIST
The focal point of the parish close, the visual account of the Passion of Christ expresses the fundamental Christian belief in the Death and Resurrection of Christ.

Christ on the Cross

Side cross

Christ Washing the Feet of His Disciples, on the east side of the calvary, shows Christ in the act of washing Peter's feet. Peter asks: "Lord, do you wash my feet?"

Peter's Denial *shows Peter lamenting his betrayal of Christ.*

Christ with the Crown of Thorns, flanked by two soldiers.

The Pietà *shows Mary holding the dead Christ in her arms.*

The Flagellation shows the naked Christ tied to a post.

The Last Supper, on the east side of the calvary.

CARDINAL POINTS
The scenes on the four sides of the calvary were intended to be read by the faithful as they processed round it. The scenes of the life of Christ are arranged in sequence from west to east, east representing Golgotha and the Resurrection.

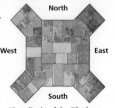

North

West

East

South

The plinth of the Pleyben calvary, in a the shape of a cross.

Granite-built house, typical of buildings in Locronan

Locronan ⑩

Road map B2. ⚄ 800.
🚉 Quimper. 🛈 Place de la Mairie;
(02) 98 91 70 14.
www.locronan.org

A legend tells that Ronan, an Irish monk, came to Cornouaille. He worked tirelessly to evangelize the area, and it became an important place of pilgrimage. In the 15th century, Locronan (*Lokorn* in Breton) developed thanks to the linen and hemp-weaving industry that provided Europe with sailcloth. Old looms and local costumes are displayed in the **Musée d'Art et d'Histoire**.

The **Église St-Ronan**, built in the 15th century, is connected to the 16th-century **Chapelle du Pénity**. The apse of the church is lit by a large 15th-century stained-glass window of the Passion of Christ, and the pulpit (1707) is carved with medallions with scenes from the life of St Ronan. There is also a Rosary altarpiece, dating from the 17th century. The chapel contains a recumbent figure of St Ronan and a magnificent *Descent from the Cross* in painted stone.

The square, in which there is a well, is lined with houses with granite façades. Built in the 17th and 18th centuries,

they were the residences of Locronan's wealthy citizens.

The **Chapelle Bonne-Nouvelle**, in Rue Moal, has a small calvary and an attractive fountain.

🏛 **Musée d'Art et d'Histoire**
Tel (02) 98 91 70 14. ⬚ varies, phone ahead. ▨

🔒 **Église St-Ronan and Chapelle du Pénity**
Place de l'Église. ⬚ daily.

🔒 **Chapelle Bonne-Nouvelle**
Rue Moal. ⬚ Easter–Sep. For other times, phone tourist office.

Douarnenez ⑪

Road map B2. ⚄ 15,820.
🚉 Quimper. ✈ Quimper-Cornouaille.
🛈 2 Rue du Dr-Mével; (02) 98 92 13 35. 🏪 Halles de la Grande-Place de Tréboul (Mon–Sat, am); Tréboul harbour (Wed & Sat am). 🎭 Rosmeur harbour, organized by the tourist office (Apr–Oct).

Douarnenez was once the largest sardine port in France, and its was here that the first canning factories opened, in 1853. Fishing, in which about 1,000 people are engaged, can no longer support the population of Douarnenez, although the fresh fish auction held here is still one of the largest in Brittany.

Remains of a *garum* factory discovered at Les Plomarc'h, a small fishing village next to Douarnenez, indicate that the site was settled in the Gallo-Roman period. *Garum* was a fish sauce highly prized throughout the Roman world

Today, it is the cove at Tréboul and the **Le Port Musée**, at Port Rhu, a centre for the preservation of the local seafaring heritage, that

Port Rhu, the maritime museum in Douarnenez, with vessels tied up at the quayside

together draw visitors to Douarnenez. Salvaged boats are also on display here. Tours of the harbour and sea fishing trips are offered by **Vedettes Rosmeur**.

Between the quays and the town centre is the 17th-century **Chapelle St-Michel**, which contains a collection of 52 mission pictures created by Michel Le Nobletz (*see p127*).

📰 **Vedettes Rosmeur**
Harbour. **Tel** (02) 98 92 83 83; tours of the harbour (Apr–Sep: am); sea fishing.

🏛 **Le Port Musée**
Place de l'Enfer. **Tel** (02) 98 92 65 20. ⬚ mid-Jun–Sep: daily; Mar–mid-Jun & Oct: Tue–Sun. ▨ ▨

🔒 **Chapelle St-Michel**
Rue du Port-Rhu. **Tel** (02) 98 92 13 35. ⬚ by arrangement.

Réserve du Cap Sizun ⑫

Road map A2. 20 km (13 miles) west of Douarnenez via the D7, Chemin de Kérisit. 🛈 64 Rue de Bruyères (02) 98 70 55 51.
Bretagne Vivante SEPNB **Tel** (02) 98 70 13 53.

This nature reserve, created in 1959 by Michel-Hervé Julien and Bretagne Vivante SEPNB (Société d'Étude et de Protection de la Nature en Bretagne), covers 25 ha (62 acres) on the north coast of Cap Sizun. It attracts many ornithologists, as, from April to the end of August, sea birds come here to breed in their thousands. Migrating birds are also seen here. There are marked footpaths to help visitors explore, and guided walks are available.

At Pont-Croix, on the right bank of the Goyen river, which runs along the southern part of Cap Sizun, stands **Notre-Dame-de-Roscudon**, founded in the 13th century. The church's Romanesque vaulting is supported by clustered columns typical of an

Pointe du Van, with Cap Sizun visible in the far distance

English-influenced architectural style that became known as the school of Pont-Croix style. Le Marquisat, a 16th-century residence, houses the **Musée du Patrimoine**.

The Goyen estuary, with salmon-rich waters and large numbers of birds, offers a walk in an unspoiled environment running for 12 km (8 miles) from Pont-Croix to Audierne.

🏛 **Musée du Patrimoine**
Tel (02) 98 70 51 86. ⬜ *varies.* 📷

Pointe du Van ❸

Road map A2. 27 km (17 miles) west of Douarnenez via the D7.

With high cliffs and the 17th-century Chapelle St-They perching on rocks, the Pointe du Van is a magnificent sight. Although the landscape here is bare, the views of Pointe de Brézellec, Cap de la Chèvre, Pointe St-Mathieu and the rocks known as the Tas de Pois (Pile of Peas) are superb. To the left is Pointe du Raz, the Phare de la Vieille and, behind it, Île de Sein. A walk along the GR34 long-distance path will reveal several small fishing villages tucked away along the coast here.

Pointe du Raz ❹

Road map A2. 16 km (10 miles) west of Audierne via the D784. 🚌 *Douarnenez, Audierne, Quimper.* ℹ️ *Maison de la Pointe du Raz, Plogoff; (02) 98 70 67 18.* 🅿️ *compulsory; pay and display.*

Wild and majestic, this spur shaped by the action of waves rises to height of more than 70 m (230 ft). Pointe du Raz (*Beg ar Raz* in Breton) is extended by a spine of submerged rocks, on the most distant of which stands a lighthouse, the Phare de la Vieille.

In fine weather, the Île de Sein and the Ar Men lighthouse are visible from here. On the north side, the sea has carved potholes known as the Enfer de Plogoff, where the legendary Princesse Dahud would cast her unfortunate lovers. The Raz de Sein, a notorious tide race, is much feared by sailors.

Pointe du Raz is now a conservation area with a network of footpaths. There is also a visitor centre, the Maison de la Pointe du Raz, which can be reached on foot or by taking a free ride in an electric-engined boat.

Environs
The Baie des Trépassés (Bay of the Dead) has a beautiful beach with caves in the cliffs that can be explored at low tide. According to local legend, the bodies of those who had died at sea would be washed up on this beach by strong currents.

The lighthouse, Phare de la Vieille, seen from Pointe du Raz

Christians processing during the Troménie in Locronan

THE TROMÈNIE, TOUR OF MONASTERY LAND

Some 2,500 years ago, Locronan was a centre of Celtic religion unlike any other in Europe. Here, Celtic astronomical points of reference were used to create a *nemeton*, a quadrilateral circuit 12 km (7.5 miles) long punctuated by 12 markers corresponding to the 12 cycles of the lunar calendar. Although Benedictine monks took over this Celtic site to build a priory, the outline of the sacred itinerary survived the imposition of Christianity. The Celtic astronomical markers became the 12 stations of the Christian procession. The word *troménie* is derived from the Breton words *tro* (tour) and *miniby* (monastery land). The oldest-established *troménie* goes back to 1299. The *grande troménie* secures pilgrims' entry into heaven and equals three *petites troménies*.

Île de Sein ⑮

🚶 250. ℹ Mairie; (02) 98 70 90 35.
⛴ Audierne (daily), Brest, Camaret
(summer only). No cars allowed on
the island. 🎪 Pardon de St-Guénolé
(Trinity Sunday, Jun), Pardon de
St-Corentin (first Sun in Aug).

This island, an extension of
Pointe du Raz, is no more
than about 2 km (1 mile) long
and 800 m (875 yds) wide,
and its highest point is just
6 m (20 ft) above sea level.
The landscape here is bare
and the small town consists
of a maze of narrow streets
that give welcome shelter
from the wind.

The Île de Sein (*Enez-Sun*
in Breton) has a few megalithic
monuments, including two
menhirs known as Les Causeurs
(The Talkers) and the Nifran
tumulus. The island may have
been a burial place for druids.

The islanders' greatest
moment in history came at
the outbreak of World War II,
when they answered the call
of General de Gaulle.

A track leads to the lighthouse and the Chapelle
St-Corentin. The **Musée Jardin
de l'Espérance** documents
daily life on the island.

Environs
The **Phare d'Ar Men**, 12 km
(7.5 miles) west of the island,
was built on a reef that is
permanently battered by the
waves. It took the islanders
14 years to build. The
unmanned lighthouse protects
shipping negotiating these
dangerous waters.

🏛 **Musée Jardin de
l'Espérance**
Quai des Paintolais. 🕒 Jun–Sep. 📷

Les Causeurs, a pair of menhirs
on the Île de Sein

The lighthouse, Phare Île de Sein, off the western tip of the Île de Sein

Audierne ⑯

Road map A2. 🚶 2,500. 🚃
Quimper-Cornouaille. 🚌 Quimper
then by bus. ℹ 8 Rue Victor-Hugo;
(02) 98 70 12 20. 🎪 Pardon (last
Sun in Aug). ⛴ Sat.
www.audierne-tourisme.com

The seafaring town of
Audierne (*Gwaien* in Breton)
still has a busy harbour, with
an inshore fishing industry
specializing in such highly
prized fish as sea bream and
monkfish caught with seine
nets, and sea bass caught on
the line, as well as crayfish.
Trips out to sea in a traditional
lobster boat are on offer
(details from the tourist office).
The boat scrapyard in the
Anse de Locquéran, with old
lobster boats, is a protected
historic site. Also of historic
interest are exhibits in the
Musée Maritime. They include
a reconstruction of a fisherman's cottage.

The 17th-century **Église
St-Raymond-Nonnat**, which
overlooks the town, is
decorated with carvings of
ships and has a striking
Baroque belfry.

The **L'Aquashow** on the
outskirts of the town, offers
the opportunity to view
marine life.

Environs
At Primelin, 3 km (2 miles)
west of Audierne on the D784,
is the beautiful **Chapelle de St-
Tugen**, built in 1535. While the
nave and square tower are
both in the Flamboyant Gothic
style, the transept and apse
date from the Renaissance.

🏛 **Musée Maritime**
Rue Lesné. **Tel** (02) 98 70 27 49.
🕒 mid-Jun–mid-Sep daily. 📷

🐟 **L'Aquashow**
Rue du Goyen.
Tel (02) 98 70 03 03. 🕒 Apr–Nov:
daily. 📷 by arrangement. ♿ 📷
🏠 **Chapelle de St-Tugen**
🕒 daily (summer only).

Audierne harbour, with the Église
St-Raymond-Nonnat on the right

Notre-Dame-
de-Tronoën ⑰

Road map B2. 9 km (5.5 miles)
west of Pont-l'Abbé, commune of
St-Jean-Trolimon. **Tel** (02) 98 82 04
63. 🕒 Apr–Sep. 📷 summer only.

A landscape of bare dunes
surrounds the chapel and
calvary of Tronoën (*Tornoan*
in Breton). The vaulted
chapel has a rose window,
and two doorways frame an
open belfry set with turrets.

The calvary (c. 1450–70) is
the oldest in Brittany, and the
detail of its carvings has been
obliterated by the passage of
time. On the platform are
Christ on the Cross, flanked
by the two thieves. The
rectangular base is decorated
by a double frieze illustrating
The Childhood of Christ and
The Passion of Christ.

The sequence of scenes
begins on the east side with
The Annunciation, continuing
on the north side with
The Visitation and The Nativity.

The scenes are carved in granite from Scaër. This stone is prone to becoming covered in lichen, as can be seen in The Last Judgment and The Last Supper (on the south side). The Visitation, The Nativity and The Three Kings bringing their gifts (north side) are carved in tougher *kersanton* (black granite).

The elegant belfry on the church of Notre-Dame-de-Tronoën

Penmarc'h ⑱

Road map B2. 12 km (7.5 miles) southwest of Pont-l'Abbé via the D785. ⬥ Quimper-Cornouaille. 🚌 🚶 6,030. 🚹 Place du Maréchal-Davout; (02) 98 58 81 44. ⚓ Pardon de Notre-Dame-de-la-Joie (15 Aug). ⛴ Jun–Sep: Fri am (St-Guénolé harbour) & Wed (Kérity harbour). **www.**penmarch.fr

The story goes that the cruel Princess Dahud cast a spell on Marc'h, legendary king of Poulmarc'h, as the result of which his head was turned into that of a horse (*penmarc'h*).

Penmarc'h consists of three parishes: that of Penmarc'h itself, and those of St-Guénolé and Kérity. St-Guénolé is the second-largest port in the Bigouden and the sixth-largest in France. The computerized fish auction that is held there is the most advanced in Europe.

The **Phare d'Eckmühl** is the pride of the town. Built in 1897 with funds provided by the daughter of Général Davout, Prince of Eckmühl, the lighthouse is in the Breton granite known as *kersanton*. Its beams carry for 50 km

GENERAL DE GAULLE'S CALL TO ARMS

The harsh existence that generations of Sénans (inhabitants of the Île de Sein) had endured gave them a fighting spirit. When, on 18 June 1940, General de Gaulle made his appeal by radio from London, calling on all Frenchmen to fight the German invasion, the men of Sein readily left the island to join other volunteers in England. When the Germans reached Sein, the only people left were women and children. In July 1940, the leader of Free France reviewed the first 600 volunteers, 150 of whom

General de Gaulle with seamen on the Île de Sein

were Sénans. "The Île de Sein therefore represents a quarter of France," exclaimed the general. Of the Sénan seamen who answered the call, only 114 returned. In 1946, de Gaulle came to the island to award it the Croix de la Libération.

(30 miles). The **Musée de la Préhistoire**, near the Plage de Pors-Carn, documents the region's prehistory.

🔦 **Phare d'Eckmühl**
Tel 06 07 21 37 38.
⬭ phone to check, depends on weather conditions. 🖼

🏛 **Musée de la Préhistoire**
Rue du Musée-Préhistorique.
Tel (02) 98 58 60 35. ⬭ Jun–Sep: Wed–Sun, Mon pm. 🖼

Le Guilvinec ⑲

Road map B2. 10 km (6 miles) south of Pont-l'Abbé via the D785 and D57. 🚶 3,040. ⬥ Quimper-Cornouaille. 🚌 🚐 🚹 62 Rue de la Marine; (02) 98 58 29 29. ⚓ Les Estivales (Jul–Aug, Fri eve). ⛴ Tue & Sun (summer).

This fishing village began to develop in the 19th century when a rail link was built as far as Quimper. It then became Quimper's main supplier of fresh fish. Today, Le Guilvinec (*Ar Gelveneg* in Breton) is still a large, traditional fishing village, and sea fishing for tourists has been introduced here. The quayside comes to life in the late afternoon when the boats return.

A seaweed oven at Pointe du Men-Meur bears witness to the importance of seaweed-harvesting in the past. Further on is the **Manoir de Kergoz**, an attractive manor built in the 15th century and now restored. It has a 16th-century dovecote. Footpaths lead to Lesconil, a charming fishing village with white houses.

The harbour at Le Guilvinec, where visitors come for sea fishing

The pleasant little fishing port of Île-Tudy

Loctudy ⑳

Road map B2. 6 km (4 miles) southeast of Pont-l'Abbé via the D2. 🏃 3,700. 🚄 Quimper-Cornouaille. 🚌 🏛 Place des Anciens-Combattants; (02) 98 87 53 78. 🎭 Pardon de St-Tudy (Sun after 11 May). 🛒 Tue am.

The well-known coastal resort of Loctudy (*Loktudi* in Breton) is pleasantly located on the Pont-l'Abbé river, with a fine view of Île Garo and Île Chevalier and of Île-Tudy, a peninsula. Loctudy's fishing port is the foremost provider of live crayfish, the famous "demoiselles de Loctudy". When the trawlers return to the harbour, there is a fish auction on the quay, which is always a high point in daily life everywhere in Armorica. Trips out to sea with rods and bait are organized by the tourist office, and visitors can also learn how to fish with nets and lay lobster pots.

The 12th-century Romanesque Église St-Tudy is very well preserved. The capitals are carved with flowers, masks, human figures and animals; the apse has an ambulatory and chapels. Beside the church is the small chapel of Pors-Bihan, and just outside the town, on the road to Pont-l'Abbé, is the pretty Chapelle de Croaziou, with a Celtic cross.

Environs

When, having sailed from Britain, St Tudy reached Brittany, he founded a monastery on what was, in the early 5th century, an island. After the saint's death, the monastery was transferred to Loctudy. **Île-Tudy**, now a peninsula, is a small, pleasant fishing village accessible by boat from Loctudy.

Manoir de Kérazan ㉑

Road map B2. 4 km (2.5 miles) south of Pont-l'Abbé via the D2. **Tel** (02) 98 87 50 10. ◯ Easter–early Jun & Sep: Tue–Sun pm; mid-Jun–Aug: daily. 🎫 groups by arrangement. 🎦 ♿ 🎭 Soirées Contes et Légendes (Jul–Aug, Thu).

This magnificent country residence, built in the 16th century and restored in the 18th, was bequeathed by Joseph Astor to the Institut de France in 1928. The manor, sturdily built in granite, is set in 5 ha (12 acres) of parkland and was obviously designed for a luxurious and sophisticated lifestyle.

The Astor family devoted themselves to the development of Bigouden culture and to local politics. In 1930, a school of embroidery was opened in the house. Later, at the instigation of his father, a patron of the arts, Joseph Astor assembled a collection of 16th- to 20th-century paintings and drawings, and a large collection of faience from the former faience factory at Porquier. These now form part of a museum collection which also includes costumes and traditional Breton furniture.

Pont-l'Abbé ㉒

Road map B2. 🏃 8,425. 🚄 Quimper-Cornouaille. 🚌 Quimper. 🚌 🏛 11 Place Gambetta; (02) 98 82 37 99. 🎭 Fête des Brodeuses (second Sun in Jul). 🛒 Thu.

The town is named after the monks (*abbés*) of Loctudy who built the first bridge (*pont*) across the river at this spot. The site had already drawn the attention of the Romans, who built a fortified camp here.

Pont-l'Abbé (*Pont-N'-Abad* in Breton) later became the capital of the Bigouden. During the Middle Ages, the lord of Pont-l'Abbé built a castle surmounted by a huge oval tower. During the Wars of the Holy League (*see p44*), the town's barons converted to Protestantism, and the castle was damaged by attacks, especially during the revolt of the Bonnets Rouges (Red Caps). In 1675, this revolt let to the uprising of hundreds of protestors in Lower Brittany. All wore red hats and all demanded the abolition of the *corvée* (unpaid labour for the feudal lord), of taxation on harvest and of the tithe paid to the clergy, and the universal right to hunt. The repression with which the governor of Brittany responded quelled further attempts at protest.

Granite buildings of the Manoir de Kerazan, built in the 16th century

Église Notre-Dame-des-Carmes, built in 1383

Îles de Glénan ㉓

Road map B3. 🚹 *49 Rue de Kérourgué, Fouesnant; (02) 98 56 00 93.* 🚢 *Port-La-Forêt, Beg-Meil, Concarneau and Benodet.*

This archipelago, 12 nautical miles (14 miles) off the mainland and opposite the Baie de La Forêt, consists of eight large islands and a dozen islets. Its white sandy beaches, clear water and plant and animal life make the archipelago an exceptionally suitable place for the sailing and deep-sea diving courses that are organized here.

Penfret, the largest island, is where the **Centre Nautique des Glénan** teaches sailing. Established in 1947, the school is world famous for its training in dinghy and catamaran sailing. Students are housed in an 18th-century fort.

The Île St-Nicolas is the base from which the **Centre International de Plongée** holds its diving courses.

The Île Guiautec is a bird sanctuary. A rare flower – the Glénan narcissus, which was brought by the Phoenicians and which flowers in April – also grows on the island.

While the main part of the castle contains the town hall, the keep houses the **Musée Bigouden**. This contains an interesting collection of traditional costumes and headdresses, as well as furniture and other objects.

The **Église Notre-Dame-des-Carmes**, built in 1383 and formerly the chapel of the Carmelite convent, has an outstanding 15th-century stained-glass window. It also contains a beautiful representation of the Virgin, embroidered in coloured silks on a banner made by the Le Minor workshop.

Not far from the quays are the ruins of the church of Lambour, which was destroyed by the Duke of Chaulnes during the Bonnets Rouges uprising. The arches and columns of the church are in the style of the Pont-Croix School (*see pp152–3*).

The towpath along the Pont-l'Abbé river makes for a pleasant walk. The river flows into an estuary dotted with small islands, Les Rats, Queffen and Garo, which are inhabited by flocks of birds, including common spoonbill and heron. At Pointe Bodillo is the largest colony of herons in Finistère.

Traditional costume, displayed in the Musée Bigouden

🏛 **Musée Bigouden**
In the castle. **Tel** *(02) 98 66 09 03.* ⬤ *Easter–May: Mon–Sat; Jun–Sep: daily.*

⛪ **Église Notre-Dame-des-Carmes**
Place des Carmes. ⬤ *varies.* ✝ *6:30pm Sat; 11am Sun.*

Centre Nautique des Glénan
Office on Place Pierre-Viannay, Concarneau. **Tel** *(02) 98 97 14 84.*

Centre International de Plongée
Office in Concarneau. **Tel** *(02) 98 50 57 02.*

Port de Cornouailles in Benodet, with the Îles de Glénan in the distance

Street-by-Street: Quimper

Historic costume

Founded by Gauls on the site of the present Locmaria district, downstream from the present city centre, the town was later named *Aquilonia* (Town of Eagles) by the Romans. For centuries, it was then known as Quimper-Corentin, after Corentine, its first bishop. The city stands at the confluence *(kemper)* of the Steir and the Odet rivers. Rampart walks, projecting towers and walls survive in the old town, although old timber-framed houses now alternate with later mansions and modern architecture. Recent building work has revealed substantial remains of the medieval city.

Musée Departemental Breton
Founded in 1846, the museum is housed in the bishops' palace.

★ Cathédrale St-Corentin
Built in the 13th and 14th centuries, on the site of a Roman temple, the cathedral was later sumptuously renovated.

René Laënnec
This statue honours the inventor of the stethoscope, who died in 1826.

★ Musée des Beaux-Arts
Built in 1872 by the Quimper architect Joseph Bigot, it contains collections of Flemish and Italian paintings.

BOULEVARD AMIRAL DE KERGUÉLEN

ODET

RUE DU ROI GRADLON

RUE DU FROUT

RUE DE LA MAIRIE

PLACE SAINT-CORENTIN

PLACE LAËNNEC

RUE KÉRÉON

RUE ÉLIE FRÉRON

RUE DU GUÉODET

RUE DES BOUCHERIES

PL. AU BEURRE

RUE DU SALLÉ

★ **Covered Market**
The market (Les Halles) is open every day except Sunday. It plays a prominent part in the life of the city.

Rue St-François
In the 18th century, crown judges lived in this street, which is lined with tall houses.

Odet River

VISITORS' CHECKLIST

🏠 67,250. ✈ Aéroport de Cornouaille, Pluguffan. 🚂 Avenue de la Gare. 🚌 📍 Place de la Résistance; (02) 98 53 04 05. 🚩 Wed & Sat. 🎭 Festival de Cornouaille (third week in Jul), Festival Le Printemps des Comidiens (late Jun), Festival Gouel Erwan (May), Les Semaines Musicales de Quimper (Aug), Festival Extérieur Cuivre (Aug), Les Jeudis de l'Évêché (mid-Jun–mid-Sep). www.mairie-quimper.fr

KEY

– – – Suggested route

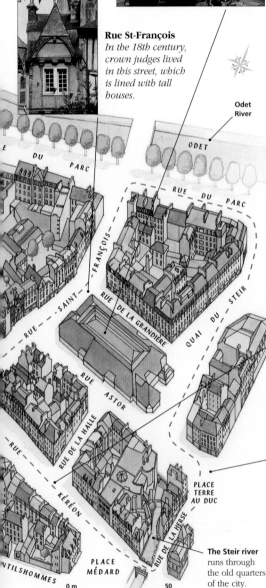

Rue Kéréon
The finest and oldest timber-framed houses in Quimper are in Rue Kéréon (Shoemakers' Street), which has a medieval atmosphere.

Place Terre-au-Duc
is lined with timber-framed houses.

The Steir river
runs through the old quarters of the city.

STAR SIGHTS

★ Cathédrale St-Corentin

★ Covered Market

★ Musée des Beaux-Arts

ODET

RUE DU PARC

DU PARC

FRANÇOIS

RUE SAINT

RUE DE LA GRANDIÈRE

QUAI DU STEIR

RUE ASTOR

RUE DE LA HALLE

KÉRÉON

RUE DE LA HERSE

PLACE TERRE AU DUC

PLACE MÉDARD

NTILSHOMMES

0 m   50

0 yards   50

Exploring Quimper

Listed as a historic town, Quimper (*Kemper* in Breton) has an unusually rich heritage, and great care is being taken to show it to best advantage. The cathedral has been restored and two squares – Places Laënnec and Place St-Corentin – have been totally remodelled. A 12th-century cemetery and 14th-century esplanades have been discovered, and Le Quartier, a newly created cultural district, has opened. Quimper has an illustrious past: it is the birthplace of Fréron (1718–76), Voltaire's famous adversary, of the adventurer René Madec (1738–84), of the poet Max Jacob (1876–1944) and of René Laënnec (1781–1826), inventor of the stethoscope. Yves de Kerguelen, the explorer, is also a native of the Quimper area. The city naturally has a strong Celtic identity, and Celtic culture is celebrated at the Festival de Cornouaille every July. It is also famous for its faience, which has been made here since 1690.

🚩 Old Town

The city's finest medieval streets are those opposite the cathedral, and they are faced with decorative ceramic tiles. Half-timbered houses, slate roofs and cobbled streets also fill this old part of the city.

Rue Kéréon (Shoemakers' Street) is lined with corbelled houses. Other street names, such as Place au Beurre (Butter Square) and Rue des Boucheries (Butchers' Street), also echo the trades that were once practised here.

At No.10 **Rue du Sallé** is the recently restored Minuellou, a former residence of the Mahaut family. Rue des Boucheries is intersected by Rue du Guéodet, which contains the famous 16th-century **Maison des Cariatides**. The faces carved into the stonework of the house are those of Quimpérois who distinguished themselves in the Wars of the Holy League. Further on, the **Rue des Gentilshommes**, which is lined with mansions, leads down to the banks of the Steir, ending at **Rue de la Herse**, which has a projecting turret.

The right bank of the Steir, on the other side of the Pont Médard, was once the

Faces on the Maison des Cariatides

territory of the dukes of Brittany. Half-timbered houses line **Place Terre-au-Duc**. Not far from here is the **Église St-Mathieu**, a church with a particularly fine 16th-century stained-glass window.

The quays along the Odet lead to **Rue St-François** and, further on, to the **Halles du Chapeau-Rouge**, where the

Banner carried in procession during the Grand Pardon

daily market is held. In Rue du Parc, which follows the Odet, is the Café de l'Épée, once patronized by writers and artists from Gustave Flaubert to Max Jacob and now a Quimper institution. On the opposite side of the Odet, footpaths lead to **Mont Frugy** (70 m/230 ft high), which offers a good view over the city centre.

The Du Plessis distillery, in the Quartier d'Ergué-Armel, contains an interesting collection of antique stills.

🏛 Musée Départemental Breton d'Art et de Traditions Populaires

1 Rue du Roi-Gradlon. *Tel* (02) 98 95 21 60. ☐ Jun–Sep daily; Oct–May: Tue–Sat.
The museum is housed in the former bishops' palace on the south side of the cathedral. The palace consists of two wings and, between them, a Renaissance tower containing a spiral staircase. The staircase gives access to all the rooms and is finished with decorative wood carvings. The tower known at the Logis de Rohan, in the Flamboyant Gothic style, was built in 1507 by Bishop Claude de Rohan and restored in the 19th century.

The museum was established in 1846 by the Société

Timber-framed houses on Place Terre-au-Duc

d'Archéologie du Finistère. Devoted to cultural anthropology, it contains an important collection of folk art. Reopened in 1999, it documents 3,000 years of Breton history.

The ground floor contains prehistoric artifacts (spear points, hand axes, Gaulish stele and weapons), a fine collection of painted wooden religious statues and two recumbent figures of knights.

The first and second floors of the museum contain magnificent displays of traditional costumes, 17th- to 19th-century furniture, including chests, box beds and wardrobes, and everyday objects, including an unusual folding spoon.

On the third floor is a collection of 300 pieces of Quimper faience *(see p164)* and stoneware dating from the 17th to the 20th centuries. Medieval and modern religious art is also exhibited. The tour of the museum ends in a room devoted to temporary exhibitions.

Le Génie à la Guirlande, by Charles Filiger, Musée des Beaux-Arts

🏛 Musée des Beaux-Arts

40 Place St-Corentin. *Tel* (02) 98 95 45 20. ☐ *Jul–Aug: daily; Sep–Jun: Wed–Mon.* ● *Sun am, Tue & public holidays.*

The gallery was built by the architect Joseph Bigot to house the collection that Jean-Marie Silguy bequeathed to the city. The gallery contains Flemish, Italian and French painting, including works by Sérusier, Denis and Lacombe, members of the Pont-Aven School *(see p169)*.

One room is devoted to the life and work of the poet and painter Max Jacob, a native of Quimper, and that of his friend Jean Moulin. Watercolours and drawings, as well as portraits of Jacob's artist friends, including Cocteau and Picasso, are displayed. Also shown are major works by Rubens, Fragonard and Corot, and 20th-century paintings (by Delaunay and Tal Coat), as well as the work of Breton painters, such as Guillou, Boudin and Noël. There are also some splendid prints and drawings, especially by Charles Filiger.

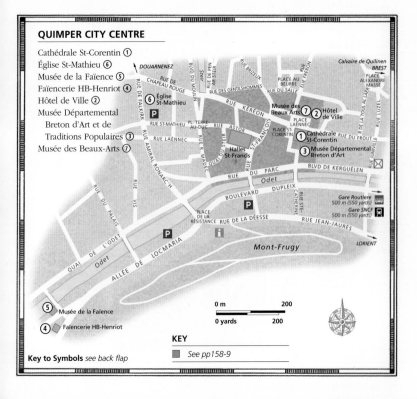

QUIMPER CITY CENTRE

Cathédrale St-Corentin ①
Église St-Mathieu ⑥
Musée de la Faïence ⑤
Faïencerie HB-Henriot ④
Hôtel de Ville ②
Musée Départemental
  Breton d'Art et de
  Traditions Populaires ③
Musée des Beaux-Arts ⑦

Key to Symbols *see back flap*

KEY

▨ See pp158–9

🏛 Musée de la Faïence

14 Rue Jean-Baptiste-Bousquet. **Tel**
(02) 98 90 12 72. 🔲 *closed for
renovations, due to reopen in 2009.*
The museum is laid out in the
Maison Porquier, a former
faience factory in the heart of
the Locmaria district, where
the 18th-century kilns are also
located. Recent building work
in this district is in keeping
with the character of the area.

The museum highlights the
elements necessary for
making pottery, namely
water, clay and fire. The
natural occurrence of clay
and water in the
vicinity is the
reason why
Quimper
became
a prime
centre of
pottery
manufac-
ture. There   **Odetta vase with
is also a   hydrangea motif**
display of
Quimper pottery, with work
by Alfred Beau, and pieces by
major throwers and painters.
The creation of the mark
Odetta HB Quimper in 1922
and the beginnings of studio
pottery are also documented.

Faïencerie HB-Henriot

16 Rue Haute. **Tel** 0800 626 510.
🔲 *Mon–Fri.* 🔲 *obligatory.*
In 1984, two Americans, Paul
and Sarah Janssens, acquired
the HB-Henriot faience
factory. Continuing Quimper's
faience-making tradition, the
factory is the only one still to
produce pieces with freehand
decoration.

Environs

The 16th-century **Calvaire de
Quilinen**, in open countryside
between Quimper and
Châteaulin, is worth a visit.
About 1 km (0.5 mile) further
on is the Gothic **Chapelle de St-
Venec**, dedicated to the brother
of St Guénolé, which has a
fountain framed by slender
twisted columns. The church
at **Cast**, 8 km (5 miles) south
of Châteaulin, is known for a
16th-century sculpture called *St
Hubert's Hunt*. The belvedere
at **Griffonez**, on a bend of the
Odet 7 km (4 miles) north of
Quimper, offers a view of the
Gorges de Stangala.

Cathédrale St-Corentin

Impressed by the religious faith of Corentine, whom he
met on Ménez-Hom, so the legend goes, King Gradlon
invited the hermit to become Bishop of Quimper and
gave him land on which to build a cathedral. History
records that in 1239 Bishop Rainaud decided to start
building the choir of his projected cathedral. The light
and airy building that resulted was achieved by means
of new construction techniques: ribbed vaulting
supported by flying buttresses. The choir was built out
of line with the nave to accommodate
an older chapel containing the tomb
of Alain Canhiart, who repelled
Norman invasions in 913.

★ **Stained-Glass Windows**
*The great vertical spaces of
the nave, the choir and the
transept are lit by superb
stained-glass windows made
in a local workshop in the
15th century.*

Small chapel

The old high altar
beneath a canopy
decorated with
seraphim, was show
at the Exposition
Universelle in Paris
in 1867.

**The apse of the cathedral and the gardens
of the former bishop's residence**

VISITORS' CHECKLIST

Place St-Corentin. **Tel** (02) 98 53
04 05. ⚐ 6:30pm Sat;
8:45am, 10am & 6:30pm Sun.
📷 ♿

★ Romanesque Nave

*Rebuilt in the 15th century, the
Romanesque nave and transept are
lit by ten windows in the Flamboyant
Gothic style. The tombs of bishops of
Quimper laid out here and in the
transept are covered by recumbent
figures of the deceased.*

Spires, in the
Pont-Croix style,
were added in 1854.

Twin towers, 76 m (250
ft) high, are pierced by
double openings.

**St-Guénolé and
St-Ronan Window**,
dating from the 19th
century, depicts the
two saints, one the
founder of the Abbaye
de Landévennec and
the other the hermit
of Locronan.

**Bell turret on
the tower**

Portal

*Seven carved archivolts
frame a rose window
above which runs a
balustrade. Between the
two square galleried
towers is a statue of
King Gradlon.*

West door

Pulpit

*Of painted and gilded wood, the
Baroque pulpit was made in 1679
by Olivier Daniel, of Quimper. It is
decorated with medallions showing
scenes from the life of St Corentine.*

STAR FEATURES

★ Romanesque Nave

★ Stained Glass

Quimper Faience

The history of Quimper faience began in 1690, when Jean-Baptiste Bousquet settled in the Locmaria district of the town. He came from Moustiers, in Provence, but competition and the lack of wood to fire the kilns had forced him to seek his fortune elsewhere. In Cornouaille, forests were more plentiful and royal permission to cut firewood easier to obtain. Clay in the area was also abundant, and the Odet provided a convenient means of transport.

Faïence by HB Henriot, Quimper

Bousquet's Manufacture de Pipes et Fayences soon prospered, and, thanks to his granddaughter's marriage, he benefited from Italian influence brought by a potter from Nevers, a leading centre of faience manufacture. He was then joined by a manufacturer from Rouen, another prestigious centre of faience production. In the 19th century, Alfred Beau, a photographer and amateur painter from Morlaix, created a new style, based on colourful scenes of daily life.

HISTORY OF FAIENCE

Faience was first made in southern France and in Italy. Faience made in Nevers, in central France, features scenes of daily life and shows a predominant use of yellow. Faience made in Rouen, a major and distinctive centre of production, is remarkably colourful and displays a variety of elaborate motifs, including flowers, trees, birds and cornucopiae. In the 19th century, faience production was dominated by the influence of Alfred Beau and by the distinctive Quimper style, with scenes of daily life depicted in bright colours by the "single stroke" technique, by which shape was defined and colour applied by a single touch of the brush.

View of the Odet at Quimper, overglaze decoration by Alfred Beau, late 19th century

Plate *in the Nevers and Moustiers style (1773).*

"Single stroke" decoration *(early 19th century).*

New style Porquier-Beau *(late 19th century).*

Vase with Odetta design (20th century)

DECORATION

After being removed from the mould and dried, the piece of faience was fired in the kiln and glazed. It was then passed to the decorators. Each design was reproduced on paper, its outline pierced with holes. The paper was applied to the glaze and the outlines transferred with charcoal. The design was then filled in with a fine brush and the piece re-fired.

Piece by Berthe Savigny, *a mid-20th century modeller.*

Statue of Quillivic (mid-20th century)

POTTING

There are several ways of modelling clay. While circular pieces are shaped on the wheel, more complex pieces are press-moulded. To make highly complex pieces, liquid clay is poured into moulds.

The potter *throws a piece on the wheel.*

The decorator *adds the finishing touches.*

Vase by Louis Garin (mid-20th century)

Dish with contemporary decoration

Bénodet ㉕

🏠 2,750. 🚊 🚶 *Quimper-Cornouaille.* ℹ️ *29 Avenue de la Mer; (02) 98 57 00 14.* 🛍️ *Place du Meneyer, Mon am.*

On the border between the Bigouden and the Fouesnant area, Bénodet (*Benoded* in Breton) is a well-known coastal resort on the Odet estuary. Comfortable residences, manor houses and chateaux line the river. The chapel in Le Perguet, just east of Bénodet, was once the parish church. It was rebuilt in the 12th century and has a Romanesque interior and a 15th-century porch.

Penfoul harbour, where boat races and regattas are held, is very lively. Cruises and trips out to sea are offered here. Cruises to Belle-Île, Ouessant, Groix and Seinon aboard the **Le Corentin**, the replica of a 19th-century coastal lugger, are also available. At Le Letty, just south of Bénodet and opposite the Îles de Glénan, is a lagoon known as the **Mer Blanche**, which attracts numerous birds.

🚤 **Vedettes de l'Odet**
Motorboats **Tel** *0825 80 08 01.*

🚤 **Le Corentin**
Tel *(02) 98 65 10 00.*

The Mer Blanche at Bénodet, a lagoon attracting many birds

Belfry of the Romanesque Église de St-Pierre, in Fouesnant

Fouesnant ㉖

🏠 8,460. 🚊 🚶 *Quimper-Cornouaille.* ℹ️ *49 Rue de Kérourgué; (02) 98 56 00 93.* 🛍️ *Wed am in Beg-Meil (summer only); Fri am, Sun am & Tue eve. in La Forêt-Fouesnant (summer only).* **www**.*ot-fouesnant.fr*

At an altitude of 60 m (300 ft) above sea level, Fouesnant (*Fouenant* in Breton) looks across the Baie de La Forêt to the Îles de Glénan. The town is in the centre of an area of lush and fertile valleys. Butter biscuits and the best cider in Brittany have largely made the reputation of the Fouesnant area.

At the Fête des Pommiers (Cider Festival), which takes place during the third week of July, the women wear traditional costumes and headdresses with large back-folded wings, waffle collar and lace wimple.

The Romanesque **Église de St-Pierre**, which was restored in the 18th century, has a pitched roof. Inside, tall semicircular arches rest on capitals carved with acanthus leaves, stars and human figures. The calvary dates from the 18th century, and the war memorial is by the sculptor René Quillivic.

Cap-Coz, on the eastern side of the Anse de Penfoulic at Fouesnant, is a pleasant place for a walk along the coast. From there it is possible to reach the resort of Beg-Meil.

Street-by-Street: Concarneau ㉗

The walled town *(ville close)*, Concarneau's
ancient centre, is set on an islet in the Moros
estuary that is just 350 m (380 yds) wide and 100 m
(330 ft) long. With narrow paved streets and
picturesque houses, the islet is very popular with
visitors. It is accessible via two bridges leading to
a postern bearing the royal coat of arms. The outer
defences here, consisting of a triangular courtyard
surrounded by high walls and flanked by two
towers, made the town impregnable. Visitors enter
this town of medieval streets by crossing an inner
moat. At the western end of Rue Vauban, with old,
crooked houses, is the Maison du Gouverneur,
one of the oldest houses in the *ville close*.

The walled town, Concarneau's historic
nucleus, seen from the fishing harbour

★ Logis du Major

*Beyond the triangular
courtyard, which is
defended by the Tour
du Major and Tour
du Gouverneur at
two of its corners, is
the Logis du Major,
built in 1730.*

Musée
de la Pêche

Maison
du Gouverneur

Postern

★ Belfry

*Fronting the towers, and
set at the third corner
of the triangle, the belfry
was once a watchtower.*

Causeway

STAR SIGHTS
★ Belfry
★ Logis du Major
★ Ramparts

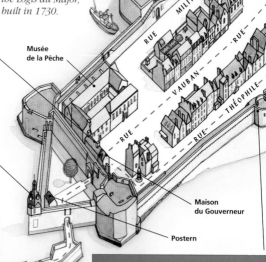

Tour de la Fortune
*The tower commands a magnificent view
of the yachting harbour.*

★ Ramparts
Beyond the two small bridges at the entrance, a stairway on the left leads to the ramparts. The wall walk gives an impressive view of the ville close.

VISITORS' CHECKLIST

Road map B3. 🚗 20,000.
ℹ 9 Quai d'Aiguillon; (02) 98 97 01 44. 🕒 Mon & Fri am. 🎉 Fête des Filets Bleus (music and dancing; Aug)
www.concarneau.org

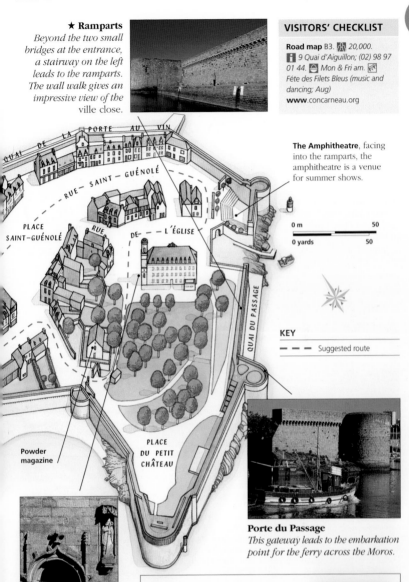

The Amphitheatre, facing into the ramparts, the amphitheatre is a venue for summer shows.

QUAI DE LA PORTE AU VIN

RUE SAINT - GUÉNOLÉ

PLACE SAINT-GUÉNOLÉ

RUE DE L'ÉGLISE

QUAI DU PASSAGE

0 m   50
0 yards   50

KEY

– – – Suggested route

Powder magazine

PLACE DU PETIT CHÂTEAU

Porte du Passage
This gateway leads to the embarkation point for the ferry across the Moros.

Façade of the former hospital
Not far from the amphitheatre, is a fine building that was once a church then later a hospital. The façade is in the late Gothic style.

VAUBAN

Sébastien Le Prestre de Vauban (1633–1707), Marshal of France and superintendent of fortifications, is France's most famous military builder. Fascinated by military techniques, he also wrote on the art of warfare and on politics. Brittany's strategic location and new methods of warfare that were current at the time led Vauban to remodel military defences on Belle-Île and at Concarneau, Port-Louis, Brest and St-Malo, and to build fortifications at Hoëdic and Houat and the Tour Dorée in Camaret.

Sébastien Le Prestre de Vauban

Exploring Concarneau

The "Blue Town", as it is known, after the blue fishing nets that were used in the early 20th century, has an important historic heritage. The islet of Le Conq was inhabited from the 10th century by monks from Landévennec, and the earliest fortifications date from the 13th century. By the 14th century, the island settlement had become the fourth-largest fortified town in Brittany. Briefly occupied by the English, the town returned to the duchy of Brittany in 1373, then, with the marriage of Anne of Brittany and Charles VIII, king of France, in 1491, it became a royal town. Vauban reinforced its defences in the 18th century. The first fish cannery opened in 1851, and 50 years later there were about 30 canning factories in Concarneau. The disappearance of sardine stocks led to hardship from 1905, but the Fête des Filets Bleus helped to raise funds for families in difficulties. The third-largest fishing port in France, Concarneau produces 25,000 tonnes of fresh fish a year.

Château de Kériolet, in a recreated Flamboyant Gothic style

Concarneau's attractive walled town, with the Îles de Glénan beyond

🏛 Musée de la Pêche

4 Rue Vauban.
Tel (02) 98 97 10 20. ◯ *Feb–Sep: daily.*
With dioramas and models complementing the displays of artifacts, the museum traces the development of Concarneau and its seafaring activities from its beginnings to the present day. Fishing methods and the town's maritime heritage are the main focus here. There is also an aquarium containing species of fish caught in the Atlantic, and, against the ramparts, an open-air maritime museum with docks where a trawler, the *Hémérica*, and a tuna boat are open to visitors.

Old-style tin of Breton sardines

⚓ Fishing Harbour

Guided tours to auctions, trawlers and canning factories Tel (02) 98 50 55 18.
Trawlers, tuna boats and sardine boats are tied up along the **Quai d'Aiguillon**. Refrigerator ships that fish in tropical waters berth along the **Quai Est**.

➤ Marinarium

Place de la Croix. *Tel (02) 98 50 81 64.* ◯ *daily.*
Created in 1859, the Marinarium du Collège de France was one of the first maritime research stations in Europe. The flora and fauna of Brittany's coasts can be seen in ten aquariums and seawater tanks. The use of

audiovisual facilities, the opportunity to view certain species under the microscope, and guided tours along the coastline make for a comprehensive understanding of marine and coastal life.

♣ Château de Kériolet

Beuzec-Conq, 2 km (1.5 miles) north of Concarneau. *Tel (02) 98 97 36 50.* ◯ *Jun–Sep.* 🎟 *groups by arrangement.*
Built in the 13th century by the architect Joseph Bigot, of Quimper, the chateau was much remodelled in the 19th century in the Flamboyant Gothic style. Among its guests was Princess Youssoupova, aunt of the last Russian tzar, Nicolas Romanov.
The chateau, surrounded by a lovely garden, is now used as a venue for artistic events.

🏰 Pointe du Cabellou

Road map B3. 3 km (2 miles) south of Concarneau via the D783.
Fine views of Concarneau and the bay can be seen from this charming promontory just a short car ride from the town. A chic residential quarter of villas and gardens, shaded by pine trees, it has a coastal footpath leading to sheltered sandy coves with quiet beaches. A 17th-century fort with a stone roof stands at the tip of the promontory. The path continues to the Minaouët river, where there is a 16th-century tidal mill.

Rosporden ❷❽

Road map B3. 10 km (6 miles) north of Concarneau via the D70. 🏠 *6,430.* 🚊 *Quimper.* 🚌 *Quimperlé.* 🛈 *Rue de Hippolyte-le-Bas; (02) 98 59 27 26 (summer), (02) 98 66 99 05 (out of season).*

In the midst of lush country-side dotted with picturesque chapels, Rosporden stands on the edge of a pond formed by the Aven river. The **Église Notre-Dame**, built in the 14th century and restored in the 17th, has a fine belfry. Inside are a notable altarpiece and several interesting statues.

The many footpaths here, as well as the disused Rosporden-Scaër railway line, allow walkers to explore the area.

Pont-Aven ❷❾

Road map B3. 🏠 *3,000.* 🚊 *Quimper.* 🚌 *Quimperlé.* 🛈 *5 Place de l'Hôtel-de-Ville; (02) 98 06 04 70.* 🐟 *Tue am, by the harbour (summer); Place de l'Hôtel-de-Ville (winter).* 🎭 *La Fête des Fleurs d'Ajonc (first weekend in Aug); Pardon de Trémalo (last Sun in Jul).*

Pont-Aven was originally a small fishing harbour set at the end of a *ria* (ancient flooded valley) and surrounded by mills. Luggers trading eastwards towards Nantes and southwards towards Bordeaux gradually transformed this small town into a busy port. The 17th- and 18th-century granite houses and paved streets that rise in tiers between Rue des Meunières and Place Royale date from this prosperous period in the port's history.

From the 1860s, Pont-Aven owed its renown to the painters who settled here. In the **Bois d'Amour** at the top of the town is the **Chapelle de Trémalo**, where the Christ on the Cross that is the subject of Paul Gauguin's *Christ Jaune* still hangs.

The quay at Quimperlé, founded in the 11th century

The **Musée de Pont-Aven** documents the town's history and has a collection of paintings by the Pont-Aven School.

Pont-Aven is also famous for its *galettes* (butter biscuits) and traditional costumes.

> 🏛 **Musée de Pont-Aven**
> Place de l'Hôtel-de-Ville.
> **Tel** *(02) 98 06 14 43.* ⭕ *Feb–Dec: daily.* 📷 📷

Quimperlé ❸⓪

Road map C3. 🏠 *11,500.* 🚌 *Quimperlé.* 🛈 *15 Place St Michel; (02) 98 96 04 32.* 🐟 *Fri in Place St-Michel; Sun am, in the covered market.* 🎭 *Fest Noz (Jul).*
www.quimperletourisme.com

This town, at the confluence of the Isole and Ellé rivers, was founded by Benedictine monks in the 11th century, although it began to develop only in the 17th century. Capuchins and Ursulines also settled here, and nobles built fine residences in **Rue Dom-Morice** and **Rue Brémond-d'Ars**, in the lower town. Other notable buildings are the **Hôtel du Cosquer** and the houses in **Rue Savary**.

Quimperlé (*Kemperle* in Breton) later expanded beyond its old boundaries, developing around the **Église Ste-Croix**, in the lower town, and Place St-Michel, in the higher town. Because of the strongly influential presence of the monks and nuns here, the principal monuments in Quimperlé are religious. They include the Baroque **Chapelle des Ursulines**, which holds temporary art exhibitions, and the **Église St-Michel** in a combined early and Flamboyant Gothic style.

THE PONT-AVEN SCHOOL

In 1866, a colony of American painters settled in Pont-Aven. Fascinated by the picturesque character of the surroundings, they painted scenes of the daily life that they observed around them. Paul Gauguin arrived in Pont-Aven in 1886, and there he met Charles Laval, Émile Bernard, Ferdinand du Puigaudeau and Paul Sérusier, artists who were later to form part of the Nabis group. Soon after, seeking refuge from the bustle of this coastal town, the group moved to the quieter surroundings of Le Pouldu, east of Pont-Aven. Influenced by primitive art, these painters used colour expressively and evocatively, and imbued images with a symbolic meaning. Their paintings were not intended to reflect reality but to embody reality itself, with line and colour producing a flat image devoid of shading and perspective. Their use of tonal contrasts, their novel approach to composition and their asceticism were at odds with Impressionism.

La Belle Angèle, by Paul Gauguin, a leading member of the Pont-Aven School

Pont-Aven's Christ on the Cross

MORBIHAN

*O*ccupying the central southern part of Brittany, the Morbihan, which means "little sea" in Breton, takes its name from the Golfe du Morbihan on the département's southeasterly side. With gentle landscapes bathed in sunshine, a deeply indented coastline washed by the Atlantic Ocean, historic towns and cities and harbours thronged with boats, the Morbihan holds many attractions.

The history of the Morbihan goes back to the remote past. Neolithic people raised an impressive number of large and mysterious standing stones here: the alignments at Carnac and Locmariaquer between them constitute the largest concentration of megalithic monuments in the world.

The Golfe du Morbihan, which is extended inland by the Auray and Vannes rivers, is almost like an inland sea. Marshland and mud flats are home to flocks of birds of various species. The gentle climate, in which a Mediterranean vegetation flourishes, the beauty of a landscape of ever-changing colours, and the soft sand beaches here combine to make the Morbihan a popular tourist destination.

The gulf is dotted with a host of small islands, whose number is said to equal that of the days in the year.

The islands include the Île d'Arz, the aptly named Belle-Île, the Île de Groix and the Île d'Houat, which are a delight for nature-lovers. The Presqu'île de Quiberon, a narrow spit of land protruding out to sea, is almost like a separate region. The peninsula's indented Côte Sauvage (Wild Coast) to the west contrasts with its more sheltered eastern side, where there are many beaches.

Great vitality characterizes towns and cities in the Morbihan, from Vannes, which was established in Gallo-Roman times, to Lorient, which was rebuilt after World War II. In the interior are such monuments to past glories as the Château de Josselin and Château de Pontivy, picturesque houses in Rochefort-en-Terre, and the fine historic covered markets in Questembert and Le Faoüet.

The Neolithic alignment of 540 menhirs at Kerlescan, outside Carnac

◁ The calvary at Rochefort-en-Terre, with a carved base and a column crowned by a Crucifixion

Exploring the Morbihan

The south of the Morbihan is crossed by the Vilaine, which flows into the Atlantic just west of La Roche-Bernard. Vannes, on the far northern side of the gulf, is the capital of the Morbihan, and a lively city with an ever-expanding student population. The Morbihan's two other major conurbations – Lorient, a port with five harbours, and Auray, a charming medieval town – are located further northwest. Water is ubiquitous in this region; countless rivers have carved deep canyons, and *rias* (ancient valleys flooded by the sea) go far inland. The Golfe du Morbihan is almost closed and is thus sheltered from the rigours of the open sea. Although the Morbihan's inland region attracts fewer visitors, it has beautiful countryside and pretty villages.

SEE ALSO

• *Where to Stay* pp227–30

• *Where to Eat* pp246–8

Basilica at Ste-Anne-d'Auray

SIGHTS AT A GLANCE

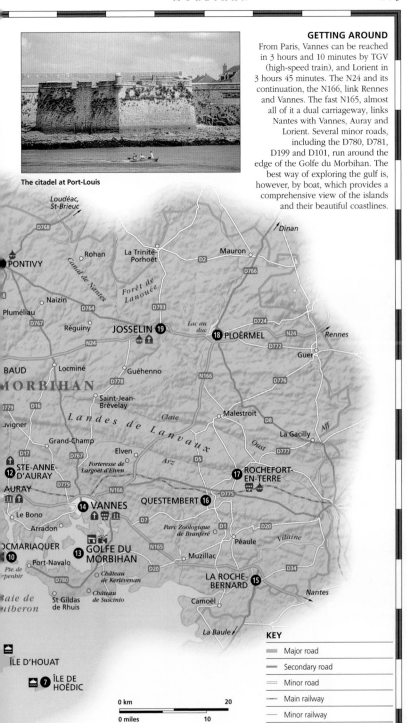

The citadel at Port-Louis

GETTING AROUND

From Paris, Vannes can be reached in 3 hours and 10 minutes by TGV (high-speed train), and Lorient in 3 hours 45 minutes. The N24 and its continuation, the N166, link Rennes and Vannes. The fast N165, almost all of it a dual carriageway, links Nantes with Vannes, Auray and Lorient. Several minor roads, including the D780, D781, D199 and D101, run around the edge of the Golfe du Morbihan. The best way of exploring the gulf is, however, by boat, which provides a comprehensive view of the islands and their beautiful coastlines.

KEY

▬▬	Major road
▬▬	Secondary road
═══	Minor road
▬▬	Main railway
──	Minor railway
▬▬	Regional border

Bagpipe-player at the Festival Interceltique held in Lorient

Lorient ❶

Road map C3. 🚶 *121,820.* 🚉 *Rue Beauvais.* 🚌 *Cour de Chazelles.* 🛳 *Rue Gahinet; (08) 20 05 60 00. Sailings to the Île de Groix (all year) and Belle-Île (Jul–Aug).* ℹ️ *Maison de la Mer, Quai de Rohan; (02) 97 21 07 84.* 🎪 *Wed & Sat.* 🎭 *Carnaval (Apr); Festival des Sept Chapelles (classical music, mid-Jul–mid-Aug); Festival Interceltique (Aug).*
www.lorient-tourisme.fr

It was in the 17th century, when the French East India Company, based in Port-Louis, needed to expand, that Lorient was created. The new port became the base for trade with the East (*l'Orient*), hence its name, and in 1770 was chosen as the site of the royal dockyard. Almost totally destroyed in World War II, Lorient has been rebuilt.

Today, Lorient is France's second-largest port. Not only a fishing port, it handles cargo and passenger ships and is a major boating centre.

Keroman harbour, with a large covered fish market, caters to the fishing industry. A 1960s marine research

vessel houses the **Bateau Musée de Thalassa**, which covers the history of Brittany's fishing industry. The **Submarine Base**, built by the Germans in 1941, is also open to the public.

The **Quayside Buildings** in the naval dockyard stand on the site of the East India Company. Old cannons are displayed in two pavilions dating from that time. The Tour de la Découverte offers a fine view of the harbour and roadstead (sheltered anchorage).

On Place Alsace-Lorraine is an **Air-Raid Shelter** *(abri)*, which could accommodate 400 people and which now gives a flavour of life during the war years (1939–45). In the Quartier de Merville are houses in the Art Nouveau and Art Deco styles that survived the bombing raids.

Teapot, 18th-century, Musée de la Compagnie des Indes

The tourist office here organizes trips to the roadstead (Rade de Lorient) and along the Blavet river, including a visit to the market at Hennebont (*see p195*).

🏛 **Bateau Musée de Thalassa**
Quai de Rohan. **Tel** *(02) 97 35 13 00.* ⭕ *daily.* 🗝

🏛 **Submarine Base**
Port de Keroman. **Tel** *06 20 17 30 82.* 🗝 *varies, phone to check.* 🗝

Painted altarpiece in the choir of the church at Larmor-Plage

🏛 **Quayside Buildings**
Porte Gabriel. 🗝 *obligatory; Jul–early Sep & school holidays: daily.* **Tel** *(02) 97 21 07 84. Admittance restricted to citizens of the EU (identification required).* 🗝

🏛 **Air-Raid Shelter**
Place Alsace-Lorraine. **Tel** *(02) 97 21 07 84.* 🗝 *Jul–Aug & school holidays: Mon–Sat.* ⬤ *Sun & public holidays.* 🗝

Environs
Larmor-Plage, to the southwest, has beaches and a fortified Gothic church that is of interest for the painted statues in the north porch and an altarpiece in the Flemish style. To the east, at the mouth of the river, lies the Barre d'Étel, a notorious sandbar. Further north, Belz leads to St-Cado, a small island that is traditionally popular with painters and where there is a Romanesque chapel.

Port-Louis ❷

Road map C3. 12 km (7.5 miles) southeast of Lorient via the D194 then the D781. 🚶 *3,000.* 🚉 *Lorient.* ℹ️ *1 Rue de la Citadelle; (02) 97 82 52 93.* 🎪 *Sat.* 🎭 *Regattas (late Jul).*

The 17th-century citadel in Port-Louis, at the entrance to Lorient's roadstead, guards the mouth of the Blavet and Scorff rivers. Begun by the Spaniards, it was completed during the reign of Louis XIII, after whom it is named. Elegant residences dating from this period can be seen in the town, although they suffered damage during World War II.

With maps, models and examples of the highly prized goods that they brought back from the East, the **Musée de la Compagnie des Indes et de la Marine**, within the citadel, describes the illustrious history of the French East India Company.

🏛 **Musée de la Compagnie des Indes et de la Marine**
Citadelle de Port-Louis. **Tel** *(02) 97 82 19 13.* ⭕ *Apr–May: Wed–Mon; Jun–Sep: daily; Oct–Mar: Wed–Mon.* ⬤ *Dec.* 🗝

Port-Tudy, on the Île de Groix, built in the 19th century

Île de Groix ❸

Road map C3. 🏘 *2,320.*
🚢 *Campagnie Océane; 0820 05 61
56.* ℹ *Quai de Port-Tudy; (02) 97 86
53 08.* 🛒 *Tue & Sat, in Loctudy.* 🎭
Fête de la Mer (late Jul).

This picturesque island, with
an area of 24 sq km (9 sq
miles), is best explored on
foot, by bicycle or on horseback. Between 1870 and
1940, tuna fishing provided
employment for up to 2,000
of the island's seamen. The
harbour at **Port-Tudy** would
then be filled with tuna boats
rather than the pleasure boats
that are moored here today.

The **Écomusée** in Port-Tudy
describes daily life on Groix
as well as its natural environment. The island's interesting
geology is the subject of the
displays in the **Maison de la
Réserve**.

At the end of the road
running south from Créhal,
a coast path leads to the
Trou de l'Enfer, an impressively deep recess in the cliff
face on the southern side of
the island.

On the west coast is the
beautiful Plage des Grands-
Sables, the only convex beach
in Europe, and there is a bird
sanctuary on the north-
westerly Pointe de Groix.

🏛 **Écomusée**
Port-Tudy. ⬜ *Apr–Nov: Tue–Sun;
Dec–Mar: Wed, Sat & Sun.*
Tel *(02) 97 86 84 60.* 📷

✂ **Maison de la Réserve**
Île de Groix. **Tel** *(02) 97 86 55 97.*
⬜ *Jun, Sep & school holidays:
Mon–Sat; Jul–Aug: Mon–Sat, Sun
am. Oct–May: Sat pm.*

Presqu'île de Quiberon ❹

Road map C4. 🚂 *Auray or Quiberon
(route served by the Tire-Bouchon
train in Jul–Aug).* 🚌 *Auray.* ℹ *14
Rue de Verdun, Quiberon; 0825 135
600.* **www**.*quiberon.com* ⬜ *Thu in
St-Pierre, Sat in Quiberon & Wed in
Port-Haliguen (mid-Jun–mid-Sep).*
🎭 *Festivale Semaines Oceanes,
Quiberon (Apr); concerts (Jul–Aug);
Fête de la Sardine, Port-Maria (Jul).*

Of all the areas of Brittany
that attract visitors, the
beautiful Presqu'Île de
Quiberon justifiably draws the
greatest number. It is also an
exceptional environment for
sailing and watersports. The
peninsula, 14 km (9 miles)
long, is linked to the mainland by a sandbank, the
Isthme de Penthièvre.

At Plouharnel, just above
the peninsula, is **La Belle
Iloise,** a sardine cannery with
a museum dedicated to the
history of this important local

Plage de Bara, near Quiberon, on
the Côte Sauvage

industry. The **Musée de la
Chouannerie**, in an old
blockhouse nearby, tells the
story of the Chouans *(see p46).*

The Fort de Penthièvre, rebuilt in the 19th century and
now owned by the French
Army, controls access to the
peninsula. To the west,
Portivy, a fishing harbour,
leads to Pointe de Percho,
from where there is a splendid
view of Belle-Île *(see pp176–7)*
and the Île de Groix.

Exposed to the rigours of
the sea, the cliffs of the **Côte
Sauvage** (Wild Coast) are indented with caves and chasms,
and on stormy days the windswept sea at Ber-er-Goalennec
is an impressive sight. Quiberon,
once a busy sardine port, is a
resort now known mainly for
its institute of thalassotherapy.
The town was launched as a
coastal resort in the early
20th century, when silk
manufacturers from Lyon built
villas on the seafront here.
From Port-Maria, once a

Alignment of menhirs
at St-Pierre-de-Quiberon

sardine port, boats sail for
Belle-Île, the Île de Houat and
Île de Hoëdic *(see pp176–7)* .
Pointe du Conguel, with the
Phare de la Teignouse, is the
peninsula's most southerly
point. During the summer,
regattas are regularly held
at Port-Haliguen.

St-Pierre-de-Quiberon, a
family holiday resort on the
eastern side, has good
beaches and interesting
prehistoric standing stones.
There are also many sailing
schools here.

🏛 **La Belle Iloise**
Zone Activité Plein Ouest. **Tel** *(02)
97 50 08 77.* ⬜ *Tue–Fri, Sat.* ♿

🏛 **Musée de la Chouannerie**
Plouharnel. On the D 768. **Tel** *(02)
97 52 31 31.* ⬜ *Apr–Sep: daily.* 📷

Belle-Île-en-Mer ❺

The largest island in Brittany, Belle-Île (Beautiful Island) well deserves its name. Its unspoiled environment, of heathland carpeted in gorse alternating with lush valleys, its beaches and well-kept villages attract numerous holiday-makers. Continually fought over on account of its strategic position south of Quiberon, the island was held by the English in 1761. It was finally exchanged for Minorca in 1763.

Pointe des Poulains
The lighthouse and its setting h_ great appeal for Sarah Bernhar

Sauzon
The town's colourfully painted houses and the steep-banked inlet here captivated painters and poets, including Victor Vasarely and Jacques Prévert in the 1950s and '60s.

Port-Donnant
is framed by sheer cliffs. The beach here is spectacular.

Grand Phare
commands a view stretching from Lorient to Le Croisic.

Port-Goulphar
The cove at Port-Goulphar and the jagged rocks at Port-Coton, where breakers foam furiously, were portrayed by the painter Claude Monet in 1886.

Bangor is a small town near some of the wildest stretches of coast.

Île de Houat ❻

Road map D4. 🏠 *345.* 🚢 *from Quiberon and Lorient; 0820 056 000; in summer, also from Port-Narvalo, La Trinité; 0825 132 100.* ℹ️ *Mairie; (02) 97 30 68 04.* 🎉 *gathering of vintage tall ships (Aug); Fête de la Mer (15 Aug).*

Cyclists riding through the quiet village of Houat

Like the neighbouring Île de Hoëdic, the Île de Houat (Duck Island in Breton) forms part of the Ponant archipelago. Just 5 km (3 miles) long and 1 km (0.5 mile) wide, Houat can be explored easily on foot. A coast path encircles the island, taking in Pointe Beg-er-Vachif, where,

at sunset, the grey granite rocks are flecked with red.

Four fifths of the island are covered with heathland. **Houat**, the island's only village, has neat whitewashed houses. The Église St-Gildas, built in 1766, is dedicated to the 6th-century saint who came to live here as a hermit. In **Port-St-Gildas**,

the harbour below Houat, fishing boats come and go.

Vestiges of Houat's former importance as a military base include the Beniguet battery, the En-Tal redoubt and a ruined fort.

The **Éclosarium**, just outside the village, is a plankton research and breeding centre where visitors can see microscopic marine life. The Plage de Treac'h-er-Goured, on the southeastern side, is one of Houat's more sheltered beaches.

🏛 **Éclosarium**
1 km (0.5 mile) from Houat. **Tel** (02) 97 52 38 38. ⬭ *Easter–Sep: daily.* 📷

Sarah Bernhardt on Belle-Île

SARAH BERNHARDT

Born Rosine Bernard in Paris, the actress known as Sarah Bernhardt (1844–1923) made her debut at the Comédie Française. From 1870 to 1900, she dominated Parisian theatre and made successful tours abroad. In 1893, she discovered Belle-Île and fell in love with the island. She purchased the Bastion de Basse-Hiot, bought land at Pointe des Poulains, and in 1909 became the owner of the Domaine de Penhoët. There is a museum in Morbihan dedicated to her life.

VISITORS' CHECKLIST

Road map C4. 👥 *5,000.*
🚢 *all year from Quiberon &
Lorient (La Morbihannaise: 0820
056 000); Apr–Oct also from
Port-Narvalo, Vannes & La Trinité
(Navix: 0825 132 100).* ℹ️ *Quai
Bonnelle, Le Palais; (02) 97 31 81
93.* 🛒 *Tue & Fri in Le Palais; Sun
in Locmaria (Jul–Aug) & Thu in
Sauzon.* 🎭 *Regattas (Jun);
Festival Lyrique (Jul–Aug), Jazz
(Jul); Fête de la Mer (Aug).*

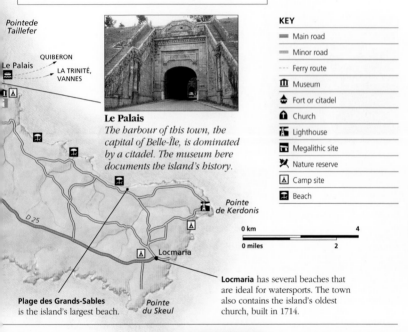

Le Palais
*The harbour of this town, the
capital of Belle-Île, is dominated
by a citadel. The museum here
documents the island's history.*

Locmaria has several beaches that
are ideal for watersports. The town
also contains the island's oldest
church, built in 1714.

Plage des Grands-Sables
is the island's largest beach.

KEY

▬	Main road
▬	Minor road
---	Ferry route
🏛	Museum
♠	Fort or citadel
🔒	Church
🔦	Lighthouse
▦	Megalithic site
✗	Nature reserve
⛺	Camp site
☄	Beach

0 km   4
0 miles   2

Île de Hoëdic ❼

Road map D4. 👥 *140.* 🚢 *from
Quiberon all year round (SMN: 0820
056 000); in summer also from La
Trinité (Navix: 0825 132 100).* ℹ️
Mairie; (02) 97 52 48 88. 🎭 *Fête de
la Mer (Aug).*

As its Breton name suggests,
the Île de Hoëdic (Little
Duck Island) is smaller than
the neighbouring Île de
Houat. It is 2.5 km (1.5 miles)
long and 1 km (0.5 mile)
wide, and like Houat, it is
easy to explore on foot.

The island's ubiquitous
heathland is scattered with
sea pinks and sea bindweed.

**Sailing off the Île de Hoëdic, an
island with a beautiful coastline**

Along the coast, superb
beaches alternate with jagged,
rocky creeks.

Le Bourg, in the centre of
Hoëdic, is a traditional village
with long, low houses, whitewashed and south-facing. The
Église St-Goustan is worth a
visit for its attractive blue and
gold ceiling and its thanks-
giving plaques. Northeast of
Bourg, the 19th-century **Fort
d'Hoëdic** contains a short-stay
gîte and exhibitions devoted
to the island's plants, animals
and local history.

🏛 Fort d'Hoëdic
Tel *(02) 97 52 48 82.*
⏺ *Jun–Aug: daily.*

Carnac ❽

Brittany's best-known prehistoric site is, without doubt, Carnac. The alignments of 3,000 standing stones – which may originally have numbered over 6,000 – are the most extraordinary group of menhirs in the world. The oldest date from the Neolithic period and the most recent from the Bronze Age. Although their significance remains unknown, they were probably connected to religion. Apart from its famous megaliths, Carnac also has wide sandy beaches and a lively commercial centre, making it a popular coastal resort for summer visitors.

The **Alignements de Kerlescan**, with 240 standing stones

Exploring Carnac

Carnac consists of the town itself and of Carnac-Plage, the beach that was created from scratch out of a lagoon in 1903.

The Renaissance **Église St-Cornély**, in the centre of the town, was built in the 17th century and is dedicated to the local patron saint of horned animals. This honour highlights the importance of agriculture, and of oxen in particular, to the local community. The figure of St Cornély, framed by oxen, can be seen above the pediment of the west door. The wooden ceiling inside the church is decorated with 18th-century frescoes, those over the nave showing scenes from the life of St Cornély.

Southwest of Carnac, overlooking the Anse du Pô, is **St-Colomban**, a picturesque fishing village where oysters are farmed. A few old houses cluster around the Flamboyant Gothic chapel, built in 1575. There is also a 16th-century fountain with two troughs, one for washerwomen and the other for animals to drink from.

🏛 Musée de Préhistoire

10 Place de la Chapelle, Carnac-Ville. **Tel** (02) 97 52 22 04. ◘ Feb–Jun & Sep–Dec: Wed–Mon; Jul–Aug: daily. ● Jan. 🖼 ✔

This important museum contains a collection of some 500,000 artifacts, although only 6,000 pieces are shown at a time. They are presented in chronological order.

The ground floor is devoted to the Palaeolithic (450,000–12000 BC), Mesolithic (12,000–5000 BC), and Neolithic (4500–2000 BC) periods. The Neolithic period, when the megaliths were built (see p35), is particularly well illustrated. Menhirs (standing stones), cromlechs (menhirs in a semicircle), dolmens (tombs consisting of two upright stones roofed by a third), cairns (galleried graves), tumuli (burial mounds), and allées couvertes (graves in the form of covered alleys) are each explained. Axes made of polished jadeite (a green stone), pottery, jewellery, bone and horn tools, and flint arrowheads, blades and handaxes provide a picture of daily life in Neolithic times.

There are also models and reconstructions.

The first floor is devoted to subsequent periods: the Chalcolithic and the appearance of the earliest bronze tools, the Bronze Age (1800–750 BC), the Iron Age, and the Gallo-Roman period, which is fittingly illustrated by objects found at the Villa des Bosséno, near Carnac.

🏛 Tumulus St-Michel

On the way out of Carnac-Ville, in the direction of La Trinité-sur-Mer. ● for excavations.

Built on a natural rise in the ground that commands a wide view of the surrounding megaliths and the Baie de Quiberon, this tumulus dates from 4500 BC and is 12 m (40 ft) high. On it stands a chapel dedicated to St Michael. The tumulus contains two burial chambers, which, when they were investigated in the 19th century, were found to contain urns filled with bones, as well as axes, jewellery and pottery.

The fountain with two troughs in St-Colomban

🏛 Alignements de Carnac

Northeast Of Carnac-Ville. 🚹 visitor centre at La Maison des Megaliths, Ménec. **Tel** (02) 97 52 29 81. ◘ all year. 🖼 ✔ obligatory, check times with visitor centre.

Carnac's standing stones, just outside the town, consist of three groups, the alignments at **Ménec**, **Kermario** and **Kerlescan**, which are framed at their eastern and western limits by cromlechs. To protect the site from large numbers of visitors, wire fencing has been erected around the alignments.

The precise purpose of the alignments remains unknown. The most likely explanation is that these were places where regular gatherings took place, and that they were great religious centres, perhaps where rituals connected to a sun god were performed.

Fresco in the Église St-Cornély, Carnac

The Alignements de Kerlescan, in the direction of La Trinité, consist of 555 menhirs arranged in 13 lines. The southwest end is marked by a cromlech of 39 stones. On the heath is the Géant du Manio, a menhir 6 m (20 ft) high.

The Alignements de Kermario consists of 1,029 menhirs laid out in ten rows. This alignment has some of the most beautiful standing stones in Carnac.

The Alignements du Ménec, further west, have the most

representative stones. The 1,099 menhirs here are arranged in 11 rows and the tallest stones are 4 m (13 ft) high.

Other megaliths here include the Tumulus de Kercado (east of Kermario), a dolmen dating from 4670 BC with a gallery leading to a burial chamber with engraved walls, and the dolmens at Mané-Kerioned.

The best time to see Carnac's menhirs is at sunrise, when the stones cast extraordinary shadows, and it is best to walk the alignment from east to west.

Carnac's tourist office supplies an itinerary and map for a 5-km (3-mile) tour of the most important sites. From

VISITORS' CHECKLIST

Road map C3-4. 4,320. Auray. 74 Avenue des Druides; (02) 97 52 13 52. Place de l'Église, Carnac-Ville (Apr–Sep). Wed & Sun. Pardon de la St-Colomban (Aug); Veillée des Menhirs (fest-noz, Jul); Breton tales legends, at the menhir known as the Géant du Manio (Tue, late Jul–early Aug); Pardon de la St-Cornély (Sep). **www**.ot-carnac.fr

April to September there is also a tourist train that makes daily 50-minute tours of the alignments and beaches. A running commentary is given in several languages, including English. Further information is available at www.petittrain-carnac.com.

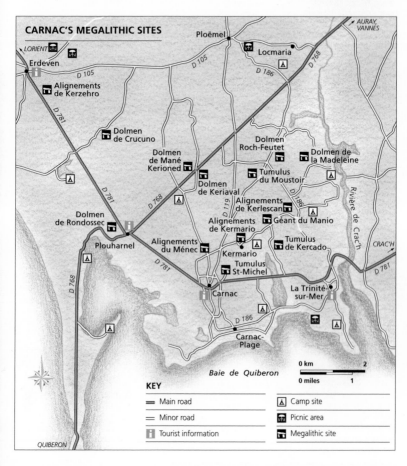

CARNAC'S MEGALITHIC SITES

AURAY, VANNES

LORIENT

Ploëmel

Locmaria

Erdeven

D 105

D 105

D 186

D 768

Alignements de Kerzehro

Dolmen de Crucuno

Dolmen Roch-Feutet

Dolmen de la Madeleine

Dolmen de Mané Kerioned

Tumulus du Moustoir

Dolmen de Keriaval

D 119

Alignements de Kerlescan

Dolmen de Rondossec

Alignements de Kermario

Géant du Manio

Rivière de Crach

Plouharnel

Alignements du Ménec

Tumulus de Kercado

CRAC'H

D 768

D 781

Kermario

Tumulus St-Michel

D 781

D 781

Carnac

La Trinité-sur-Mer

D 186

QUIBERON

Carnac-Plage

Baie de Quiberon

0 km 2

0 miles 1

KEY

Main road

Minor road

Tourist information

Camp site

Picnic area

Megalithic site

The Grand Menhir Brisé (Great Broken Menhir) at Locmariaquer, 5 m (16 ft) wide and originally 20–30 m (65–98 ft) high

La Trinité-sur-Mer ❾

Road map C3–4. 1,530. *Auray. Navix; (02) 97 55 81 00. Sailings to Belle-Île & Île de Houat Jul–Aug & cruises in the Golfe du Morbihan. 30 Cours des Quais; (02 97 55 72 21). Tue & Fri. Spi Ouest France (regattas; Easter); Fête du Nautisme (May); Claire Fontaine Regatta (Sep); Fête de l'Été (15 Aug).* **www**.ot-trinite-sur-mer.fr

Nestling in a sheltered *ria*, La Trinité-sur-Mer is the time-honoured meeting place of sailing enthusiasts. The town's sailing club, founded in 1879, is one of the oldest in France, and it was here that Éric Tabarly, Peyron and other yachtsmen began their careers. From April to September, regattas take place in the harbour, which is large enough to accommodate 1,200 yachts. La Trinité also has a fishing industry, which supplies the town's lively fish market.

A coast path leads from the harbour to the beaches, taking in Pointe de Kerbihan. The Pont de Kérisper, in the direction of Carnac and spanning the Crac'h river, offers a breathtaking view of the river, which incorporates both the oyster farms further upstream and the marina further downstream. Trips out to sea in an old sailing boat and boat rides on the Crac'h are available in summer.

The Table des Marchands, a Neolithic galleried grave

Locmariaquer ❿

Road map C–D 3. 10 km (6 miles) east of La Trinité-sur-Mer via the D 781. *1,400. Auray. Navix; (02) 97 57 36 78. Trips to Belle-Île & cruises in the Golfe de Morbihan (Jul–Aug). Rue de la Victoire; (02) 97 57 33 05. Tue & Sat (Jul-Aug). Pardon (Jun); Randonnée des Mégalithes (Jun–Sep); Fête de l'Huître (Aug).*

This charming coastal resort also has some of the most impressive megalithic monuments in Brittany. Just outside the town is the **Table des Marchands**, a Neolithic galleried grave dating from 3700 BC. Its stones are engraved with scrolls, an axe shape and depictions of cattle. Behind the Table des Marchands, a path leads to the Mané-Lud tumulus, consisting of 22 engraved stones forming a corridor. The Er-Grah Tumulus, 140 m (460 ft) long, is a burial mound.

These monuments date from a time when people were using polished stone axes, had learned to make pottery, and had begun to keep animals and plant crops. Having adopted a settled way of life, they turned to raising impressive monuments.

The **Grand Menhir Brisé**, dating from 4500 BC, is 20 m (65 ft) long and weighs 350 tonnes. It lies broken into four pieces, but is the largest known menhir in the western world.

Megaliths (Grand Menhir Brisé, Table des Marchands & Er-Grah Tumulus)
At the entrance to the town, near the cemetery. ***Tel*** *(02) 97 57 37 59. daily. 20 Dec–10 Jan.*

Environs

The Pointe de Kerpenhir, opposite Port-Navalo *(see p184)*, southeast of Locmariaquer, offers a panoramic view of the Golfe du Morbihan. The granite statue of Notre-Dame de Kerdro protects sailors and yachtsmen. Behind Plage de Kerpenhir is the Allé Couverte des Pierres-Plates *(free access)*, a corridor grave with two burial chambers engraved with motifs, which are connected by a long passage.

Auray ⓫

Road map D3. *10,590. 2 km (1 mile) from the town centre. Chapelle de la Congrégation, 20 Rue du Lait; (02) 97 24 09 75. Jul–Aug: Thu. Mon on Place de la République; Fri on Place Notre-Dame; Sun at the railway station; Wed eve. (Jul-Aug) at St-Goustan farm. Les Not'en Bulles (theatre & music; mid-Jul).* **www**.auray-tourisme.com

Tucked away at the end of a *ria*, Auray stands on a promontory overlooking the Loch river. With its old houses and attractive harbour, this is a delightful town. It also has

Detail of the 17th-century altarpiece in the Église St-Gildas in Auray

THE IMP OF THE HIGH SEAS

Éric Tabarly (1931–98), once a captain in the French Navy, was the ultimate yachtsman of the second half of the 20th century. Such eulogy would have embarrassed this shy man, who would face cameras with a modest smile. He had a long list of victories to his name. His first came in 1964, sailing in the *Pen Duick II*, when he won the second Solo Transatlantic Race, beating the British. Tabarly became a French yachting legend in the process and, as the newly popular art of sailing gripped the nation, others were inspired to emulate him.

Éric Tabarly aboard the *Côte d'Or*

Timber-framed houses in the Quartier St-Goustan, Auray

its place in the history of Brittany. It was the Battle of Auray, in 1364, that brought an end to the War of the Breton Succession (*see p40*) .

The **Église St-Gildas** has a Renaissance doorway (1636) and contains a remarkable Baroque altarpiece (*see p64*) made by a sculptor from Lavalle in 1657. Place de la République is surrounded by elegant houses, including the Maison Martin and the Hôtel de Trévegat, both dating from the 17th century, and the town hall, built in 1776.

From the belvedere and the promenade above the Loch, where terraced gardens are laid out in tiers below the castle, there is a beautiful view of the river and the harbour.

A 17th-century stone bridge at the bottom of the town leads to **St-Goustan**, which was once Auray's port. Here, medieval timber-framed

houses line the quay, whose peaceful atmosphere has captivated many painters.

The **Goélette-Musée *St-Sauveur*** is a schooner moored on Quai Martin. Containing displays of seafaring equipment and models of ships, it is now a museum of coastal shipping. It also traces the seafaring history of St-Goustan. The steep narrow streets behind the harbour are also worth exploring.

🏛 Goélette-Musée St-Sauveur
Quai Martin, St-Goustan harbour.
Tel *(02) 97 56 63 38.* ⬜
Easter–Sep: daily; Oct–Easter & school holidays: Sat–Sun. 🎟

Environs
The picturesque fishing village of Le Bono lies 6 km (4 miles) southeast of Auray. The view from the suspension bridge (1840) is magnificent.

The 17th-century cloisters at Ste-Anne-d'Auray

Waxwork of John Paul II in the Musée de Cire, Ste-Anne-d'Auray

Ste-Anne-d'Auray ⑫

Road map D3. 7 km (4 miles) north of Auray via the D17. 🚂 *1,950.*
🚊 *Auray.* ℹ️ *26 Rue de Vannes; (02) 97 57 69 16.* 🛒 *Wed.*
🎉 *Grand Pardon (late Jul).*

The second-greatest shrine in France after Lourdes, and honoured by a visit from Pope John Paul II in 1999, Ste-Anne-d'Auray became a major place of pilgrimage in the 17th century.

St Anne, mother of the Virgin Mary, appeared numerous times to a humble ploughman, Yves Nicolazic, whom she instructed to build a chapel. When a statue was discovered at the spot that she had indicated, a church was built there. It was replaced by the present basilica in 1872. The church contains stained-glass windows depicting scenes from the life of St Anne and of the ploughman. The **Trésor** (Treasury) in the cloisters contains votive plaques, seascapes and model ships, and statues dating from the 15th to the 19th centuries.

The **Musée de Cire de l'Historial**, opposite the basilica, traces the origins of the town as a place of pilgrimage and describes the life of Nicolazic. The town is also the site of the Monument aux Morts, a memorial to the 250,000 Bretons who died in World War I.

⛪ Trésor de la Basilique
Tel *(02) 97 57 68 80.*
⬜ *Tue–Sun.* 🎟
🏛 Musée de Cire de l'Historial
6 Rue de Vannes. ***Tel*** *(02) 97 57 64 05.* ⬜ *Mar–mid-Oct: daily, phone to check opening hours.* 🎟

Golfe du Morbihan ⓭

This large bay was created 9,000 years ago, when global warming caused the sea level to rise. About 15,000 years earlier, the sea level was 100 m (330 ft) lower than it is today, and Belle-Île was attached to the mainland. The rising sea gradually created hundreds of islands, the largest of which are the Île d'Arz and the Île aux Moines. The Golfe du Morbihan consists of two parts: an eastern basin, which is flatter, rather like a lagoon; and a western basin, which is defined by a rocky coastline and where there are strong currents. Here, the sea bed is uneven, particularly around Port-Navalo, where depressions can be as much as 30 m (100 ft) deep. The constant ebb and flow of the tide circulates volumes of water from the Atlantic, encouraging thousands of species of marine plant and animal life to thrive. These in turn provide food for indigenous and migratory birds.

Sailing boat off Île Berder

Île Berder
At low tide, it is possible to walk across the sand to the island.

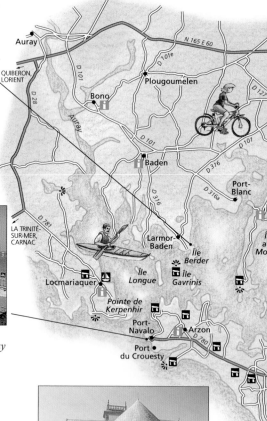

★ Port-Navalo
This small port is also a holiday resort. The coast path offers beautiful views in all directions.

0 km		5
0 miles		3

STAR SIGHTS

★ Château de Suscinio

★ Pointe d'Arradon

★ Port-Navalo

Église St-Gildas-de-Rhuys
Founded in the 11th century, the church still has its original transept and choir.

★ Pointe d'Arradon
This promontory commands spectacular views of the Île aux Moines and the Île d'Arz.

VISITORS' CHECKLIST

Road map D 3-4. 🚉 *Auray & Vannes.* 🛈 *Auray (02) 97 24 09 75; Locmariaquer (02) 97 57 33 05; Sarzeau (02) 97 41 82 37; Vannes 0825 13 56 10.* 🚢 *Arradon, Arzon, Baden, Île aux Moines, Île d'Arz, Locmariaquer, Sarzeau.* 🚶 🚴

Île d'Arz
A walk around the island takes in this old restored tidal mill.

KEY

═══	Main road
══	Minor road
-- --	Ferry route
🛈	Tourist information
♟	Castle
🔲	Megalithic site
🗡	Nature reserve
🏄	Sailing
☀	View point

★ Château de Suscinio
In the Middle Ages, the castle was the main residence of the dukes of Brittany. It was abandoned after the Revolution but, at the suggestion of the writer Prosper Mérimée, it was classified as a historic monument in 1835. Now under municipal ownership, it contains a museum of Breton history.

Exploring the Golfe du Morbihan

Focal point of the Morbihan region, the Golfe du Morbihan is 20 km (12 miles) wide and covers 12,000 ha (30,000 acres). The gulf, with its deeply indented coastline and many islands, can be explored by boat from Vannes, Port-Navalo, Auray, La Trinité or Locmariaquer. Tourism, together with shellfish and oyster farming, are major industries here, and, although fishing, sailing and other activities have also developed, the gulf is a haven for bird life. The land around it is dotted with menhirs, dolmens and tumuli.

Detail of the stoup in the Église St-Gildas-de-Rhuys

🦅 Pointe d'Arradon

Road map D3. 9 km (6 miles) south-west of Vannes via the D101 then the D101a. 🅸 *2 Place de l'Église, Arradon; (02) 97 44 77 44.* 🚌 *Tue & Fri.*

The "Riviera of the Gulf", the Pointe d'Arradon can be reached via the D101 west from Vannes. There are some superb houses here and the view takes in the Îles Logoden, Île Holavre and Île aux Moines.

🦅 Île d'Arz

Road map D4. 🚢 *15 mins from Vannes-Conleau, (02) 97 01 22 80; Navix, 0825 16 21 00.* 🅸 *Mairie,*

Île d'Arz; (02) 97 44 31 14. 🎉 *Pardon, on Île d'Hur (late Jul); regattas (Aug).*

The Île d'Arz (Bear Island), which attracts fewer visitors than the Île aux Moines, can be explored on foot as it is only 3 km (2 miles) long and 1 km (0.5 mile) wide. The low, whitewashed, slate-roofed houses and lush vegetation here create a typical image of Brittany.

The island is dotted with menhirs and dolmens, with a particular concentration on Pointe de Liouse. The Église Notre-Dame, in the town, has

Romanesque capitals decorated with grotesque figures. Boating enthusiasts will find no fewer than five sailing schools on the island.

🪦 Cairn de Gavrinis

Road map D4. Île Gavrinis. 🅸 *(02) 97 57 19 38.* 🚢 *Larmor-Baden.* 🕐 *Oct–Mar: daily pm; Apr, Jun–Sep: daily; May: Mon–Fri pm, Sat & Sun.* 📷 ✔️

Discovered in 1832, this single-chambered passage grave is considered to be unusual both on account of its construction – of a type that makes it one of the oldest in

CAIRN DE GAVRINIS

Measuring 16 m (52 ft), the Cairn de Gavrinis is the longest dolmen in France. The gallery leading to the burial chamber consists of 29 stones, some of which are engraved with symbolic motifs including shields, scrolls, axes, horn shapes and other signs. Inferences about the significance of these signs gives an insight into the meaning of such inscriptions.

Carved Stone No. 8 has engravings in which the central motif is a shield. This is usually a schematic depiction of an anthropomorphic deity.

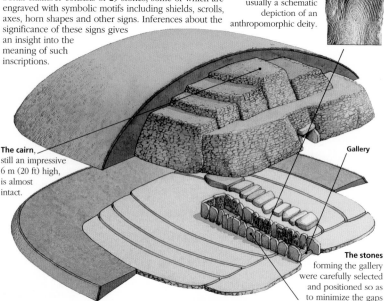

The cairn, still an impressive 6 m (20 ft) high, is almost intact.

Gallery

The stones forming the gallery were carefully selected and positioned so as to minimize the gaps between each of them.

the region – and because of its engravings. When the writer Prosper Mérimée visited it in 1835, he was struck by "stones covered in peculiar drawings... curved, straight, broken and wavy lines combined in a hundred different ways".

Île aux Moines
Road map D4. ☒ from Port-Blanc, or Izenah Crosières (02) 97 26 31 45. ℹ The harbour; (02) 97 26 32 45. ☒ summer: daily; winter: Wed & Fri. ☒ Semaine du Golfe (gathering of old sailing ships, Ascension, 40th day after Easter); Festival de Voile (Aug).

This cruciform island, 6 km (4 miles) long and 3 km (2 miles) wide, once belonged to the Abbaye de St-Sauveur in Redon (see p64). The largest island in the Golfe du Morbihan, it has been inhabited since Neolithic times, and it has several megalithic sites. The most notable are the cromlech at Kergonan, the largest in France, and, further south, the dolmen of Pen-Hap.

Like the neighbouring Île d'Arz, the Île aux Moines has fine 17th- and 18th-century houses. Its mild microclimate supports a vegetation associated with more southerly climes. Eucalyptus, mimosa, camellia and fig all thrive here. As for the island's forests – Bois d'Amour (Wood of Love), Bois des Soupirs (Wood of Sighs) and Bois des Regrets (Wood of Regrets) – their names alone are conducive to gentle reverie.

Each of the promontories on the island's indented coastline offers spectacular views of the gulf.

Presqu'île de Rhuys
Road map D4. South of the Golfe du Morbihan, via the D780 from Vannes. ℹ Sarzeau, (02) 97 41 82 37; St-Gildas-de-Rhuys, (02) 97 45 31 45; Port du Crouesty, (02) 97 53 69 69. ☒ Sun in St-Gildas-de-Rhuys); Tue in Port du Crouesty; Mon in Port du Crouesty (Jul–Aug). ☒ Semaine du Golfe (gathering of old sailing boats; Ascension, 40 days after Easter, every 2 years from 2007); Fête Médiévale (Château de Suscinio, Jul); Festival de Théâtre (Château de Suscinio, Aug); Fête de la Mer (Aug).

Like Quiberon (see p175), this peninsula has two

An attractive 18th-century house on the Île aux Moines

different aspects: a sheltered north-facing side, and a southern side that is exposed to the rigours of the Atlantic.

The Italianate **Château de Kerlévenan** dates from the 18th century. Only its park is open to visitors. The **Château de Suscinio**, on the south side, is surrounded by marshland. Built as a hunting lodge in the 13th century, it was converted into a fortress in the 14th century. It has a drawbridge flanked by towers, walls set with watchtowers, and a moat fed by the sea. In the 15th century, Francis II and his daughter, Anne of Brittany, chose Nantes rather than Suscinio as their place of residence, and the castle fell into neglect. It now houses a museum on Brittany's history.

St-Gildas-de-Rhuys, further west, is named after an English monk who established a monastery here in the 6th century. The **Musée des Arts**

et des Métiers, at the Le Net roundabout, contains reconstructions of workshops and shops dating from the 1600s to the 1950s. Between here and Arzon stands the Tumulus de Tumiac, also known as Caesar's Mound because the future Roman emperor is reputed to have used it as a lookout.

At the western tip of the peninsula, Port-Navalo and Port du Crouesty are modern coastal resorts. The coast path here commands impressive views of the gulf. It is also worth calling at the pretty little port of Le Logeo, opposite the Îles Branec.

Sarzeau, in the centre of the peninsula, has fine 17th- and 18th-century residences with ornate dormer windows. The chapel at Penvins, nearby, dates from 1897.

Migratory birds can be observed from footpaths on the peninsula's north coast.

⚜ **Château de Kerlévenan**
On the D780. **Tel** (02) 97 26 46 79. **Park** ☐ Jul–mid-Sep: Sat–Thu pm; mid-Sep–Jun: by arrangement. ☒

⚜ **Château de Suscinio**
From Sarzeau, take the D198. **Tel** (02) 97 41 91 91. ☐ daily. ☒ ☒ **www**.suscinio.info.fr

🏛 **Musée des Arts et Métiers**
Le Net roundabout. **Tel** (02) 97 53 68 25. ☐ Jul–Aug: Mon–Sat & Sun pm; Sep–Jun: Tue–Sun pm. ☒

The chapel at Penvins, near Sarzeau, in the form of a Greek cross

Street-by-Street: Vannes

The medieval centre of Vannes is a honeycomb of narrow streets which, like those around the Cathédrale St-Pierre, are lined with well-restored timber-framed houses. The main entrance into the walled town, a busy commercial district, is Porte St-Vincent, near Place Gambetta. The walls on the eastern side offer a fine view of the town, with formal gardens laid out below, and also pass the city's old wash houses. The harbour, to the south, is a lively centre of activity.

★ City Walls and Gardens
Part of the Gallo-Roman walls around the old town survives.

Place Gambetta
This square, opposite the marina, is always busy. It is a central meeting place for the inhabitants of Vannes, who fill the café terraces here.

The fish market takes place twice a week, on Wednesdays and Saturdays

Château de l'Hermine
The chateau was built in the 18th century on the site of the residence of the dukes of Brittany. It is fronted by extensive formal gardens, where it is pleasant to walk.

The new market was opened in 2001.

Porte Poterne leads to the gardens beneath the city walls.

RUE LE HELLEC

RUE DE LA POISSONNERIE

RUE NOÉ

PLACE GAMBETTA

PLACE DU POIDS PUBLIC

RUE SAINT — VINCENT

PLACE DES LICES

RUE DE LA PORTE POTERNE

RUE D

Wash Houses
Located beside the Marle river, the city's wash houses date from 1820. They were still in use after World War II.

STAR SIGHTS

★ City Walls and Gardens

★ Doorway of the Cathédrale St-Pierre

★ Place des Lices

Place Henri-IV

The square is lined with timber-framed houses dating from the 15th and 16th centuries, the oldest in Vannes. In the Middle Ages, a popular bird market was held here.

Musée d'Histoire

VISITORS' CHECKLIST

Road map D3. 🏠 *54,000.*
🛈 *Office du Tourisme du Pays de Vannes, 1 Rue Thiers, 0825 13 56 10.* 🚆 *Wed & Sat am.* 🎭 *Fêtes Historiques (Jul); Festival de Jazz (Jul); Nuits Musicales du Golfe (Jul–Aug); Fêtes d'Arvor (traditional dancing and music, Aug).*
www.tourisme-vannes.com

Musée de la Cohue is an art gallery that also contains displays of artifacts relating to seafaring.

★ **Doorway of the Cathédrale St-Pierre**

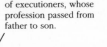

Built in the 16th century in the Flamboyant Gothic style, the doorway is lined with niches that, in keeping with Breton tradition, contain statues of the Apostles.

Porte St-Jean was the home of executioners, whose profession passed from father to son.

★ **Place des Lices**

The square is surrounded by well-kept timber-framed houses, the most recent dating from the 17th century.

Porte Prison, dating from the 13th and 15th centuries, was the main gateway into Vannes. Criminals were imprisoned there.

Tour du Connétable

The tower, the highest in Vannes, was built in the 16th century and is now owned by the city authorities, who have restored it. It has a pointed roof and mullioned windows.

0 m	100
0 yards	**100**

KEY

– – –   Suggested route

Exploring Vannes

The history of Vannes goes back to Roman times, when it was known as Darioritum. In the 5th century, it was a diocese and, in the Middle Ages, a city of major importance. Vannes expanded during the 14th century, when it became the capital of Brittany. As a university town, an administrative centre and the capital of the Morbihan, it is again expanding rapidly today. The city also attracts large numbers of sightseers and holiday-makers.

Porte Poterne, the city's postern gate, built in the 17th century

🚩 Town Walls

Vannes was once completely surrounded by defensive walls. Two thirds of these remain, and some have been incorporated into more recent buildings. Part of the Gallo-Roman walls survive on the north side of the city.

Vannes' finest gateway is on its southern side, opposite the harbour. This is Porte St-Vincent, built in 1624. It was restored in 1747, when the gate's existing arrow slits and machicolation were replaced by niches with shell motifs and columns with capitals.

From here to Porte Prison, on the north side of the town, the wall walk overlooks formal gardens laid out in the former moat. It also passes Porte Poterne (1678), and the historic wash houses nearby. Other towers in the town walls include Tour de la Trompette, Tour de la Poudrière, Tour de la Joliette, and Tour du Bourreau. The highest is Tour du Connétable.

🔒 Cathédrale St-Pierre

🕐 8:30am–6:30pm daily.

From a vantage point on the Colline du Mené, the Cathédrale St-Pierre dominates the old town. It was built in the Flamboyant Gothic style, but has neo-Gothic additions dating from the 19th century.

A rotunda chapel dedicated to the Holy Sacrament is built into the north aisle. A jewel of Renaissance architecture, it has a double tier of niches with pediments and high windows framed by semicircular arches. It contains the tomb of St Vincent-Ferrier, a Spanish monk renowned for his preaching. A Gobelins tapestry decorates the wall and there is an outstanding 16th-century Flemish altarpiece.

The cathedral treasury contains some fine metalwork.

🚩 Old Town

Place Henri-IV, at the heart of the old town, is lined with 15th- and 16th-century half-timbered houses, the oldest in Vannes. Many of the houses in the area around the square have sumptuous decoration. The house at No. 13 Rue Salomon has animal carvings and, on the corner of Rue Noé, is the famous inn sign in the form of "Vannes et sa Femme", the couple who ran the tavern.

In the 17th century, when the Breton parliament was exiled in Vannes, many fine granite or stone town houses (*hôtels*) were built here. The Hôtel de Lannion, in Impasse de la Psalette, flanked by a projecting turret, was once the residence of the governors of Vannes and Auray. The Hôtel de Limur, in Rue Thiers, with a Neo-Classical façade, is a three-storey residence with a courtyard and a garden.

🏛 Musée de la Cohue

9 & 15 Place St-Pierre. **Tel** (02) 97 01 63 00. 🕐 mid-Jun–Sep: daily; Oct–mid-Jun: daily pm. ● public holidays.

The museum is laid out in a restored covered market (*cohue*) whose origins go back to the 13th century. While market stalls occupied the ground floor, the first floor housed the ducal courts of the Breton parliament, when the latter was exiled to Vannes in 1675 on the orders of Louis XIV. The building was then used as a theatre until the 1950s.

The Musée de la Cohue is an art gallery whose most highly prized exhibit is Delacroix's *Crucifixion*. Millet, Corot and Goya are also represented. The work of Breton painters, including Maufra, Henri Moret, Paul Helleu, and of engravers native to Vannes, such as Frélaut and Dubreuil, are also displayed, as is that of contemporary artists, including Tal Coat, Soulages and Geneviève Asse. Two other rooms in the museum are devoted to pieces relating to seafaring.

Statue of the Virgin in the Cathédrale St-Pierre

For hotels and restaurants in this region see pp227–30 and pp246–8

🏛 Musée d'Histoire

Château Gaillard, 2 Rue Noé. *Tel (02) 97 01 63 00.* ☐ *mid-Jun–Sep: daily; mid-May–mid-Jun: daily pm.* ▨
Housed in the 15th-century Château Gaillard, which once accommodated the Breton parliament, this archaeological museum contains prehistoric artifacts from sites in the Morbihan. These include axes of polished jadeite and jewellery made of variscite (a kind of turquoise). Coins struck by the Veneti, a local Gaulish tribe, pieces from Roman Gaul, and medieval and Renaissance artifacts are also displayed.

🚇 Place Gambetta

This semicircular square, lined with the white façades of residential blocks, was laid out in the 19th century and is today one of the liveliest parts of Vannes. The harbour lies immediately to the south, so that pleasure boats can sail right up into the heart of the city.

From the square, Promenade de la Rabine, a wide walkway which is continued by a coast

The marina in Vannes, just south of Place Gambetta

road, leads to the Presqu'île de Conleau, 4 km (3 miles) downstream.

Environs

The **Forteresse de Largoët d'Elven**, 14 km (9 miles) northeast of Vannes, is an example of medieval Breton architecture. The fortress has two towers and a curtain wall dating from the 13th century, a 14th-century keep, a gatehouse and a 15th-century circular tower. The surrounding **Landes de Lanvaux**, heathland with lakes and woods, is traversed by footpaths and cycle tracks.

⛪ Forteresse de Largoët d'Elven

From Vannes, take the N166 then the D135 at St-Nolff. The fortress is about 3 km (2 miles) further north. *Tel (02) 97 53 35 96.* ☐ *Jul–Aug: daily; May: Sat & Sun; Jun–Sep: Wed–Mon.* ☐ *Oct–Apr.* ▨

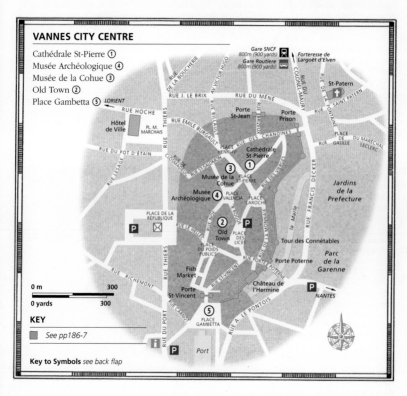

VANNES CITY CENTRE

Cathédrale St-Pierre ①
Musée Archéologique ④
Musée de la Cohue ③
Old Town ②
Place Gambetta ⑤

KEY

☐ See pp186–7

Key to Symbols see back flap

The 16th-century town hall in La Roche-Bernard

La Roche-Bernard ⓯

Road map D3. 34 km (21 miles) southeast of Vannes on the N165. 🚉 *Ponchâteau*. 🛈 *14 Rue du Docteur-Cornudet; (02) 99 90 67 98.* 🚍 *Thu.*

Perched on a rocky spur, La Roche-Bernard stands at an important intersection on the estuary of the Vilaine. In the 11th century, a village grew up around the fortress and, six centuries later, Richelieu ordered naval dockyards to be installed. It was here that the three-decker *La Couronne*, pride of the French navy, was built in 1634.

The port consists of a marina, along the Vilaine, and of the old harbour that was later abandoned in favour of the Quai de la Douane. Salt, corn, wine, quicklime and chestnut wood once passed through the docks here. In the old town, which rises in tiers, is the 16th-century Maison du Canon, which houses the town hall, and the Auberge des Deux Magots, on Place du Bouffay. There are former salt ware- houses in Rue de la Saulnerie.

The **Musée de la Vilaine Maritime** is laid out in the 16th-century Maison des Basses-Fosses, where the ground floor is carved out of the living rock. The museum traces the history of navigation on the Vilaine and documents the rural life of the region.

Environs
The **Parc Zoologique de Branféré**, 20 km (12 miles) northwest of La Roche-Bernard, has over 100 species of animals that roam in relative freedom.

🏛 **Musée de la Vilaine Maritime**
6 Rue Ruicard. **Tel** *(02) 99 90 83 47.* ⏰ *early Jun: daily pm; mid-Jun–mid-Sep: daily; mid– end Sep & school holidays: daily pm.* 📷

🐾 **Parc Zoologique de Branféré**
Le Guerno, via the N165. **Tel** *(02) 97 42 94 66.* ⏰ *Feb, Mar, Oct, Nov: daily pm; Apr–Sep: daily.* 📷

Questembert ⓰

Road map D3. 28 km (17 miles) east of Vannes, via the N165, the D775 and the D5. 🚉 *Bel Air.* 🛈 *Hôtel Belmont; (02) 97 26 56 00.* 🚍 *Mon.* 📷 *Pardon in Bréhardec (15 Aug); Soirées Estivales (fest-noz, songs of the sea, Sat in Jul–Aug).*

This small town, whose name means "chestnut-tree land" in Breton, owes its former prosperity to the fairs that took place here, in the covered market (1675). Nearby is the former Hostellerie Jehan le Guenego, built in 1450 and the oldest house in the town. The 16th-century Hôtel Belmont next door, now the tourist office, is enlivened by some remarkable wooden caryatids. There are many producers of duck foie gras in the area.

Rochefort-en-Terre ⓱

Road map D3. 33 km (20 miles) east of Vannes via the N166, the D775 and the D774. 🚉 *Bel Air.* 🛈 *Place du Puit; (02) 97 43 33 57.* 📷 *Pardon (mid-Aug); Festival de Musique (late Aug).* **www**.rochefort-en-terre.com

Built on a promontory above the Gueuzon river, this village has a medieval atmosphere. Because of its strategic position, the sitehas been fortified since Roman times.

A keep overlooking Rochefort was built in the 12th century, and in the 15th the town was enclosed by walls. Demolished on three previous occasions, the **castle** was again destroyed during the Revolution. In 1907, Alfred Klots, an American painter, restored it and moved into the castle's 17th-century outbuildings. The castle **museum** contains antique furniture, paintings by Alfred Klots and various items illustrating life in the area. The moat walk offers a good view of the surroundings.

The finest houses in Rochefort, with granite or schist façades carved with decorative motifs, are in Grande-Rue and Place du Puits. The Église Notre-Dame-de-la-Tronchaye, built on the hillside and dating from the 15th and 16th centuries, has a façade in the Flamboyant Gothic style. Features of interest within include beams decorated with monsters,

Wooden roof of the 17th-century covered market in Questembert

Place du Puits, in the flower-filled village of Rochefort-en-Terre

woodcarvings on the theme of death (left of the pulpit) and a Renaissance altar-piece. A 16th-century calvary stands on the church square.

⚜ **Castle and Museum**
Tel (02) 97 43 31 56. ☐ *May: Sat–Sun & public holidays, pm; Jun: daily pm; Jul–Aug: daily; Sep: daily pm.* ☐ *Oct–Apr.* 📷

Ploërmel ⑱

Road map D3. 🚉 *Vannes.*
🏠 *8,000.* ℹ️ *5 Rue du Val; (02) 97 74 02 70.* 🛒 *Jul–Aug: Mon–Sat.* 🚢 *Fri.* 🎭 *Songs of the sea (late Jul); Semaines Arthuriennes (late Jul–early Aug).*

This town was one of the places of residence of the dukes of Brittany. The tombs of John II and Jean III lie in the 16th-century Église St-Armel, near the tomb of Philippe de Montauban. The fine stained-glass window with the Tree of Jesse is the work of Jehan le Flamand. The north entrance is decorated with some strikingly expressive reliefs depicting the vices and the Last Judgment.

The **Maison des Marmousets** (1586), opposite the tourist office in Rue Beau-manoir, has some unusual reliefs. Next door is the Hôtel des Ducs de Bretagne, which, built in 1150,

Figure, Maison des Marmousets

is the town's oldest building. The astronomical clock (1855), near the Lycée Lamennais, was made by a member of the Ploërmel brotherhood, which was founded by the older brother of the writer Félicité de Lamennais (*see pp25 & 47*).

Environs
The Circuit de l'Hortensia is a walk around the Lac au Duc, 1 km (0.5 mile) northwest of Ploërmel. The lake is bordered by 2,000 hydrangeas representing 12 different types of these colourful flowering shrubs.

Josselin ⑲

Road map D3. 🚉 *Vannes.*
🏠 *2,500.* ℹ️ *Place de la Congrégation; (02) 97 22 36 43.* 🚢 *Sat.* 🎭 *free concerts (Jul–Aug); Pardon St Eloi (8 Sep).*
www.paysdejosselin-tourisme.com

Linen weaving and the linen trade created Josselin's wealth. The town has at least two important buildings: the **Château de Josselin** (*see pp192–3*) and the **Basilique Notre-Dame-du-Roncier**, with legendary origins.

A miraculous statue of the Virgin was found under brambles (*ronces*) and a church was built on the holy spot. The basilica that now stands on this legendary site is in the Flamboyant Gothic style, with typically Gothic gargoyles, but Romanesque columns survive in the choir. Recumbent statues of Olivier de Clisson (*see p192*) and of his wife, Marguerite de Rohan, lie near the miraculous statue.

Rues des Vierges, Olivier-de-Clisson and Trente are lined with fine 16th- and 17th-century houses. The **Musée des Poupées**, at No. 3 Rue Trente, contains some 600 wax, wooden and porcelain dolls dating from the 17th and 18th centuries. Chapelle Ste-Croix (1050), on the banks of the Oust, is the oldest chapel in the Morbihan.

Marguerite de Rohan, Basilique Notre-Dame-du-Roncier, Josselin

Environs
From the Middle Ages, the Forêt de Lanouée, 10 km (6 miles) north of Josselin, provided firewood for the ironworks where cannon balls were made. They were at their most productive in the 18th century.

The parish close at Guéhenno, 11 km (7 miles) southwest of Josselin, is the only complete example in the Morbihan. Two statues of soldiers guard the entrance to the ossuary, where there is a figure of the resurrected Christ. The calvary is the most spectacular part of the close. It dates from 1550 but was badly damaged in the Revolution. Eventually a parish priest undertook its restoration. A column with the symbols of the Passion of Christ stands in front of it.

🏛 **Musée des Poupées**
3 Rue Trente. *Tel* (02) 97 22 36 45. ☐ *Apr–mid-Jul & Sep: daily pm; mid-Jul–Aug: daily; Oct: Sat & Sun.* ☐ *Nov–Mar.* 📷

Château de Josselin

Perched on rocks opposite the Oust river, the Château de Josselin, once the stronghold of the Rohan dynasty, is an impressive sight. It is defended by four towers built by Olivier de Clisson in the 14th century. The castle's military severity is softened by the more delicate inner façade, dating from the early 16th century and looking onto gardens. A fine Flamboyant Gothic building, the castle has delicately carved granite galleries, pinnacles, balustrades and chimneypieces, and is decorated with a range of motifs, including fleurs-de-lis, stoats and lozenges.

Detail of the chimneypiece, with the Rohans' motto, "A Plus"

Ten dormer windows rising through two storeys cover almost half the façade.

★ Library
Containing 3,000 volumes, the library was remodelled in the neo-Gothic style in the 19th century.

★ Interior North Façade
This side of the castle has dormer windows with ornamental pediments. Each window is different, and together they embody the decorative repertoire of the time.

Prison tower

OLIVIER DE CLISSON

One of the most illustrious owners of the Château de Josselin was Olivier de Clisson (1336–1407). He married Marguerite de Rohan and in 1370 acquired the castle. De Clisson harboured a long hatred of the king of France, who had ordered his father's execution because of his support of the English. During the War of the Breton Succession, de Clisson sided with the English. However, he later transferred his allegiance to the French, befriending Bertrand du Guesclin and succeeding him as constable of France. De Clisson finally gave his daughter in marriage to the son of Charles of Blois, his erstwhile enemy.

Equestrian statue of Olivier de Clisson

STAR FEATURES

★ Grand Salon

★ Interior North Façade

★ Library

★ Grand Salon
The room has a chimneypiece decorated with garlands and hunting scenes, as well as 18th-century furniture and a portrait of Louis XIV painted by Rigaud.

VISITORS' CHECKLIST

Place de la Congrégation. *Tel*
(02) 97 22 36 45. **Ground floor:**
Apr–May: 2–6pm Wed, Sat–Sun;
Jun: 2–6pm daily; Jul–Aug: 10–6pm
daily; Sep: 2–6pm daily; Oct:
2–6pm Wed, Sat–Sun; school
hols: 2–6pm daily. Nov–Mar.

The main courtyard is an ideal place from which to take in this fine Gothic building.

Façade over the Oust
The fortress stands on an outcrop of schist at the foot of which runs the Oust river. Only four of the nine towers raised by Olivier de Clisson survive.

Entrance gate

Entrance Gate
Beyond the entrance gate is an inner façade with a wealth of intricate carving.

Dining Room
The neo-Gothic furniture in the dining room is the work of a local cabinetmaker and the design of the chimneypiece echoes that in the Grand Salon.

Machicolated defences at the Château des Rohan in Pontivy

Baud ⑳

Road map D3. 24 km (15 miles) north of Auray via the D768. 🚌 Auray. 👥 4,930. 🛈 Chemin de Karmarec; (02) 97 39 17 09. 🚌 Sat.

The small town of Baud overlooks the Evel valley. In the upper town is the Chapelle Notre-Dame, with an interesting 16th-century apse.

Fontaine Notre-Dame-de-la-Clarté in Baud

In the lower town, is the 16th-century **Fontaine Notre-Dame-de-la-Clarté**, which provides water for the old wash houses here.

Also of interest is the **Cartopole Conservatoire de la Carte Postale**, with a collection of 20,000 old postcards depicting the crafts of the past and local history.

Environs

About 2 km (1 mile) southwest of Baud, near a ruined castle, is a statue known as the Vénus de Quinipily. Standing about 2 m (7 ft) high, the almost naked figure is inscribed with the mysterious letters "LIT". Either Egyptian or Roman, it may represent Isis, a fertility goddess revered by Roman legionaries.

Public footpaths traverse the woods around Baud. The Blavet valley also contains a large number of interesting calvaries, fountains and chapels. In summer, exhibitions of contemporary art are held in many of the villages.

🏛 **Cartopole Conservatoire de la Carte Postale**
Rue d'Auray. **Tel** (02) 97 51 15 14.
🕐 mid-Jun–mid-Sep: daily; mid-Sep–mid-Jun: Wed; Thu; Sat & Sun pm. ● Nov–Easter. 🖼

Pontivy ㉑

Road map D3. 🚌 🚌 Rue d'Iéna. 👥 14,500. 🛈 Rue du Général-de-Gaulle; (02) 97 25 04 10. 🚌 Mon. 🎭 Kan ar Bol (Breton tales and songs, late Mar).

This town, the capital of the Rohan dynasty, consists of two distinct parts: the medieval town, with timber-framed houses and a great castle; and an imperial town, with straight avenues arranged around Place Aristide-Briand. This latter district was laid out on the orders of Napoleon, who aimed to make Pontivy a base from which to fight back against the Chouans (see p46).

The **Château des Rohan**, which was begun in 1479 by John II de Rohan, is a fine example of military architecture. The seignorial living quarters overlooking the courtyard were remodelled in the 18th century. Exhibitions and shows take place at the castle in summer.

The old town spreads out around the castle. Of the old town walls, only la Porte de Carhaix survives. The finest houses here, built in the 16th and 17th centuries, are those on Place du Martray and along Rue du Fil and Rue du Pont.

A canal runs alongside Pontivy, making the town an important intersection for river traffic. The towpath also offers the chance of walks through beautiful countryside.

🏰 **Château des Rohan**
Tel (02) 97 25 12 93. 🕐 Feb–mid-Jun & mid-Sep–Nov: Wed–Sun; mid-Jun–mid-Sep: daily. 🖼

NAPOLEON-VILLE

In 1790, Pontivy sided with the Republicans and the town became the focus of the Chouan royalists' war (see p46). In March 1793, 10,000 recalcitrant peasants attacked the town. Napoleon chose Pontivy as a base from which to lead a counter-attack. He also decided to canalize the Blavet river between Brest and Nantes and built a new town. When the Napoleonic Empire collapsed, the project was still unfinished. An imperial district was, however, built during the reign of Napoleon III.

Mairie de Pontivy, built during the Napoleonic period

Guéméné-sur-Scorff ㉒

Road map C–D3. 19 km (12 miles)
west of Pontivy via the D782.
🚉 *Lorient.* 🏠 *1,500.* ℹ️ *Rue
Bisson; (02) 97 39 33 47 (Jun–Sep).*
🛍 *Thu.* 🎉 *Fête de l'Andouille
(late Aug).*

Now a centre of *andouille*
(sausage) production, the
town was the object of bitter
dispute during the War of the
Breton Succession *(see p40)*.
The houses on Place Bisson
reflect its former prosperity.

Frescoes in the choir of the
church in Kernascléden

Kernascléden ㉓

Road map D3. 30 km (19 miles)
southwest of Pontivy via the D782.

It is worth stopping at this
little village to visit the
15th-century church, which
contains frescoes that are
among the finest of their
period. The choir is decorated
with scenes of the life of the
Virgin and of the childhood
of Christ. In the crossing is a
chillingly realistic depiction of
the Dance of Death, similar to
that in the Chapelle Kermaria-
an-Iskuit *(see p101)*, in the
Côtes d'Armor.

Le Faouët ㉔

Road map C3. 35 km (22 miles)
north of Lorient via the D769.
🚉 *Quimperlé.* 🏠 *3,000.* ℹ️ *3 Rue
de Cendres; (02) 97 23 23 23.*
🛍 *first and third Wed in the month.*
🎉 *Pardons (last Sun in Jun, third Sun
in Aug); folk festival (mid-Aug).*

Isolated in undulating
wooded landscape, the
village of Le Faouët has a fine
16th-century covered market.
The **Musée des Peintres du
Faouët**, in a former convent,
contains 19th-century paintings
of country life in Brittany and
Breton landscapes. In the
Musée de l'Abeille Vivante,
visitors can observe bees in
glass-sided hives.

Environs
The chapels in the vicinity of Le
Faouët – St-Nicolas, Ste-Barbe
and St-Fiacre – are each worth
a visit. The most interesting is
the Chapelle St-Fiacre, 3 km
(2 miles) southeast of Le
Faouët, in the Flamboyant
Gothic style and with a
gabled belfry. It also contains
a beautiful rood screen.
The **Parc Aquanature
Le Stérou**, 6 km (4 miles)
southeast of Le Faouët, is a
70-ha (170-acre) nature park
with a population of deer.

🏛 **Musée des Peintres
du Faouët**
1 Rue de Quimper. **Tel** (02) 97 23 23
23. ⬜ *varies, call ahead.* 📷

🏛 **Musée de l'Abeille Vivante**
Kercadoret, Le Faouët. **Tel** (02) 97
23 08 05. ⬜ *varies, call ahead.* 📷

🦌 **Parc Aquanature Le Stérou**
Route de Priziac. **Tel** (02) 97 34 63 84.
⬜ *Apr–Oct: daily.* 📷

The stud at Hennebont, housed in
a former Cistercian abbey

Hennebont ㉕

Road map C3. 13 km (8 miles)
northeast of Lorient, via the D769
then the D769 bis. 🚉 🏠 *14,000.*
ℹ️ *9 Place du Maréchal-Foch; (02) 97
36 24 52.* 🛍 *Thu.* 🎉 *Medieval
festivals (late Jul); Pardon (late Sep).*

Overlooking the steep
banks of the Blavet river,
Hennebont was once one of
the largest fortified towns in
the area. On Place Foch, with
a central well (1623), is the
Basilique Notre-Dame-du-
Paradis, built in the 16th
century. The walled town,
damaged during World War II,
is defended by the Porte du
Broërec'h. This 13th-century
gatehouse contains a **museum**
of local history. A view of the
gardens and the river can be
enjoyed from the rampart walk.
The **Haras National**
(National Stud), where 75
thoroughbreds (including
Breton post-horses, Arabs and
Selle Français) are kept, is
housed in a former Cistercian
abbey. Visitors can see the
farrier's forge, the tack room,
the stables, the school and a
collection of carriages.
The Forges d'Hennebont, at
Inzinzac, are ironworks that
operated from 1860 to 1966,
and were important to the
local economy. The
Écomusée Industriel here
describes metalworking
techniques, as well as
worker's living and working
conditions at the time.

🏛 **Musée des Tours
Broërec'h**
Rue de la Prison. **Tel** (02) 97 36 29
18. ⬜ *Jun–Sep: daily.*

🐴 **Haras National**
Rue Victor-Hugo. **Tel** (02) 97 89 40
30. ⬜ *Jul–Aug: daily; May, Jun,
Sep: Tue–Fri, Sat, Mon pm.*

🏛 **Écomusée Industriel**
Inzinzac, Zone Industrielle des Forges.
Tel (02) 97 36 98 21. ⬜ *Jul–Aug:
daily; Sep–Jun: Mon–Fri & Sun pm.*

The Oratoire St-Michel, attached to the Chapelle Ste-Barbe, near Le Faouët

LOIRE-ATLANTIQUE

Between Ancenis in the east and St-Nazaire in the west, the great Loire river winds lazily, cutting through verdant lands and flowing through Nantes, the region's capital, before broadening into an estuary as it empties into the Atlantic. While the north of the Loire-Atlantique is a region of lakes and woodland, the south is characterized by mud flats, especially on the Guérande peninsula to the west.

Both in historical and in geographical terms, the Loire-Atlantique is assuredly Breton. Yet, incorporated into the Pays de la Loire in 1969, the region is also oriented towards the south and the Vendée, to the southwest.

The central axis of the Loire-Atlantique is the Loire estuary, which provides a link with the Atlantic. On it stands Nantes, the former capital of the dukes of Brittany, and today not only the capital of the Pays de la Loire but also the largest city in western France. Until the mid-19th century, the Loire was a major artery for the transport of commercial goods: salt from Guérande and fish from the Atlantic were transported inland by boat.

The Loire-Atlantique is made up of a mosaic of distinct areas. While the Presqu'île de Guérande and the coastal town of Le Croisic grew rich long ago from salt-panning, La Baule and the surrounding coastal resorts came into their own in the late 19th century. The industrial city of St-Nazaire enjoyed a golden age in the first half of the 20th century.

While the Pays de Retz, to the west, is a land of pasture, beaches and mud flats fringed by the sea, the Pays d'Ancenis, to the east, is a major wine-producing area, where hillsides are dotted with terracotta-roofed houses. The Forêt de Gâvre and the countryside around Châteaubriant, to the north, offer yet more lush landscapes.

Le Croisic, with the former residences of wealthy merchants lining the quay

◁ Interior of the 9th-century Carolingian abbey church of St-Philibert-de-Grand-Lieu

Exploring the Loire-Atlantique

Named after the river that traverses it from east to west, flowing into the Atlantic Ocean at St-Nazaire, the Loire-Atlantique is Brittany's most southerly region. The northwest of this *département*, consisting of the Presqu'île de Guérande and the great nature reserve of La Brière, is dominated by heathland with outcrops of granite, by marshland and by a rocky coastline. Slate-roofed or thatched houses are ubiquitous here. The area around Châteaubriant, in the north, contains a central expanse of woodland with outcrops of blue-grey schist. This is good walking country. South of the Loire, vineyards where Muscadet and Gros Plant are grown stretch as far as the eye can see. In the Pays de Retz, which borders the Atlantic in the west, wide sandy beaches alternate with marshes where salt has been gathered since ancient times.

Villa Ker Souveraine in Pornichet

KEY

══	Motorway
══	Major road
──	Secondary road
┈┈	Minor road
┄╌	Main railway
──	Minor railway
══	Regional border

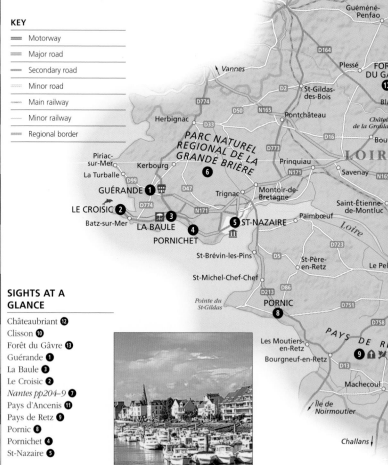

SIGHTS AT A GLANCE

Châteaubriant ⑫
Clisson ⑩
Forêt du Gâvre ⑬
Guérande ❶
La Baule ❸
Le Croisic ❷
Nantes pp204–9 ❼
Pays d'Ancenis ⑪
Pays de Retz ❾
Pornic ❽
Pornichet ❹
St-Nazaire ❺

Tour

Parc Naturel Régional
  de la Grande Brière ❻

The harbour at Le Croisic

SEE ALSO

- *Where to Stay* pp230–31

- *Where to Eat* pp248–9

Allée Turenne, in Île Feydau, Nantes

GETTING AROUND

Nantes has an international airport and is also only 2 hours 15 minutes from Paris by TGV (high-speed train). The most direct road route from Paris to Nantes is the A11 motorway. From there, the N165, which becomes the N171, leads to St-Nazaire. The Pays de Retz, in the west, can be explored by taking D213 from St-Nazaire or the D751 from Nantes. The N137 leads to the Pays de Gâvre, in the north, while the D178 runs north to Châteaubriant. The N23, along the Loire, leads to Ancenis, to the east. To the south, the N249 then the D763 run to Clisson.

The ruins of Château de Clisson

Porte St-Michel, the main entrance into
the walled town of Guérande

Guérande ❶

Road map D4. 🏠 12,000.
🚉 La Baule. ✈ Nantes-Atlantique.
ℹ 1 Place du Marché-aux-Bois;
(02) 40 24 96 71. ♦ Wed & Sat.
🎭 Remontée du Sel de Guérande
(Apr–May), Fête Medievale (May), La
Salicorne (Mar & Jun).

Overlooking extensive salt
marshes on the Presqu'Île de
Guérande, this town has long
depended on the salt-panning
industry. Although this
industry began in Roman
times, it became important
only in the 15th century.
   The old town is enclosed
within 14th- and 15th-century
ramparts. The Porte St-Michel,
the gatehouse and main
entrance on the eastern side,
contains the **Musée Château
du Pays de Guérande** in which
local furniture, costumes,
faience and religious art are
displayed. The Collégiale St-
Aubin, the collegiate church
in the centre of the old town,
was built in the 13th century

and later remodelled.
The interior has 14th-
and 15th-century
stained glass, and
Romanesque capitals
carved with scenes
of martyrdom and
fantastic animals.
The **Musée de la
Poupée et du Jouet
Ancien** contains
dolls and toys
dating from 1830 to
the present day.

Environs
The D99 running
northwest out of Guérande
leads to La Turballe, the
largest sardine port on the
Atlantic coast. The market
where the fish auction takes
place has an exhibiton on
fishing. Past Pointe du Castelli,
the road reaches the resort of
Piriac-sur-Mer, where a
granite-built church stands
amid narrow streets.
   The D774 south from
Guérande winds through salt
marshes, leading to Saillé, a
typical salt-panning village.
The **Maison des Paludiers**
documents the history of salt-
panning on the peninsula.

🏛 **Musée Château du Pays
de Guérande**
Porte St-Michel. **Tel** (02) 28 55 05
05. ☐ Apr–Oct: daily. ● Mon am
(outside school holidays). 🎫

🏛 **Musée de la Poupée**
23 Rue de Saillé. **Tel** (02) 40 15 69
13. ☐ May–Oct: daily; Nov–Apr:
daily pm. 🎫

🏛 **Maison des Paludiers**
18 Rue des Prés. Garnier, Saillé.
Tel (02) 40 62 21 96. ☐ varies,
phone ahead. 🎫

Le Croisic ❷

Road map D4. 🏠 4,450. 🚉
🚉 La Baule. ✈ Nantes-Atlantique.
ℹ Place du 18 Juin-1940; (02) 40 23
00 70. ♦ Thu & Sat. 🎭 Fête de la
Mer (Aug), Les Vieux Métiers de la
Mer (Jun–Sep). www.ot-lecroisic.fr

Set on a peninsula reaching
5 km (3 km) into the Atlantic,
Le Croisic is both an active
fishing port and a popular
resort. The old town has
some fine houses dating from
the time when salt was
shipped from Le Croisic to
destinations as distant as the
Baltic. In the **Océarium du
Croisic**, one of the largest
private aquariums in France,
the marine life of the Atlantic
coast can be observed.
   The Flamboyant Gothic
Église St-Guénolé has a high
tower from which Batz-sur-
Mer can be seen. The granite
Chapelle Notre-Dame-du-
Mûrier, built in the 15th
century, is now in ruins.

Environs
The **Musée des Marais Salants**
in Batz-sur-Mer, 5 km (3 miles)
southeast of Le Croisic, documents the history of the salt
marshes and the lives of salt
panners in the 19th century.

🏛 **Océarium du Croisic**
Avenue de St-Goustan, Le Croisic.
Tel (02) 40 23 02 44.
www.ocearium-croisic.fr ● Three
weeks in Jan. 🎫 ♿

🏛 **Musée des Marais Salants**
29 bis, Rue Pasteur, Batz-sur-Mer.
Tel (02) 40 23 82 79. ☐ Jun–Sep &
school holidays: daily; Oct–May:
Sat–Sun. 🎫

The harbour at Le Croisic, with active fishing and shellfish-farming industries

For hotels and restaurants in this region see pp230–31 and pp248–9

The beautiful 8-km (5-mile) beach at La Baule

La Baule ❸

Road map D4. 🏠 *16,400.*
🚉 🚌 🛈 *8 Place de la Victoire; (02)
40 24 34 44.* 🏪 *Apr–Sep & school
holidays: daily am (Jul & Aug all day);
Oct–Mar: Tue–Sun, am.* 🎭 *Pardon
d'Escoublac (Aug). Fireworks on
beach Jul-Aug.* **www**.labaule.fr.

This resort is famous for
its exceptionally long
beach, which stretches
for some 8 km (5 miles).
It became a holiday
resort when the rail link
with the interior opened
in 1879. Residential districts
were then created, and a
multitude of villas and
luxury hotels sprang up.
The seafront promenade was
opened in 1929. Later,
however, apartment blocks
replaced the seaside villas,
although a few fine examples
survive, particularly in the
resort's eastern extension, La
Baule-les-Pins. About 10 km
(7 miles) inland is the large
Forêt d'Escoublac, which is
traversed by footpaths.

Pornichet ❹

Road map D4. 🏠 *8,160.* 🚉 🚌 *La
Baule.* 🛈 *3 Boulevard de la République;
(02) 40 61 33 33.* 🏪 *Wed & Sat;
covered market daily Jun–Sep.*

Occupying the eastern third
of a wide bay, Pornichet is
extended on its eastern side

by several beaches and
smaller bays. "Port Niché"
(Nestling Harbour) began to
grow into a fashionable resort
in 1860, when publishers and
other literary people came to

**Detail from an elegant
villa in Pornichet**

enjoy the coast here. The
Plage des Libraires (Booksellers'
Beach) recalls those days.
   This smart resort boasts a
number of elegant villas built
between 1880 and 1930.

St-Nazaire ❺

Road map E4. 🏠 *66,000.*
🚉 🚌 ✈ *Nantes-Atlantique.*
🛈 *Submarine base; (02) 40 22 40 65.*
🏪 *Tue, Fri & Sun.* 🎭 *Les Escales,
Festival de Musiques du Monde (Aug),
Consonances (chamber music; Sep).*
www.saint-nazaire-tourisme.com

The great shipyards of St-
Nazaire began to develop in
the 19th century, when ships
too large to sail up the Loire
to Nantes would dock here.
The port is still a major
industrial and shipbuilding
centre today.
   The **Écomusée**, in the
harbour, illustrates the wildlife
and history of the Loire
estuary. It also gives access
to *L'Espadon*, a French
submarine built in 1957, in
which the life of submariners
is re-created. A monument
commemorating the abolition
of slavery stands near the
ecomuseum.
   The **Alstom Chantiers de
l'Atlantique**, shipyards from
which such legendary liners
as *Normandie* (1932) and
France (1960) were launched,
and where impressive cruise
liners are still built today, are
open to visitors.
   Escal-Atlantic, an exhibition
tracing the history of ocean
liners, is laid out in a huge
Nazi blockhouse in the
submarine base here.

🏛 **Alstom Chantiers de
l'Atlantique, Ecomusée,
Escal'Atlantic, L'Espadon
submarine**
Port de St-Nazaire. **Tel** (08) 10 88
84 44. ⬤ *Each site has different
opening hours, call for more
detailed information.* 📷

Pont de St-Nazaire over the Loire estuary, the longest bridge in France

Tour of the Parc Naturel Régional de la Grande Brière ❻

Consisting of a landscape of reed beds crossed by canals, the Parc Naturel Régional de la Grande Brière occupies the centre of the Presqu'île de Guérande. This natural environment of 40,000 ha (99,000 acres) was made a protected area in 1970. It has an abundant population of birds, and also contains about 2,000 traditional stone-built, thatched houses. One way of exploring the park is by boat, accompanied by local guide. Alternative ways to enjoy it are on foot, by bicycle, on horseback or by horse-drawn carriage.

Château de Ranrouet ①
The origins of this imposing fortress, now in ruins, go back to the 13th century.

Les Fossés-Blancs ②
This is Grande Brière's most northerly barge port. The botanical nature walk that has been created here follows the canal and then penetrates deep into the reed beds. Boats, with a guide, can be hired here.

St-Lyphard ③
From the belfry of the church in the village of St-Lyphard, there is a stunning view of Grande Brière.

Kerhinet ④
This village came to life again when Grande Brière was declared a protected area. It consists of a cluster of 18 thatched houses, one of which contains a restored bread oven. About 1 km (0.5 mile) further west is a well-preserved Neolithic galleried grave.

Bréca ⑤
This barge port is located at the western extremity of the Bréca Canal, which opened in 1937–8 and which crosses Grande Brière from east to west, starting at Rozé.

La Barbière ⑩
The Dolmen de la Barbière at Crossac testifies to human habitation of this area 5,000 years ago. There are also megaliths at Herbignac and St-Lyphard.

Chapelle-des-Marais ⑪
The Maison du Sabotier (Clogmaker's House) here is open to visitors. The church contains a statue of St Cornély, protector of horned animals, and in the village hall *(mairie)* the fossilized stump of a tree that grew in the marshes is on display.

Île de Fédrun ⑨
The centre of the island, inhabited since ancient times, was reserved for growing staple crops. A road running around the edge links the island's houses. The Maison de la Mariée (Bride's House), at No. 30, displays bridal headdresses.

Rozé ⑧
This port, with a lock on its west side, is the point from which the water level is controlled. It was through Rozé that peat, Grande Brière's "black gold", was transported. The Maison de l'Éclusier (lock-keeper's cottage) and Parc Animalier (small animal park) are open to the public.

Pont de Paille at Trignac ⑦
With its locks and pounds (holding areas for barges), Trignac is the largest barge port in Grande Brière. It is also known for its excellent fishing. The bridge spans the Canal de Rozé, one of the major canals across the reserve.

La Chaussée-Neuve ⑥
This barge port, which once handled consignments of peat, now attracts people who come to the park to fish and shoot. At the beginning of each year, reed-cutters land their harvest here. The reeds are used to roof the houses in Grande Brière.

Map labels:
D 50
⑪ Ste-Reine-de-Bretagne
D 33
PONTCHÂTEAU
D 4
D 50
Crossac
⑩
D 16
St-Joachim
⑨
Canal du Nord
Canal de Rozé
⑧
éca
Canal de Trignac
St-Malo-de-Guersac
D 50
Montoir-de-Bretagne
SAVENAY, NANTES
⑦
D 971
ST-BRÉVIN-LES-PINS
N 171

| 0 km | | 5 |
| 0 miles | | 3 |

KEY

▬ Suggested route

═ Other routes

☀ Viewpoint

Nantes ⑦

Historic capital of the dukes of Brittany, Nantes is today capital of the Pays de la Loire. Such dual importance enhances the cultural diversity of this vibrant city. Connected to the Atlantic via the wide lower reaches of the Loire, Nantes is a port city, and historically the slave trade ensured its prosperity. But, in the heart of vegetable-growing country, Nantes is now focused on a land-based economy. A stately city but

Cicada motif at La Cigale

also a modern metropolis, an industrial and cultural centre with a well-respected university, Nantes is one of the most dynamic towns in France, with a steadily growing population and pleasant, well-kept districts.

Doorway and balcony in Rue Kervégan

⌂ Place du Bouffay

This is the heart of Nantes, where the founders of the future city settled, near the confluence of the Loire and the Erdre. In the Middle Ages, a fortress (destroyed in the 18th century) was built to serve as a prison and law tribunal, and executions took place on the square.

The street names in the vicinity echo the past: Rue de la Bâclerie (Bolt Street), with 15th-century timber-framed houses, Rue de la Juiverie (Jewry Street), Rue des Halles (Market Street), Place du Pilori (Stocks Square). The Église Ste-Croix, on Place Ste-Croix, was begun in the 17th century and completed 200 years later. The clock and bell were transferred from the destroyed Tour du Bouffay in 1860. This pedestrianized area is a part of Nantes that has been least affected by the city's rapid development.

⌂ Quartier Graslin

Place Royale links the medieval quarter of Nantes with the Neo-Classical Quartier Graslin. Laid out by the architect Mathurin Crucy in 1790, the square is lined with tall residential buildings of elegant restrained design. The blue granite fountain, dating from 1865, is decorated with personifications of the Loire and its tributaries.

Statue in Passage Pommeraye

Place Graslin, nearby, is named after Jean Graslin, a Parisian barrister who came to seek his fortune in Nantes in 1750. A shrewd speculator, he purchased land and commissioned Crucy to develop the district. Part of this development was the Neo-Classical **theatre**, centre-piece of the square. The building, fronted by eight Corinthian columns crowned with eight muses, is a focal point of cultural life in Nantes.

Opposite stands **La Cigale**, a famous brasserie that opened in 1895. The decoration of the interior, by Émile Libaudière, is in the Art Nouveau style: large areas of dark wood carvings are surrounded by motifs in ceramic, wrought iron, mosaic and plaster, featuring stylized cicadas (cigales). This is somewhere to go as much to feast the eyes as to enjoy good food.

⌂ Île Feydeau

This district, a former island, was created when branches of the Loire were filled in in the 1930s and 1940s, and it is here that the wealth gener-ated by a profitable trade in slaves and sugar is most evident. The luxurious private residences here were built in the 18th century by traders who bought slaves with cheap jewellery, sold them and then returned from Africa with vessels loaded with sugar.

Allée Turenne, Allée Duguay-Trouin, Allée Brancas, **Rue Kervégan** and Place de la Petite-Hollande are lined with houses decorated with masks, shells, the faces of bearded spirits and ears of corn, and faced with wrought-iron balconies – all outward signs of wealth.

⌂ Passage Pommeraye

Opened in 1843, this unusual arcade is named after the man who built it. Pommeraye, a lawyer, joined forces with Guilloux, a restaurateur, to create the arcade, designed on the model of those that were built in Paris at the time.

The Neo-Classical theatre on Place Graslin

For hotels and restaurants in this region see pp230–31 and pp248–9

The shops, cafés and restaurants that opened here soon attracted Nantes' wealthy inhabitants. The film-maker Jacques Demy, who was born in Nantes, chose the arcade as the location for two of his films, *Lola* and *Une Chambre en Ville*. An elegant wooden staircase, decorated with lamps and statues, gives access to the arcade's three galleries, on different levels. Between those on the upper floor is a Neo-Classical porch decorated with medallions.

🏛 Musée Thomas Dobrée

18 Rue Voltaire. **Tel** (02) 40 71 03 50. ◯ *Tue–Fri, Sat & Sun pm. Renovation planned, call ahead.* 🖼

At the age of 28, Thomas Dobrée (1810–95), heir to a family business going back 300 years, turned down a career as a shipowner to concentrate on collecting art. In time, his collection came to encompass painting, sculpture and drawings, tapestries, furniture and porcelain, arms and armour, and religious art.

Painting of Louis XII and Anne of Brittany, Musée Thomas Dobrée

From 1862 until his death, Dobrée devoted himself to creating a suitable building in which to house the 10,000 pieces that his collection by then comprised. For this he commissioned the architect Viollet-le-Duc, who built the Neo-Gothic chateau that is now the Musée Thomas Dobrée.

Among the finest pieces on display here are a gold reliquary with a crown containing the heart of Anne of Brittany (1514), enamels, such as the 12th-century Reliquary of the True Cross, and the 13th-century Reliquary of

St Calminius. Engravings by Dürer, Schongauer, Rembrandt, Ruysdael and Jacques Callot are among the museum's masterpieces.

Two other buildings stand in the palace precinct. One is the Musée Archéologique is devoted to prehistory, ancient Egyptian and Greek artifacts and local Gaulish and Gallo-Roman history. The other is the Manoir de la Touche, which documents local history during the Revolution, especially the Vendée Wars.

NANTES CITY CENTRE

0 m 400
0 yards 400

Key to Symbols *see back flap*

Around the Chateau and Beyond

LU logo of c. 1930

The Château des Ducs de Bretagne *(see pp208–9)*, with Place du Bouffay and the Cathédrale St-Pierre-et-St-Paul, once formed the hub of Nantes. This nucleus is on the eastern side of the present city. The Jardin des Plantes, the Musée des Beaux-Arts and the picturesque Lieu Unique are other landmarks. The Musée Jules-Verne, devoted to this famous native of Nantes, is on the western side of the city, well beyond the port.

The Musée des Beaux-Arts, late 19th-century façade

⛪ Cathédrale St-Pierre-et-St-Paul

Place St-Pierre. ☐ *daily.* 📷
Standing on the site of a Roman building, vestiges of which remain in the crypt, the Flamboyant Gothic cathedral was begun in 1434. Its construction continued until the 19th century, when the apse was completed.

The cathedral has richly decorated doorways and an impressively lofty nave, 37 m (120 ft) high. The choir and ambulatory are lit by contemporary stained-glass windows. A fine example of the Renaissance style, the black and white marble tomb of Francis II and his wife Marguerite de Foix was carved by Michel Colombe in 1507. It is surrounded by allegorical statues; that of Justice is thought to portray their daughter, Anne of Brittany.

Porte St-Pierre, next to the cathedral and once part of the walls that surrounded Nantes, leads to Cours St-Pierre, a walkway where there are remains of the 13th-century ramparts. Impasse St-Laurent, on the left of the cathedral, leads to La Psalette, a charming Gothic house dating from the 15th century.

🏛 Musée des Beaux-Arts

10 Rue Georges-Clemenceau. **Tel** *(02) 51 17 45 00.* ☐ *Wed–Mon.* ⬤ *public holidays.* 📷
Built by the architect Josso, a native of Nantes, in the late 19th century, this is one of best designed museums of its period. The building is arranged around a large courtyard lit by natural light.

The ground floor, of simple design, is devoted to modern and contemporary art, from Impressionism to the present day, and including abstract art of the 1950s. Besides paintings by the Fauves and the Nabis, there are two Monets *(Waterlilies* and *Gondolas in Venice), Lighthouse at Antibes* by

Statue of Marguerite de Foix, Cathédrale St-Pierre-et-St-Paul

Signac, and works by Dufy, Émile Bernard, Mauffra and the Pont-Aven School *(see p169),* as well as 11 paintings by Kandinsky. Works by Manessier, Soulages and Bazaine represent more recent developments.

The first floor is devoted to major periods in the history of art from the 13th century to the first half of the 19th. The collection of early Italian painting includes a *Virgin in Majesty* by the Master of Bigallo (13th century), a *Madonna with Four Saints* (c. 1340) by Bernardo Daddi and *St Sebastian and a Franciscan Saint* (15th–16th century) by Perugino. A typically full-blooded Rubens, *Judas Maccabaeus*

THE REVOLUTION IN NANTES

During the civil war fought between royalists and republicans during the French Revolution, one man in particular stood out in the political climate that prevailed in Nantes. Jean-Baptiste Carrier, a member of the Convention (revolutionary assembly), was sent to Brittany on a mission to pacify the region. After the royalist Chouans were defeated at Savenay, he inflicted on the citizens of Nantes a cruel repression. He designed boats with a hull that could be opened when the vessel reached the middle of the Loire, drowning as many as 100 people at a time. "Republican weddings" consisted of tying a man and a woman together and tossing them into the river. Some 5,000 people lost their lives under this regime. Executions of royalists also took place on Place Viarme, in Nantes.

Mass drownings organized by Jean-Baptiste Carrier in Nantes in June 1793

Praying for the Dead (1635), provides a dramatic and strong contrast to peaceful Dutch and Flemish landscapes and still-life paintings.

French painting of the 17th century is represented by

Le Gaulage des Pommes, by Émile Bernard, Musée des Beaux-Arts

three works by Georges de la Tour, a master of the depiction of light: *The Hurdy-Gurdy Player, St Peter's Denial* and *Apparition of the Angel before St Joseph*.

Highlights of the 19th-century collections include works by Ingres, particularly his beautiful portrait of *Madame de Senonnes* (1814), by Delacroix *(Caid, Moroccan Chief)*, and by Corot *(Democrites and the Abderitans)*, as well as paintings by the Barbizon School. In the room devoted to Courbet, the subject-matter and composition of *The Gleaners* demonstrates his skill as a realist.

🏛 Usine LU, Lieu Unique

Rue de la Biscuiterie, Quai Ferdinand-Favre. *Tel (02) 40 12 14 34.* ☐ Tue–Sun pm. 🎫 📷

The history of Nantes is inseparable from that of the almost legendary biscuit, the Petit-Beurre LU, which people have enjoyed for over a century.

In 1846, the Lefèvre-Utile, a couple from Lorraine who settled in Nantes, opened their first pâtisserie. To challenge competition from British imports, they began making biscuits on an industrial scale and in 1885 built a factory. The Petit-Beurre was launched, followed by the Paille d'Or. From 1913, the factory turned out 20 tonnes of biscuits per day. When it became too small to meet the growing demand, the site was abandoned.

Threatened with demolition in 1995, the factory was rescued and, since 1999, what became known as the Lieu Unique (Unique Place) has become a cultural centre where festivals, shows and exhibitions take place. It is very popular with the people of Nantes.

🌿 Jardin des Plantes

Boulevard Stalingrad & Place Sophie-Trébuchet. ☐ daily.

Opened in the early 19th century, the botanical garden – the second-largest in France after the Jardin des Plantes in Paris – covers 7 ha (17 acres) and contains 12,000 species of plants. It was originally a garden of mostly medicinal plants, but sea captains brought back exotic specimens that rapidly broadened its scope. Today, the garden contains over 200 varieties of camellia,

which flourish beneath the oldest magnolias in Europe. In the tropical greenhouses flourish a great many species of orchid.

🏛 Musée Jules-Verne

3 Rue de l'Hermitage. *Tel (02) 40 69 72 52.* ☐ Wed–Mon. ● Tue, Sun am & public holidays. 🎫 📷 Jul–Aug.

This small house at the top of a steep street is the birthplace of the writer Jules Verne. The museum that it now contains gives a detailed account of his life and work, and of the peculiar world that he created in his novels. Books, souvenirs, quotations, humorous drawings, cards, magic lanterns and models draw the visitor into the imaginary world created by the writer. There is also furniture from his house in Amiens, where Verne spent most of his life.

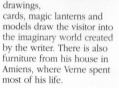

Jules Verne, born in Nantes in 1828

Environs

The 11th-century **Château de Goulaine**, 13 km (8 miles) southeast of Nantes, contains a collection of tropical butterflies, and an exhibition documenting the history of the LU biscuit factory. The reception rooms are sumptuously decorated.

♣ Château de Goulaine

Haute-Goulaine. *Tel (02) 40 54 91 42.* ☐ Easter–Nov: Sat–Sun & public holidays: pm; mid-Jul–mid-Sep: Wed–Mon pm. 🎫 📷 for groups, all year round by arrangement. ♿

The Jardin des Plantes, botanical gardens laid out as a park in the English style

Château des Ducs de Bretagne

On the banks of the Loire, the Château des Ducs de Bretagne was founded in the 13th century, and served both as a residential palace and military fortress. Anne of Brittany was born here in 1477, and it is here that Henry IV is supposed to have signed the Edict of Nantes in 1598. Over the centuries, the castle was continually remodelled. The sturdy towers and drawbridge, part of the fortifications, are counterbalanced by delicate Renaissance buildings facing on to the courtyard. Converted into barracks in the 18th century, the castle passed into state ownership after World War I. A restoration programme to return the buildings to their original appearance was carried out between 1993 and 2006, and the castle now contains a major museum of the history of Nantes.

★ Grand Logis
The façade bears the coat of arms of Louis XII and Anne of Brittany.

Tour du Port was hidden by a bastion for 200 years. The bastion was demolished in 1853.

Entrance to museum

Courtine de la Loire, the wall linking Tour de la Rivière and Tour du Port, was built in the 15th and 16th centuries.

Petit Gouvernement
Built in the 16th century, during the reign of Francis I, the king's apartments are now known as the Petit Gouvernement (Governor's Small Palace). The dormer windows are typical of the Renaissance.

ILLUSTRIOUS GUESTS

**Henry IV
(1553–1610)**

Many famous people have passed through the gates of the Château des Ducs de Bretagne. The wedding of Francis II of Brittany and Marguerite de Foix took place here in 1471, and it was also here that their daughter, Anne, Duchess of Brittany, was married to Louis XII in 1499. In 1532, Francis I of France came here to mark the "permanent union of the duchy and country of Brittany with the kingdom of France", as an inscription in the courtyard recalls. Henry II, then Charles IX, also stayed in the castle. In 1598, Henry IV thrashed out the terms of the Edict de Nantes, which legalized Protestantism. He may even have signed the edict at the castle. Louis XIV also stayed here when he came to Nantes in 1661, during a gathering of the States of Brittany.

Tour de la Rivière
Forming part of the castle's system of defences, the Tour de la Rivière consists of two floors with a terrace above.

For hotels and restaurants in this region see pp230–31 and pp248–9

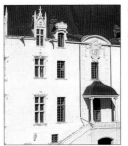

Grand Gouvernement
The ducal palace, known since the 17th century as the Grand Gouvernement (Governor's Great Palace), has been restored to its original splendour. The double staircase leads up to a single row of steps beneath a porch.

VISITORS' CHECKLIST

4 Place Marc-Elder.
Tel *08 11 46 46 44.*
Ramparts and courtyard *daily.* **Musée d'Histoire** *Wed–Sun.* *(museum only; moat ditches, courtyard and sentry walk free).*
www.chateau-nantes.fr

The castle museum is devoted to regional folk art of the 16th to 20th centuries.

★ Vieux Donjon
The polygonal keep, built in the 14th century on the orders of John IV de Montfort, is the oldest part of the castle. It is attached to the 18th-century caretaker's lodge.

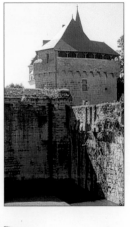

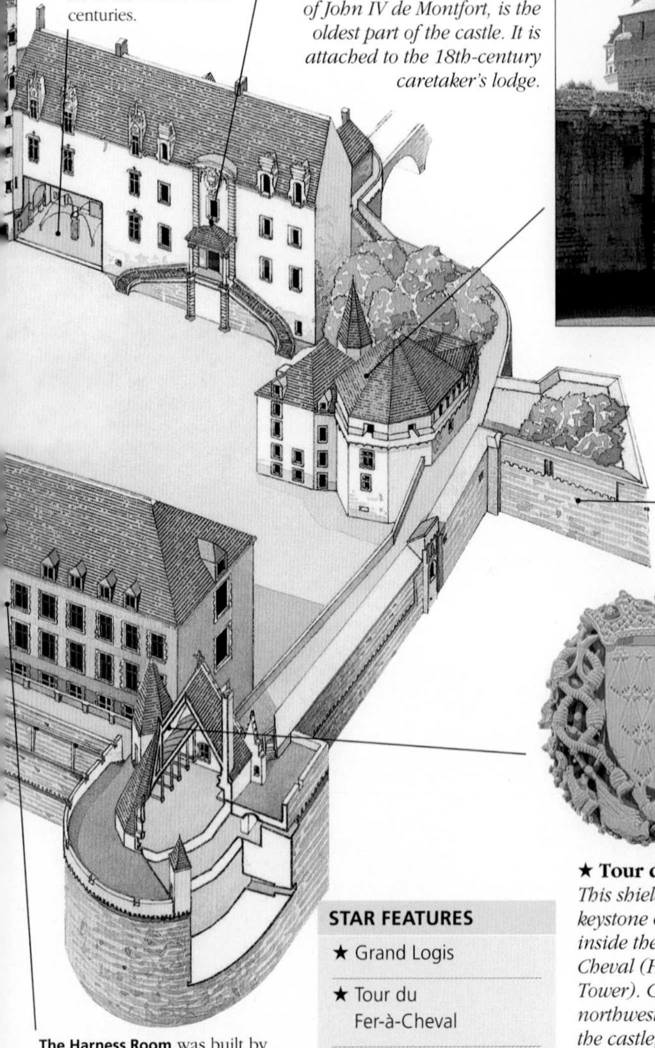

Bastion St-Pierre, built in the 16th century, was levelled off in 1904

★ Tour du Fer-à-Cheval
This shield decorates the keystone of the vaulting inside the Tour du Fer-à-Cheval (Horseshoe Tower). Guarding the northwest corner of the castle, it is a fine example of 15th-century military architecture.

STAR FEATURES

- ★ Grand Logis
- ★ Tour du Fer-à-Cheval
- ★ Vieux Donjon

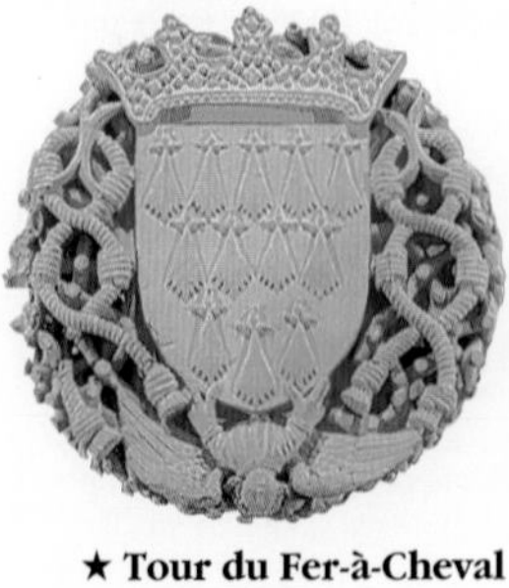

The Harness Room was built by the army in the 17th and 18th centuries.

The thalassotherapy centre on Plage de l'Alliance, in Pornic

Pornic ❽

Road map E5. 🏠 *14,000.* 🚉 🚌
🛥 ℹ️ *Place de la Gare; (02) 40 82 04 40.* 🏪 *Thu & Sun.* 🎭 *spring carnival (Apr), free festivals (Jul–Aug).*

A small fishing harbour, Pornic is also a coastal resort with yachting harbours and a **thalassotherapy centre**. The lower town, with brightly painted fishermen's houses, is dominated by the outline of the castle, which was owned by Gilles de Rais *(see p41)* in the 15th century. It was remodelled by Viollet-le-Duc in the 19th century. The coast road beyond Pornic is lined with 19th-century villas where the writers Michelet and Flaubert, as well as the painter Renoir, once stayed.

St-Michel-Chef-Chef, 9 km (5 miles) further north, is renowned for its biscuits made with salted butter, and for its wide beach.

Pays de Retz ❾

Road map E5. Machecoul. Between the D751 and the D13. 🚉 🚌 *Nantes.*
ℹ️ *3 Chausée du Pays de Retz Bernerie; (02) 40 82 70 99.*

Machecoul, once the capital of the Pays de Retz, was the fiefdom of Gilles de Rais, the local Bluebeard *(see p41).* The ruins of one of his castles still stand here.

The **Musée du Pays de Retz** at Bourgneuf-en-Retz, 12 km (9 miles) further west on the D13, describes the local salt-panning and fishing industries, as well as the crafts of the past. Les Moutiers-en-Retz, on the

coast, owes its name to two 11th-century monasteries. Vestiges of these buildings can be seen in the Église St-Pierre, which was built in the 16th century in the Gothic style. Close to this church is an 11th-century lantern whose flame was intended to cast light into the darkness for the benefit of the dead.

The Lac de Grand-Lieu, to the east, is an unusually rich bird sanctuary. The **Maison du Lac** here documents the local wildlife, including 225 species of birds, among which are heron and teal. Built in the 9th century, the Carolingian abbey church of **Abbaye de St-Philbert**, at St Philbert-de-Grand-Lieu, is one of the oldest churches in France. In the crypt lies the tomb of St Philbert, the abbey's founder.

🏛 **Musée du Pays de Retz**
Rue des Moines, Bourgneuf-en-Retz.
***Tel** (02) 40 21 40 83.* ⏰ *Apr–Oct: Tue–Sun.* ⬤ *Dec–Mar.* ♿

🏹 **Maison du Lac**
St-Philbert-de-Grand-Lieu.
***Tel** (02) 40 78 73 88.* ⏰ *Apr–Sep: daily; Oct–Mar: Tue–Sat, Sun pm.*

⛪ **Abbaye de St-Philbert**
ℹ️ *St-Philbert de Grand-Lieu; (02) 40 78 73 88.* ⏰ *daily.*

Clisson ❿

Road map F5. *20 km (12 miles) south of Nantes via the D59.* 🏠
5,900. 🚌 *Place du Minage; (02) 40 54 02 95.* 🏪 *Tue, Wed & Fri.* 🎭 *Les Italiennes de Clisson (theatre, music & film, Jul), Les Médiévales (Aug).*

A romantic dream led to the development of Clisson. In the 19th century, the Cacault brothers, natives of Nantes who loved Italy, built themselves a Tuscan-style villa here. This set a trend, and ochre-walled, red-roofed houses, in contrast to those roofed in the customary slate, began to spring up.

Although it is in ruins, the **Château de Clisson** here, built in stages between the 13th and the 16th centuries, well illustrates the evolution of military architecture.

La Garenne Lemot, an estate on the eastern exit from the town, has two further examples of the Italianate style: the estate office, by the architect Crucy (1815), and the Villa Lemot, designed by the sculptor Lemot (1824). The surrounding parkland is decorated with antique columns, obelisks, follies and other ornaments.

Muscadet and Gros Plant vines are grown in the vineyards between Clisson and the Loire.

♟ **Château de Clisson**
Place du Minage. ***Tel** (02) 40 54 02 95.* ⏰ *Oct–Apr: Wed–Sun pm; May–Sep: Wed–Mon.* 🖼 📷

🌿 **La Garenne Lemot**
Gétigné. ***Tel** (02) 40 54 75 85.*
⏰ *Park: daily.* **Estate office:** *Apr–Sep: daily; Oct–Mar: Tue–Sun pm.* **Villa Lemot:** *temporary exhibitions.*

Château de Clisson at Place du Minage

Pays d'Ancenis ⑪

Road map F4. Ancenis. 30 km
(19 miles) east of Nantes via the A11
or the N23. 🏠 *7,000*. 🚉 🚌 *Nantes-
Atlantique*. 🛈 *27 Rue du Château;
(02) 40 83 07 44*. 🎪 *Fête de la Loire
et des Vins (every two years in May,
next festival 2011)*. 🛒 *Thu*.

This area of countryside,
whose focal point is the town
of Ancenis, flanks a stretch of
the Loire that in places runs
between high cliffs.

Ancenis, set in the midst of
vineyards, has some elegant
wine merchants' houses and a
16th-century **chateau**.

Further downstream is the
Donjon d'Oudon, a 14th-
century keep. Overlooking
Ancenis, the keep is also
ideally situated to survey the
Loire, once the main traffic
artery in western France.
Further upstream is Varades.
The elegant 19th-century
Italian-style **chateau** here was
built by an engineer who had
made his fortune during the
reign of Napoleon III.

♦ **Château d'Ancenis**
Rue du Pont. **Tel** *(02) 40 83 87 00.*
🗓 *exterior of the castle, Jul–Aug.*

♦ **Donjon d'Oudon**
Rue du Pont-Levis. **Tel** *(02) 40
83 60 17.* ⬭ *Mar: Sun & public
hols; Apr–Sep: daily; Oct: Sat &
Sun.* 🎫

♦ **Château de Varades**
Palais Briau. **Tel** *(02) 40 83 45 00.*
⬭ **Park:** *Apr–Sep: daily pm.* **Palais:**
*Apr–Sep: Sat, Sun & public holidays
pm; Aug: daily pm.* 🎫

The Nantes–Brest Canal at Blain, just south of the Forêt du Gâvre

Châteaubriant ⑫

Road map F3. 🏠 *13,380*.
🚉 🚌 🛈 *Rue de Couéré
(02) 40 28 20 90.* 🛒 *Wed am.*
🎪 *Foire de Béré (Sep).*
www.tourisme-chateaubriant.fr

The few surviving schist-built
medieval houses here give
the walled town of
Châteaubriant a historic
atmosphere. Two **chateaux**
stand in close proximity on a
hill overlooking the Chère

South gallery of the Renaissance
chateau in Châteaubriant

river: a medieval fortress,
with a keep, and an elegant
Renaissance chateau with a
main building flanked by wings.

The Romanesque Église
St-Jean-de-Béré, built in
contrasting blue schist and
red granite, contains a 17th-
century Baroque altarpiece.

♦ **Chateaux**
Access via Place Charles-de-Gaulle.
Tel *(02) 40 28 20 20.* ⬭ *May–Sep:
Wed–Mon.* 🗓 *interiors of the
castles.* 🎫 *(entry to the park is free)*

Forêt du Gâvre ⑬

Road map E4. Blain. 35 km (22
miles) north of Nantes via the N137
then the D164. 🏠 *7,450.* 🛈 *2 Place
Jean-Guilhard; (02) 40 87 15 11.* 🛒
Tue & Sat am. 🎪 *St-Laurent (Aug).*

Covering a large massif
enclosed by the Don, Isac
and Brivet rivers, the forest is
good walking country. There
is also an interesting museum
and a chateau to explore here.

The **Musée des Arts et
Traditions Populaires**, in
Blain, on the D164, is devoted
to daily life in the early 20th
century. The **Château de la
Groulais**, in the direction of
St-Nazaire, was the residence
of the Clisson and Rohan
families during the Middle
Ages. Temporary exhibitions
are held here.

🏛 **Musée des Arts et
Traditions Populaires**
2 Place Jean-Guilhard, Blain. **Tel** *(02)
40 79 98 51.* ⬭ *Tue–Sat, pm.* 🎫

♦ **Château de la Groulais**
South exit from Blain. **Tel** *(02) 40 79
07 81.* ⬭ *May–Oct: Tue–Sun.* ⬤
*Nov–Mar: groups only, by
arrangement.* 🎫

VENDÉE WARS

In 1793, the persecution of the clergy, the execution of
Louis XVI and a rise in taxation provoked an anti-republican
uprising in the Vendée. Royalists soon followed up with acts
of barbarism, and the execution of republicans in Machecoul
began on 11 March. Catelineau, a carter, and Stofflet, a

Republican prisoners being
given their freedom

gamekeeper, joined by various
aristocrats, stirred up revolt
among the peasantry. In June,
the Armée Catholique et Royale
Vendée seized control of the
Vendée, as well as the towns of
Saumur and Angers, but it was
defeated by the republicans at
Cholet on 17 October. On the
orders of General Turreau, the
latter led punitive expeditions
in the Vendée in 1794–5.

TRAVELLERS' NEEDS

WHERE TO STAY

For many decades, Brittany has been among the most popular tourist destinations in France. As a result, the region is well equipped to cater for the needs of visitors. From grand chateaux to basic camping sites, and including establishments in the familiar hotel chains, there is accommodation to suit every taste and budget, and even in individual locations the choice is wide.

Accommodation in Brittany's coastal resorts is, of course, more varied and plentiful than that available inland, even though there is much to interest visitors in areas away from Brittany's coasts. While the resorts are oriented towards holiday-makers' enjoyment of beaches, watersports and sailing, a warm welcome at a guesthouse inland brings visitors closer to the soul of Brittany.

RESERVATIONS

In the summer holiday season, Brittany, like any other area that attracts large numbers of visitors, becomes very crowded. This particularly applies during school holidays and over long holiday weekends, and also when local festivals and other events take place.

It is therefore essential to book your accommodation well in advance. Branches of the French Tourist Office hold a list of hotels in Brittany and can make a reservation for you. Outside the busiest periods, it is best to make a reservation by contacting your chosen hotel direct. Whether you would like to stay in a hotel of character and atmosphere, or prefer guesthouse accommodation *(chambres d'hôtes)*, and whether you have in mind a particular area of Brittany or simply need a suggestion for a weekend break, the **Maison de la Bretagne** can provide all the necessary information.

HOTEL CATEGORIES

The French Ministry of Tourism grades hotels into five categories, with a rating of one to five stars. This

The Hôtel Castel Marie-Louise in La Baule *(see p230)*

rating gives an idea both of the size of the rooms on offer, and also of the facilities available.

A two-star hotel, for example, will have a lift if there are four or more floors, and there will be a telephone in each room. Some of the more modest establishments have a no-star rating.

PRICES

In Brittany, as in the rest of France, advertised prices include tax and service. Charges are per room rather than per person, except when board or half-board is offered. In country areas, half-board may be compulsory, or indeed may even be the sole option when the hotel is the only place in the town or village where visitors can have a meal.

Most establishments through all categories make a small charge for a third person or a child sharing a double room.

A room with shower is usually about 20 per cent cheaper than one with bath.

Some establishments may close during the winter. However, those that stay open may offer advantageous rates during the low season. Information on off-season rates and deals is available from travel agents or directly from the hotels themselves.

CHAIN HOTELS

The large hotel chains have establishments all over Brittany. Among them is **Groupe Envergure**, which includes hotels forming part of the Balladins, Campanile, Climat de France, Kyriad, Bleu Marine, Première Classe, Nuit d'Hôtel, Clarine and Côte à Côte sub-chains.

As with those in the older-established **Ibis**, **Mercure** and **Novotel** chains, strict controls ensure that these establishments offer a high standard of comfort and cleanliness and an excellent range of facilities. **Formule 1** and **B+B Hotels** are hotel chains designed to provide basic facilities at a low price.

Villa Kerasy in Vannes *(see p230)*
◁ Interior of La Cigale, Nantes

TRADITIONAL FAMILY-RUN HOTELS

Establishments affiliated to **Logis de France**, the leading independent association of hotels in Europe, will suit visitors who prefer smaller hotels with local character. Identifiable by a green and yellow logo *(see p217)*, hotels in this chain offer a more personal welcome and an authentic flavour of their particular locality. The hotels themselves are usually buildings of character that are very much in keeping with their surroundings.

Relais du Silence is an affiliation of distinguished hotels with a friendly atmosphere and where peace and relaxation are a prime consideration. They have a two-star to five-star rating.

LUXURY HOTELS

Those who like a little luxury and a memorable gastronomic experience will not be disappointed by the finest hotels in Brittany. A number of chateaux and listed buildings have been converted into upmarket hotel-restaurants, some of which employ the services of prestigious chefs. Such hotels are ideal for visitors seeking the very best in French hospitality and cuisine.

Establishments of this type belong to either of two main associations. One is **Relais et Châteaux**, with eight hotel-restaurants in Brittany, including the Château de

The Grand Hôtel des Thermes in St-Malo *(see p220)*

Locguénolé in Hennebont *(see p228)*, the Auberge Bretonne in La Roche-Bernard *(see p229)* and Le Castel Marie-Louise in La Baule *(see p230)*. The other is **Châteaux et Hôtels de France**, with nine establishments in Brittany, including the Hôtel Reine Hortense in Dinard *(see p218)*.

THALASSOTHERAPY

This therapeutic treatment uses the curative powers of sea water, which is rich in iodine and trace elements, and whose curative effects and revitalizing properties are widely known. Between St-Malo in the north and La Baule in the south, there are 11 thalassotherapy centres along the coasts of Brittany. Among the best known are the Institut de Thalassothérapie de Quiberon *(see p175)* and the Thermes Marins in St-Malo, where there are six sea-water swimming pools.

Thalassotherapy centres offer several options that also include accommodation. There are, for instance, anti-stress treatments, cures to

combat the effects of smoking, and post-natal courses. Full details on thassalotherapy in Brittany is available from the **Comité Régional du Tourisme de Bretagne** *(see p216)*.

CHAMBRES D'HÔTES

Private houses with rooms to let *(chambres d'hôtes)* are becoming increasingly numerous in Brittany. This option has many advantages. Staying in a private house provides the opportunity to meet local people and to experience Breton culture at a more authentic level than is possible when staying in a hotel.

When guesthouses provide meals, this is also an opportunity to enjoy local specialities in informal surroundings and for considerably less than the price of a restaurant meal.

A list of private houses offering *chambres d'hôtes* is available from local tourist offices. *Chambres d'Hôtes en Bretagne*, a full listing giving all details, is published by **Gîtes de France**.

The Hôtel Reine Hortense in Dinard *(see p218)*

The Hôtel Ker Moor in St-Quay-Portrieux *(see p222)*

COUNTRY GÎTES

Often on farm premises, country gîtes *(gîtes ruraux)* are fully furnished, fully equipped houses or apartments built in the local rural style. Their setting and immediate surroundings are far superior to that of most other types of rented accommodation.

One of the best-known organizations to which country gîtes are affiliated is **Gîtes de France**, which has several local offices in Brittany and which publishes four handbooks, listing gîtes in the Côtes d'Armor, the Morbihan, Finistère and Ille-et-Vilaine respectively.

Gîtes de France also issues lists of specific types of accommodation in Brittany: these are *gîtes de caractère* (picturesque houses), *gîtes de pêche* (for fishing), *gîtes d'étape* (dormitory accommodation for groups), *gîtes Panda* (in the Parc Naturel Régional d'Armorique; *see pp140–1), chalets loisirs* (for outdoor activities), gîtes for people with disabilites and gîtes suitable for elderly

people. The association also issues a free guide, *Bienvenue à la Ferme en Bretagne*.

SELF-CATERING ACCOMMODATION

Local estate and letting agents hold lists of houses and apartments that can be rented for holidays. Rental is by the week, usually starting on Saturdays. Weekend bookings may also be possible, except in the high season. Local tourist offices in Brittany will provide lists of self-catering accommodation with contact details for booking. It is advisable to obtain full information, including the name of the local organization in charge of self-catering accommodation.

DIRECTORY

French Government Tourist Offices

UK: *Lincoln House, 300 High Holborn, London WC1V 7JH.* **Tel** *020 7062 6600 (within UK only).*
www.franceguide.com
www.en-france.com
US (east coast):
825 Third Avenue, 29th floor, New York 10022.
Tel *514 288 1904.*
US (mid-west): *205 North Michigan Ave, Suite 3770, Chicago, IL 60601.*
Tel *(312) 0327 0290.*
US (west coast): *9454 Wilshire Bd, Suite 210, Beverly Hills, CA 90212.*
Tel *(210) 514 288 1904.*

Comité Régional de Tourisme de Bretagne
1 Rue Raoul-Ponchon, 35069 Rennes.
Tel *(02) 99 36 15 15.*
www.brittanytourism.com

Maison de la Bretagne
203 Bd St-Germain, 75007 Paris.
Tel *(01) 53 63 11 50.*
www.tourisme bretagne.com

YOUTH HOSTELS

Youth Hostel Association (YHA)
Trevelyan House, Dimple Road, Matlock, Derbyshire DE4 3YH.
Tel *01629 592 600.*
www.yha.org.uk

Hostelling International-American Youth Hostels (HI-AYH)
8401 Colesville Road, Suite 600, Silver Spring MD 2091D.
Tel *301 495 1240.*
www.hiusa.org

CROUS
2 Avenue le Gorgeu, BP 88710, 2987 Brest.
Tel *(02) 98 03 86 28.*
7 Place Hoche, BP 115, 35002 Rennes Cedex.
Tel *(02) 99 84 31 31.*
www.crous-rennes.fr

CAMPING

Fédération Française de Camping et de Caravaning
78 Rue de Rivoli, 75004 Paris.
Tel *01 42 72 84 08.*
www.ffcc.fr

CHAIN HOTELS

B&B Hotels
Tel *08 92 78 29 29.*
www.hotel-bb.com

Groupe Envergure
Tel *(02) 96 62 72 01.*
www.envergure.fr

Formule 1
Tel *0892 685 685.*
www.hotelformule1.com

Ibis, Novotel, Sofitel, Mercure
Tel *0870 609 0961 UK.*
www.accorhotels.com

TRADITIONAL HOTELS

Logis de France
Tel *(01) 45 84 83 84.*
www.logis-de-france.fr

Relais du Silence
Tel *(01) 44 49 90 00.*
www.relaisdusilence.com

LUXURY HOTELS

Relais et Châteaux
Tel *0825 32 32 32.*
www.relaischateaux.com

Châteaux et Hôtels de France
84 Avenue Victor Cresson, 92441 Issy-les-Moulineaux.
Tel *(01) 58 00 22 00.*
www.chateauhotels. com

GÎTES DE FRANCE

59 Rue St-Lazare, 75439 Paris. **Tel** *(01) 49 70 75 75.*
www.gites-de-france.fr

Côtes d'Armor
7 Rue St-Benoît, BP 4536, 22045 St-Brieuc.
Tel *(02) 96 62 21 73.*

Finistère
5 Allée Sully, 29322 Quimper.
Tel *(02) 98 64 20 20.*

Ille-et-Vilaine
107 Avenue Henri Fréville, BP 70336, 35203 Rennes.
Tel *(02) 99 22 68 68.*

Loire-Atlantique
3–5 Rue Félibien, BP 93218, 44032 Nantes.
Tel *(02) 51 72 95 65.*

Morbihan
42 Avenue Président Wilson, BP 30318, 56403 Auray. **Tel** *(02) 97 56 48*
12.Gîtes de France brochures are obtainable from French Government Tourist Offices.

A pretty youth hostel close to the old town district of Quimper

YOUTH HOSTELS

Some of the least expensive accommodation is provided by youth hostels *(auberges de jeunesse)*. This is available to everyone, regardless of age, as long as they have a **Youth Hostel Association** or *Hostelling International* card. If you are not a member of the YHA in your home country, you will have to pay a surcharge each time you stay in a French youth hostel.

A full list of youth hostels is available from the association. During the summer, students may also stay in rooms at student lodgings at universities. These rooms can be booked through **CROUS (Centre Régional des Oeuvres Universitaires)**.

CAMPSITES

Many campsites in Brittany have exceptionally fine locations, perhaps beside the sea or, inland, deep in a forest.

Lists of campsites are available from the tourist offices of each *département* of Brittany. Advance booking is advised.

The **Fédération Française de Camping et de Caravaning** publishes an official guide of approved campsites. The Association des Gîtes de France also provides a guide to campsites on farms and publishes *Campings Verts en Bretagne (Green Campsites in Brittany)*.

Campsites are subject to an official classification system, which runs from a one-star to a four-star rating according to toilet, washing and facilities such as public telephones, swimming pools and television. Three- and four-star sites are usually impressively spacious with plenty of amenities and electricity connections for tents and caravans. One- and two-star sites, often in more

Gîtes de France logo

remote areas, always have toilets, a public phone and running water (sometimes only cold on one-star sites). It is sometimes possible to hire tents and camper vans, or rent bungalows.

Camping rough at one of the unofficial camp sites along the coast also has its attractions. Such sites often have stunning locations and charge very little.

DISABLED TRAVELLERS

Various organizations provide information on holidays and establishments with facilities for disabled people. The **GIHP** (Groupement pour l'Insertion des Personnes Handicappés Physiques), the **Association des Plysés de France** and its travel branch, APF Evasion, **Voyages ASAH** and the **EPAL** (Association Évasion en Pays d'Accueil et de Loisirs) all organize holidays for disabled people. The **CNRH** (Comité National pour la Réadaptation des Handicapés) and the Association des Paralysés de France have local offices that issue lists of establishments adapted for people with disabilities. **Gîtes de France** publish a list of gîtes with wheelchair access and special equipment.

The **CIDJ** (Centre d'Information et de Documentation Jeunesse) has information for young disabled travellers. For details, *see p264*.

Camper vans at a site on Pointe de l'Arcouest, on the Côtes d'Armor *(see p99)*

Choosing a Hotel

Hotels have been selected across a wide price range on the basis of their facilities, good value, and location. Hotels in Brittany are generally not air-conditioned unless stated here. Check ahead also for wheelchair access and disabled facilities. The hotels in this chart are listed by area. For map references, *see inside back cover.*

PRICE CATEGORIES
The following price ranges are for a standard double room and taxes per night during the high season. Breakfast is not included, unless specified.

€ under 60 euros
€€ 60–80 euros
€€€ 80–110 euros
€€€€ 110–150 euros
€€€€€ over 150 euros

ILLE-ET-VILAINE

BAZOUGES-LA-PÉROUSE Château de la Ballue
P €€€€€

Bazouges-la-Pérouse, 35560 **Tel** *02 99 97 47 86* **Fax** *02 99 97 47 70* **Rooms** *5*   **Map** *F2*

Situated just 14 km (9 miles) north of Combourg, this elegant 17th-century château is set in landscaped gardens with topiary twists, a labyrinth and sculptures. The large, luxurious rooms are decorated with period furnishings, canopied beds, antiques and works of art. Closed Jan–mid-Feb. **www.laballue.com**

CANCALE Le Grand Large
€€

4 Quai Jacques Cartier, 35260 **Tel** *02 99 89 82 90* **Fax** *02 99 89 79 03* **Rooms** *13*   **Map** *E1*

In a quaint ivy-clad building, this hotel has panoramic views of the sea. The comfortable, well-maintained rooms are traditionally furnished, with a dash of colour in the decor adding a modern touch. The restaurant has tables on the terrace overlooking the bay and serves good seafood platters. **www.hotellegrandlarge.com**

CANCALE La Maison de la Marine
P €€€€

23 Rue de la Marine, 35260 **Tel** *02 99 89 88 53* **Fax** *02 99 89 83 27* **Rooms** *5*   **Map** *E1*

Not far from the Sentiers de Douaniers, this 17th-century stone building has recently renovated rooms that are sumptuous with period furniture, parquet floors and rich Baroque-style fabrics, but also have wireless Internet access. There is a pretty garden with a large sunny terrace and gazebo. Closed Jan. **www.maisondelamarine.com**

CHÂTEAUBOURG Pen'Roc
€€€

La Penière en St Didier, 35221 **Tel** *02 99 00 33 02* **Fax** *02 99 62 30 89* **Rooms** *29*   **Map** *F3*

A short drive from Rennes, this family hotel is located in the Vitré countryside. It was originally an old Breton farmhouse, but the rooms are modern and there are excellent facilities that include a sauna, *hammam* (Turkish bath) and Jacuzzi. Regional dishes are served in the restaurant. **www.penroc.fr**

COMBOURG Hôtel du Château
P €€

1 Place Chateaubriand, 35270 **Tel** *02 99 73 00 38* **Fax** *02 99 73 25 79* **Rooms** *33*   **Map** *E2*

Near Chateaubriand's former home, this granite stone hotel has comfortable, individually decorated rooms, some of which are quite spacious. The restaurant serves regional specialities, and romantic candle-lit dinners can be reserved in the adjoining tower room. Closed mid-Dec–mid-Jan. **www.hotelduchateau.com**

DINARD Hôtel Printania
€€

5 Ave Georges V, 35801 **Tel** *02 99 46 13 07* **Fax** *02 99 46 26 32* **Rooms** *57*   **Map** *E1*

This friendly family-run hotel is decorated in typical Breton style with ornate box beds, Quimper faience *(see pp164–5)* and carved wooden furniture. Located near the beach, it offers fine sea views. The restaurant specializes in seafood and fish, served by staff in traditional costume. **www.printaniahotel.com**

DINARD Hôtel Reine Hortense
P €€€€€

19 Rue Malouine, 35800 **Tel** *02 99 46 54 31* **Fax** *02 99 88 15 88* **Rooms** *8*   **Map** *E1*

Built by a Russian Prince in 1907 as a tribute to Queen Hortense of the Netherlands, this charming *belle époque* villa offers both a stunning view of St-Malo and an intimate atmosphere. The rooms are decorated with many period pieces. There is private access to the Plage de L'Ecluse. Closed Oct–Mar. **www.villa-reine-hortense.com**

DOL DE BRETAGNE Domaine des Ormes
€€€

Epiniac, 35120 **Tel** *02 99 73 53 00* **Fax** *02 99 73 53 55* **Rooms** *45*   **Map** *E2*

The hotel is part of a privately-owned holiday resort with an 18-hole golf course, aquaparc, horseriding school and adventure park. It has charming guestrooms – there are even five cosy tree-houses with rooms, accessible by rope ladder! The restaurant serves classic French food. **www.lesormes.com**

FOUGÈRES Les Voyageurs
€€

10 Place Gambetta, 35300 **Tel** *02 99 99 08 20* **Fax** *02 99 99 99 04* **Rooms** *37*   **Map** *F2*

Located near the ramparts in the heart of the upper town, this is a fine 1900s hotel. The rooms are prettily decorated, and the modern facilities include wireless Internet access. A copious buffet breakfast is served. Closed over Christmas and New Year. **www.hotel-fougeres.fr**

Key to Symbols *see back cover flap*

HÉDÉ Hostellerie du Vieux Moulin

P **11** **杰** €

La Vallée du Moulin **Tel** *02 99 45 45 70* **Fax** *02 99 45 44 86* **Rooms** *13* **Map** *E2*

A 17th-century creeper-clad long, stone building, which was once a miller's residence, has simply furnished and bright bedrooms. All have a private bathroom and overlook the attractive garden that contains the ruins of a watermill. The restaurant, with traditional Breton furniture and oak beams, is a little sombre in style. Closed Jan.

LA GUERCHE DE BRETAGNE Hôtel Calèche

P **11** €€

16 Avenue Générale Leclerc, 35130 **Tel** *02 99 96 21 63* **Fax** *02 99 96 49 52* **Rooms** *12* **Map** *F3*

Ideally situated for visiting the Roche aux Fées, this delightful manor house is set in a peaceful garden planted with ancient plane trees. The rooms are pleasant, simply furnished and unpretentious. The restaurant serves traditional cuisine. The village market on Tuesdays is one of the best in Brittany.

LE VIVIER-SUR-MER Hôtel de Bretagne

P **11** **杰** **灯** €€

Rond-Point du Centre, 35960 **Tel** *02 99 48 91 74* **Fax** *02 99 48 81 10* **Rooms** *17* **Map** *E2*

Recently renovated, this traditional Breton hotel offers a good view of the bay of St-Michel and is good value. Its guestrooms are well-maintained and pleasant, and there is a panoramic restaurant specializing in seafood dishes, as well as a sauna and a gym. Closed mid-Nov–Feb. **www.logisdefrance.com**

MONT-ST-MICHEL Croix Blanche

11 **杰** €€€

16 Grand Rue, 50116 **Tel** *02 33 60 14 04* **Fax** *02 33 48 59 82* **Rooms** *9* **Map** *F2*

Sheltered by the ramparts, this quaint hotel has small, yet cosy, bedrooms that are tastefully furnished, with small but functional bathrooms. The view from the rooms on the top floor is well worth the climb up several flights of stairs. The restaurant serves good seafood and has some tables with a sea view. **www.auberge-saint-pierre.fr**

MONT-ST-MICHEL Terrasses Poulard

P **11** **杰** €€€

Grand Rue, 50116 **Tel** *02 33 89 02 02* **Fax** *02 33 60 37 31* **Rooms** *29* **Map** *F2*

A building with old-world charm houses this popular hotel, situated on the main street. The rooms, some with a view of the bay, are tastefully decorated and are very comfortable and well-equipped. The restaurant serves local specialities, and some tables have a panoramic view. **www.terrasses-poulard.fr**

PAIMPONT Le Relais de Brocéliande

11 **杰** €

5 Rue des Forges, 35380 **Tel** *02 99 07 84 94* **Fax** *02 99 07 80 60* **Rooms** *24* **Map** *E3*

Nestling in the Fôret de Paimpont, this hotel has two privately owned lakes and hires out boats and tackle for fishing. The rooms are traditionally furnished, some having exposed oak beams. The restaurant, decorated with stags' heads, serves dishes that use the locally caught fish and game. Closed mid-Dec–mid-Jan. **www.le-relais-de-broceliande.fr**

PANCE La Chatellerie

P **灯** €

1 Rue des Charrières, 35320 **Tel** *02 99 43 06 13* **Fax** *02 99 43 06 13* **Rooms** *3* **Map** *E3*

This guesthouse *(chambre d'hôtes)* is in the heart of a rural village, just 25 km (16 miles) from Rennes. Ideally located for walking in the surrounding countryside, it has comfortable rooms, all with a private bathroom. The owners are very friendly and serve a copious breakfast in the dining room and garden. **www.chatellerie.com**

PLEURTUIT Manoir de la Rance

P €€€

Jouvente, 35730 **Tel** *02 99 88 53 76* **Fax** *02 99 88 63 03* **Rooms** *9* **Map** *E2*

The former Château de Jouvente is a stylish 19th-century manor house, overlooking the Rance river. Its rooms, which are individually decorated, are spacious and comfortable, and some have river views. The enchanting gardens descend right down to the river banks, providing an ideal setting to unwind. Closed Jan–Mar. **www.manoirdelarance.com**

REDON Hôtel Chandouineau

P **11** **杰** €€

1 Rue Thiers, 35600 **Tel** *02 99 71 02 04* **Fax** *02 99 71 08 81* **Rooms** *7* **Map** *E3*

Situated in the heart of Redon, this stylish establishment has guestrooms located above the dining room of the renowned restaurant. The attractive, comfortable attic rooms are tastefully decorated and well-equipped. Make a reservation for the restaurant, which offers specialities based on local produce.

RENNES Hôtel des Lices

灯 **杰** **目** €€

7 Place des Lices, 35000 **Tel** *02 99 79 14 81* **Fax** *02 99 79 35 44* **Rooms** *45* **Map** *E3*

In a great location just steps away from the old town, this modern hotel has stylish, pleasant rooms furnished in "Philippe Starck" style. Nearly all have balconies. The soundproofing, however, proves essential, especially on Saturday when the square comes alive for the market. A public car park is close by. **www.hotel-des-lices.com**

RENNES Hôtel Anne-de-Bretagne

灯 **P** **目** €€€

12 Rue Tronjolly, 35000 **Tel** *02 99 31 49 49* **Fax** *02 99 30 53 48* **Rooms** *42* **Map** *E3*

A modern building that lacks architectural charm but is in the heart of the city, not far from the old town, houses this hotel. The recently renovated rooms are fully equipped and have soundproofing and wireless Internet access. The decor and furnishings are pleasant. A good buffet breakfast is served. Closed Dec–Jan. **www.anne-de-bretagne.fr**

RENNES Le Coq-Gadby

灯 **11** **杰** €€€€€

156 Rue d'Antrain, 35700 **Tel** *02 99 38 05 55* **Fax** *02 99 38 53 40* **Rooms** *11* **Map** *E3*

An elegant 17th-century building, five minutes' drive from the city centre, provides a calm and intimate atmosphere with the aid of classic period furnishings, polished parquet floors and ornate mirrors. The guestrooms "Olympe", "Louis VI" and "Anglaise" are vast and elegant. A spa and sauna are next door. Closed mid-Jul–mid-Aug. **www.lecoq-gadby.com**

ST-MALO La Villefromoy
7 Boulevard Hébert, 35400 **Tel** *02 99 40 92 20* **Fax** *02 99 56 79 49* **Rooms** *21*   **Map** *E1*

In a quiet location just a few paces from the seafront promenade, this hotel comprises two elegant Second Empire villas. Some rooms have balconies facing the sea. The recently renovated interior is sophisticated and decorated in the style of the period. A buffet breakfast is served. Closed mid-Nov–mid-Dec, mid-Jan–mid-Feb. **www.villefromoy.fr**

ST-MALO Le Beaufort
25 Chaussée du Sillon, 35400 **Tel** *02 99 40 99 99* **Fax** *02 99 40 99 62* **Rooms** *22*   **Map** *E1*

Built in 1850 and with uninterrupted sea views, this comfortable hotel was thoroughly renovated in 2001 but – with its restful beige and white tones – it has retained the charm of a private residence. Just a few minutes' walk from the walled town, it also has direct access to the beach. Some rooms have a private terrace. **www.hotel-beaufort.com**

ST-MALO Le Grand Hôtel des Thermes
Grand Plage du Sillon, 35401 **Tel** *02 99 40 75 75* **Fax** *02 99 40 76 00* **Rooms** *171*   **Map** *E1*

A comfortable, classic seaside hotel, with direct access to the thalassotherapy centre, this 19th-century palace has a good range of rooms. The most spacious, and most expensive, offers a suite with a balcony facing the sea. There are excellent children's facilities and two restaurants. **www.thalassotherapy.com**

ST-MALO Hôtel de la Cité
26 Rue Sainte Barbe, 35412 **Tel** *02 99 40 55 40* **Fax** *02 99 40 10 04* **Rooms** *41*   **Map** *E1*

Situated in the old town, this tastefully refurbished hotel has very comfortable, soundproofed rooms, some with a lovely view of the sea and Le Grand Bé, the burial place of Chateaubriand. There are also some large family rooms. A buffet breakfast is served in an attractive dining room. The private garage is at extra charge. **www.hotelcite.com**

ST-MÉLOIR-DES-ONDES Tirel Guérin
Gare de la Gouesnière, 35350 **Tel** *02 99 89 10 46* **Fax** *02 99 89 12 62* **Rooms** *49*   **Map** *E2*

A flower-adorned façade and landscaped gardens are notable features of this former railway hotel located 10 km (6 miles) from Cancale and St-Malo. With modern and spacious rooms, it is a haven of peace. There are also good leisure facilities and an excellent restaurant serving classic dishes. Closed mid-Dec–mid-Jan. **www.tirelguerin.com**

ST-REMY-DU-PLAIN Château la Haye d'Irée
35560 **Tel** *02 99 73 62 07* **Rooms** *4*   **Map** *F2*

This luxury guesthouse (*chambre d'hôtes*) occupies an 18th-century property on a hill 15 km (9 miles) east of Combourg, with magnificent views of the surrounding countryside. A warm welcome is provided by the viscomte and viscomtesse. The rooms are furnished in rustic Louis XVI style. Closed Oct–Mar. **www.chateaubreton.com**

CÔTES-D'ARMOR

BRÉHAT (ILE DE) Hôtel-Restaurant Bellevue
Port-Clos, 22870 **Tel** *02 96 20 00 05* **Fax** *02 96 20 06 06* **Rooms** *17*   **Map** *D1*

A popular spot on the island, this hotel is only five minutes' walk from the beach. Some of the large, pleasant and bright rooms have splendid views. The restaurant is perched on an overhanging veranda, and there is a pretty terrace too. Bicycles for exploring the island are available. Closed Jan–mid-Feb. **www.hotel-bellevue-brehat.fr**

BRÉLIDY Château de Brélidy
22140 **Tel** *02 96 95 69 38* **Fax** *02 96 95 18 03* **Rooms** *10*   **Map** *C2*

This imposing 16th-century manor house is one of the best places to stay in the Côtes-d'Armor. The bedrooms are spacious and elegantly decorated. Some rooms, with private terrace, open on to the extensive parkland. There is also private fishing, and a billiard room, library and Jacuzzi. Closed mid-Nov–Easter. **www.chateau-brelidy.com**

CAP FRÉHEL Le Relais de Fréhel
Route du Cap, Plévenon, 22240 **Tel** *02 96 41 43 02* **Fax** *02 96 41 30 09* **Rooms** *5*   **Map** *E1*

This guesthouse (*chambre d'hôtes*) is in a lovely renovated Breton longhouse, with the breakfast room in the former stables. Surrounded by woodland and a garden with tennis courts, it has large, comfortable and attractively furnished rooms that can sleep up to four people. There are also two gîtes. Closed mid-Nov–Mar. **www.relaiscapfrehel.fr**

DINAN Hôtel Arvor
5 Rue Augustus-Pavie, 22120 **Tel** *02 96 39 81 88* **Fax** *02 96 39 83 09* **Rooms** *23*   **Map** *E2*

In the heart of the old town, near the tourist office, this 18th-century building, on the site of a former convent, houses a modern hotel with up-to-date decor. The decent-sized rooms are functional, but not soulless, and there is a very comfortable lounge with an open fireplace. Closed Jan. **www.hotel-arvor-dinan**

DINAN Moulin de la Fontaine des Eaux
Vallée de la Fontaine des Eaux, 22100 **Tel** *02 96 87 92 09* **Fax** *02 96 87 92 09* **Rooms** *5*   **Map** *E2*

Set in a wooded valley five minutes from the port of Dinan, this converted 18th-century watermill overlooks its own lake and grounds. It has guestrooms (*chambres d'hôtes*) only; there is no restaurant, but breakfast is provided. The rooms are simply furnished and have disabled access. **www.dinanbandb.com**

Key to Price Guide *see p218* **Key to Symbols** *see back cover flap*

GUINGAMP La Demeure de Ville Blanche €€€

5 Rue du Général-de-Gaulle, 22200 **Tel** *02 96 44 28 53* **Fax** *02 96 44 45 54* **Rooms** *7*   **Map** *C2*

An outstanding 17th-century house, this guesthouse *(chambre d'hôtes)* combines comfort with elegant decor and period furniture. The rooms are fully-equipped and the suites have their own kitchen. A large lounge and attractive garden help to create a relaxing atmosphere, making it a great place to unwind. **www.demeure-vb.com**

HILLION Château de Bonabry €€€

Hillion, 22120 **Tel** *02 96 32 21 06* **Fax** *02 96 32 21 06* **Rooms** *2*   **Map** *D2*

Not far from St-Brieuc, this chateau by the sea, with two large suites for four and five people, has been in the same family for five generations. Standing in woodland and combining a timeless hunting-lodge atmosphere with modern amenities, it has direct access to the beach. Closed Nov–Easter. **www.bonabry.fr.st**

LAMBALLE Hôtel de Lion d'Or €

3 Rue de Loin d'Or, 22400 **Tel** *02 96 31 20 36* **Fax** *02 96 31 93 79* **Rooms** *17*   **Map** *D2*

Housed in a lovely stone building in a quiet street near the market square, this hotel has recently renovated and bright rooms with gaily patterned furnishings. A buffet breakfast is served in the no-frills dining room. Access to the Internet and a warm welcome make this a good-value option. **www.leliondor-lamballe.com**

LANNION Manoir du Launay €€

Chemin de Ker-ar-Faout, 22300 **Tel** *02 96 47 21 24* **Fax** *02 96 47 26 04* **Rooms** *5*   **Map** *C1*

At the end of a tree-lined alley, just five minutes from the beach, sits this lovely manor house with five superb guestrooms *(chambres d'hôtes)*, each decorated in a different theme. The best room is "Morgane", but all are attractive with parquet floors and stylish modern decor, and breakfast is copious. **www.manoirdulaunay.com**

PAIMPOL Repaire de Kerroc'h €€

29 Quai Morand, 22500 **Tel** *02 96 20 50 13* **Fax** *02 96 22 07 46* **Rooms** *13*   **Map** *D1*

This former 18th-century home of a wealthy pirate, near the port, has pleasant rooms, many with parquet flooring and some with views. Drinks can be taken around a roaring fire in winter, or on the pretty terrace in summer. Fish specialities are served in the restaurant. **www.repaire-kerroch.com**

PAIMPOL K'Loys €€€

21 Quai Morand, 22500 **Tel** *02 96 20 40 01* **Fax** *02 96 20 72 68* **Rooms** *17*   **Map** *D1*

Sitting at the edge of the marina, this pleasant hotel, a former sea merchant's house, is ideally located for exploring the Goëlo coast. Decorated in chintzy English style, it has a cosy atmosphere. Breakfast is served in the dining room or outside on the terrace in fine weather. There is public parking by the port.

PERROS-GUIREC Les Feux des Iles €€€

53 Boulevard Clémenceau, 22700 **Tel** *02 96 23 22 94* **Fax** *02 96 91 07 30* **Rooms** *18*   **Map** *C1*

In a typical 1930s stone-built house, with stunning views of the sea and islands, this hotel is well away from the bustle of the main resort. The rooms are comfortable, some with terraces facing the sea; there are modern rooms in the annexe. The decent restaurant serves seasonal local produce. Closed 23 Dec–4 Jan. **www.feux-des-iles.com**

PERROS-GUIREC Le Manoir du Sphinx €€€€

67 Chemin de la Messe, 22700 **Tel** *02 96 23 25 42* **Fax** *02 96 91 26 13* **Rooms** *20*   **Map** *C1*

The cliff-edge location of this 1900s manor house is spectacular. The rooms are bright, elegant and refined, and have furnishings in contemporary style. All have a view of the sea and the lovely flower-filled gardens that stretch down to the beach. Closed Jan–Feb. **www.lemanoirdusphinx.com**

PLANCOËT Hôtel L'Ecrin €€€€

20 Les Quais, 22130 **Tel** *02 96 84 10 24* **Fax** *02 96 84 01 93* **Rooms** *7*   **Map** *E2*

Presentation in both the bedrooms and the highly acclaimed restaurant is meticulous. Rooms are individually decorated with pretty fabrics and traditional furniture. Reflecting the gastronomic standards, the Breton breakfast, or brunch, includes pastries, oysters, cured meats and tripe *à la Bretonne*. There is a sauna and solarium. **www.crouzil.com**

PLANCOËT-PLOREC Château Le Windsor €€

Le Bois-Billy, 22130 **Tel** *02 96 83 04 83* **Fax** *02 96 83 05 36* **Rooms** *23*   **Map** *E2*

Just 20 km (12 miles) from the beaches of the Côte d'Emeraude, this chateau is ideally located between the coast and woodlands. The interior has fine period furniture and art works, and is tastefully decorated throughout. The restaurant serves delicious seafood dishes. Closed mid-Jan–mid-Feb. **www.chateau-le-windsor.fr**

PLANGUENOUAL Domaine du Val €€€€

Le Val, 22400 **Tel** *02 96 32 75 40* **Fax** *02 96 32 71 50* **Rooms** *28*   **Map** *D2*

Set in woodland, and with direct access to the sea just a short walk away, this is a superb hotel. The decor is elegant and each room is individually decorated. The restaurant is in the original dining room and serves gourmet cuisine. Squash, tennis, swimming and a sauna are all on offer, as is Internet access. **www.chateau-du-val.com**

PLÉNEUF-VAL-ANDRÉ Georges €€€

131 Rue Clémenceau, 22370 **Tel** *02 96 72 23 70* **Fax** *02 96 72 23 72* **Rooms** *24*   **Map** *D2*

In the centre of the resort, a short way from the beach, this is a typical seaside hotel. Recently completely renovated, the rooms are bright, and decorated in soft cream and beige tones with modern dark wood furniture. The best rooms are those at the front with balconies and sea views. Closed Dec–Jan.

PLÉVEN Manoir du Vaumadeuc
P 🏃 €€€€€

22130 **Tel** 02 96 84 46 17 **Fax** 02 96 84 40 16 **Rooms** 13 · **Map** E1

This grand old manor house nestles in the Fôret de la Hunaudaye. The building dates from the 15th century, and a magnificent granite staircase inside leads to the first-floor bedrooms. The surrounding wooded park has a beautiful rose garden and lake. There is also a heliport. **www.vaumadeuc.com**

PLOUGRESCANT Manoir de Kergrec'h
P €€€

Kergrec'h, 22820 **Tel** 02 96 92 59 13 **Fax** 02 96 92 51 27 **Rooms** 8 · **Map** C1

A magnificent 17th-century manor house – facing the sea and set in extensive grounds – has rooms beautifully furnished with pieces from the Louis XV, Louis XVI, *Directoire* and Rococo periods. The owners are hospitable, and guests who use of the main lounge, while breakfast is served in the dining room. **www.manoirdekergrech.com**

QUEMPER GUÉZENNEC Le Manoir de Kermodest
P 🍴 🏊 🏃 €€€

22260 **Tel** 02 96 95 38 46 **Fax** 02 96 95 30 73 **Rooms** 7 · **Map** C1

The hotel is situated in an old, granite-built manor house not far from Pontrieux. The bedrooms range from those that accommodate families comfortably and have a kitchenette, to more luxurious suites. Comfortable, relaxing country house atmosphere with leather armchairs encircling an open fireplace in the lounge. **www.kermodest.com**

QUINTIN Hôtel du Commerce
🍴 €€€

2 Rue Rochenon, 22800 **Tel** 02 96 74 94 67 **Fax** 02 96 74 00 94 **Rooms** 11 · **Map** D2

Housed in a vine-clad 18th-century building, this is a traditional hotel in the centre of a charming medieval city. The decor in each of the carefully renovated and individually decorated rooms is cheerful and bright. The rustic dining room, with its period chimney piece, offers good local dishes. Good value for money. **www.hotelducommerce.fr.cc**

SABLES-D'OR-LES-PINS La Voile d'Or
P 🍴 🏃 €€€

Allée des Acacias, 22240 **Tel** 02 96 41 42 49 **Fax** 02 96 41 55 45 **Rooms** 22 · **Map** D1

Located on the edge of the resort overlooking a lovely tidal lagoon, this hotel offers a peaceful stay. The rooms are very comfortable and decorated in an attractive contemporary style. There is a sheltered panoramic terrace and solarium. The restaurant, also with sea views, has a good reputation for seafood dishes. Closed Dec–mid-Feb. **www.la-voile-dor.fr**

ST-BRIEUC Hôtel le Relais de Beaucemaine
P 🍴 €

Ploufragan, 22440 **Tel** 02 96 78 05 60 **Fax** 02 96 78 08 33 **Rooms** 24 · **Map** D2

A friendly establishment in a peaceful setting only 5 km (3 miles) from St-Brieuc, this charming old farm building has simple yet comfortable rooms, some with a private terrace overlooking the garden. Breakfast can be taken in the garden in fine weather. There is also a bar and restaurant (dinner only). Excellent value. **info@hotel-beaucemaine**

ST-BRIEUC Hôtel de Clisson
P 📶 €€€

36 Rue Gouët, 22000 **Tel** 02 96 62 19 29 **Fax** 02 96 61 06 95 **Rooms** 25 · **Map** D2

In the old town, but away from the bustling centre, this pleasant hotel is in a plain white building but has a charming garden with a pond and fountain. The diversely decorated rooms are well-maintained and comfortable. The most spacious rooms are those with a Jacuzzi bath. Closed mid-Dec–early Jan. **www.hoteldeclisson.com**

ST-CAST-LE-GUILDO Hôtel Les Arcades
📶 🍴 🏃 €

15 Rue-du-Duc-D'Aiguillon, 22380 **Tel** 02 96 41 80 50 **Fax** 02 96 41 77 34 **Rooms** 32 · **Map** E1

Close to the beach and on a busy pedestrianized street, this hotel offers a warm welcome and well-equipped rooms with adequate, simple furnishings. There is a popular restaurant that serves classic dishes, and also a bar serving snacks and crepes. Unpretentious and good value. Closed mid-Nov–Mar. **hotel.arcades@wanadoo.fr**

ST-QUAY-PORTRIEUX Ker Moor
🍴 **P** €€€€

13 Rue-du-Président-le-Sénéchal, 22410 **Tel** 02 96 70 52 22 **Fax** 02 96 70 50 49 **Rooms** 28 · **Map** D1

This cliff-top hotel was originally a flamboyant Moorish-style villa built by a Breton diplomat in the early 20th century. The rooms are smartly furnished with bright modern fabrics and furniture. The most attractive and stylish also have a panoramic view of the Armor coast. Closed mid-Nov–Mar. **www.ker-moor.com**

TRÉBEURDEN Manoir de Lan-Kerellec
P 🍴 🏃 €€€€€

Main street in Lan-Kerellec, 22560 **Tel** 02 96 15 47 47 **Fax** 02 96 23 66 88 **Rooms** 19 · **Map** C1

A pretty hotel with gardens facing the sea, this tastefully renovated 19th-century Breton manor house has comfortable well-priced rooms. Those on the first floor are more spacious, some having balconies. Imaginative cuisine is served in the restaurant. Tennis is available. Closed mid-Nov–mid-Mar. **www.lankerellec.com**

TRÉGASTEL Park Hôtel Bellevue
P 🍴 €€

20 Rue-Des-Calculots, 22730 **Tel** 02 96 23 88 18 **Fax** 02 96 23 89 91 **Rooms** 31 · **Map** C1

Built in the 1930s and sitting in a pretty flower-filled garden, this hotel overlooks the sea and is close to the beach. The rooms are well-maintained and most have a good view. There is a diversity of styles in the furnishings, from typically Breton to contemporary. Closed mid-Nov–mid-Mar. **www.hotelbellevuetregastel.com**

TRÉGUIER Aigue Marine
📶 **P** 🏊 🏃 📺 €€€

5 Rue-M-Berthelot, 22220 **Tel** 02 96 92 97 00 **Fax** 02 96 92 44 48 **Rooms** 43 · **Map** C1

The bedrooms are functional in this hotel, which is situated at the Port de Plaisance. Some have views of the port, others the swimming pool or garden, and some have balconies too. There is a good buffet breakfast, and a decent restaurant for dinner. **www.aiguemarine.fr**

Key to Price Guide *see p218* **Key to Symbols** *see back cover flap*

NORTHERN FINISTÈRE

BREST Hôtel de la Corniche
1 Rue Amiral-Nicol, 29200 **Tel** *02 98 45 12 42* **Fax** *02 98 49 01 53* **Rooms** *16* **Map** *B2*

This modern hotel, built of local stone in the Breton style, is on the west side of the city near the naval base. It is conveniently located for walks along the scenic coastline. The rooms are simply furnished. The hotel restaurant offers a set menu Monday–Thursday evenings, for which reservations are required. **www.hotel-la-corniche.com**

BREST Hôtel Continental
Square de la Tour-d'Auvergne, 29200 **Tel** *02 98 80 50 40* **Fax** *02 98 43 17 47* **Rooms** *73* **Map** *B2*

Le Conti, as it is known by its regular clients, was first built in 1913, destroyed during the war, and rebuilt in the 1950s. Don't be put off by the vast and unwelcoming reception area. The soundproofed rooms are comfortable and spacious, and have authentic Art Deco furnishings. There is also wireless Internet access. **www.oceaniahotels.com**

CARANTEC Hôtel de Carantec-Patrick Jeffroy
20 Rue de Kelenn, 29660 **Tel** *02 98 67 00 47* **Fax** *02 98 67 08 25* **Rooms** *12* **Map** *B1*

This elegant Breton house is perched on a cliff top with a splendid view of the bay. The rooms are individually decorated, in a variety of styles. The best rooms are those with a terrace facing seawards. The restaurant, in which Patrick Jeffroy makes imaginative use of local produce, is excellent. Closed Jan. **www.hoteldecarantec.com**

GUISSÉNY L'Auberge de Keralloret
29880 **Tel** *02 98 25 60 37* **Fax** *02 98 25 69 88* **Rooms** *11* **Map** *B1*

A collection of beautifully restored old stone houses make up this hotel. Each room is original, inspired by legendary people or the region's scenery, and is meticulous in every detail, with bed linen embroidered to match the theme. The restaurant, with open fireplace, serves Breton cuisine. Closed Jan. **www.keralloret.com**

HUELGOAT Hôtel du Lac
12 Rue de Général-du-Gaulle, 29690 **Tel** *02 98 99 71 14* **Fax** *02 98 99 70 91* **Rooms** *15* **Map** *C2*

Near to the Forêt de Huelgoat and beside a lake, this is one of the few hotels to have survived the decline in tourism after the hurricane of 1999 destroyed large areas of the ancient forest. Rooms are well-refurbished and prettily decorated. The restaurant has a refectory feel about it, but it serves good traditional food. Closed Jan.**www.hoteldulac-huelgoat.com**

LANDÉDA La Baie des Anges
350 Routes des Anges, Port de L'Aber Wrac'h **Tel** *02 98 04 90 04* **Fax** *02 98 04 92 27* **Rooms** *22* **Map** *A2*

This seaside resort hotel overlooks the bay and a splendid coastline, where out to sea the Île Vierge lighthouse blinks in the night. The rooms are smartly decorated and comfortable, and the hotel is well equipped with sauna, Internet access and a salon bar. The breakfasts are ample. Closed Jan. **www.baie-des-anges.com**

PLOUJEAN-MORLAIX Le Manoir de Roch Ar Brini
29600 **Tel** *02 98 72 01 44* **Fax** *02 98 88 04 49* **Rooms** *3* **Map** *C1*

This hotel is housed in a 19th-century manor house, once owned by a local writer and ship-owner, and is situated just 3km (2 miles) from Morlaix, near the port of Dourduff. Bright, airy rooms are decorated with contemporary fabrics, and there is a billiards room. Horse-riding and bicycles are available. **www.brittanyguesthouse.com**

LE CONQUET Le Relais deu Vieux Port
1 Quai du Drellac'h, 29217 **Tel** *02 98 89 15 91* **Fax** *02 98 97 84 04* **Rooms** *7* **Map** *B1*

Located at the port, this family-run hotel has a nautical theme and a relaxed, friendly atmosphere. The fresh, bright rooms have modern furnishings and some have canopied beds and sea views. There is a terrific crêperie on the ground floor terrace, overlooking the port. **www.lerelaisduvieuxport.com**

LOCQUIREC Grand Hôtel des Bains
15 Rue de l'Eglise, 29240 **Tel** *02 98 67 41 02* **Fax** *02 98 67 44 60* **Rooms** *36* **Map** *C1*

Sheer luxury and elegance prevail in this early 20th-century seaside resort hotel, which has a seawater therapy and fitness centre. Most rooms open on to terraces with stunning sea views. The service is irreproachable, and the food, which uses organic produce, is excellent. There is also a spa and indoor pool. **www.grand-hotel-des-bains.com**

MOLÈNE (ÎLE DE) Hôtel Kastell an Daol
Le Quai, 29259 **Tel** *02 98 07 39 11* **Rooms** *10* **Map** *A2*

This is the only hotel on the island and it is set in a typical house dating from 1880. The rooms are well-maintained and well-equipped. Two brothers run the hotel: one is famous for his Johnny Halliday collection, the other for his Breton lobster dish. The restaurant is 150m away from the main hotel. Closed Jan–Feb. **www.kastell-an-daol.com**

MORLAIX Hôtel de l'Europe
1 Rue d'Aiguillon, 29600 **Tel** *02 98 62 11 99* **Fax** *02 98 88 83 38* **Rooms** *60* **Map** *C1*

This Second Empire hotel, located in the city centre, has an elegant and richly decorated interior. Rooms are well-equipped and soundproofed. Each is different, with styles ranging from traditional to modern. Service is attentive. A buffet breakfast is provided and there is a good-value brasserie. **www.hotel-europe-com.fr**

MORLAIX Le Port
€€
3 Quai de Léon, 29600 **Tel** *02 98 88 07 54* **Fax** *02 98 88 43 80* **Rooms** *25*
Map *C1*

Housed in a 19th-century Breton building on the quay, not far from the former tobacco factory and viaduct, this hotel has soundproofed and simply furnished rooms; some are quite small. The best have a view of the viaduct and port. A good buffet breakfast is served and there is a bar for residents. Wireless Internet access is available.

OUESSANT ÎLE D' Le Ti Jan Ar C'Hafe
P   €
Kernigou, 29242 **Tel** *02 98 48 82 64* **Fax** *02 98 48 88 15* **Rooms** *8*
Map *A2*

In this wonderfully renovated house, named after the owner's grandmother "Jan", the marine theme has been abandoned despite the building's closeness to the sea. Each of the delightful rooms is decorated in warm tones of red, orange and green. Outside there is a neat garden and wooden deck-style terrace. Closed mid-Nov–Feb.

PLOUDIER Hôtel de la Butte
€€€€
10 Rue de la Mer, 29260 **Tel** *02 98 25 40 54* **Fax** *02 98 25 44 17* **Rooms** *24*
Map *B1*

A family-run establishment, situated in a private garden with views out to the Baie de Goulven, this hotel offers rooms that are simply decorated in a modern nautical style. Some have a sea view. There is a lounge-bar and a restaurant whose menu features classic seafood. Closed Jan. **www.labutte.fr**

PLOUGONVELIN Hostellerie de la Pointe St-Mathieu
€€€€
Pointe de St-Mathieu, 29217 **Tel** *02 98 89 00 19* **Fax** *02 98 89 15 68* **Rooms** *25*
Map *B2*

Splendidly situated, with views of both the sea and the ancient ruins of St-Mathieu Abbey, this hotel offers modern, bright rooms decorated in a marine theme. The restaurant, with an open fireplace, serves rich, seasonal cuisine based on local produce. There is an indoor pool and sauna. Closed Feb. **www.pointe-saint-mathieu.com**

PLOUGONVEN La Grange de Coatélan
P   €€
D109, Coatélan, 29640 **Tel** *02 98 72 60 16* **Fax** *02 98 72 60 16* **Rooms** *5*
Map *C2*

A peaceful stay is guaranteed at this 16th-century Breton farmhouse. The ancient farm buildings have been tastefully converted and house five individually decorated bedrooms. Enjoy grilled meats and local recipes at the restaurant, housed in the former barn and with a roaring fire in winter. **www.legrangedecoatelan.com**

ROSCOFF Hôtel Aux Tamaris
€€
49 Rue Edouard Corbière, 29680 **Tel** *02 98 61 22 99* **Fax** *02 98 69 74 36* **Rooms** *26*
Map *B1*

Built in 1935, this hotel is on the seafront close to the thalassotherapy centre. Successive refurbishments have turned it into a modern resort hotel, and behind the stark façade there are comfortable rooms. Breakfast, which may include *crêpes* and Breton biscuits, can be taken in the dining room with its panoramic view. **www.hotel-aux-tamaris.com**

ROSCOFF Hôtel Bellevue
€€
Boulevard Ste Barbe, 29681 **Tel** *02 98 61 23 38* **Fax** *02 98 61 11 80* **Rooms** *18*
Map *B1*

Just a few minutes from the ferry terminal, this old Breton house enjoys fine views of the sea and old port. The bedrooms are a little cramped, but bright and quiet. At the back of the building is a pleasant patio garden where breakfast is served on warm days. Closed Dec–Feb. **hotelbellevue.roscoff@wanadoo.fr**

ROSCOFF Le Brittany
€€€€
Boulevard Ste-Barbe, 29681 **Tel** *02 98 69 70 78* **Fax** *02 98 61 13 29* **Rooms** *25*
Map *B1*

Located in a fine Breton manor house that looks out over the Île de Batz, this hotel is furnished with authentic period pieces. However, the amenities are up-to-date and include a heated indoor pool and sauna. The restaurant, "The Yachtsman", is renowned for its sophisticated cuisine. Closed mid-Nov–mid-Mar. **www.hotel-brittany.com**

SIZUN Le Clos de Quatre Saisons
€
2 Rue de la Paix, 29450 **Tel** *02 98 68 80 19* **Fax** *02 98 24 11 93* **Rooms** *19*
Map *B2*

Although very close to the town centre, this hotel provides peace and quiet in a private walled garden. The rooms are simply but pleasantly decorated, and well-equipped. The restaurant is beside the main building and serves up good-quality classic cuisine. Closed Oct. **www.restaurant-4saisons.com**

ST-JEAN-DU-DOIGT Le Ty Pont
P   €
Place Robert Le Meur, 29630 **Tel** *02 98 67 34 06* **Fax** *02 98 67 85 94* **Rooms** *22*
Map *C1*

A welcoming, family-run traditional Breton hotel in the centre of the village of St-Jean-Du-Doigt offers well-maintained and comfortable bedrooms. The restaurant serves good and filling traditional dishes. Just a stroll away is the church, which houses the relic of John the Baptist's finger. Closed Nov–Easter.

ST-THÉGONNEC Ars Presbital Coz
P   €
18 Rue de Gividic, 29410 **Tel** *02 98 79 45 62* **Fax** *02 98 79 48 47* **Rooms** *6*
Map *B2*

This comfortable guesthouse (*chambre d'hôtes*) occupies a former 18th-century presbytery, and has six spacious rooms. There is no television. Breakfast can be taken on the terrace in the large garden. Except on bank holidays and Sundays, a three-course dinner is served to guests who reserve before midday. **andre.prigent@wanadoo.fr**

STE-ANNE-DU-PORTZIC Belvédère
€€€
380 Rue Pierre Rivoalon, 29200 **Tel** *02 98 31 86 00* **Fax** *02 98 31 86 39* **Rooms** *30*
Map *A2*

Housed in a modern building near the beach and overlooking the Rade de Brest, this hotel has comfortable, light, airy rooms with contemporary furnishings. The decoration sometimes lacks a personal touch, but the view compensates. The panoramic restaurant offers classic seafood dishes. **www.belvedere.brest.com**

Key to Price Guide *see p218* **Key to Symbols** *see back cover flap*

ST-POL-DE-LEON Hôtel de France

29 Rue Minimes, 29250 **Tel** *02 98 29 14 14* **Fax** *02 98 29 10 57* **Rooms** *22*   **Map** *B1*

An elegant house, with a whitewashed exterior, this hotel is in a quiet location in extensive gardens. It was completely renovated only a few years ago, and now offers attractive and well-equipped rooms. Breakfast can be taken in the shady garden in fine weather. The atmosphere is relaxed and friendly.

SOUTHERN FINISTÈRE

AUDIERNE Au Roi Gradlon

3 Avenue Manu-Brusq, 29770 **Tel** *02 98 70 04 51* **Fax** *02 98 70 14 73* **Rooms** *19*   **Map** *A1*

This functional, modern box-shaped hotel has an unusually fine location right on the beach. The rooms have all been renovated and are decorated in a simple traditional style, and most have splendid views of the Atlantic Ocean. There is a panoramic view from the restaurant. Closed mid-Dec–Jan. **www.auroigradlon.com**

AUDIERNE Le Goyen

Place Jean-Simon, 29770 **Tel** *02 98 70 08 88* **Fax** *02 98 70 18 77* **Rooms** *26*   **Map** *A1*

Most of the bedrooms in this restored old building overlook the fishing port that supplies the hotel's superb restaurant. The old-fashioned decor is cosy, with frilly floral hangings and well-worn armchairs. The rooms, however, are comfortable and well-equipped. Pay parking is opposite. Closed mid-Jan–mid-Mar. **www.le-goyen.com**

BÉNODET Domaine de Kereven

Kereven, 29950 **Tel** *02 98 57 02 46* **Fax** *02 98 66 22 61* **Rooms** *12*   **Map** *B3*

Comprising a hotel and holiday cottages in the heart of the countryside, this family-run establishment is just 1.5 km (1 mile) from the sea. The hotel is in a former farmhouse building dating from 1742. The rooms are comfortable and decorated in soothing tones, and the cosy lounge has an open fire. Internet access is provided. **www.kereven.com**

BÉNODET Armoric

3 Rue Penfoul, 29950 **Tel** *02 98 57 04 03* **Fax** *02 98 57 21 28* **Rooms** *30*   **Map** *B3*

Standing in attractive private gardens close to the harbour, beach and casino, this classic hotel has spacious rooms that are elegantly furnished. A copious buffet breakfast is provided, while at other times the restaurant serves succulent local seafood. **www.armoric-benodet.com**

CHATEAUNEUF-DU-FAOU Relais de Cornaille

9 Rue Paul Sérusier, 29520 **Tel** *02 98 81 75 36* **Fax** *02 98 81 81 32* **Rooms** *29*   **Map** *B2*

This traditional hotel with a friendly atmosphere is ideally located for touring the Montagnes Noires and Mont d'Arrée regions. The functional and simple rooms are well maintained. The bar is a regular haunt for the locals, and in the rustic dining room homely dishes are served using regional produce. Closed Oct. **www.lerelaiscornaille.com**

CONCARNEAU Ker Mor

Plage des Sables-Blancs, 29900 **Tel** *02 98 97 02 96* **Fax** *02 98 97 84 04* **Rooms** *11*   **Map** *B3*

Originally an early 20th-century seaside villa, this charming hotel is ideally located on the beach. Inside are furnishings recovered from the demolition of cargo ships. All the rooms are comfortable, but the best are those with decked terraces facing the sea. The breakfast room has sea views too. **www.hotel-kermor.com**

DOUARNENEZ Auberge de Kerveoc'h

42 Route de Kerveoc'h, 29900 **Tel** *02 98 92 07 58* **Fax** *02 98 92 03 58* **Rooms** *12*   **Map** *B2*

This former farm estate is now a charming hotel and restaurant. The original farmhouse, built in 1838, houses the restaurant and four bedrooms. The other rooms are in the former estate owner's house, built in 1927. The reception is in the ancient cider press room, while the bar is in the barn. **www.auberge-kerveoch.com**

DOUARNENEZ Hostellerie Le Clos de Vallombreuse

7 Rue d'Estienne-d'Orves, 29100 **Tel** *02 98 92 63 64* **Fax** *02 98 92 84 98* **Rooms** *25*   **Map** *B2*

Overlooking the Baie de Douarnenez and standing in a small, quiet park in the town centre, this early 20th-century house exudes elegance. The lawns and flowerbeds are well-kept, and the light, airy rooms are smartly decorated. Gourmet cuisine is served in the good restaurant. Closed mid-Nov–mid-Dec. **www.closvallombreuse.com**

FORÊT FOUESNANT Le Manoir du Stang

29940 **Tel** *02 98 56 97 37* **Fax** *02 98 56 97 37* **Rooms** *24*   **Map** *B3*

Built in the 15th and 17th centuries, this elegant manor house stands in parkland a short walk from the sea. Inside are oak beams and carved stone fireplaces, and rooms that are beautifully furnished with antiques and have a view of the gardens or a lake. There is also tennis and fishing. Closed mid-Sep–mid-May. **www.manoirdustang.com**

FOUESNANT Mona Lisa à Cap Coz

Plage de Cap Coz, 29170 **Tel** *02 98 51 18 10* **Fax** *02 98 56 03 40* **Rooms** *49*   **Map** *B3*

Only minutes from Concarneau, this seafront hotel has direct access to the beach. The rooms are bright and cheerful, decorated in a nautical style with polished wood. Most have balconies with a sea view, and there are some family rooms. The restaurant has an outside terrace. Closed Nov–Feb. **www.monalisahotels.com**

ÎLE DE SEIN Hôtel d'Ar Men

Route du Phare, 29170 **Tel** *02 98 70 90 77* **Fax** *02 98 70 93 25* **Rooms** *10*   **Map** *A2*

On the western tip of the small Île de Sein, not far from the lighthouse on the reef, is this charming, friendly establishment with a peaceful and calm atmosphere. The attractively renovated rooms have ocean views and the guests' lounge is well-stocked with literature on the island. Closed 2 weeks early Oct. **hotel.armen@wanadoo.fr**

LANDUDEC Château de Guilguiffin

29710 **Tel** *02 98 91 52 11* **Fax** *02 98 91 52 52* **Rooms** *6*   **Map** *B3*

On a family-owned estate stands this magnificent 18th-century chateau, whose owners welcome their guests warmly. The rooms are individually decorated with period furniture. There are special themed weekends – cooking, health and thalasso – and horses can be stabled at an extra charge. Closed mid-Jan–Feb. **www.chateau-guilguiffin.com**

MOËLAN-SUR-MER Manoir de Kertalg

Route de Riec-sur-Belon, 29350 **Tel** *02 98 39 77 77* **Fax** *02 98 39 72 07* **Rooms** *9*   **Map** *C3*

This ivy-covered manor house stands in picturesque parkland. The grand interior is elegantly furnished with period pieces. The rooms are luxurious and decorated in soothing cream tones. The breakfast room is bright and looks out on to the gardens, where there is a terrace for fine weather. Closed mid-Nov–Easter. **www.manoirdekertalg.com**

MORGAT Grand Hôtel de la Mer

12 Rue d'Ys, 29160 **Tel** *02 98 27 02 09* **Fax** *02 98 27 02 39* **Rooms** *78*   **Map** *A2*

Souvenirs of the *belle époque* pervade this 1920s hotel built by the Peugeot family. The interior decor is basic, and the bedrooms functional, but the views of the wooded park or bay compensate for the lack of luxurious furnishings. There is also a tennis court in the grounds and a restaurant with a panoramic view. Closed Nov–Mar.

NEVEZ Hôtel Ar Men Du

Raguenez Plage, 29920 **Tel** *02 98 06 84 22* **Fax** *02 98 06 76 69* **Rooms** *15*   **Map** *B3*

All the rooms in this smart hotel-restaurant, with an exceptional beachfront location, have a sea view. They are also well-presented and decorated in a contemporary nautical theme. The restaurant, which looks out on to a tidal islet, serves succulent dishes based on the local seafood. Closed Nov–late Dec, Jan–mid-Mar. **www.men-du.com**

PLONÉOUR DE LANVERN Hôtel des Voyageurs

1 Rue Jean-Jaurès, 29720 **Tel** *02 98 87 61 35* **Fax** *02 98 87 67 05* **Rooms** *12*   **Map** *B3*

Situated in the centre of a pretty Bigouden village, this small, unpretentious hotel has simply decorated rooms with rustic furnishings. Guaranteeing peace and quiet, it also provides good value for money and good regional cuisine in the restaurant. Closed 2 weeks Nov, 1 week Dec. **www.hotelrestaurant-lesvoyageurs.fr**

PLONÉOUR DE LANVERN Manoir de Kerhuel

Route de Qiumper, 29720 **Tel** *02 98 82 60 57* **Fax** *02 98 82 61 79* **Rooms** *26*   **Map** *B3*

An enchanting old manor house and converted outbuildings sit at the end of a drive lined with 100-year-old beech trees. All rooms are spacious and elegantly decorated. There is a tennis court, sauna and gamesroom, plus Internet access. The restaurant serves traditional dishes. Closed mid-Nov–Mar. **manoir-kerhuel@wanadoo.fr**

PLONOVEZ-PORZAY Le Manoir de Moëllien

29550 **Tel** *02 98 92 50 40* **Fax** *02 98 92 56 54* **Rooms** *18*   **Map** *B2*

About 3 km (2 miles) from the beaches of Douarnenez and the medieval town of Locronan, this 17th-century granite manor house has a tranquil atmosphere. The rooms, the majority of which are in the converted outbuildings, have character and are attractively decorated. Closed Feb. **www.moellien.com**

PONT AVEN Roz Aven

11 Quai Theodore-Botrel, 29930 **Tel** *02 98 06 13 06* **Fax** *02 98 06 03 89* **Rooms** *24*   **Map** *B3*

In the harbour and by the Aven river, this hotel is in a 16th-century thatched cottage with a modern extension. The rooms are simply and attractively furnished and well maintained. There is one ground-floor room for guests with limited mobility. The bar serves snacks throughout the day. Closed Nov–late Feb. **www.hotelpontaven.com**

PONT L'ABBÉ Hôtel de Bretagne

24 Place de la République, 29120 **Tel** *02 98 87 17 22* **Fax** *02 98 82 39 31* **Rooms** *18*   **Map** *B3*

Centrally located in the capital of Bigouden, this family-run hotel has attractively furnished rooms. The largest are at the front of the building. The atmosphere is friendly, especially in the restaurant where the two brothers serve regional seafood dishes. There is also an attractive decked terrace. Closed mid-Jan–early Feb. **www.hoteldebretagne29.com**

QUIMPER Hotel Escale Oceania

6 Rue Théodore Le Hars, 29000 **Tel** *02 98 53 37 37* **Fax** *02 98 90 31 51* **Rooms** *63*   **Map** *B3*

Modern and functional, this hotel near the Odet River is ideally located for visiting the historic town of Quimper. The decor is basic in the practical but small rooms. The largest rooms are situated at the front of the building, but the quietest are at the rear. A decent buffet breakfast is served in the dining room. **www.oceaniahotels.com**

QUIMPER Hôtel Gradlon

30 Rue de Brest, 29000 **Tel** *02 98 95 04 39* **Fax** *02 98 95 61 25* **Rooms** *22*   **Map** *B3*

Just two minutes' walk from the historic city centre, this hotel has charming, peaceful rooms – a few overlooking the enclosed flower garden and fountain. Some disabled access. Breakfast can be taken on the pretty veranda, and there is a cosy salon bar with an open fire. **www.hotel-gradlon.com**

Key to Price Guide *see p218* **Key to Symbols** *see back cover flap*

STE-MARINE Hôtel Sainte Marine

19 Rue du Bac, 29120 **Tel** 02 98 56 34 79 **Fax** 02 98 51 94 09 **Rooms** 13

Map B3

At Ste-Marine port this hotel-restaurant sits on the quay. The charming interior was designed by a regional artist, and each room is decorated in a nautical theme with pretty hand-painted frescoes and hand-picked furnishings. The restaurant serves good innovative seafood dishes. Closed 15 Nov–15 Dec. **www.hotelsaintemarine.com**

TRÉBOUL Hôtel Ty Mad

Plage St-Jean, 29100 **Tel** 02 98 74 00 53 **Fax** 02 98 74 15 16 **Rooms** 16

Map B2

Housed in the former presbytery of the St-Jean chapel, and overlooking the beach, this hotel has an eclectic decor. Polished parquet floors, contemporary art and older objets d'art create an intimate atmosphere. Home-made pastries are served at breakfast; the menu for dinner changes daily. Closed mid-Nov–mid-Mar. **www.hoteltymad.com**

TRÉGUNC Les Grandes Roches

Rue des Grandes Roches, 29910 **Tel** 02 98 97 62 97 **Fax** 02 98 50 29 19 **Rooms** 17

Map B3

Peaceful and picturesque, and located on the Artists' Trail, this hotel has lovely gardens. The rooms in the main building are charming, and there are two suites in thatched cottages. The terrace is perfect for breakfast; the restaurant has seasonal menus. There is Internet access. Closed mid-Dec–Jan. **www.hotel-lesgrandesroches.com**

MORBIHAN

AURAY Hôtel du Loch

2 Rue François-Guhur, La Forêt, 56400 **Tel** 02 97 56 48 33 **Fax** 02 97 56 63 55 **Rooms** 30

Map D3

In a quiet residential area, on the edge of a forest, this contemporary hotel has a calm atmosphere. The building appears stark from the outside but bedrooms are spacious and tastefully furnished. The excellent restaurant, which opens out on to the garden, serves traditional gourmet dishes. Closed Christmas. **www.hotel-du-loch.com**

AURAY Hôtel du Golf Saint-Laurent

Golf de Saint-Laurent, 56400 **Tel** 02 97 56 88 88 **Fax** 02 97 56 88 28 **Rooms** 42

Map D3

This modern hotel has its own golf course. The rooms are practical, bright and pleasantly furnished, each with a private terrace overlooking the gardens and green. Breakfast is served on the terrace beside the pool. There is also a comfortable bar, billiards room, Jacuzzi and solarium. Closed 19 Dec–9 Jan. **www.hotel-golf-saint-laurent.com**

BELLE-ÎLE-EN-MER Hostellerie La Touline

Rue de Port-Vihan, Sauzon, 56360 **Tel** 02 97 31 69 69 **Fax** 02 97 31 66 00 **Rooms** 5

Map C4

Painted in pinks and blues, this typical Breton house is close to the port, yet has a peaceful atmosphere. The rooms are stylish and individually decorated, mainly with a nautical theme, and there is a Jacuzzi in the flower-filled garden. The hosts are friendly and the ambience cosy. Closed 9 Oct–Mar. **www.hostellerielatouline.com**

BELLE-ÎLE-EN-MER La Désirade

Bangor, 56360 **Tel** 02 97 31 70 70 **Fax** 02 97 31 89 63 **Rooms** 30

Map C4

A good base for exploring the island, this friendly hotel comprises several traditional longhouses, which are decorated in soothing pastel tones. The rooms are large and comfortable, and most have views of the garden and pool. The good restaurant serves gourmet local dishes. Closed mid-Nov–Apr. **www.hotel-la-desirade.com**

BELLE-ÎLE-EN-MER Castel Clara

Port-Goulphar, 56360 **Tel** 02 97 31 84 21 **Fax** 02 97 31 51 69 **Rooms** 59

Map C4

A luxurious hotel, the Castel Clara has an idyllic location looking out over the Goulphar cove and thalassotherapy centre. The large rooms are elegantly furnished with impeccable attention to detail. The restaurant has a panoramic view and serves excellent food, including sublime seafood dishes. Closed mid-Nov–Feb. **www.castel-clara.com**

BILLIERS Domaine de Rochevilaine

Pointe de Pen-Lan Sud, 56190 **Tel** 02 97 41 61 61 **Fax** 02 97 41 44 85 **Rooms** 35

Map D4

Consisting of converted 16th- and 17th-century Breton buildings, this hotel complex includes a balneotherapy (water treatment) centre. Located on a rocky point facing the ocean, the rooms have sophisticated decor, both contemporary and period, and are well-equipped. The restaurant is renowned. **www.domainederochevilaine.com**

BONO LE Le Manoir de Kerdréan

Just outside Le Bono, 56400 **Tel** 02 97 57 84 00 **Fax** 02 97 57 83 00 **Rooms** 69

Map C3

Hidden away in parkland and overlooking a golf course, this hotel has an exceptional location. The rooms, with rustic furnishings, are in the main manor house and in the recently built annexe that looks out on the pool. Some have balconies with a view of the woodland and tennis court. Closed 1st week Jan. **www.abbatiales.com**

CARNAC Hôtel An Ti Gwenn

2 Rue Poulperson, 56340 **Tel** 02 97 52 00 73 **Fax** 02 97 52 81 88 **Rooms** 11

Map C4

Ideally situated in a quiet corner not far from the Grande Plage and at the foot of the Tumulus St-Michel, An Ti Gwenn (the white house) has gaily decorated rooms with modern furnishings. Television is on request and bikes are available. The pool and local restaurant are a short stroll away. **www.hotel-antigwenn.com**

CARNAC Hôtel Celtique

€€

17 Avenue Kermario/82 Avenue des Druides, 56190 **Tel** *02 97 52 14 15* **Fax** *02 97 52 71 10* **Rooms** *73* **Map** *C4*

This modern building is a short walk from one of the most beautiful beaches in the bay. The bright, well-equipped rooms look out on to an extensive garden with ancient pine trees. The pool is open-air in the summer but converted to an indoor one in the winter. There is also a fitness centre and Jacuzzi. **www.hotel-celtique.com**

CARNAC Lann Roz

€€

36 Avenue de la Poste, 56340 **Tel** *02 97 52 10 48* **Fax** *02 97 52 24 36* **Rooms** *13*   **Map** *C4*

Just ten minutes' walk from the beach, this is a friendly hotel with a pretty garden. The rooms are fresh and bright, and decorated in pale blues and pinks. The typical Breton dining room with oak beams and open fireplaces serves local specialities. There is a terrace and garden. **www.lannroz.com**

CARNAC Les Ajoncs d'Or

€€€

Route de Plouharnel, Kerbachique, 56340 **Tel** *02 97 52 32 02* **Fax** *02 97 52 40 36* **Rooms** *17*   **Map** *C4*

A tiny hamlet just 2 km (1 mile) from the centre of Carnac is the location of this pretty granite farmhouse with old-fashioned, but comfortable, rooms, some of which are family rooms. The rustic dining room serves regional specialities, and there are chairs and loungers in the delightful garden. Closed Nov–Mar. **www.lesajoncsdor.com**

FAOUËT LE La Croix d'Or

€

9 Place Bellanger, 56320 **Tel** *02 97 23 07 33* **Fax** *02 97 23 06 52* **Rooms** *13*   **Map** *D1*

This small friendly hotel, built in the late 19th century, faces the fine 16th-century covered marketplace in the village centre. A market is still held twice a month. The hotel has a convivial atmosphere, traditional decor, and rooms that are simple, neat and comfortable. The rustic restaurant serves regional dishes. **www.lacroixdor.com**

GROIX ÎLE DE Hôtel de la Marine

€€

7 Rue de Général de Gaulle, 56590 **Tel** *02 97 86 80 05* **Fax** *02 97 86 56 37* **Rooms** *22*   **Map** *C3*

Expect a warm welcome at this hotel in the middle of the beautiful island of Groix. A relaxing hideaway, it has charming bedrooms that overlook either the sea or the garden terrace. In the restaurant, great care is taken in the preparation of fine fish dishes. **www.hoteldelamarine.com**

HENNEBONT Château de Locguénole

€€€€

1 km (half a mile) south of Hennebont, 56700 **Tel** *02 97 76 76 76* **Fax** *02 97 76 82 35* **Rooms** *22*   **Map** *C3*

An 18th-century chateau and manor house, surrounded by parkland lining a wide coastal inlet, provide elegant rooms with antique furniture, woodcarvings and tapestries. Some are decorated in a romantic style; others are more refined. There is a tennis court, hammam and sauna. Closed Jan–mid-Feb. **www.chateau-de-locguenole.com**

JOSSELIN La Butte de St-Laurent

€

La Butte de St-Laurent, 56120 **Tel** *02 97 22 22 09* **Rooms** *4*   **Map** *D3*

A small, cosy guesthouse (*chambre d'hôtes*) sits on top of the hillock (*butte*), from where there are splendid views of the chateau and village famous for its linen weaving. Each of the comfortable attic rooms has a private bathroom. A family room is available, and there is also a pleasant garden. Closed mid-Sep–Mar.

LOCMARIAQUER Les Trois Fontaines

€€€

Rosnarho, Golfe de Morbihan, 56470 **Tel** *02 97 57 42 70* **Fax** *02 97 57 30 59* **Rooms** *18*   **Map** *D4*

At the edge of an oyster-farming village, this charming hotel is well situated for visiting the region. All the elegantly decorated rooms face in the same direction, towards flowerbeds and a sheltered terrace. Both they and the pleasant lounge are furnished in mahogany. Closed mid-Nov–Mar. **www.hotel-troisfontaines.com**

LORIENT Les Pecheurs

€

7 Rue Jean La Garde, 56100 **Tel** *02 97 21 19 24* **Fax** *02 97 21 13 19* **Rooms** *21*   **Map** *C3*

This convivial and traditional one-star hotel is conveniently situated near to the marina and on a quiet side street. The rooms are not exceptional, but are clean and neat with simple furnishings. The hosts are friendly and helpful and serve a complimentary breakfast. The bar is lively and fills up with locals. **www.bar-hotel-les-pecheurs.fr.st**

LORIENT Hôtel Victor Hugo

€€

36 Rue Lazare-Carnot, 56100 **Tel** *02 97 21 16 24* **Fax** *02 97 84 95 13* **Rooms** *30*   **Map** *C3*

Small yet well-equipped and comfortable rooms are provided by this hotel in the new town, next to the embarkation point for boats to the Île de Groix marina. The rooms are also well insulated against noise and are traditionally furnished. A friendly welcome is a further bonus at this good-value hotel. **www.hotelvictorhugo-lorient.com**

MOINES ÎLE AUX Le San Francisco

€€€

Rue de Port, 56780 **Tel** *02 97 26 31 52* **Fax** *02 97 26 35 59* **Rooms** *8*   **Map** *D4*

A short walk from the beach and overlooking the pretty harbour is this building belonging to Franciscan sisters, with recently renovated and simply furnished rooms. Some have sea views; others are in the attic. The restaurant serves traditional dishes, and there is a lovely terrace with sea views. Closed Nov–Easter. **www.le-sanfrancisco.com**

NOYAL-MUZILLAC Manoir de Bodrevan

€€€

2 km (1 mile) northwest on D153, 56190 **Tel** *02 97 45 62 26* **Rooms** *6*   **Map** *D3*

A former hunting lodge, with a rustic interior and huge open stone fireplaces, offers guestooms (*chambres d'hôtes*) that are comfortable and individually decorated. The good buffet breakfast can be taken on the outside terrace; dinner can be reserved. Closed Nov–mid-Dec; Jan–mid-Feb. **www.manoir-bodrevan.com**

Key to Price Guide *see p218* **Key to Symbols** *see back cover flap*

PLOEMEUR Le Vivier
P | ¶| | €€€

Lomener, 4 km (2 miles) south on D163, 56270 **Tel** *02 97 82 99 60* **Fax** *02 97 82 88 89* **Rooms** *14* **Map** *C3*

Built on a rocky outcrop with a superb view of the ocean and the Île de Groix, this hotel is a delightfully tranquil place to stay. The well-maintained rooms are modern and smartly furnished; all have sea views. The restaurant serves wonderfully fresh seafood dishes. Closed 2 weeks Mar; Christmas–mid-Jan. **www.levivier-lomener.com**

PLOËRDUT Château du Launay
P | ¶| | | | €€€

56160 **Tel** *02 97 39 46 32* **Fax** *02 97 39 46 31* **Rooms** *6* **Map** *D3*

Set in the heart of the legendary land of the Druids, this guesthouse *(chambre d'hôtes)* has an irresistible charm. The spacious rooms are each decorated in a different style. There is a colonial atmosphere, especially in the lounge where you can play bridge, chess or the piano. There is also a hammam and fitness facilities. **www.chateaudulaunay.com**

PLOËRMEL Hôtel Le Cobh
P | ¶| | | €€€

10 Rue des Forges, 56800 **Tel** *02 97 74 00 49* **Fax** *02 97 74 07 36* **Rooms** *12* **Map** *D3*

In this recently renovated hotel the decor has been inspired by the legends of Broceliande to create three types of room: sacred rites and literature in blue tones, the forest in green tones and opalescence in red tones. There is also a garden, children's play area and Internet access. The hosts provide a pleasant welcome. **www.hotel-lecobh.com**

PONTIVY Hôtel de l'Europe
| P | ¶| | | €€

12 Rue François-Mitterand, 56300 **Tel** *02 97 25 11 14* **Fax** *02 97 25 48 04* **Rooms** *19* **Map** *D3*

Located in the centre of Napoléonville, this stately 19th-century mansion house has pleasant, well-kept rooms. Soundproofing and Internet access have been installed, but the furnishings maintain an ambience from the period. In the restaurant a young chef produces inspirational dishes. Closed Christmas–New Year. **www.hotellerieurope.com**

PONTIVY Le Rohan
P | €€€

90 Rue Nationale, 56300 **Tel** *02 97 25 02 01* **Fax** *02 97 25 02 85* **Rooms** *17* **Map** *D3*

Ideally located for visiting both inland and coastal Brittany, this Napoléon-style building is situated on Pontivy's main street. Gaily decorated with contemporary wicker furniture, the rooms are modern and bright. In summer, breakfast is served in a pretty courtyard terrace. **www.hotelpontivy.com**

QUESTEMBERT Le Bretagne
P | ¶| | | €€€

13 Rue St-Michel, 56230 **Tel** *02 97 26 11 12* **Fax** *02 97 26 12 37* **Rooms** *9* **Map** *D3*

Set in lush gardens and with a much-praised restaurant, this is a smart country house hotel. The decor of the comfortable rooms is elegant and sophisticated, and the interior decorations include paintings by the chef-artist and sculptures. A delicious breakfast is served. Closed 3 weeks Jan. **www.paineaulebretagne.com**

QUIBERON PRESQU'ÎLE DE Hôtel Bellevue
P | ¶| | | | €€€

Rue de Tiviec, 56173 **Tel** *02 97 50 16 28* **Fax** *02 97 30 44 34* **Rooms** *38* **Map** *C4*

Located near the seafront, casino and thalassotherapy centre, this modern hotel forms an L-shape around the heated swimming pool. The bedrooms are comfortable, while the restaurant is airy and bright. There is a choice of a buffet breakfast by the pool or breakfast in your room. Closed Oct–Mar. **www.bellevuequiberon.com**

ROCHE-BERNARD LA L'Auberge Bretonne
| P | ¶| | | €€€€

2 Place du Guesclin, 56130 **Tel** *02 99 90 60 28* **Fax** *02 99 90 85 00* **Rooms** *11* **Map** *E4*

This luxury hotel-restaurant complex consists of three beautifully renovated Breton houses. The bedrooms, with soft creamy-coloured furnishings, are light and airy and the atmosphere is relaxed. Creative cuisine is served in the dining room, which encircles the vegetable garden. Closed mid-Nov–mid-Jan. **www.auberge-bretonne.com**

ROCHEFORT-EN-TERRE Château de Talhouët
P | ¶| | | €€€

56220 **Tel** *02 97 43 34 72* **Fax** *02 97 43 35 04* **Rooms** *7* **Map** *D3*

A genuine Breton manor house with private chapel, built in the 15th and 17th centuries, offers unusually large rooms that are both comfortable and tastefully furnished. The peace of the location is enhanced by the surrounding park. Dinner is served every evening for guests. **www.chateaudetalhouet.com**

SARZEAU Le Mur de Roy
| P | ¶| €€€

Penvins, 56370 **Tel** *02 97 67 34 08* **Fax** *02 97 67 36 23* **Rooms** *10* **Map** *D4*

Situated on the Presqu'île de Rhys, with direct access to the beach, this friendly hotel has recently renovated rooms decorated in bright, fresh colours. All have modern, attractive furnishings; some have sea views. The restaurant has a panoramic view and serves local seafood dishes. Closed mid-Dec–mid-Jan. **www.lemurderoy.com**

TRINITÉ-SUR-MER LA Le Lodge Kerisper
P | | €€€

4 Rue de Latz, 56470 **Tel** *02 97 52 88 56* **Fax** *02 97 52 76 39* **Rooms** *16* **Map** *C4*

This former farm building has been transformed into a charming hotel with a lovely conservatory. The interior has original parquet flooring and elegant designer furniture. Also provides wireless Internet access, a heated pool, beauty and massage facilities, and access for persons with limited mobility. **www.lodgekerisper.com**

VANNES Hôtel La Marébaudière
| P | | €€€

4 Rue Aristide Briand, 56000 **Tel** *02 97 47 34 29* **Fax** *02 97 54 14 11* **Rooms** *41* **Map** *D3*

Conveniently situated a short walk from the beautifully preserved old walled town, this is a stylish hotel with a peaceful atmosphere and bedrooms overlooking the garden. Breakfast can be taken in the dining room or in your room. There is a wide choice of restaurants nearby. **www.marebaudiere.com**

VANNES Le Roof Hôtel-Restaurant
📶 P ⑪ 👤   €€€€

At the end of Presqu'Île de Conleau, 56000 **Tel** *02 97 63 47 47* **Fax** *02 97 63 48 10* **Rooms** *42*   **Map** *D3*

Virtually at the water's edge beside the port, this modern hotel is 4.5 km (3 miles) from the centre of Vannes. The rooms, some with superb views, are comfortable and large. Service is attentive and friendly. The restaurant, decorated in nautical style, offers a good range of simple seafood dishes. Closed Nov–Dec. **www.bestwestern.fr**

VANNES Villa Kerasy
P   €€€€€

20 Avenue Favrel & Lincy, 56000 **Tel** *02 97 68 36 83* **Fax** *02 97 68 36 84* **Rooms** *13*   **Map** *D3*

Near the medieval city centre, this hotel recalls the past of the East India Company. Each room is named after a port along the spice route and is furnished with oriental items. There is a lovely terrace and Japanese garden, plus modern facilities that include Internet access. Closed Jan. **www.villakerasy.com**

LOIRE-ATLANTIQUE

BAULE LA Castel Marie-Louise
📶 P ⑪   €€€€€

1 Avenue Andrieu, 44500 **Tel** *02 40 11 48 38* **Fax** *02 40 11 48 35* **Rooms** *31*   **Map** *D4*

This superb 1910s manor house, surrounded by gardens, overlooks the bay. Inside is both contemporary decor and beautiful rooms furnished with antiques. The atmosphere is luxurious yet relaxed. The restaurant is excellent and offers gourmet dishes. Internet access is provided. Closed mid-Nov–mid-Dec. **www.castel-marie-louise.com**

BAULE LA Saint-Christophe
P ⑪ 👤   €€€

1 Avenue Alcyons, 44500 **Tel** *02 40 62 40 00* **Fax** *02 40 62 40 40* **Rooms** *45*   **Map** *D4*

Located in a quiet corner of a busy resort, this ivy-covered collection of early 20th-century villas has elegantly furnished rooms. Some have air-conditioning, others balconies, and some adjoining rooms for families. All have a comfortable country-house atmosphere. There is a pretty garden and summer terrace. **www.st-christophe.com**

BERNERIE-EN-RETZ Château de la Gressière
P ⑪ 👤   €€

Rue Noue-Fleurie, 44500 **Tel** *02 51 74 60 06* **Fax** *02 51 74 60 02* **Rooms** *15*   **Map** *D4*

Elegant, Regency-style furnishings feature throughout this classic 19th-century manor house on a hill overlooking the sea and Île de Noirmoitier. The well-appointed rooms have a view of the beach or garden, and traditional regional dishes are served in the restaurant. There is also a tennis court and sauna. **www.lagressiere.com**

CHÂTEAUBRIANT Le Châteaubriant
📶 P 📄   €€

30 Rue de 11-Novembre, 44110 **Tel** *02 40 28 14 14* **Fax** *02 40 28 26 49* **Rooms** *36*   **Map** *F3*

In an elegant stone building that has a practical central location for visiting Châteaubriant, this hotel has pleasant and comfortable bedrooms with Louis XVI-style furnishings. The modern amenities include Internet access. The service is friendly and efficient, and there are good restaurants nearby. **www.hotellechateaubriant.com**

CROISIC LE Les Nids
P 🏊 👤   €€

15 Rue Pasteur, Port-Lin, 44490 **Tel** *02 40 23 00 63* **Fax** *02 40 23 09 79* **Rooms** *26*   **Map** *D4*

Close to the beach, this modern seaside resort hotel has pleasant, freshly decorated rooms with attractive furnishings, most with balconies. Family orientated, it has a children's play area and gamesroom. Tropical plants flourish at the edges of the indoor pool. A buffet breakfast is served. Closed mid-Nov–Mar. **www.hotellesnids.com**

CROISIC LE Fort de l'Océan
📶 P ⑪ 🏊 👤 📺   €€€€€

Pointe de Croisic, 44490 **Tel** *02 40 15 77 77* **Fax** *02 40 15 77 80* **Rooms** *9*   **Map** *D4*

Ramparts dating from the 17th century enclose this hotel facing the sea, which was once a fortress designed by Vauban. Nothing remains of the harsh military lifestyle; comfort is foremost. The stylish bedrooms include one equipped for the disabled. The restaurant serves wonderful seafood dishes. **contact@fort-ocean.com**

GUÉRANDE La Guérandière
P   €€

5 Rue Vannetaise, 44350 **Tel** *02 40 62 17 15* **Rooms** *7*   **Map** *D4*

In a walled garden, beneath the ramparts of the city, stands this carefully restored *hôtel particulier*. Most of the original features – stained glass windows, wood-carved panels, parquet floors and a grand wooden staircase – have been preserved. The cosy rooms are individually decorated with charm. Closed Jan–Mar. **www.laguerandiere.com**

MISSILLAC La Bretesche
📶 P ⑪ 🏊 👤   €€€€€

Domaine de Bretesche, 44780 **Tel** *02 51 76 86 96* **Fax** *02 40 66 99 47* **Rooms** *32*   **Map** *E4*

In one of the most beautiful hotel-restaurants in Brittany, the rooms are in converted outbuildings beside a majestic crenellated castle. A truly sumptuous ambience is created by the rich furnishings. Adding to guests' enjoyment is the extensive parkland, lake, private golf course and superb restaurant. Closed Feb–mid-Mar. **www.bretesche.com**

NANTES Amiral
📶 P   €€

26bis Rue Scribe, 44000 **Tel** *02 40 69 20 21* **Fax** *02 40 73 98 13* **Rooms** *49*   **Map** *F4*

Located in a functional 19th-century building, this city-centre hotel has a diversely decorated interior featuring Art Deco mosaics, 17th- and 18th-century fittings, ornate ceilings and stained-glass windows. The pleasant bedrooms are spacious, well-equipped and elegantly furnished. **amiral@hotel-nantes.fr**

Key to Price Guide *see p218* **Key to Symbols** *see back cover flap*

NANTES Hôtel de la France

24 Rue Crébillon, 44000 **Tel** *02 40 73 57 91* **Fax** *02 40 69 75 75* **Rooms** *74*

Map *F4*

On a busy street in the heart of the city centre, opposite the Opéra, the soundproofing is essential for a peaceful night in this former 18th-century *hôtel particulier*. Choose from rooms with ornately decorated Louis XVI- or Regency-style decor and Internet access. There is also a bar and restaurant. **www.oceaniahotels.com**

NANTES Hôtel La Pérouse

3 Allée Duquesne, 44000 **Tel** *02 40 89 75 00* **Fax** *02 40 89 76 00* **Rooms** *47*

Map *F4*

Named after a French navigator, this chic city-centre hotel with a zen atmosphere opened in 1993. The rooms have glossy wooden flooring and contemporary-design furniture, and are reasonably quiet. A good choice is available at the buffet breakfast. Guests also have free access to a nearby gym club. **www.hotel-laperouse.fr**

NANTES Jules Verne

3 Rue de Couëdic, 44000 **Tel** *02 40 35 74 50* **Fax** *02 40 02 09 35* **Rooms** *65*

Map *F4*

A modern hotel, functional rather than attractive, the Jules Verne is in a busy pedestrian square in the city centre. The rooms are reasonably sized and comfortable and have satellite TV. Disabled facilities are available. A good buffet breakfast is served in the basement dining room. Service could be better. **www.bestwestern.fr-nantes**

PORNIC Hôtel Beau Soleil

70 Quai Leray, 44210 **Tel** *02 40 82 34 58* **Fax** *02 40 82 43 00* **Rooms** *18*

Map *E5*

In a modern building on the harbour, this hotel has rooms that are not very big but have bright, fresh decor and are well maintained. Breakfast is served in the cheerful dining room. It can be noisy in the peak season, but the rooms are soundproofed and most have a sea view. Service is friendly. **www.annedebretagne.com/beausoleil**

PORNICHET Le Régent

150 Boulevard des Océanides, 44210 **Tel** *02 40 61 05 68* **Fax** *02 40 61 25 53* **Rooms** *22*

Map *D4*

Built early in the 20th century, this smart spa resort house has a dining room, terrace and some rooms with a view of the beach. The decor in the rooms is contemporary and bright; the suites have extras such as whirlpool baths and air-conditioning. The restaurant serves tasty fish dishes. Closed Oct–Feb. **www.le-regent.fr**

PORNICHET Villa Flornoy

7 Avenue Flornoy, 44210 **Tel** *02 40 11 60 00* **Fax** *02 40 61 86 47* **Rooms** *30*

Map *D4*

Tucked away in a quiet residential side street, this large period villa has been converted into a hotel with an English cottage-style atmosphere. The decor of the well-kept rooms is a little old-fashioned and floral, but charming. There is also a pretty garden. Internet access is provided. Closed Nov–early Feb. **www.villa-flornoy.com**

SORINIÈRES Abbaye de Villeneuve

Route de La Roche-Sur-Yon, 44840 **Tel** *02 40 04 40 25* **Fax** *02 40 31 28 45* **Rooms** *23*

Map *F4*

Located just 8 km (5 miles) from Nantes, this is a beautiful abbey that was fully restored in 1977. An 18th-century building now houses grand bedrooms with sumptuous furnishings and bathrooms. The restaurant, in the 13th-century cloisters, serves gourmet regional cuisine. **www.abbayedevilleneuve.com**

ST-JOACHIM La Mare Aux Oiseaux

162 Île de Fredun, **Tel** *02 40 88 53 01* **Fax** *02 40 91 67 44* **Rooms** *10*

Map *E4*

This hotel-restaurant nestles in the middle of the marshlands of the Grande Brière. The stylish bedrooms, three of which occupy a wood cabin in the grounds, are named after birds. The contemporary furnishings are well chosen and the restaurant is excellent. Barge trips are organized. Closed Jan, Mar. **www.mareauxoiseaux.com**

ST-LYPHARD Les Chaumières du Lac

Rue Vignonnet, facing lake St-Lyphard, 44410 **Tel** *02 40 91 40 30* **Fax** *02 40 91 30 33* **Rooms** *20*

Map *D4*

Situated in the Parc Régional de la Brière, this establishment comprises three recently converted and whitewashed thatched cottages. The bedrooms, with lake views, are vast and pleasantly decorated. The restaurant, "Les Typhas", serves delicious food in its cheery dining room. Closed mid-Nov–early Feb. **www.leschaumieresdulac.com**

ST-MARC-SUR-MER Hôtel de la Plage

97 Rue du Commandant-Charcot, 44600 **Tel** *02 40 91 99 01* **Fax** *02 40 91 92 00* **Rooms** *30*

Map *D4*

Just southwest of St-Nazaire, in a small, traditional coastal resort, this quiet and comfortable classic seaside hotel has direct access to the beach made famous by "Monsieur Hulot". The bedrooms are furnished with simplicity; some have stunning sea views. The restaurant serves good local produce. Currently undergoing renovations – phone to check if it is open.

ST-NAZAIRE Au Bon Acceuil

39 Rue Marceau, 44600 **Tel** *02 40 22 07 05* **Fax** *02 40 19 01 58* **Rooms** *17*

Map *E4*

This enchanting hotel is housed in a small building in a peaceful corner of the city centre that escaped the destruction of World War II. The bedrooms are simple, modern and functional. The dining room is a little gloomy, but serves dishes such as oysters with steamed beans, and scallops. The atmosphere is friendly and welcoming. **www.aubonacceuil44.com**

ST-SAVEUR DE LANDEMONT Château de la Colaissière

49270 **Tel** *02 40 98 75 04* **Fax** *02 40 98 74 15* **Rooms** *15*

Map *F4*

A noble Renaissance chateau encircled by a moat and parkland has rooms in three styles: Louis XV, Louis XVI and Louis-Philippe. The gourmet restaurant overlooks the moat, and there are stunning lounges with immense fireplaces. Helicopter tours can be arranged from the grounds. **www.colaissiere.com**

WHERE TO EAT

The foremost agricultural region of France, Brittany abounds in produce that is the basis of the region's cuisine. Brittany is best known for its fish and shellfish, but locally produced cooked meats and free-range poultry are also on the menu. Excellent fruit and vegetables, including strawberries and artichokes,

Logo of Coreff beer, brewed in Morlaix

are grown in Brittany. Breton cider and prized Muscadet from the vineyards around Nantes are other specialities. From the finest meals served in some of the most highly reputed establishments in France to a plate of pancakes enjoyed in a simple *crêperie*, Brittany's restaurants cater for all tastes and all pockets.

The Auberge Bretonne in La Roche-Bernard *(see p248)*

TYPES OF RESTAURANTS

Bretons are fond of good food, and locally grown produce provides plenty of opportunity for creating excellent dishes. Away from the coasts, especially, there are restaurants that offer genuine Breton cuisine at reasonable prices. Some hotels, particularly those affiliated to **Logis de France** *(see p215)*, serve high-quality regional food. The *fermes-auberges* (farmhouse inns) and *tables d'hôtes* offer the opportunity of enjoying simple, inexpensive dishes made with local produce.

On the coasts, the choice is wider but the quality may not be the highest. There are fast-food outlets, pizzerias, snack bars and *crêperies* (pancake houses) as well as upmarket restaurants.

Tables et Saveurs de Bretagne is an association of 40 restaurants in Brittany that offer original cuisine based on local produce. Information on these restaurants is available from the **Comité Régional du Tourisme**.

LOCAL PRODUCE

Such is the abundance and variety of Brittany's fish and seafood and of locally grown fruit and vegetables that it is impossible to mention any more than the most popular.

Breton cuisine is renowned chiefly for its fish dishes. Because of the freshness of local catches, the grilled mackerel and sardines served in Brittany are particularly delicious. Monkfish, sea bass, yellow pollack, turbot, red mullet, sole or sea bream, gently baked or served with *beurre blanc* (a butter, vinegar and shallot sauce), are succulent dishes. In the Loire-Atlantique, shad, elvers and lamprey also appear on the menu. Seafood, such as oysters from Cancale, Paimpol, Aven-Belon, Quiberon and Croisic, and mussels from Vivier and Pénestin, as well as whelks, winkles, shrimps, spider crabs and lobsters, are piled high in almost every market near the coast. Lovers of seafood never tire of scallops, that highly prized delicacy, while top chefs are beginning to use edible seaweed and samphire in their dishes.

According to the season, Brittany's inland areas also offer a range of culinary

Art Nouveau interior of La Cigale in Nantes *(see p249)*

DIRECTORY

FERMES-AUBERGES

Chambre d'Agriculture de Bretagne

ZAC Atalante Champeaux,

Rond Point Maurice Le Lannou,

35042, Rennes Cedex.

Tel (02) 23 48 27 50.

Comité Régional du Tourisme

Information on

Tables et Saveurs de Bretagne

Tel (02) 99 28 44 30.

www.tourismebretagne.com

Les Forges, a restaurant near the Forêt de Brocéliande (see p237)

delights. Potatoes, a basic ingredient in all Breton cuisine, artichokes, cauliflowers, beans (such as those known as *coco de Paimpol*), lamb's lettuce from the Nantes area, asparagus, onions from Roscoff, turnips and leeks are all popular ingredients. Locally grown fruit includes apples, pears and kiwi fruit, and succulent melons from the Rennes area.

BRETON SPECIALITIES

Brittany is famous for its traditionally made butter biscuits and delicious pancakes *(see pp232–3)*, as well as for the tempting *plateau de mer* (seafood platter) and *homard à l'armoricaine* (lobster served in a hot garlic and tomato sauce). Another great classic, albeit in a different league, is a dish of mussels, such as *moules marinière* (mussels cooked in wine).

Because it is a prime producer of pork, Brittany also offers a range of products made from pig meat. Two of the most prominent are *andouilles* (chitterling sausages made with lard) from Guéméné-sur-Scorff, and, from Baye, sausages and pâté (including the famous Hénaff brand).

As for meat dishes, there is the succulent *agneau de pré-salé* (salt-pasture lamb) from

Mont-St-Michel, roast duckling and cold duck galantine.

Breton salted butter (French butter is otherwise unsalted) is also highly prized. In the days before refrigerators existed, salt was added to butter as a preservative, and to this day salted butter is an essential ingredient in Breton cuisine. Salt from Guérande, meanwhile, is recognized as the best in the region.

Breton cakes include *kouign amann*, a delicious cake made with wheat flour, butter and sugar, which is eaten warm. *Far*, Breton prune flan, and *quatre-quarts*, a rich fruit cake, are other deservedly famous specialities, along with Traou-Mad de Pontaven (cookies), Pleyben or St-Michel *galettes* (butter biscuits) and the wafer-thin *crêpes-dentelles* from Quimper.

As for liquid refreshment, cider is the most popular drink in Brittany. Although many people like sweet cider *(cidre doux)*, connoisseurs prefer dry *(cidre brut)*. The best cider-producing regions of Brittany are the areas around Dol-de-Bretagne and the Arguenon, Rance, Messac, Fouesnant and Domagné valleys. *Chouchen*, a kind of mead (or hydromel) is also worth sampling, as is the locally brewed beer. Among the best brands are Coreff, of Morlaix, and Telenn Du, a wheat beer. Muscadet from the Loire-Atlantique is a delicate, crisp, dry wine.

A chef working at Les Maisons de Bricourt (see p236)

PRACTICALITIES

In the high season, it is always advisable to book a restaurant table in advance. While informal dress is perfectly acceptable in most restaurants, such casual wear as shorts is likely to attract disapproval in higher-class establishments. Swimming costumes are definitely unacceptable, except in beach-side restaurants.

Most restaurants offer children's menus, and almost all accept the main bankers' cards. However, in country areas, it is a wise precaution to have cash with you in case any other form of payment is not accepted.

Tables outside a *crêperie* on the Rue St-Georges in Rennes

WHEELCHAIR ACCESS

Unfortunately, few restaurants have proper wheelchair access. When booking, inform the restaurant staff that extra space for a wheelchair will be needed. Organizations providing information for disabled travellers are listed on page 217.

CHILDREN

Children are welcomed in Brittany, and many restaurants, such as creperies, are suitable for families. Most establishments offer special menus for children, and some provide highchairs for toddlers.

The Flavours of Brittany

Although the food most commonly associated with this part of France is the simple *crêpe*, visitors will easily find a good range of far more gastronomic fare, much of it based around the region's top quality vegetables and seafood. Brittany has an extensive coastline – around 1,700 km (1,055 miles) long – and really fresh fish is readily available. Of particular note are the fine oysters, reared in penned-off areas close to the shore. Not surprisingly, given the region's many pig farms, charcuterie features strongly on the Breton menu. Hearty stews made with lamb and beef are also good, especially washed down with the local cider.

Globe artichokes

Mussel-cultivation beds in the Baie de Cancale

MEAT AND CHARCUTERIE

Brittany is France's main pig-rearing region. Look out for *porc fermier*, meat from pigs raised in the open on a cereal-based diet, and for the region's superb charcutérie, which includes a variety of cooked and smoked hams, garlic sausage, *boudin noir* (black pudding), *pâté breton*, a coarsely textured pork terrine, and *andouille de Guémené*, a smoked sausage made from pigs' intestines.

On the marshy fields just inland from the coast, *pré-salé* (salt-marsh) lamb is raised. Most Breton farms rear cows for dairying, especially the black and white *pie noire* breed, but there are some cattle, mostly Charolais or Charolais crosses, that are reared for their excellent beef.

FISH AND SHELLFISH

The sea off Brittany is rich in fish. Loctudy is a major port for mackerel, while Audierne is noted for langoustines, as Erquy and Loguivy-de-la-Mer are for scallops. Lobsters, crabs, prawns (shrimp), mussels, clams, whelks, cockles and oysters are also found in abundance. Huge platters of seafood are served at restaurants all along the coast. Breton

Oysters   Prawns (shrimp)   Lobster   Mackerel   Sardines   Mussels

Selection of typical Breton fish and seafood

LOCAL DISHES AND SPECIALITIES

Meals often start with fish or shellfish. Fish soups, *moules marinières* and stuffed clams or scallops are popular, as are oysters, especially when served with rye bread spread with Breton salted butter. A lobster or crab with mayonnaise, or one of the massive platters of mixed seafood, make a meal in themselves. The main course may be fresh fish baked in sea salt, braised in cider or *à l'armoricaine* (in a herby tomato sauce). Meat dishes include hearty stews, roast pork and lamb *à la bretonne* (with haricot beans, garlic, shallots and tomatoes). Prawns (shrimp) may come with cauliflower and *boudin noir* (black pudding) with slices of apple. Favoured desserts include *crêpes, far aux pruneaux* (a prune and batter pudding) and Plougastel strawberries.

Salted butter

Homard à l'armoricaine *Fresh lobster pieces are cooked in a sauce of tomato, garlic and herbs, enriched with cognac.*

Disaplay of vegetables at a market stall in Vannes

oysters are highly prized. Two basic types are on offer: the more common, crinkled creuse variety and the flat, rounded *belons*, reared at Riec-sur-Belon in the south and at Cancale on the north coast. The mussels that are cultivated in the Vilaine estuary and the Baie de Cancale, are also popular.

BUTTER AND DAIRY PRODUCE

Salted butter is a Breton speciality and is excellent on rye bread to accompany oysters. It is also used in regional delicacies such as salt butter caramels and ice cream.

Brittany also produces much of France's fresh milk. Curiously, though, cheese production is only on a small scale. Local offerings include several fine goat cheeses as well as the mild, semi-soft cheeses, Campénéac, Timadeuc and St-Paulin.

FRUIT AND VEGETABLES

Brittany's mild winters make it an important area for winter and early spring vegetables. Globe artichokes

Sign outside a *crêperie* in the medieval village of Locronan

fill local market stalls from October to May and most of France's cauliflowers come from Northern Finistère. Other important crops include onions, shallots, haricot beans, asparagus, broccoli, potatoes and tomatoes. Plougastel is famous for its sweet succulent strawberries.

BAKED GOODS

An array of delicious baked goods can be found in Brittany including *Kouign-aman* (a sweet bread), *sablé* (shortbread) biscuits, *quatre-quarts* (a rich buttery cake), and *crêpes dentelles* (thin, sugary pancakes, rolled up and baked until crispy).

ON THE MENU

Crêpes Both savoury and sweet, with fillings such as cheese, ham, honey and jam

Bisque de homard A smooth creamy lobster soup

Feuilleté aux fruits de mer Shellfish in puff pastry

Fricassée de pétoncles Clams and leeks fricasséed with white wine and cream

Gigot à la bretonne Leg of lamb with white haricot beans, tomatoes and garlic

Kig ha fars Meat and vegetable hotpot with buckwheat dumpling

Roulade sévigné A roulade of guinea fowl, apples and ham

Moules marinières *Mussels are steamed with dry white wine, shallots, parsley and butter until their shells open.*

Cotriade *This traditional stew of fish, cooked with potato and onion, is often served with slices of toast.*

Far aux pruneaux *Prunes, first soaked in tea, rum or apple eau-de-vie, are baked in a thick sweetened batter.*

Choosing a Restaurant

The restaurants in this section have been selected across a wide price range for their excellent food, good value and interesting location. Most restaurants in Brittany offer set menus which may work out cheaper than the price category. For *Flavours of Brittany see pp234–5*. For map references *see inside back cover*.

ILLE-ET-VILAINE

BILLE Ferme de Mésouboin   P ☂   €
On the D179 direction Fougères to Vitré, 35113 **Tel** *02 99 97 61 57*   **Map** *F2*

This charming 17th-century manor house, complete with chapel, only 8 km (5 miles) from Fougères, offers authentic farmhouse cooking. Specialities include home-made paté, duck in cider, *gratin fougerais* (a local dish), and wonderful house desserts. Home-made cider and apple juice are also available. Telephone to reserve in advance.

CANCALE La Cancalaise   ☂   €
3 Rue Vallée-Porçon, 35260 **Tel** *02 99 89 71 22*   **Map** *E1*

Exceptional both for the local atmosphere and the food, this *crêperie* has been used as a film set, where Joe Cocker sings "N'oubliez jamais" in a Gérard Jugnot film. The *crêpes* (pancakes) are delicious and the local produce is well-chosen: sausages from a neighbouring farm, scallops from the catch of the day, and strawberries from St-Éloir.

CANCALE Le Surcouf   ☂ ♿ 🍴 ☂   €€
7 Quai Gambetta, 35260 **Tel** *02 99 89 61 75*   **Map** *E1*

One of the best restaurants along the quay, Le Surcouf makes an effort to prepare more than the standard tourist dishes. Great care is taken in the choice of produce. The seafood platter, bass *à la plancha* and the turbot are especially recommended. The good wine list has some excellent Bordeaux wines at reasonable prices. Closed Jan–Dec.

CANCALE Les Maisons de Bricourt   P ☂ ♿ ☂   €€€€
1 Rue Duguesclin, 35260 **Tel** *02 99 89 64 76*   **Map** *E1*

The acclaimed chef Olivier Roellinger takes diners on a worldwide adventure, combining to perfection local seafood with exotic spices, such as the lobster dish or bass cooked with flower-scented oils. Recommended meat dishes include saddle of lamb roasted with exotic spices. Closed mid-Dec–mid-Mar.

CHATEAUBOURG Ar Milin'   P ☂ ♿ ☂   €€€
30 Rue de Paris, 35220 **Tel** *02 99 00 30 91*   **Map** *F3*

This restaurant, in an ancient flour mill, has a lovely view out on to the Vilaine river and parkland. The chef, a pupil of Alain Ducasse, offers superbly prepared dishes, such as rabbit with red pepper and baby marrows, or a red fruit tiramisu. There is also a bistro and modern guestrooms. Closed Christmas–mid-Jan.

COMBOURG L'Ecrivain   P ☂ ♿ 🍴   €
Place St-Gilduin, 35270 **Tel** *02 99 73 01 61*   **Map** *E2*

The decor evokes memories of Chateaubriand and has a selection of second-hand books for sale. The cuisine is imaginative and uses local produce. Specialities include fish smoked on the premises, tuna perfumed with basil, and delicious home-made pastries and desserts (also sold to take away). Closed 2 weeks Jun; 2 weeks Oct.

DINARD La Passerelle   €€
Promenade de Clair de Lune, 35800 **Tel** *02 99 16 96 37*   **Map** *E1*

Refined cuisine is served in elegant, contemporary surroundings and at night the view is spectacular. Dishes include carpaccio of bass seasoned with vanilla, tuna kebabs or crayfish ravioli served with Puy lentils. Leave room for desserts such as warm chocolate tart served with tea flavoured ice cream. Closed Sun dinner, Mon & Tue lunch.

DINARD Didier Méril   ☂ 🍴 ☂   €€€
1 Place Général de Gaulle, 35800 **Tel** *02 99 46 95 74*   **Map** *E1*

This elegant restaurant, with an attractive terrace and close to La Plage de l'Ecluse, has a dynamic talented chef. The inventive menu includes shellfish and lobster dishes in succulent sauces, and there is an interesting selection of Breton cheeses. There is also a good selection of wines. Closed 2 weeks Dec; 2 weeks Jan.

FOUGÈRES Les Voyageurs   ☂   €
10 Place Gambetta, 35300 **Tel** *02 99 99 14 17*   **Map** *F2*

The urban location is not this restaurant's most attractive feature, but it serves good gourmet cuisine. The dining room has recently been decorated in a bright, contemporary design that complements the imaginative dishes. The carefully selected ingredients are sourced from local producers. Making a reservation is recommended.

Key to Symbols *see back cover flap*

FOUGÈRES Le Haute-Sève
37 Boulevard Jean-Jaurès, 35300 **Tel** *02 99 94 23 39*   €€€

Map F2

The enthusiastic chef creates interesting dishes with finesse, using local produce, at this restaurant whose menus reflect both Norman and Breton influences. Dishes include crispy camembert with herbs, bass served with an iced ratatouille, and crab and herb ravioli. The dessert menu has a good choice. Closed 3 weeks Aug.

HÉDÉ L'Hostellerie de Vieux Moulin
Ancienne Route de St-Malo, 35630 **Tel** *02 99 45 45 70*   €€

Map E2

In a building erected in the 19th century as part of a complex to supply water power, this restaurant overlooks the Hédé castle, with the ruins of the old watermill in the grounds. Good-value lunchtime menus include pan-fried scallops, lightly grilled langoustines, and succulent duck. There are also rooms available.

HÉDÉ La Vieille Auberge
La Vallée, 35630 **Tel** *02 99 45 46 25*   €€

Map E2

The setting for this restaurant, in a 17th-century stone house with a view of a lake and pretty garden, is idyllic. Among the dishes of the experienced chef, who specializes in seafood, are tartare of crab and salmon, spicy roast monkfish and risotto of scallops and mushrooms with parmesan "tuiles". Closed 3 weeks end Feb; end Aug–beginning Sep.

MONT-ST-MICHEL Relais St-Michel
On the causeway 2 km (1 mile) from the mount, 35260 **Tel** *02 33 89 32 00*   €€€

Map F2

In the same chain as Hôtel-Restaurant de la Mère Poulard, this is the only one with a superb view of Mont-St-Michel. The traditional and regional cuisine includes Breton lobster with *sauce armoricaine* (tomato and garlic sauce), and roast leg of lamb. Each fixed-price menu includes an omelette flambéed with calvados, and caramelized apples.

MONT-ST-MICHEL Mère Poulard
Grande-Rue, 50170 **Tel** *02 33 89 68 68*   €€€€

Map F2

Frequented mainly by tourists, this deluxe brasserie was founded in 1888 by Mère Poulard and is a legend. Famous for omelettes cooked over a wood fire, it now offers fine dishes such as *agneau de pré-salé* (salt-pasture lamb) and roast piglet. The menu is slightly over-priced, but the restaurant has an old-world charm that is worth experiencing.

NOYAL SUR VILLAINE Auberge du Pont d'Acigné
Route d'Acigné, 35530 **Tel** *02 99 62 52 55*   €€€

Map F3

Regional cuisine with a modern twist is served in this charming restaurant on the banks of the Vilaine River, 12km from Rennes. The menu specializes in fish and includes dishes such as crunchy tomatoes served with a paella sorbet or lobster ravioli with rhubarb. The lunchtime menu is good value. Closed Sat lunch, Sun dinner & Mon.

PAIMPONT Les Forges
Les Forges, 35380 **Tel** *02 99 06 81 07*   €€

Map E3

In a magical location on the edge of the Forêt de Brocéliande, this restaurant serves traditional dishes, perfected by the chef for over three decades. The menu specializes in game dishes such as roast pigeon and partridge, and venison. There is cheese from the nearby Abbaye de la Trappe and a good choice of desserts. Closed Mon, Tue dinner.

REDON Le Moulin de Via
Route de Lagacilly, 35600 **Tel** *02 99 71 05 16*   €€€

Map E3

An authentic *longère* (Breton farm building) houses this restaurant set in its own garden, close to the town centre. The chef uses the best of local produce to create dishes such as pan-fried Breton lobster, stuffed Sainte-Anne d'Auray pigeon and Plougastel strawberries served with spices and chocolate. Closed first 2 weeks Sep; one week Mar.

RENNES Léon Le Cochon
1 Rue Maréchal-Joffre, 35000 **Tel** *02 99 79 37 54*   €€

Map E3

This traditional city bistro is decorated with humour – there is an illuminated tree and the original oak beams are painted bright green. Pork is on the menu in all its forms: *charcuterie*; *a la plancha*; with a rich wine sauce. There is also a good choice of other meat dishes including veal and pigeon, as well as fish. Excellent local cheeses too.

RENNES L'Escu de Runfao
11 Rue de Chapitre, 35000 **Tel** *02 99 79 13 10*   €€€

Map E3

Situated in the picturesque old quarter of Rennes, this oak-timbered building houses a cosy, old-fashioned, refined restaurant. In the summer there is a peaceful outside courtyard. Dishes include Breton turbot, John Dory, crayfish and game in season. There is also a good selection of wines. Closed Sat lunch, Sun dinner.

RENNES L'Ouvrée
18 Place des Lices, 35000 **Tel** *02 99 30 16 38*   €€€

Map E3

In this chic yet traditional restaurant – splendidly located on a square lined with timber-framed houses – the menu includes superb foie gras, turbot with assorted shellfish, and a mousseline of *fromage blanc* with strawberries. The wine list features a different wine producer each month. Closed first 2 weeks Aug.

RENNES La Fontaine aux Perles
Le Manoir de la Poterie, 96 Rue de la Poterie, 35200 **Tel** *02 99 53 90 90*   €€€€

Map E3

A passionate, enthusiastic chef produces dynamic cuisine in this restaurant on the eastern outskirts of Rennes. The freshest local produce is used. Artichoke heart with crayfish, veal served with a creamy morelle mushroom sauce and Breton lobster braised in a sweet Layon wine are just some of the exceptional dishes on offer. Closed one week in Aug.

ST-GREGOIRE Le Saison

P 🏃 ♿ 🖼   €€€€

Impasse de Vieux-Bourg, 35760 **Tel** *02 99 68 79 35*   **Map** *E2*

Originally from the Basque country, the chef here has lots of personality. Located in the smart suburbs of Rennes, the dining room is bright and modern. The menu can change at the whim of the chef, who conjures up stunning dishes such as bass accompanied by a vegetable sausage, and pig's trotters with sea snails.

ST-JOUAN DES GUERETS Ferme de la Porte

P 🏃 ♿   €

Centre-ville, 35430 **Tel** *02 99 81 10 76*   **Map** *E1*

Just 3 km (2 miles) from St-Malo, this farmhouse has an exceptional view of the Rance estuary. Home-made charcuterie, terrines, foie gras, duck, piglet and lamb spit roasted in the open fireplace are just some of the delicious dishes on offer. Guestrooms *(chambres d'hôtes)* and gîtes are also available. Telephone to reserve in low season.

ST-MALO La Coquille d'Œuf

🏃   €

20 Rue de la Corne-de-Cerf, 35400 **Tel** *02 99 40 92 62*   **Map** *E1*

Behind the turquoise façade of this restaurant there is a family atmosphere and homely cuisine. The simple but well-presented dishes on the menu include the inescapable *oeuf* (egg) *cocotte* with sorrel to start, followed by a cooked-to-perfection pollock steak with chives. Closed 2 weeks Jun, 2 weeks Dec.

ST-MALO Restaurant L'Epicerie

🏃   €

18 Rue de la Herse, 35400 **Tel** *02 23 18 34 55*   **Map** *E1*

Situated within the ramparts, near to the Grande Porte, this bistro-style restaurant serves locally sourced produce and freshly caught fish from Erquy port. The kitchen and dining room almost merge into each other. The menu depends on the season and the pick of the market, and therefore changes daily.

ST-MALO La Chalut

🏃   €€€

8 Rue de la Corne de Cerf, 35400 **Tel** *02 99 56 71 58*   **Map** *E1*

One of St-Malo's best restaurants, La Chalut has a chef who excels in fish dishes and well-chosen produce simply prepared. Assorted fish seasoned with orange and saffron-flavoured oil, and John Dory with fresh coriander are examples of the delicious dishes on offer. There is also a good selection of cheeses. Book ahead.

ST-MALO La Saint Placide

♿   €€€

6 Place Poncel, St Servan sur Mer 35400 **Tel** *02 99 81 70 73*   **Map** *E1*

This is one of the best places to eat outside the ramparts of St Malo and the contemporary decor contrasts well with the traditional building. The promising chef creates dishes such as crispy crayfish, basil and parmesan tart, and bass with a potato and truffle emulsion. Closed Wed (except Jul & Aug) and Tue.

ST-MALO A La Duchesse Anne

🖼   €€€€

5 Place Guy-la-Chambre, 35400 **Tel** *02 99 40 85 33*   **Map** *E1*

Long-established and with an appealingly nostalgic setting, this restaurant serves traditional, classic cuisine. Dishes include Chateaubriand with *béarnaise* sauce, filet of beef with its marrow bone, and grilled or poached turbot – followed by a fabulous tarte tatin. Closed Dec–Jan.

ST-MÉLOIR DES ONDES Tirel Guérin

P 🏃 ♿ 🍴   €€€€

Gare de la Gouesnière, 35350 **Tel** *02 99 89 10 46*   **Map** *E2*

A countryside restaurant just 10 km (6 miles) from Cancale and St-Malo features a culinary team renowned for their light classic dishes. Specialities include seared lobster served with salad and sherry vinegar dressing, loin of lamb, and wild oysters. Also delicious are the inventive desserts. Dress smartly. Closed 22 Dec–20 Jan.

VITRÉ La Taverne de l'Ecu

🏃   €€€€

12 Rue Baudairie, 35500 **Tel** *02 99 75 11 09*   **Map** *F3*

This half-timbered Renaissance house provides an historic ambience for a meal in one of two dining rooms. The menu changes seasonally. Try the venison cooked in wine served with mushrooms and a chestnut flan, fish with sorrel sauce and courgette crumble, roast rabbit or one of the other fish dishes. Home-made bread accompanies your meal.

CÔTES D'ARMOR

BRÉHAT ÎLE DE L'Oiseau des Îles

🏃 🖼   €

Rue du Port, 22870 **Tel** *02 96 20 00 53*   **Map** *D1*

A popular *creperie*, the best on the island, L'Oiseau des Îles is in a colourful blue-shuttered building. The dining room is bright, and there is also an outdoor terrace. On the menu are typical pancake fillings, along with more unusual ones such as *andouillette* (chitterling sausage). A good choice of salads too. Reserve in peak season. Closed Jan–Feb.

DINAN Crêperie Ahna

🏃 🖼   €

7 Rue de la Poissonnerie, 22100 **Tel** *02 96 39 09 13*   **Map** *E2*

This *crêperie*, located on one of the pedestrianized streets in the heart of the city, has a faithful following. There is a grill menu, as well as a vast choice of fillings such as lamb, turkey, smoked ham and mushrooms for the substantial *galettes de blé noir* (buckwheat pancake). The sweet flambéed *crêpes* are irresistible. Closed Mar, Nov.

Key to Price Guide *see p236* **Key to Symbols** *see back cover flap*

DINAN Le Bistrot de Viaduc

P 🖶 💡   ©

22 Rue du Lion d'Or, Lanvallay, 22100 **Tel** *02 96 85 95 00*   **Map** E2

In a pleasant setting off the tourist track, overlooking the Rance valley just 2 km (3 miles) east of the centre of Dinan, this up-market bistro has a relaxed atmosphere. The staple bistro dishes, such as the herring salad and grilled belly pork, are very tasty, and there is a classic well-chosen wine list. Closed mid-Jun–mid-Jul; 3 weeks Christmas.

DINAN La Mère Pourcel

©©©

3 Place des Merciers, 22100 **Tel** *02 96 39 03 80*   **Map** E2

This restaurant in a stunning timbered Gothic building, with tables on the cobbled street, is a Dinan landmark. It serves generous portions of seasonal gourmet cuisine, which includes locally reared lamb along with more innovative dishes such as cod with truffles. There is a good selection of wines.

ERQUY Restaurant L'Escurial

💡   ©©©

21 Boulevard de la Mer, 22430 **Tel** *02 96 72 31 56*   **Map** D1

Since the arrival of the new chef in 2002, the cuisine of this restaurant – with a panoramic view of the port – has been inspired. Scallops marinated in *fleur de sel* (sea salt), with a spicy cream sauce and vinaigrette of beetroot juice, and leg of rabbit with prunes are some of the succulent dishes on the quintessentially seafood menu. Closed mid-Nov–mid-Feb.

FRÉHEL Le Victorine

🚹 ♿ 🖶   ©©

Place de la Mairie, 22240 **Tel** *02 96 41 55 55*   **Map** E1

Friendly and frequented by local people, this restaurant is in the town square. The chef uses the best local produce. The menu offers tasty dishes such as roast brill, or leg of rabbit with prunes. Make sure to leave room for the remarkable desserts. Closed mid-Nov–mid-Dec.

LANNION Les Filets Bleus

©©

Port de Loquémeau, Tredez, 23000 **Tel** *02 96 35 22 96*   **Map** C1

Situated just 12km (7 miles) from Lannion, this mainly seafood restaurant is in an idyllic setting. The dining room lacks a little charm, but the freshness of the ingredients more than makes up for it. Mouth-watering dishes include pollock with cinnamon and turbot with lemongrass. Open lunchtime only.

LANNION La Ville Blanche

P 🚹 🖶 💡   ©©©©

3 km (2 miles) from Lannion on the road to Tréguier, 22300 **Tel** *02 96 37 04 28*   **Map** C1

In this restaurant, with an excellent and unusual menu devised by Jean Yves Jaguin, dishes such as roast lobster with salted butter, the claws served as ragout, are served up. Simpler dishes include monkfish in cider sauce served with local vegetables. There is a good selection of Loire wines. Closed first week Jul, mid-Dec–Jan.

LOGUIVY-DE-LA-MER Au Grand Large

🚹 🖶   ©©

5 Rue de la Jetée, 22620 **Tel** *02 96 20 90 18*   **Map** D1

In a picture postcard port just 5 km (3 miles) north of Paimpol, this restaurant sits on the jetty looking out over the fishing boats. It also serves wonderful straightforward seafood dishes, such as the langoustines. It is slightly expensive, but the freshness of the produce is exceptional. Closed Jan, mid-Nov–mid-Dec.

MÛR DE BRETAGNE L'Auberge Grand'Maison

P 🚹   ©©©

1 Rue Léon Le Cerf, 22530 **Tel** *02 96 28 51 10*   **Map** D2

On this restaurant's menu are dishes that remind the chef of his childhood: Breton pig, scallops, and early asparagus. He also prepares innovative dishes such as sole and red mullet dressed with asparagus and a poppy vinaigrette. Dress smartly. Closed Sun dinner, Mon, Tue lunch (except Jul–Aug); 2 weeks Oct; 2 weeks Feb.

PAIMPOL L'Islandais

🚹   ©

19 Quai Morand, 22500 **Tel** *02 96 20 93 80*   **Map** D1

In this popular *crêperie* overlooking the lively Paimpol harbour, the chef serves up a good selection of traditional Breton *galettes* (savoury pancakes), which are always a favourite with children and a good option for vegetarians. Shellfish is abundant, and includes fresh oysters, mussels, lobsters and langoustines.

PAIMPOL La Vieille Tour

🚹 💡   ©©

13 Rue de l'Eglise, 22500 **Tel** *02 96 20 83 18*   **Map** D1

In the old town, this restaurant is cosy and friendly. The menus include the catch of the day, and the specialities include original and classic dishes such as a gratin of sardines, cod steak with herring purée, and brill with assorted shellfish. There is an interesting wine list. Closed Mon lunch, Wed mid-Nov–Mar; Sun dinner Sep–Apr; last week Jun.

PAIMPOL Le Repaire de Kerroc'h

©©

29 Quai Morand, 22500 **Tel** *02 96 20 50 13*   **Map** D1

A former 18th-century corsaire's residence on the port, this classic restaurant serves imaginative gourmet food. Star anise, honey and fennel are used to flavour several fish and seafood dishes, while a typical meat dish is duck with apricots, honey and prunes. There is also a cosy bar bistro. Closed Tue, Wed lunch.

PAIMPOL Restaurant Hôtel de la Marne

P 💡   ©©

30 Rue de la Marne, 22500 **Tel** *02 96 20 82 16*   **Map** D1

Close to the railway station, this restaurant is improving all the time, with the talented chef adding personal touches to classic dishes. Specialities include fillet of pollock with a delicately flavoured crust, and a Normandy *teurgoule* (spiced rice pudding). The cellar has some real gems. Dress smartly. Closed Sun dinner, Mon (except Jul–Aug).

PERROS-GUIREC Le Soroît
81 Rue Ernest-Renan, 22700 **Tel** *02 96 23 23 83*

Map C1

Located on the harbour, opposite the fresh fish auction, this restaurant serves seafood whose freshness and quality is assured. The enjoyable, well-prepared cuisine focuses on fish and seafood classics, served in a comfortable dining room in front of an open fire. Service is friendly and attentive. Closed Sun dinner, Mon.

PERROS-GUIREC La Crémaillère
13 Place de l'Eglise, 22700 **Tel** *02 96 23 22 08*

Map C1

Seasonal menus, based on seafood and grilled meats, are served in the rustic interior of this 17th-century building with a convivial atmosphere. The seafood kebabs with smoked duck breast are recommended, as is the succulent roast beef. The desserts are imaginative. Reservation is advisable in peak season. Closed Mon lunch.

PLANCOËT Jean-Pierre Crouzil
20 Les Quais, 22130 **Tel** *02 96 84 10 24*

Map E2

The experienced chef has a passion for creating innovative menus. Try imaginative and tasty dishes such as turbot with baby vegetables in a light black truffle sauce or roast Breton lobster. There is also a well-stocked cellar with some good finds from the south. Closed Sun dinner–Tue.

PLÉLO Au Char à Bancs
Moulin de la Ville-Geffroy, 22170 **Tel** *02 96 74 13 63*

Map D2

In this family-run farmhouse restaurant in an ancient mill, homely comfort dishes are simmered in the open fireplace. The speciality is a pork stew served with home-grown vegetables. Wash down the well-garnished *galettes* with a glass of local cider. Closed Tue Jul–Aug, Mon–Fri rest of year. Reservation is advisable.

PLÉNEUF VAL-ANDRÉ Au Biniou
121 Rue Clémenceau, 22370 **Tel** *02 96 72 24 35*

Map D2

Near the casino and the beach at Val-André, this restaurant is a favourite with the locals. High-quality, interesting cuisine is served in elegant surroundings. Particularly recommended are the braised sea bass and the seafood kebabs. Closed Tue dinner, Wed; Feb.

PLÉRIN La Vieille Tour
75 Rue de la Tour, 22190 **Tel** *02 96 33 10 30*

Map D2

This energetic chef produces succulent dishes such as foie gras with raspberry ketchup. Leave room for the original desserts such as chestnut tiramisu. There is also a good selection of wines. Dress smartly. Closed Sat lunch, Sun dinner, Mon; mid-Aug–mid-Sep; 2 weeks Feb.

PLOUMANAC'H Castel Beau Rivage
Place St-Guirec, 22700 **Tel** *02 96 91 40 87*

Map C1

In a grand granite building with a superb location by the beach, this recently established restaurant holds promise. The chef produces well-prepared unpretentious dishes. Try the marinated tuna, or red mullet served with a *provençale tian* (baked dish), followed by a *clafoutis* (sweet batter pudding). Closed Mon, Tue lunch, Sun dinner.

POMMERIT LE-VISCOUNT Le Traon
8 Kervaudry, 29580 **Tel** *02 96 21 78 53*

Map D2

This farm raises its own pigs for the *assiette campagnarde* (plate of cold meats and patés), and goats for the cheese board. The copious menus feature traditional dishes such as *jambon au foin* (ham cooked with hay) and *kig ha fars* (see p234). An apéritif and coffee is included in the price. Reservations only for Sat dinner, Sun lunch.

SABLES D'OR LES PINS La Voile d'Or
Allée des Acacias, 22240 **Tel** *02 96 41 42 49*

Map D1

The chef transforms simple produce into imaginative dishes that make the most of the local produce. The result is dishes such as Erquy scallops with fresh herbs, succulent Breton lobster and *sablé* Breton with caramel and butter. Dress smartly. Closed Sun dinner–Tue.

ST-BRIEUC Amadeus
22 Rue de Gouët, 22000 **Tel** *02 96 33 92 44*

Map D2

Housed in one of the oldest buildings in the historic town of St-Brieuc, this elegant gourmet restaurant specializes in fish. Dishes such as truffle-topped sea bass, tuna ratatouille and fillet of sole are all outstanding. The wide range of tempting desserts includes Amaretto chocolate cake, and Breton butter biscuits with fruit.

ST-BRIEUC Bistrot du Port
15 Rue des Trois-Frères-Le-Goff, 22000 **Tel** *02 96 33 83 03*

Map D2

Although it doesn't actually have a sea view, as it is located on a small street leading to the port, this restaurant is still recommended. The interior is typical bistro, bordering on kitsch, but the atmosphere is relaxed and friendly. The chef prepares savoury dishes using fresh produce direct from the market. Closed Sun.

ST-BRIEUC La Croix Blanche
61 Rue de Genève, Cesson, 22000 **Tel** *02 96 33 16 97*

Map D2

In a large white house with a pretty garden, this elegant restaurant serves well-prepared dishes delicately enriched with exotic flavours. Expect dishes such as a lasagne of lobster and grapefruit or strawberry salad with mint cream, Bergamot and griotte cherries. Dress smartly. Closed Sun dinner, Mon; 3 weeks Aug.

Key to Price Guide *see p236* **Key to Symbols** *see back cover flap*

ST-BRIEUC Restaurant Aux Pesked €€€

59 Rue de Légué, 22000 **Tel** *02 96 33 34 65* **Map** *D2*

A short walk from the cathedral, this gourmet city-centre restaurant has elegant decor, and a lovely view of the Légué valley from the terrace. The remarkable, creative cuisine is mainly fish-based. Specialities include roast tandoori langoustines with a fennel emulsion and fillet of John Dory with a curry emulsion.

ST-QUAY-PORTRIEUX Fleur de Blé Noir €

9 Rue du Commandant Malbert, 22410 **Tel** *02 96 70 31 55* **Map** *D1*

This *crêperie* has diverse fillings for the fine *galettes* and *crêpes*. There are basically two menus: *de la terre* (from the land) and *de la mer* (from the sea). The former features *andouillette* (chitterling sausage) and ham; the latter has such specialities as flambéed scallops with sardines, and fillet of sole with camembert. Closed Sun, Wed; Jan.

TRÉBEURDEN Ker An Nod €€

2 Rue de Porz-Termen, 22560 **Tel** *02 96 23 50 21* **Map** *C1*

With a great location facing the sea and with a view of the islands offshore, this is a traditional family-run restaurant whose specialities are fish and seafood. The chef produces excellent dishes such as warm oysters with Muscadet-flavoured butter, Breton lobster, a *papillote* of cod and Trégor chicken with crayfish. Closed early Jan–late Mar.

TRÉBEURDEN Le Manoir de Lan Kerellec €€€€€

Allée Centrale de Lan Kerellec, 22560 **Tel** *02 96 15 00 00* **Map** *C1*

A beautiful rotund dining room with magnificent views of the sea, and a ceiling in the form of ship's hull, is the setting for elegant dishes such as puréed artichokes and langoustines, oysters and *andouille* (chitterling sausage), and white pudding and scallops. Desserts are equally good. Dress smartly. Closed Mon–Thur lunch; mid-Nov–Mar.

TRÉGASTEL Auberge Vieille Eglise €

Place de l'Eglise, 22730 **Tel** *02 96 23 88 31* **Map** *C1*

In the old village, a flower-covered Breton inn offers exceptionally good traditional cuisine. Walk through the bar to the rustic dining room, where dishes such as foie gras with Granny Smith apples, and panfried bass served with artichoke mousse are on offer. The service is good. Reserve in peak season. Closed Mon (except Jul–Aug), Tue dinner, Sun; Mar.

TRÉGUIER Des Trois Rivières €€

Port de Plaisance, 22220 **Tel** *02 96 92 97 00* **Map** *C1*

Part of the Hôtel Marine, beside the harbour, this gourmet restaurant offers good value for money. Both seafood and meat feature on the menu, with dishes such as veal with olive-flavoured juices served with polenta, and pollock in a chorizo crust. The cheese course is interesting. Closed Sat lunch, Sun dinner, Mon except Jun–Sep; Jan–mid-Feb.

TREVOU-TEGUIGHEC Kerbugalic €€

1 Vieille-Côte-de-Trestel, 22660 **Tel** *02 96 23 72 15* **Map** *C1*

A typical Breton auberge facing the sea with a homely family atmosphere, this establishment likes to steer clear of the banal tourist trade fare. Uncomplicated dishes with well-chosen local produce, such as a seafood platter and plainly grilled fish, are carefully prepared and served. Closed lunch except Sun, Mon; Oct–Mar.

NORTHERN FINISTÈRE

BATZ ÎLE DE Crêperie La Cassonade €

Le Débarcardère, 29253 **Tel** *02 98 61 75 25* **Map** *B1*

Located on a pretty terrace with the smell of honeysuckle in the air. The menu has a wide selection of dishes, ranging from mussels and chips (made from organic potatoes) to tasty buckwheat crepes. In the afternoon, return for Breton cake or a refreshing ice-cream. Service is non-stop.

BREST Ma Petite Folie €€

Port de Plaisance du Moulin-Blanc, 29200 **Tel** *02 98 42 44 42* **Map** *B2*

The menu of this restaurant, on a former lobster-fishing boat moored in the pleasure port, features abundant seafood platters, local oysters, grilled lobster and simply prepared but excellent fish dishes. The wine list could be more interesting. Reservation is essential at weekends and in high season. Closed 1–10 Jan.

BREST La Fleur de Sel €€€€

15bis Rue de Lyon, 29200 **Tel** *02 98 44 38 65* **Map** *B2*

This is a modern bright city-centre restaurant, with simple, comfortable furnishings. The dishes are prepared with precision. Try the lobster *parmentier* with truffle juice, the warm oysters with a cider *sabayon* and the walnut ice-cream. The set menu at midday is particularly good value for money. Service is a little stuffy.

BREST Le Nouveau Rossini €€€€

22 Rue Commandant Drogou, 29200 **Tel** *02 98 47 90 00* **Map** *B2*

This restaurant is located in the former Maritime Prefecture that housed Générale de Gaulle during the Liberation. The menu focuses mainly on fish and seafood such as roast Loctudy langoustines and tartare of salmon. The vaulted cellar is used for wine tastings. There is a pretty garden too. Closed Sun dinner & Mon.

CARANTEC La Chaise de Curé   €€

3 Place de la République, 29660 **Tel** *02 98 78 33 27*   **Map** *B1*

Situated in the church square, and with an elegant dining room, this restaurant has a young but experienced chef. The dishes, such as Carantec oysters, tuna carpaccio and swordfish steak, use the best ingredients. Homage is paid to the desserts too. Service is good. Closed Wed, Thu except Jul–Aug; 2 weeks Nov; mid-Jan–mid-Feb.

CARANTEC Restaurant Patrick Jeffroy   €€€€€

20 Rue Kélénn, 29660 **Tel** *02 98 67 00 47*   **Map** *B1*

There is a magnificent view over Kélénn beach from this restaurant in a fabulous 1930s manor house hotel. Shellfish is in abundance, with classic and modern cuisine combining to perfection in dishes such as fillet of sole with cider butter, pig's trotters served with artichokes, and a fig tart served with mango sorbet. There is an extensive choice of Loire Valley wines.

CONQUET LE Le Relais de Vieux Port   €

1 Quai Drellach, 29217 **Tel** *02 98 89 15 91*   **Map** *A2*

You can almost dangle your feet in the water as you sit and choose the fillings for your *crêpe*. Seafood is the house speciality. Try a *crêpe* filled with fresh scallops or prawns accompanied by a green salad. Leave room for dessert, especially the *Bonne Maman* with caramelized apples and whipped cream.

CONQUET LE Ferme de Keringar   €€

Lochrist, 29217 **Tel** *02 98 89 09 59*   **Map** *A2*

In an authentic Breton farmhouse hearty dishes are prepared using local cider and seaweed to flavour the sauces. Breton dish *kig ha fars*, a meat and vegetable stew with buckwheat dumplings, is the speciality. The atmosphere is friendly and relaxed; there are also snug, comfortable guestrooms. Open only weekends out of season.

GUIMILIAU Ar Chupen   €

43 Rue de Calvaire, 29400 **Tel** *02 98 68 73 63*   **Map** *B2*

After admiring the richly decorated church, step down the road to this restaurant in a renovated Breton farmhouse. Traditional lacy *galettes* (savoury pancakes) made with sarrazin flour, and *crêpes* are prepared to order. The choice of fillings seems endless. Good place for children and vegetarians. Friendly staff.

LAMPAUL-GUIMILIAU L'Escapade   €

8 Place de Villiers, 29400 **Tel** *02 98 68 61 27*   **Map** *B2*

A traditional restaurant and *crêperie*, L'Escapade has two large spacious dining rooms. Specialities on the classic menu include goulash soup and *coquilles* (scallops) *à la Bretonne*. The *galette* and *crêpe* menu includes some unusual fillings, such as prunes and smoked bacon, or for dessert, cherry, chocolate and whipped cream. Closed Mon.

LAMPAUL-PLOUARZEL Auberge de Vieux Puits   €€€

Place de l'Eglise, 29810 **Tel** *02 98 84 09 13*   **Map** *A2*

Although on the well-beaten tourist track, on the coast north of Le Conquet, the chef here does not serve up anything slapdash. The good-value menus include a variety of well-prepared dishes. Prawns grilled with rosemary, pork fillet *au colombo*, and veal sweetbreads in port-flavoured sauce are recommended. Closed Sun dinner, Mon.

PLOUDALMÉZEAU-PORTSALL Le Caïman   €

44 Rue du Port, 29830 **Tel** *02 98 48 69 77*   **Map** *B1*

As the name of this restaurant and the gaily decorated dining room suggests, the chef has spent some time in the tropics. There is a lively, trendy atmosphere with jazz and blues musical evenings. The terrace, on the water's edge, is a great place to enjoy grilled seafood or stuffed mussels.

LOCQUIREC Le Grand Hôtel des Bains   €€€

15 bis Rue de l'Eglise, 29241 **Tel** *02 98 67 41 02*   **Map** *C1*

Tucked away from the bustle of the crowds and in an early 20th-century building that has recently been renovated, this hotel-restaurant has a dining room with contemporary decor and a view of gardens and the sea. It offers sophisticated cuisine focusing on seafood and organic vegetables. Only open for dinner.

MORLAIX Brasserie de l'Europe   €

1 Rue d'Aiguillon, 29600 **Tel** *02 98 88 81 15*   **Map** *C1*

Part of the Hôtel de l'Europe, this typical up-market brasserie serves good-quality traditional dishes. They include platters of cold meats and salads, terrines, savoury tarts, and beef in many guises: *tartare* or carpaccio, or *bavette* steak grilled with shallots. Good selection of ultra-classic desserts. The service is efficient and pleasant. Closed Sun.

MORLAIX La Marée Bleue   €€€

3 Rampe St-Mélaine, 29600 **Tel** *02 98 63 24 21*   **Map** *C1*

This restaurant is in one of the oldest houses in the area around St-Mélaine church, near the viaduct. Decorated in fresh colours, the rustic dining room is charming and is occasionally used to exhibit local artists' work. On the menu is traditional cuisine with seafood and shellfish specialities. Closed Sun dinner, Mon.

OUESSANT ÎLE DE Ty Korn   €

Lampaul village centre, 29217 **Tel** *02 98 48 87 33*   **Map** *A2*

Live music and a good beer selection are provided in the bar, which is favoured by local residents. The cosy unpretentious restaurant prepares simple, uncomplicated regional dishes that include langoustines, sea bass and an excellent fish soup. The menus are hearty and good value and the atmosphere friendly. Closed Sun dinner, Mon.

Key to Price Guide *see p236* **Key to Symbols** *see back cover flap*

PLOUDIER La Butte

P ⚡ €€€

10 Rue de la Mer, 29260 **Tel** *02 98 25 40 54* **Map** *B1*

A stunning view of the Baie de Goulven is a bonus feature of a restaurant that offers such refined fish dishes as turbot with three *fruits vanillés*, and meat dishes such as young pigeon *kig ha fars (see p235)* and roast beef with Chinon-flavoured sauce. There are also classic desserts. Closed Sun, Mon.

PLOUGASTEL-DAOULAS Le Chevalier de l'Auberlac'h

⚡ 🖼 €

5 Rue Mathurin Thomas, 29470 **Tel** *02 98 40 54 56* **Map** *B2*

Offering traditional cuisine, this is the best restaurant on the peninsula. A good selection of both meat and fish dishes includes fish sauerkraut, salmon with *beurre blanc* or flambéed langoustines. The lunchtime weekday menu offers plenty of choice and is very good value. Closed Mon dinner (Apr–Sep); Mon (Oct–Mar).

ROSCOFF Le Surcouf

⚡ €

14 Rue Amiral Révellière, 29680 **Tel** *02 98 69 71 89* **Map** *B1*

Close to the church, this brasserie-style restaurant serves regional cuisine. The fixed-price menus have a wide choice of local coastal produce. Start with a plate of mussels, sea snails, whelks and six oysters. For the main course, choose a lobster from the tank, or the delicious seafood casserole.

ROSCOFF L'Ecume des Jours

⚡ 🖼 €€

Quai d'Auxerre, 29680 **Tel** *02 98 61 22 83* **Map** *B1*

In an ancient Breton building near to the lighthouse are two dining rooms: one with a view of the sea, and the other intimate and rustic with stone walls and oak beams. Regional dishes are prepared with a touch of imagination. The shellfish served with smoked duck breast are delicious. Closed Tue–Wed (except Jul–Aug); Dec–Jan.

ROSCOFF Le Temps de Vivre

⚡ ♿ 🖼 €€€

17-19 Place Lacaze-Douthiers, 29680 **Tel** *02 98 61 27 28* **Map** *B1*

The acclaimed chef Jean-Yves Crenn creates some inspired seafood and vegetable dishes in this restaurant facing the sea. Specialities include roast crab claws and panfried langoustines with artichoke *galette*. There is a good selection of wines and the staff are friendly.

ST-POL-DE-LÉON La Pomme d'Api

€€€

49 Rue Verdrel, 29250 **Tel** *02 98 69 04 36* **Map** *B1*

Gastronomic cuisine is served in a fine mid-16th-century house. The talented chef creates elaborate dishes using local produce. Dishes include a tart of Roscoff onions and artichokes, and whiting with *andouille* (sausage) accompanied by local new potatoes. Dress smartly. Closed Sun dinner, Mon, Tue dinner; 2 weeks Nov; 3 weeks Feb.

ST-THÉGONNEC Auberge de St Thégonnec

⚡ €€

6 Place de la Mairie, 29410 **Tel** *02 98 79 61 18* **Map** *B2*

In this smart hotel-restaurant the spacious dining room is both rustic and stylish. The menu has a good selection of fish and meat dishes. Try the steamed turbot with leeks, seaweed and *beurre blanc* sauce, or the fillet of beef with port. Closed Mon, Sat lunch out of season, Sun dinner Sep–Jun; mid-Dec–1st week Jan.

ST-VOUGAY Crêperie du Château

P ⚡ ♿ 🖼 €

Kerfao, 29440 **Tel** *02 98 69 93 09* **Map** *B1*

In a typical farmhouse surrounded by wonderful gardens, neighbouring the magnificent Château de Kerjean, there is something for everyone: *galettes* and *crêpes* with interesting fillings, pizzas, salads, fish, grilled meats and seafood platters. There is even a children's play area outside. Closed Mon, Tue, and Fri in winter.

SOUTHERN FINISTÈRE

AUDIERNE Le Goyen

⚡ ♿ €€€

Place Jean-Simon, 29770 **Tel** *02 98 70 08 88* **Map** *A1*

Classic seafood cuisine is served at this hotel-restaurant facing the sea. Deliciously fresh oysters and seafood platters are a good choice. The menu also includes roasted monkfish on a bed of spinach with a vermouth sauce, or panfried *coquilles St-Jacques* (scallops) accompanied by asparagus.

CARHAIX-PLOUGUER Auberge de Poher

⚡ 🖼 €€

Port de Carhaix, 29270 **Tel** *02 98 99 51 18* **Map** *C2*

In a village in the heart of the Brittany countryside, this restaurant serves simple, hearty cuisine. The decor may leave a lot to be desired but the tasty home-made terrines, the well-prepared noisette of lamb with garlic, and desserts such as pear Charlotte, more than make up for the surroundings. Closed Tue, Wed & Sun dinner, Mon.

CLÉDON-CAP SIZUN L'Etrave

P ⚡ ♿ €

Route de la Pointe du Van, 29770 **Tel** *02 98 70 66 87* **Map** *A2*

Located on Cap Sizun, and with contemporary decor, this restaurant offers delicately prepared dishes that are simple and full of flavour. The menus, which are good value for money, are based on the local sea produce. Dishes such as *langoustines à la crème* and stuffed spidercrab are perfectly executed. Closed Tue, Wed; Oct–Apr.

COMBRIT Villa Tri Men
P 🚶 ♿ 🛒   €€
16 Rue du Phare, 29120 **Tel** *02 98 51 94 94*   **Map** *B3*

This restaurant has an idyllic location overlooking the Port Ste Marine. The dining room is modern and attractive. Featuring seafood and fish, the menu is not extensive but changes frequently. Expect to find dishes such as pan-fried abalone, and fresh tuna with spices. Good desserts. Closed Mon, Sun, lunch; mid-Nov–mid-Dec, mid-Jan–mid-Feb.

CONCARNEAU Le Petit Chaperon Rouge
🚶   €
7 Place Duguesclin, 29900 **Tel** *02 98 60 53 32*   **Map** *B3*

Following the theme of "Little Red Riding Hood", with its wicker baskets and red tablecloths, this *crêperie* near the harbour has a delicious choice of savoury and sweet fillings, such as *La Blandette* (goat's cheese, spinach, ham and cream) and *Mère Grande* (banana and honey flambéed with rum).

CONCARNEAU Chez Armande
🚶 🛒   €€
15 bis Avenue du Dr-Nicolas, 29900 **Tel** *02 98 97 00 76*   **Map** *B3*

The new chef in this restaurant, just opposite the walled town, has given a breath of fresh air to the menu. Specialities include a ragout of lobster with girolle mushroom sauce, and Saler's beef with sauce *velours*. There is also an extensive dessert menu. Closed Tue, Wed; Feb; 1st week Sep; Christmas.

CONCARNEAU Le Buccin
🚶 ♿   €€
1 Rue Duguay-Trouin, 29900 **Tel** *02 98 50 54 22*   **Map** *B3*

There is a pleasant relaxed atmosphere in this restaurant that has a good choice of both meat and fish dishes, although it specializes in seafood. The fixed-price menus are good value. The starters include a delicious bass served with tomatoes and basil and a salad of foie gras, crab and langoustine. Closed Thu, Sat lunch, Sun dinner.

CROZON Le Mutin Gourmand
🚶 ♿ 🍽   €€€
Place de l'Eglise, 29160 **Tel** *02 98 27 06 51*   **Map** *B2*

At this well-regarded restaurant the menu changes with the seasons, ensuring the produce is fresh. There are interesting land-sea combinations – such as the salads of foie gras and langoustines with artichoke – impeccably cooked grilled fish, and great desserts. There's also a large choice of wines. Closed Sun dinner, Mon, Tue lunch.

DOARNENEZ Au Gouter Breton
🚶   €
36 Rue Jean-Jaurès, 29100 **Tel** *02 98 92 02 74*   **Map** *B2*

This is one of the best crêperies in the region and it offers a wide range of fillings, plus a good selection of ciders to complement them. There is a pretty dining room with interior garden and service continues until the late evening. Closed Sun.

FOUESNANT La Pointe-du-Cap-Coz
🚶 ♿ 🛒   €€€
153 Avenue de la Pointe-du-Cap-Coz, 29170 **Tel** *02 98 56 01 63*   **Map** *B3*

The young chef at this hotel-restaurant has created a menu with personality. Simple ingredients are prepared with care to produce dishes such as mackerel toasts, and codling with a cauliflower *fricassée*. There are also more expensive items, such as foie gras and lobster. Closed Sun dinner, Mon lunch, Wed; Jan–mid-Feb; 1 week Nov.

LA FÔRET FOUESNANT Auberge St-Laurent
P 🛒   €€
Route de Concarneau, La Foret Fouesnant, 29940 **Tel** *02 98 56 98 07*   **Map** *B3*

A pretty stone-built Breton auberge, set in the countryside, with traditional furniture, exposed beams and an open fireplace. The menu offers a wide choice, from buckwheat pancakes to a more elaborate rumpsteak with a blueberry sauce. Lovely terrace overlooking the garden. Closed Mon & Tue dinner, Wed.

MOËLAN SUR MER Les Moulins du Duc
P 🛒   €€€
Routes des Moulins, 29350 **Tel** *02 98 96 52 52*   **Map** *C3*

Set in a former mill amongst pretty parkland, Les Moulins du Duc serves delicious gourmet cuisine. Subtle, light dishes marry the flavours of the land with those of the Mediterranean and Atlantic seas. Expect such delicacies as lamb served with tapenade or tartare of lobster. Closed Dec–Feb.

PLEYBEN Crêperie de l'Enclos
🚶 ♿   €
52 Place Charles-de-Gaulle, 29190 **Tel** *02 98 26 38 68*   **Map** *B2*

This gourmet *crêperie* offers an immense choice of fillings, including gastronomic choices such as the "Mausanne"(a delicious combination of courgette and tomato) and the "Concarnoise" (a tuna mousse with herbs). There is a large range of regional beers. Closed Mon–Thu eve; 2 weeks Mar, May, & Jun; mid-Nov–early Jan.

PLOGOFF Hôtel de la Baie des Trépassés
P 🚶   €€
Baie des Trépassés, 29770 **Tel** *02 98 70 61 34*   **Map** *A2*

A large white building, sheltering in the bay, houses this pleasant coastal hotel-restaurant. There are spectacular views of the Pointe du Raz from the dining room, in which good-value seafood and fish dishes are served. Local freshly sourced produce is handled adeptly. Reservation advised in peak season.

PLOMODIERN Les Glazicks
P 🚶 🍽   €€€€
7 Rue de la Plage, 29550 **Tel** *02 98 81 52 32*   **Map** *B2*

Acclaimed as "Brittany's best young chef", Olivier Bellin blends flavours to perfection using both local produce and ingredients from further afield. His constantly changing menus include creations such as lobster with extra large chips and tomato-chorizo sauce. Dress smartly. Closed Mon & Tue; Wed–Thu dinner Jan; 3 weeks Mar; Oct.

Key to Price Guide *see p236* **Key to Symbols** *see back cover flap*

PLUGUFFEN La Roseraie de Bel Air   P ♿   €€
Impasse de la Bossière, 29700 **Tel** *02 98 53 50 80*   **Map** *B3*

Two chefs produce a cuisine that is full of vitality. Brittany, Provence and areas far further afield are evoked by dishes such as a mixture of both cooked and uncooked scallops, langoustines *à la plancha,* and bitter chocolate dessert with wild mint ice-cream. Dress smartly. Closed Sat lunch, Sun dinner, Mon; mid-Sep–Feb.

PONT-AVEN La Taupinière   P ♥   €€€€
Croissant Saint-André, 29930 **Tel** *02 98 06 03 12*   **Map** *B3*

This unique restaurant couples a festive atmosphere with remarkable cuisine. The specialities include Concarneau langoustines prepared in many ways, including being served with foie gras or flambéed in eau-de-vie of cider. Tempting desserts include *millefeuille* of crêpes and strawberries. Dress smartly. Closed Mon, Tue; mid-Sep–mid-Oct.

PONT-AVEN Le Moulin de Rosmadec   P ♿ 🍽 ♥   €€€€
Venelle de Rosmadec, 29930 **Tel** *02 98 06 00 22*   **Map** *B3*

The Sébilleau brothers prepare traditional ingredients with originality in this restored 15th-century mill. The focus is on seafood and fish. Dishes include crispy langoustines with creamy risotto, as well as classics such as *crêpe soufflées au citron.* Dress smartly. Closed Wed, Sun dinner; 2 weeks end Oct, 3 weeks Feb.

QUIMPER L'Ambroisie   ♿   €€
49 Rue Elie Fréron, 29000 **Tel** *02 98 95 00 02*   **Map** *B3*

Located just at the end of one of the tiny streets in the centre of Quimper, a short walk from the cathedral, this restaurant provides good simple cuisine using quality produce. Try the oysters in an artichoke broth, smoked salmon and egg rolled in a buckwheat pancake, and crispy almond cake with strawberries.

QUIMPER Erwan   ♿ ♿   €€€
3 Rue Aristide-Briand, 29000 **Tel** *02 98 90 14 14*   **Map** *B3*

This restaurant has a deserved reputation for being reliable. Traditional cuisine is served in a brightly decorated dining room. Specialities include Breton dishes such as *kig ha fars (see p235),* and a *blanquette* (white-sauce stew) of monkfish. The portions are generous and the atmosphere friendly. Closed Sat lunch, Sun, Mon.

QUIMPER Les Acacias   P   €€€
88 Blvd Creach Gwen, 29000 **Tel** *02 98 52 15 20*   **Map** *B3*

This modern restaurant is situated just outside Quimper and has its own pretty, flower-filled garden. The dining room is bright and contemporary and the cuisine is classic. The menu has dishes such as quail breast braised with cabbage. Closed mid-Aug–Sep, Sun dinner, Mon dinner & Sat.

QUIMPERLÉ Le Bistro de la Tour   ♿ ♿ ♥   €€
2 Rue Dom-Morice, 29300 **Tel** *02 98 39 29 58*   **Map** *C3*

This restaurant, with a tastefully decorated dining room, is well-known for the quality of both its cuisine and choice of over 600 wines, the best of which are from the Rhône and Loire. There is a wide selection of wines by the glass, plus good fish and casseroled meat dishes. Also has guestrooms. Closed Sat lunch, Sun dinner, Mon lunch.

QUIMPERLÉ Ty Gwechall   ♿   €€
4 Rue Mellec, 29300 **Tel** *02 98 96 30 63*   **Map** *C3*

In this delightful *crêperie* the chef, a former baker, knows his dough, and the *galettes* are perfect – light and lacy. There is a wide variety of fillings, including the traditional favourites, and they are well-priced. The drinks menu is decidely Breton, with beers and ciders from Cornouaille. Closed Mon and Sun dinner.

RIEC-SUR-BÉLON Domaine de Kerstinec Kerland   P ♿ ♿   €€€€€
Route de Moëlan, 29340 **Tel** *02 98 06 46 20*   **Map** *C3*

In a renovated 18th-century farmhouse surrounded by parkland, this elegant hotel-restaurant has a superb view of the Bélon River which inspires the menu. Lovely setting to enjoy Bélon oysters, grilled lobster, John Dory, or turbot with a langoustine and truffle sauce. Dress smartly. Closed 1 week before Christmas.

ROSNOEN Ferme Auberge du Seillou   P ♿ ♿   €€
On the D791, 5.5 km (3 miles) from Faou, 29580 **Tel** *02 98 81 92 21*   **Map** *A2*

On the Crozon Peninsula, this delightful auberge-farm prepares its own home-grown produce. Beef, chicken and pork are all on the menu; also the traditional *kig ha fars (see p235)* on reservation. Desserts can be washed down with a glass of farm cider. Guestrooms are available. Open daily for dinner Jul–Aug, weekends for lunch out of season.

SEIN ÎLE DE Chez Brigitte   ♿   €
14 Quai des Paimpolais, 29990 **Tel** *02 98 70 91 83*   **Map** *A2*

There is a spectacular view of the sea, facing the Pointe du Raz, from the windows of the first-floor dining room. The menu features superb seafood, including wonderfully fresh oysters and simply grilled fish direct from the boat – plus the stunning lobster dishes for which Brigitte's has a well-earned reputation. Closed Mon, Sun dinner; Nov–Easter.

STE-ANNE DE LA PALUD Hôtel de la Plage   P ♿ ♿   €€€€
Beach road, 29550 **Tel** *02 98 92 50 12*   **Map** *B2*

In this restaurant in a peaceful, attractive hotel, the chef, originally from Marseille, adds a Mediterranean touch to local Breton produce. He creates interesting food combinations, such as roast turbot with wakame and cauliflower or roast pigeon with mango. Dress smartly. Closed Tue, Fri lunch, Wed dinner; Nov–Mar.

MORBIHAN

ARRADON Les Vénètes
€€€   **Map** D3

9 Rue Carrière, 56610 **Tel** *02 97 44 85 85*

The dining room of this hotel-restaurant has a splendid view of the Golfe du Morbihan. Tasty dishes using local produce are prepared with respect for the natural flavours. Try the pan-fried king prawns *à l'orange* or clams in a thyme-infused cream sauce. Closed Sun dinner, Mon lunch; 2 weeks Jan.

ARZON Grand Largue
€€€€   **Map** D4

1 Rue du Phare, 56640 **Tel** *02 97 53 71 58*

Situated only 2 km (1 mile) northeast of Port Navalo, the chef buys his fish each morning at the port. Superb Belon oysters, cooked-to-perfection red mullet, and local brill just unhooked from the line are among the simply prepared dishes he then produces. Freshness is the key. Closed Mon, Tue; mid-Jan–mid-Feb, mid-Nov–Dec.

AURAY La Closerie de Kerdrain
€€€€   **Map** D3

20 Rue Louis-Billet, 56400 **Tel** *02 97 56 61 27*

Fine cuisine is served in an 18th-century dining room with elegant furnishings. The enthusiastic chef likes to add a dash of flavour with home-grown herbs. Among the dishes on the menu are a gateau of langoustines and *andouille* (sausage) and warm lobster with a basil and celery *remoulade*. Closed Mon and Tue lunch.

AURAY L'Eglantine
€€€€   **Map** D3

17 Place St Saveur, St-Goustan, 56400 **Tel** *02 97 56 46 55*

Right on the port of St-Goustan, with its medieval timber-framed houses, this restaurant offers a variety of fish and meat dishes. Delicious sole and turbot are simply prepared, while sea bass and monkfish medallions are accompanied by elaborate sauces. The seafood platters are exquisite. Other dishes include pigeon and succulent steak. Closed Wed.

BADEN Hôtel Restaurant Gavrinis
€€€   **Map** D4

Toulbroch, 56870 **Tel** *02 97 57 00 82*

Recently taken over by a new husband and wife team, this comfortable hotel-restaurant is undergoing renovations. The new menu offers tasty dishes such as the saddle of rabbit served with houmous and pimento-enhanced sauce, crab cannelloni and *millefeuille* of scallops and beetroot. Closed Mon, Sat lunch, Sun dinner; mid-Jan–mid-Feb.

BELLE-ÎLE-EN-MER Roz Avel
€€   **Map** C4

Rue du Lt Riou, Sauzon, 56630 **Tel** *02 97 31 61 48*

Just behind the church, this is one of the best places to eat in picturesque Sauzon. The set menus are excellent value. They are also very popular in high season, so making a reservation is advisable. Simply prepared fillets of fish, grilled langoustines with vegetables, and roast monkfish are among the dishes on offer.

BELLE-ÎLE-EN-MER Le Contre Quai
€€€   **Map** C4

Rue St-Nicolas, Sauzon, 56360 **Tel** *02 97 31 60 60*

A chef passionate about the region's produce creates dishes with wonderfully fresh ingredients, whether it's a carpaccio of fish with seaweed condiment, or brill with spidercrab sauce. Dishes that are favourites with the regulars include stuffed crab and local lamb raised on the island. Delicious desserts too. Closed Sun, Mon; Sep–Mar.

BELLE-ÎLE-EN-MER Castel Clara
€€€€€   **Map** C4

Port-Goulphar, Bangor, 56360 **Tel** *02 97 31 84 21*

There is a nautical atmosphere at this hotel-restaurant with impressive views of the cliffs at Port-Goulphar. The menu focuses on seafood and fish dishes. The cuisine is refined and consists of subtle preparations of the best the sea has to offer, such as lobster, crayfish and turbot. Service is attentive. Dress smartly. Closed mid-Jan–Feb.

BILLIERS Domaine de Rochevilaine
€€€€€   **Map** D4

On the Pointe de Pen-Lan-Sud, 56190 **Tel** *02 97 41 61 61*

At the tip of a rocky promontory, this is a traditional luxury establishment with a slightly staid atmosphere but a constantly evolving menu. The talented chef produces imaginative dishes such as bass in a salt crust served with a fennel béarnaise sauce. Dress smartly.

CARNAC La Bavolette
€€€   **Map** C4

9 Allée du Parc, 56340 **Tel** *02 97 52 19 69*

One of the more classy eating places in the popular seaside resort of Carnac-Plage, La Bavolette serves a number of dishes that are particular favourites with customers, including *brochettes* (skewers) of fish, and sardine terrine. Among its specialities are fish soup served with a rich garlicy aïoli and croutons, and flambéed langoustines. Closed Tue & Wed.

CARNAC La Côte
€€€   **Map** C4

Kermario, 56340 **Tel** *02 97 52 02 80*

A pretty old farmhouse surrounded by a garden, this is a gourmet restaurant serving tasty, subtle dishes such as roast bass and asparagus flavoured with aniseed, and pigeon marinated in olive oil and lime juice. The weekday menu is particularly good value. Closed Sun dinner, Mon, Sat lunch; mid-Jan–mid-Feb, 1 week Nov, Dec, Mar.

Key to Price Guide *see p236* **Key to Symbols** *see back cover flap*

GROIX ÎLE DE La Marine

⚐ ©©

7 Rue de Général-de-Gaulle, 56590 **Tel** *02 97 86 80 05*

Map *C3*

Near to the harbour, this excellent-value hotel-restaurant serves simple, well-prepared dishes. Specialities include marinated squid, mussels *à la crème d'ail* (in garlic cream), and *brandade* (a salt cod dish) with local white beans. There are also traditional favourites such as *far Breton* (a stew). Closed Sun dinner, Mon except Apr–Sep; Jan.

HENNEBONT Château de Locguénolé

☐⚐☐☐☐ ©©©©©

Route de Port-Louis, 56700 **Tel** *02 97 76 76 76*

Map *C3*

This splendid restaurant set in parkland combines reliable cuisine with faultless presentation. Luxury produce is used for dishes such as sardines marinated in basil-flavoured oil and lobster. The veal and lamb dishes are also superb. The wine list includes all the greats, but at accessible prices. Closed lunch, Mon dinner; Jan–mid-Feb.

JOSSELIN La Marine

⚐☐ ©

8 Rue du Canal, 56120 **Tel** *02 97 22 21 98*

Map *D3*

The interior is decorated in a nautical style and there is a pretty terrace with splendid views of the chateau and River Oust. This *crêperie* offers a choice of fillings with a seasonal theme, such as "L'Automne", which is sweet chestnut purée, apple and pear. There is also a good lunchtime menu. Can get busy in summer. Closed Mon, Tue dinner and 2 weeks Nov.

JOSSELIN La Table d'O

⚐ ©©

9 Rue Glatinier, 56120 **Tel** *02 97 70 61 39*

Map *D3*

The dynamic chef changes his menus according to both the season and his mood and produces excellently prepared dishes such as rabbit and prunes served with a *crème brûlée* of foie gras. The pleasant dining room has large windows overlooking the valley and chateau. Closed Sun dinner, Wed except Jul–Aug; 2 weeks Nov, 1 week Jun.

LOCMINÉ Auberge de la Ville au Vent

☐⚐☐☐☐ ©©

9 Rue Olivier-de-Clisson, 56500 **Tel** *02 97 60 08 40*

Map *D3*

A charming and rustic dining room in a lovely restored farmhouse is the setting for good meat dishes, such as young pigeon served with turnips, or more ambitious fish dishes, such as monkfish tournedos, sautéed artichokes and haricots with herbs. Closed Sun dinner, Mon, Tue–Thu dinner (Sep–May); 1 week Mar; 3 weeks Nov.

LORIENT Le Jardin Gourmand

⚐☐☐☐ ©©

46 Rue Jules-Simon, 56100 **Tel** *02 97 64 17 24*

Map *C3*

Excellent cuisine is served in an attractive dining room that opens on to a terrace and garden. The choice of fish or meat for the main course changes daily, depending on what's available at the market. There's a fine Breton cheeseboard and over 40 wines. Closed Sun dinner, Mon & Tues; 2 weeks Feb, 3 weeks end Aug–Sep.

LORIENT Le Neptune

⚐ ©©

15 Avenue de la Perrière, 56100 **Tel** *02 97 37 04 56*

Map *C3*

The haul at the nearby fishing port of Keroman determines the dish of the day at this restaurant with a modern interior, and some tables in a pretty conservatory at the rear of the dining room. The menu includes flambéed lobster and fricassée of monkfish. The portions are generous and the service friendly.

LORIENT L'Amphitryon

☐☐ ©©©©©

127 Rue du Colonel-Müller, 56100 **Tel** *02 97 83 34 04*

Map *C3*

This restaurant, with modern decor and masterchef Jean-Paul Abadie, is one of the best in Brittany. Each dish retains a purity of flavour, whether elaborate or simple. The specialities include clams with a sabayon of Muscat de Rivesaltes. The wine list is remarkable. Dress smartly. Closed Sun, Mon; first 2 weeks Nov, first 2 weeks May.

MALESTROIT Le Canotier

⚐☐ ©©

Place de Docteur Queinner, 56140 **Tel** *02 97 75 08 69*

Map *D3*

The best restaurant in a small town in the heart of the Brittany countryside, Le Canotier offers a good choice of dishes in a cosy, comfortable dining room. The specialities include seafood, such as red mullet and scallops. There are also good grilled meats. Closed Mon, Tue–Sat dinner in low season.

MOINES ÎLE AUX Les Embruns

⚐☐ ©©

Rue Commerce, 56780 **Tel** *02 97 26 30 86*

Map *D4*

On a picturesque island, the largest in the Golfe du Morbihan, this delightful bar-restaurant serves unpretentious dishes that are based on the local produce. The cuisine is straightforward and simple, the menus are good value, and the service is friendly. Closed Wed; first 2 weeks Oct; Jan–Feb.

PONTIVY La Pommeraie

⚐ ©©©

17 Quai du Couvent, 56300 **Tel** *02 97 25 60 09*

Map *D3*

A chef with lots of personality, who respects seasonal ingredients to the letter, is responsible for precise cuisine combining land and sea produce. Dishes include charlotte of crab, young pigeon and a fillet of mullet accompanied by a mussel risotto. The wine list is well-chosen, if not extensive. Closed Mon; end Aug–early Sep.

PORT-LOUIS Avel Vor

⚐☐ ©©©

25 Rue de Locmalo, 56290 **Tel** *02 97 82 47 59*

Map *C3*

The contemporary dining room has a lovely view of the port. The ambitious cuisine is based on local produce and the freshest ingredients the port can offer. Crab with virgin olive oil, red mullet fillet, and lobster all feature on the good-value menu. There are also good traditional desserts and a classic wine list. Closed Sun dinner, Mon, Tue.

QUESTEMBERT La Bretagne
P 🏠 ♿ 🍷   €€€€€

13 Rue St-Michel, 56230 **Tel** *02 97 26 11 12*   **Map** *D3*

A chef of long-standing acclaim is in charge at this former inn with a charming dining room and garden. The menu is classic, but with some contemporary influences, and has such dishes as a crumble of saddle of lamb, and lobster with glazed turnips. Dress smartly. Closed Tue, Sun dinner; 3 weeks Jan; 1 week Mar.

QUIBERON Le Relax
🏠 ♿   €

27 Boulevard Castéro, 56170 **Tel** *02 98 50 12 84*   **Map** *C4*

With lovely sea views and a pretty garden, this restaurant is guaranteed to make you relax. It offers a wide selection of superbly cooked seasonal fish, as well as mussels, langoustines, crabs, oysters and tasty seafood sauerkraut. There's also a good wine cellar and a very knowledgeable sommelier.

QUIBERON La Chaumine
🏠 🏡   €€€

36 Place du Manémeur, 56170 **Tel** *02 97 50 17 67*   **Map** *C4*

A convivial atmosphere reigns in this small family-run inn in the heart of the fishermen's quarter. The good-value menu features the catch of the day and good seafood platters, as well as simple, well-cooked dishes such as crayfish in mayonnaise. Service is friendly. Closed Sun dinner, Mon; 3 weeks Mar; Nov–early Dec.

ROCHE BERNARD L'Auberge Bretonne
P ♿ 🍷   €€€€€

2 Place Duguesclin, 56130 **Tel** *02 99 90 60 28*   **Map** *E4*

At what is certainly the best farm-auberge in Brittany, the produce is home-grown. A subtle balance between the rusticity of the countryside and city-based refinement is achieved in dishes such as lobster with a mango and citrus fruit sauce spiked wirh Jamaican pepper. Reservation is advised. Dress smartly. Closed Mon, Tue, Fri lunch, Thu; mid-Nov–mid-Jan.

ST-AVÉ Le Pressoir
🏠 ♿ 🍷   €€€

7 Rue de l'Hôpital, 56890 **Tel** *02 97 60 87 63*   **Map** *D3*

This restaurant's gourmet cuisine is both sea-based and daring. Expect to find dishes such as *kouign patates* (potato pancake) with chitterling sausage and pigs' trotters, and *kouign amann* (speciality cake) of Granny Smith apples. The wine list has some interesting choices. Dress smartly. Closed Sun dinner, Mon, Tue; 3 weeks Oct; 2 weeks Mar.

ST-COLOMBIER Le Tournepierre
🏠   €€€€€

Le Bourg, 56370 **Tel** *02 97 26 42 19*   **Map** *D4*

Authentic and exacting cuisine is served in a rustic dining room in a typical Breton village. The Breton chef works with pure local products and offers dishes such as brill roasted with hazelnuts, and veal with *cocos* (white beans). It is very popular, so making a reservation is advisable. Dress smartly. Closed Sun dinner, Mon, Tue; Nov.

TRINITÉ-SUR-MER L'Azimut
P 🏠 ♿ 🏡 🍷   €€€

1 Rue du Men-Du, 56470 **Tel** *02 97 55 71 88*   **Map** *C4*

In this coastal inn the menu changes with the season; in October, for example, it includes three different scallop dishes. The reliable no-risk cuisine offers such dishes as John Dory with saffron-flavoured potatoes, grilled fish or a plate of oysters. There are also interesting wines, some by the glass. Dress smartly. Closed Tue lunch, Wed.

VANNES La Saladière
🏠   €

36 Rue de Port, 56000 **Tel** *02 97 42 52 10*   **Map** *D3*

Located on the harbourside, this restaurant serves big bowls of cooked-to-order mussels. Try the exceptionally tasty mussels with Muscadet and parmesan sauce. The salads are large and there is an interesting choice. The wine list is small but focuses on some decent Loire and Bordeaux wines. Closed Sun dinner.

VANNES Table des Gourmets
🏠   €€€

6 Rue Alexandre-le-Pontois, 56000 **Tel** *02 97 47 52 44*   **Map** *D3*

Tasty meals at reasonable prices are served in this restaurant opposite the ramparts. The chef uses regional ingredients with originality. Try the sautéed lobster with girolle mushrooms, or the *croustillant* of pigeon with perfumed rice. The wine list includes organic producers.

VANNES Le Richemont
🏠   €€€

24 Place de la Gare, 56000 **Tel** *02 97 42 61 41*   **Map** *D3*

This restaurant's unusual cuisine combines traditional Breton produce with exotic flavours discovered on the chef's travels. Expect to find original contemporary dishes with a Mediterranean influence, such as melted mozzarella and tomato chutney with red mullet salad or Andalusian-style tripe. Closed Sun, Mon; 2 weeks Feb; 1 week Jun, 2 weeks Nov.

LOIRE-ATLANTIQUE

BAULE LA Le Billot
🏠 🏡   €€

17 Allée des Pétrels, 44500 **Tel** *02 40 60 00 00*   **Map** *D4*

Near to the market place, this bistro has a lively atmosphere and serves superb meat-based dishes. The dish of the day could be lamb with a confit of onion, or a succulent piece of beef. Seafood is not forgotten altogether: there are delicious scallops and king prawns. Closed Sun dinner, Mon except Jul–Aug; first 2 weeks Jan.

Key to Price Guide *see p236* **Key to Symbols** *see back cover flap*

BAULE LA Le Castel Marie Louise   🅿 🚶 🍷   €€€€€

1 Avenue Andrieu, 44504 **Tel** *02 40 11 48 38*   **Map** *D4*

This *belle époque* hotel-restaurant with contemporary decor offers a cuisine focused on local sea produce. Dishes include excellent sole, delicious crab, and pan-fried cod seasoned with Guérande salt. Originally from Lyon, the chef prepares good pork dishes too. Dress smartly. Closed lunch except Sun; mid-Nov–mid-Dec.

CLISSON La Bonne Auberge   🅿 🚶 🖥   €€€

1 Rue Olivier de Clisson, 44190 **Tel** *02 40 54 01 90*   **Map** *F5*

Located in the city centre, this comfortable auberge has three attractive dining rooms. Wonderful things are done to classics. Specialities include scallops with oyster sauce, puff pastry filled with langoustines in a creamy sauce and sea bass with potatoes flavoured with truffles. Delicate desserts. Closed Sun dinner, Mon, Tue lunch, Wed dinner; 3 weeks Aug.

CROISIC LE La Bouillabaisse Bretonne   🚶 ♿   €€

12 Quai de la Petite Chambre, 44490 **Tel** *02 40 23 06 74*   **Map** *D4*

Housed in an attractive building in the port, and with a magnificent view of the ocean, this restaurant offers good-value and interesting menus inspired by the local produce. Dishes include bouillabaise with five different fish, grilled brill with fennel, and scallops and langoustines roasted with peanut oil. Closed Sun dinner, Tue, Mon; Jan–mid-Mar.

GUÉRANDE Roc-Maria   🚶 ♿   €

1 Rue Vieux-Marché aux Grains, 44350 **Tel** *02 40 24 90 51*   **Map** *D4*

This friendly *crêperie* lies within the ramparts of the town of Guérande. The dining room is in a charming 15th-century building, which also has cosy guestrooms. Well-made *crêpes* and savoury *galettes* are served with a good choice of fillings. Closed mid-Nov–mid-Dec.

HAUTE GOULAINE Manoir de la Boulaie   🅿 🚶 ♿ 🍷   €€€€€

33 Rue de la Chapelle Saint-Martin, 44115 **Tel** *02 40 06 15 91*   **Map** *F4*

In the middle of vineyards, this imposing manor house serves creative cuisine. The chef, Laurent Sardeau, combines the best local produce to create specialities such as yoghurt of foie gras and mushrooms, and red mullet and oysters with a chorizo compôte. Good choice of Muscadet wines. Dress smartly. Closed Sun dinner, Mon, Wed; mid-Dec–mid-Jan, Aug.

NANTES Bistro de l'Ecrivain   ♿   €

15 Rue Jean-Jacques-Rousseau, 44000 **Tel** *02 51 84 15 15*   **Map** *F4*

There is a warm atmosphere in this city-centre bistro with a terrace, and walls covered by books and portraits of authors. The fine cuisine includes many traditional dishes to which the chef has added a personal touch. The menu changes regularly and there is a good choice of wines by the glass. Good desserts. Closed Sun.

NANTES La Cigale   ♿ 🖥 🍷   €€

4 Place Graslin, 44000 **Tel** *02 51 84 94 94*   **Map** *F4*

This ornate *belle époque* brasserie dates from 1895 when it was frequented by celebrated writers and the elite of Nantes. The quality and choice of the cuisine, which includes oysters, carpaccio of salmon and beef *à la plancha*, match the exceptional interior. Open all day serving breakfast, brunch and afternoon tea. Extensive wine list.

NANTES Les Temps Changent   ♿ 🖥 🍷   €€

1 Place Aristide-Briand, 44000 **Tel** *02 51 72 18 01*   **Map** *F4*

In this welcoming venue an excellent chef who has a forward-looking vision of modern cuisine creates quality French dishes that combine classic produce with inventive cooking. Typical dishes are foie gras *a la plancha* served with a confit of baby vegetables and hot and cold red mullet with mini fennel and tapenade. Closed Sat, Sun; 3 weeks Aug.

NANTES L'Atlantide   🅿 ♿ 🍷   €€€€€

16 Quai Ernest-Renaud, 44000 **Tel** *02 40 73 23 23*   **Map** *F4*

Innovative cuisine is served in a vast fourth-floor dining room with a superb view of the river and port. Typical dishes are frogs' legs and smoked eel brandade, pan-fried scallops and goose foie gras in cabbage parcels, and pigeon and lobster kebabs. Simply the best place in town to eat. Remarkable wine list. Dress smartly. Closed Sat lunch, Sun; Aug; Christmas.

PORNIC Beau Rivage   🚶 🍷   €€€

Plage de la Birochère, 44210 **Tel** *02 40 82 03 08*   **Map** *E5*

The chef of this restaurant overlooking the beach picks the best from each season and region for his vast menu – including seafood and fish from the ports of Guilvinec and Croisic, Challans duckling and Noirmoutier potatoes. Good selection of Loire wines, especially Muscadet. Closed Sun & Wed dinner except Jul–Aug, Mon; mid-Dec–Jan.

ST-JOACHIM La Mare aux Oiseaux   🅿 🚶 ♿ 🖥 🍷   €€€€€

162 Île de Fédrun, 44720 **Tel** *02 40 88 53 01*   **Map** *E4*

Imaginative cuisine is served in this attractive auberge, using the best offered by the marshlands: pigeon, eel, duck, frog and wild mint, and the sea: sardines, crab and edible seaweed. Specialities include pigeon and frogs' legs in mint sauce and frogs' legs with Breton seaweed. Dress smartly. Closed Mon lunch; 2 weeks Jan, 3 weeks Mar.

ST-LYPHARD L'Auberge de Kerbourg   🅿 ♿ 🖥 🍷   €€€

Village de Kerbourg, 44410 **Tel** *02 40 61 95 15*   **Map** *D4*

This charming old farmhouse restaurant has a talented chef who prepares seasonal produce with a respect for tradition and creates such dishes as hare *à la royale* and duck from the Breton region. Good selection of muscadet wines. Dress smartly. Closed Sun dinner, Mon, Tue lunch, Fri lunch; mid-Dec–mid-Feb.

SHOPS AND MARKETS

From the stalls laid out on a Saturday in Vitré to the great covered market in Plouescat, Brittany's weekly food markets are key events in the region's gastronomic life. It is here that the best and freshest local produce – crisp young vegetables, glistening seafood,

Tin of Breton sardines

farm-produced cheeses, cider and charcuterie – is to be found. There are also many fascinating shops to be explored, offering other Breton goods, among the most distinctive being striped sailors' sweaters, Quimper faience and craft items, such as ship models, with a marine theme.

Artichokes, sold in every market in Brittany

MARKETS

The regular weekly markets are the major outlet for local produce and local, or even family, specialities. But they are not the only choice. To promote their own produce, certain growers have set up small farmers' markets on their own farm premises, where they sell goat's cheese, buttermilk and other produce from local farms.

There are farmers' markets in Planguenoual, Milizac, Plouzélambre and Notre-Dame-du-Guildo. *Circuits gourmands* (gastronomic tours) are also organized by local producers in an initiative to promote local delicacies. A list of these markets and the addresses of the relevant producers are available from tourist offices.

LOCAL DRINKS

Thanks to a small group of cider-makers, such as **Éric Baron**, who use traditional methods, cider has undergone

a revival in popularity since the 1980s. The Cornouaille region produces an excellent cider, which has an AOC classification. Robust and with an orange hue, it goes very well with seafood.

Some producers, such as **Fisselier** and **Dassonville**, also offer a wide range of liqueurs made from strawberries and other suitable kinds of fruit, as well as coffee liqueurs made with cider brandy, *chouchenn*, a mead made with cider and honey, *pommeaux* (sparkling apple wines) and Breton whisky. There is also *lambig*, made by distilling cider brandy and ideal for lobster flambé.

There were once 75 breweries in Brittany and, following a decline, there has been a resurgence of small independent breweries since 1985. The beers that they produce – such as Coreff, a pale ale, Blanche Hermine and Telenn Du, a wheat beer – easily equal more famous brands.

PRODUCE OF THE SEA

Fresh fish auctions are held in many harbours all along the coast of Brittany. If the idea of attending one does not appeal, there are

Coreff beer

alternatives. Oysters can be bought at oyster farms, such as that at the **Château de Belon**. Fish and seafood can also be bought from wholesalers and from fish farms (*viviers*), such as those in Audierne, Camaret and **Roscoff**. Although wholesale prices fluctuate, they are always sure to be lower than retail prices.

The best kinds of oysters are Nacre des Abers and Morlaix-Penzé, which have a sweet taste; Aven-Belon, which are crisp and sweet; Cancale, firm with a nutty aftertaste; Paimpolaise, salty with a flavour of the sea; and the plump Ria d'Étel.

Easier to take home are sardines, mackerel fillets, slices of tuna and traditionally cured sprats, which are canned in factories, such as **Gonidec**, on the south coast of Brittany. Guérande salt, jars of samphire and seaweed products are also good buys. With 800 different varieties, the coast of Finistère is one of the largest seaweed-growing areas in the world. The benefits of seaweed are many and varied. **Thalado**, for example, makes seaweed bath salts, soap, tonic lotions and nutritional supplements.

Oysters on a stall in Vivier-sur-Mer

SAILORS' CLOTHING

In most harbours there is a fishermen's cooperative where traditional sailors' clothing, labelled "Made in Breizh" is on sale. This ranges from thick pullovers, indigo-and-cream striped sweaters and smocks, to waxed jackets and seamen's watch jackets with double waterproof collars. Perfectly suited for sailing and for fishing trips, these tough, weatherproof clothes are derived from traditional Breton clothing. The *kabig*, a jacket made of heavy cloth, evolved from the *kab an aod* that Breton seaweed-gatherers once wore.

The best-known brands of seamen's clothing are Captain Corsaire, **Armor Lux** and **Guy Cotten**, the leading manufacturer of clothes for professional seamen.

Stall selling *Kouign amann*, the traditional Breton cake

Retail outlet of the Faïencerie Henriot in Quimper

HANDICRAFTS

Colourful Quimper Faience *(see pp164–5)*, particularly that produced by the Faïencerie Henriot, is without doubt Brittany's best known hand-crafted product. The Île de Bréhat is also renowned for its glassware and Pont-l'Abbé for its embroidered linen, such as that offered for sale in **Le Minor**.

There are also craftsmen's workshops that are open to the public in Brasparts *(see p141)*, in Locronan *(see p152)*, in Guérande *(see p200)*, in the villages around Pont-Scorff, 7 km (4 miles) from Lorient, and in St-Méloir, 17 km (10 miles) from Dol-de-Bretagne.

Browsing in shops selling marine antiques may also turn up some interesting finds, as may a visit to woodworkers such as **Thierry Morel** in Plouvien, **Frères Douirin** in Plozévet, and Francis Tirot in Fougères, all of whom make wooden ship models.

Most shops are open from 9am to 12.30pm and 2.30 to 7pm, Monday to Saturday.

DIRECTORY

REGIONAL SPECIALITIES

FINISTÈRE

Fédération Régionale des Pays Touristiques de Bretagne
2 Place Bisson, Pontivy.
Tel *(02) 97 51 46 16.*
Strong, traditionally brewed beers.

Château de Belon
On the right bank of the river, Riec-sur-Bélon.
Tel *(02) 98 06 90 58.*
Oysters.

Dassonville
Pen-ar-Ros, Plouegat-Moysan.
Tel *(02) 98 79 21 25.*
Chouchenn (mead) & honey.

Éric Baron
Kervéguen, Guimaec.
Tel *(02) 98 67 50 02.*
Cider made by traditional methods.

Gonidec
2 Rue Henri Fabre, Concarneau.
Tel *(02) 98 97 07 09.*
Canned fish.

Thalado
5 Avenue Victor Hugo, Roscoff.
Tel *(02) 98 69 77 05.*
Edible seaweed and seaweed for use in thalassotherapy.

Viviers de Roscoff
Pointe Ste-Barbe, Roscoff.
Tel *(02) 98 61 19 61.*
Crustacean farms.

ILLE-ET-VILAINE

Fisselier
56 Rue du Verger, Rennes-Chantepie.
Tel *(02) 99 41 00 00.*
Liqueurs made by traditional methods.

CLOTHES & HANDICRAFTS

FINISTÈRE

Bonneterie d'Armor
21–3 Rue Louison Bobet, Quimper.
Tel *(02) 98 90 05 29.*
Head office of Armor Lux (for sailors' clothing).

Faïencerie H-B Henriot
Place Bérardier, Quimper.
Tel *(02) 98 52 22 52.*
Quimper faience

Frères Douirin
9 Impasse de la Poste, Plozevet.
Tel *(02) 98 91 42 04.*
Miniature Breton furniture.

Guy Cotten
Pont Minaouët, Trégunc.
Tel *(02) 98 97 66 79.*
www.guycotten.com
Sailors' clothing.

Le Minor
3 Quai St-Laurent, Pont-l'Abbé.
Tel *(02) 98 87 07 22.*
Embroidery, lace & tulle.

Thierry Morel
183 Rue Emile Salaun, Plouvien. **Tel** *(02) 98 40 99 24.* Ship models.

What to Buy in Brittany

Quimper faience seated figure

Brittany projects a distinctive image. This is reflected in the seamen's striped sweaters and yellow oilskins and the pretty Quimper faience that are the staple of so many souvenir shops. But there is, in fact, far more to Breton craftsmanship than this. Not only are there countless delicacies – butter made in the churn, local pâtisserie, cooked meats and traditionally made cider – but also many high-quality items with a marine theme. Ranging from seaweed balm to antique sextants and sailors' chests, these are redolent of the high seas and, of course, of Brittany itself.

Handmade toy boat

SOUVENIRS

In the most popular coastal resorts, a little discrimination is sometimes needed to distinguish good-quality pieces from cheap souvenirs. It is best to choose locally made items, or to look round old chandlers' shops. CDs of traditional Breton songs are another reliable buy.

Nautilus shells *make attractive ornaments and, like other souvenirs with a marine theme, they bring a taste of the sea to any décor.*

The sailor's almanac, *giving the times of tides, is an essential accessory for anglers and yachting enthusiasts.*

Pipe

Plaster figures *of a Breton couple, sold in many local shops.*

Lighthouse

Bowl

Breton pennant

FAIENCE

Continuing a tradition established in the 17th century (*see pp164–5*), Quimper's faience factories produce wares in a range of shapes, decorated with patterns such as *petit breton* and *à bords jaune*, painted in various colours.

Quimper faience tray

Quimper faience salt cellar and pepper pot

Faience pitcher *decorated with a classic Quimper floral pattern.*

Quimper faience, *like this colourful plate with floral border, is decorated entirely freehand, without the use of transfers. Good-quality pieces are signed by the decorator.*

CLOTHES

Sturdy and weather-resistant, traditional sailors' clothing conjures up images of the open sea and ocean spray. With the rise in popularity of sailing and water sports, it has become essential wear both for yachting enthusiasts and for casually chic town-dwellers.

Seaman's woolly hat, *ideal for keeping out a sea fret.*

Sailors' sweaters

Kabig, *a hooded jacket made of heavy waterproofed cloth.*

SWEETS AND BISCUITS

Among Breton specialities are many kinds of sweets and biscuits, some owing their distinctive taste to Brittany's excellent butter. These treats include pancakes (packaged in foil), butter toffees, butter biscuits, especially *petits-beurre* made in Nantes, and *berlingots,* handmade sweets also from Nantes.

Butter toffees

Traou Mad, butter biscuits, made in Pont-Aven

Box of Leroux toffees

Berlingots *are twisted sweets made by traditional methods.*

Tins of coloured *berlingots,* **made in Nantes**

SKINCARE PRODUCTS

A wide range of skincare products, including seaweed-based cosmetics and creams made with extracts of oyster, are on sale in thalassotherapy centres all along the coasts of Brittany.

Traditional Breton cider

Fleur de caramel

Fraise de Plougastel

Phytomer for skincare

Bath salts

ALCOHOLIC DRINKS

Brittany is renowned for its ciders and liqueurs, including *fleur de caramel* liqueur and *fraise de Plougastel,* a strawberry liqueur.

ENTERTAINMENT IN BRITTANY

Bretons are fond of festivals and celebrations, and they are also enthusiastic communicators. Music, film and cartoon festivals, as well as live performances, take place all over Brittany throughout the year. The region also has a great variety of museums, art galleries and other cultural centres. Those who do not wish to spend all their time on the beach will find more than enough to entertain them. For details of local festivals, see Brittany Through the Year *(pp28–31)*.

Musician at the Festival des Vieilles Charrues

GENERAL INFORMATION

The regional newspapers and magazines *(see p263)* are the best source of information regarding festivals and other events *(see pp28–31)*. Lists of upcoming events are also available from the Comité Régional du Tourisme, for the whole of Brittany, and the relevant Comité Départemental, for each region of Brittany. Local tourist offices are another convenient source of information.

BUYING TICKETS

Tickets for shows and festivals for which there is an admission charge are usually available direct from the organizers. Shops run by FNAC (Fédération Nationale d'Art et de Culture), which can be found in large towns, also have ticket offices.

It is worth bearing in mind that most major events usually draw very large crowds, and it may be necessary to book tickets several months in advance.

MUSIC

The passionate enthusiasm that Bretons have for music *(see pp22–3)* goes back to their ancient roots. Many solo musicians and groups who began their careers in Brittany have gone on to achieve much wider fame. In this respect, **Ubu**, the arts centre in Rennes, stands out for its policy of promoting avant-garde musicians.

Brittany also hosts many major music festivals. Among the greatest is the Festival des Vieilles Charrues in Carhaix *(see p29)*, the Route du Rock in St-Malo *(see p29)*, the Rencontres Transmusicales in Rennes *(see p31)*, the Festival Astropolis in Concarneau, and the Festival Art Rock in St-Brieuc *(see p28)*. For jazz enthusiasts there is the Festival du Jazz in Vannes *(see p29)*.

Traditional Breton music is celebrated at the Festival Interceltique in Lorient *(see p29)*, which draws 4,500 performers and 450,000 spectators each year. The focus of the Festival de Cornouaille in Quimper is world music.

THEATRE

Besides the high-quality programme of plays performed by the **Théâtre National de Bretagne** in Rennes, theatre in Brittany comes to the fore at the annual Festival Tombées de la Nuit *(see p28)*, which takes place in the city in July. Other theatres with dynamic programmes are in Nantes and Brest.

CINEMA

Several annual film festivals take place in Brittany. Established over ten years ago, the **Festival du Film Britannique** in Dinard *(see p30)* shows feature films and organizes retrospectives. Prominent people from the world of film, including actors, directors, producers and distributors, attend.

Travelling, a week-long film festival that takes place in Rennes in January, highlights the work of filmmakers from a particular city, such as London, Berlin or Tokyo. This is an opportunity to see some

Dancers at the Rencontres Transmusicales in Rennes

unusual productions. The **Festival du Cinéma des Minorités Nationales**, meanwhile, shows films on the theme of various civilizations.

EXHIBITIONS

Brittany has a wealth of museums and art galleries, with interesting or unusual permanent collections and temporary exhibitions.

Some of the best temporary exhibitions can be seen at two venues in Rennes – the Musée des Beaux-Arts *(see p59)* and La Criée, a centre for modern art. There are also the **Centre d'Art Passerelle** in Brest, the Musée des Jacobins in Morlaix *(see p117)*, the contemporary art centre in Kerguehennec, the **Galerie Dourven** in Trédrez-Locquémeau, the Musée de La Cohue in Vannes *(see pp187–8)* and the Musée des Beaux-Arts in Quimper *(see pp158 and 161)*.

Participants in the Festival Interceltique in Lorient

DIRECTORY

VENUES

CÔTES D'ARMOR

Le Masque en Mouvement
(theatre)
13 Rue de la Gare,
22250 Broons.
Tel *(02) 96 84 75 19.*

La Passerelle
(theatre)
Place de la Résistance,
22000 St-Brieuc.
Tel *(02) 96 68 18 40.*

Théâtre des Jacobins
Rue de l'Horloge,
22100 Dinan.
Tel *(02) 96 87 03 11.*

FINISTÈRE

Le Quartz de Brest
(theatre, music and dance)
4 Avenue Clemenceau,
29200 Brest.
Tel *(02) 98 33 70 70.*

Théâtre de Cornouaille
(regional theatre in Quimper)
4 Place de la Tour-d'Auvergne,
29000 Quimper.
Tel *(02) 98 55 98 55.*

ILLE-ET-VILAINE

Opera
Place de l'Hôtel-de-Ville, 35000 Rennes.
Tel *(02) 99 78 48 78.*

Salle de la Cité
(music and dance)
10 Rue St-Louis,
35000 Rennes.
Tel *(02) 99 79 10 66.*

Théâtre National de Bretagne
1 Rue St-Hélier,
35000 Rennes.
Tel *(02) 99 31 12 31.*

Théâtre de la Parcheminerie
23 Rue de la Parcheminerie,
35000 Rennes.
Tel *(02) 99 79 47 63.*

Le Triangle
(music and dance)
30 Boulevard de Yougoslavie,
35000 Rennes.
Tel *02 99 22 27 00.*

Ubu
(music and dance)
1 Rue St-Hélier,
35000 Rennes.
Tel *(02) 99 30 31 68.*

LOIRE-ATLANTIQUE

Cité International des Congrès de Nantes-Atlantique
(theatre, music and dance)
5 Rue Valmy,
44000 Nantes.
Tel *(02) 51 88 20 00.*

Le Grand T
(theatre, music and dance)
84 Rue du Général-Buat,
44000 Nantes.
Tel *(02) 28 24 28 00.*
www.legrandt.fr

Lieu Unique
(theatre, music and dance)
Quai Ferdinand-Favre,
44000 Nantes.

Tel *(02) 51 82 15 00.*
www.lelieuunique.com

Théâtre Graslin
(Opera)
1 Rue Molière,
44000 Nantes.
Tel *(02) 40 41 90 77.*

MORBIHAN

Le Grand Théâtre
Place de l'Hôtel de Ville,
56100 Lorient.
Tel *(02) 97 02 22 77.*

Plateau des 4 Vents
(theatre)
2 Rue du Professeur-Mazé,
56100 Lorient.
Tel *(02) 97 37 53 05.*

ART GALLERIES

CÔTES D'ARMOR

Galerie Dourven
Domaine Départemental du Dourven,
22300 Trédez-Locquémeau.
Tel *(02) 96 35 21 42.*

FINISTÈRE

Centre d'Art Passerelle
41 bis Rue Charles-Berthelot,
29200 Brest.
Tel *(02) 98 43 34 95.*

ILLE-ET-VILAINE

La Criée
Halles Centrales,
Place Honoré-Commeurec,
35000 Rennes.
Tel *(02) 23 62 25 10.*

MORBIHAN

Domaine de Kerguehennec
Centre d'Art Contemporain Bignan,
56500 Locmine.
Tel *(02) 97 60 44 44.*
www.art-kerguehennec.com

LOIRE-ATLANTIQUE

Le Grand T
10 Passage Pommeraye,
44000 Nantes.
Tel *(02) 51 88 25 25.*

CINEMA

Festival du Film Britannique
Organizer's office:2 Bd Féart, 35800 Dinard.
Tel *(02) 99 88 19 04.*
Fax *(02) 99 46 67 15.*
www.festivaldufilm-dinard.com

Festival Travelling de Rennes
5 Rue de Lorraine, 35000 Rennes. **Tel** *(02) 23 46 47 08.* **www**.travelling-festival. com

Festival du Cinéma des Minorités Nationales
20 Rue du Port-Rhu, BP 206,
29172 Douarnenez Cedex.
Tel *(02) 98 92 09 21.*
Fax *(02) 98 92 28 10.*
@ fdz@wanadoo.fr
www.kerys.com/festival

OUTDOOR ACTIVITIES

With beautiful bays and beaches, dramatic promontories and cliffs, and picturesque islands, Brittany is well endowed with areas of natural beauty. The region's coast is its best-known feature, and many watersports are available *(see pp258–9)*.

Brittany's spectacular coastline should not, however, obscure the attractions of the interior. These include the Monts d'Arrée and the Montagnes Noires, as well as heathland, forests, lakes, rivers, canals, valleys and marshland. These landscapes can be explored on foot, by bicycle or on horseback. Brittany's nature reserves and coastal areas offer plenty of opportunities for birdwatching, and, with more than 30 fine golf courses, the region is also attractive to keen golfers.

Cyclists at Fort de La Latte, a 13th-century fortress on Cap Fréhel

WALKING

Running both along coastlines and inland, France has over 60,000km (37,000 miles) of long-distance footpaths (Sentiers de Grande Randonnée, or GR) and 80,000km (50,000 miles) of Promenade et Randonnée (PR) routes. These are maintained and marked out by volunteers of the **Fédération Française de la Randonnée Pédestre**.

Most of the best footpaths in Brittany are mentioned in the appropriate entries in this guide. Various organizations, such as **Rando Breiz** and the Comité Régional du Tourisme, offer walking programmes with overnight stays in gîtes (some of which have received an award for their standards of comfort), or in *chambres d'hôtes* (guest rooms) or small, family-run hotels.

CYCLING

The Blavet valley, the Cornouaille region and the Baie du Mont-St-Michel have been identified as prime areas for mountain biking (Sites VTT) by the **Ligue de Bretagne de Cyclotourisme**.

As with long-distance walking *(see above)*, gîte and other en-route accommodation can be arranged through local cycling organizations or the Comité Régional du Tourisme.

Walkers near the Phare du Paon, Isle de Bréhat

HORSEBACK RIDING

Those who prefer to explore Brittany on horseback will enjoy following Équibreizh, a long-distance bridleway that traverses Brittany. It is clearly marked and covers over 2,000 km (1,250 miles) of varied and scenic terrain. The *Topo-Guide Équibreizh*, published by **CRTEB** (Régionale Comité pour le Tourisme Équestre de Bretagne), includes detailed maps indicating routes, overnight stopping places, riding centres, farriers and horse transporters. Accommodation can also be arranged through the **Comité Régional** in the revelant area of Brittany.

BIRD-WATCHING

Brittany is one of the best places in Europe for birdwatching. The diversity of the region's landscapes attracts a great variety of birds *(see pp16–17)*, from the ubiquitous herring gull and crested cormorant, to the marsh harrier and ringed plover. There is much for nature-lovers to see, and almost 20 bird sanctuaries and other protected areas to explore.

Bretagne Vivante-SEPNB (Société pour l'Étude et la Protection de la Nature en Bretagne) and **Vivarmor Nature** both organize a variety of bird-watching trips, in winter as well as in summer. Useful information is also available from **LPO (Ligue pour la Protection des Oiseaux)**.

GOLF

There are 32 golf courses in Brittany, providing golfing enthusiasts with a wide choice. The **Ligue de Golf de Bretagne** and the Comité Régional du Tourisme publish a guide listing all the golf courses in the region. Many options, from a day's play to a full week, are available. The association **Formule Golf** offers tailor-made golfing programmes spread over several days.

SPORT AND TOURISM FOR DISABLED PEOPLE

Brittany has several organizations that arrange holidays and sports activities for people with disabilites. Founded in 1982 by UFCV (Union Francaise des Centres de Vacances et de Loisirs), of which it is a member, the **Association EPAL** (Évasion en Pays d'Accueil et de Loisirs, *see p264*) organizes sightseeing and sporting holidays for disabled people.

Golf course at Les Rochers-Sévigné in Vitré

Two other organizations – **RADAR**, based in London, and **MDLF** *(see pp264)*, based in Canada – offer a very similar service.

Comprehensive information relevant to activities organized in Brittany is available from the **Comité Régional de Sport Adapté de Bretagne** and the **Comité Régional de Handisport de Bretagne**. The names and contact details of other organizations that arrange a variety of sports and holidays for people with disabilities is given on p264.

Bird-watching at Cap Sizun, in southern Finistère

DIRECTORY

WALKING

Fédération Française de la Randonnée Pédestre
13B Ave Cucille, 35760 St-Gregoire.
Tel (02) 99 54 67 61.
www.ffrandonee.fr

Rando Breiz
1 Rue Raoul-Ponchon, 35000 Rennes.
Tel (02) 99 27 03 20.
@ info@randobreizh.com

CYCLING

Ligue de Bretagne de Cyclotourisme
11 Rue Alphonse-Guérin, 35000 Rennes.
Tel 08 77 98 13 99.

HORSEBACK RIDING

CRTEB
5 bis Rue Waldeck-Rousseau,
BP 307, 56103 Lorient.
Tel (02) 97 84 44 03.
www.equibreizh.com

Tourisme Équestre des Pays de la Loire
3 Rue Bossuet, 44000 Nantes.
Tel 08 79 65 77 42.
www.terre-equestre.com

BIRD-WATCHING

Bretagne Vivante-SEPNB (Société pour l'Étude et la Protection de la Nature en Bretagne)
186 Rue Anatole-France, BP 32,29276, Brest cedex.
Tel (02) 98 49 07 18.
www.bretagne-vivante.asso.fr

LPO (Ligue pour la Protection des Oiseaux)
Corderie Royale, BP 90263 17305 Rochefort cedex.
Tel (05) 46 82 12 34.
www.ipo.fr

Vivarmor Nature
10 Boulevard Sévigné, 22000 St-Brieuc.
Tel (02) 96 33 10 57.
www.assoc.wanadoo.fr/vivarmor/

GOLF

Formule Golf
2 Rue Jacques Daguerre, EUROPARC de la Chantrerie, 44306 Nantes Cedex 3.
Tel (02) 40 12 55 95.
www.formule-golf.com

Ligue de Golf de Bretagne
130 Rue Eugéne Pottier, 35000 Rennes.
Tel (02) 99 31 68 80.

VISITORS WITH DISABILITIES

RADAR
12 City Forum, 250 City Road. London EC1V 8AF.
Tel 020 7250 3222.
www.radar.org.uk

Comité Régional de Handisport de Bretagne
Rue Auguste Fresnel, 29490 Guipavas.
Tel (02) 98 42 61 05.

Comité Régional de Sport Adapté de Bretagne
9 Rue Jean Daudin, 75015 Paris.
Tel (01) 42 73 90 00.
www.ffsa.asso.fr.

Watersports

From the illustrious seafaring traditions of the past to the prestigious regattas that take place in its major coastal harbours today, Brittany has a close association with the sea. This, together with a spectacular coastline, makes it an ideal environment in which to enjoy watersports. Of the variety of watersports practised in Brittany, yachting, canoeing, scuba-diving, sand yachting and surfing are by far the most popular. For beginners and experienced alike, the opportunities for enjoying them are many, and each in its different ways reveals the power and beauty of the sea.

Sailing boat bear Phare de la Vieille, off southern Finistère

SAILING

With hundreds of sailboards, catamarans, dinghies and traditional sailing boats invading its coastal waters each summer, Brittany is one of the best places in the world for sailing. It has more than 70 marinas and mooring for a total of 22,120 pleasure boats. Sailing courses and cruises are also available.

Brittany's sailing schools, of which there are over 70, together with several dozen watersports associations, have high standards of tuition and safety. The only conditions for joining are the ability to swim 50 m (55 yds), which can be proved either by showing a certificate or by completing a test, and the production of a medical certificate of fitness.

The main sailing centres are St-Malo, St-Cast-Le Guildo, Pléneuf-Val-André, Perros-

Guirec, Rade de Brest, Crozon-Morgat and Lorient. Information on sailing schools is available from **Nautisme** or the Comité Départemental in the relevant area of Brittany.

For coastal and ocean sailing, there are schools that offer high standards of tuition in a friendly atmosphere. Groups are organized according to participants' ability, and the schools cater for all levels, including introductory tuition for children, and theory and competitions for more experienced sailors. Information is available from **Formules Nautiques Bretagne**. During school holidays, this organization also offers residential courses for children aged six to 17, running from six days to one month. Any parents wishing to accompany their children are able to stay in gîtes, apartments or hotels.

SURFING

Cap Fréhel, Le Dossen, Le Petit-Minou, La Palue, La Torche, Guidel, the Presqu''île de Quiberon and other places along the coasts of Brittany attract some 15,000 surfers each year.

Catering for all abilities, Brittany's eight surfing schools offer tuition in long-boarding, body-boarding, skim-boarding and body-surfing. They are located in Dinard, Brest, Crozon-Morgat, Audierne, La Torche, Larmor-Plage, Guidel and Plouharnel. The **ESB (École de Surf de Bretagne)** and **WSA (West Surf Association)** jointly constitute the regional surfing federation.

DIVING

About 190 diving clubs in Brittany and the Loire area are affiliated to the **Comité Inter-Régional de Plongée de Bretagne et des Pays de la Loire**.

The organization Plongée Label Bretagne has eight diving centres. Catering for children, families, individuals and groups, they offer tuition for beginners as well as tailor-made dives, underwater photography sessions, and visits to local shipwrecks. These centres are based in St-Malo, Erquy, Trébeurden, Brest, Camaret, Audierne, Lorient and Concarneau. Their details are available from the Comité Inter-Régional de Plongée.

Kayaks around the Île de Batz, in northern Finistère

Sand yachts in Plestin-les-Grèves, on the Côtes d'Armor

CANOEING

Neither canoeing nor kayaking require a high degree of skill. The boats are ideal for exploring bays and inlets accessible only from the sea.

To ensure good standards of equipment and safety, the **Comité Régional de Bretagne** has set up Point Kayak de Mer, an affiliation with 15 centres. These are based in St-Malo, St-Pierre de Quiberon, St-Armel, La Roche-Derrien, Paimpol, Loguivy, Plestin-les-Grèves, Ploudalmezeau, Perros-Guirec, Crozon, St-Lunaire, Pontrieux, Plouhinec, Erdeven and Moelan-sur-Mer.

Brittany's canals and rivers are also worth exploring by canoe. Special kayaking and rafting centres have been set up in Lannion, Cesson-Sévigné and Inzinzac-Lochrist. The canoeing centres in Pont-Réan and Quimper-Cornouaille have both been made a Point Canoë Nature, a mark of quality bestowed by the Comité Régional de Bretagne.

SAND YACHTING

Now an international sport, sand yachting has several sub-disciplines, each using a different type of equipment.

There are over 15 sand-yachting clubs in Brittany. Most bear the name "École de Char à Voile", which means they are affiliated to the **Ligue de Char à Voile de Bretagne**.

Full information on sand yachting is available from this organization.

SAFETY AT SEA

Sailing is not a sport for the uninitiated. Many accidents are caused by a lack of knowledge or by negligence.

Before setting out on a sailing trip, it is essential to obtain a local weather forecast, as weather conditions can change rapidly. Novice sailors must be supervised by professionals at all times.

The *Almanach du Marin Breton*, an annual navigational handbook, is available from all good newsagents. Published by **Œuvre du Marin Breton**, a non-profit-making association, it contains information aiding the safety of vessels, a map of local currents, tidetables, astral and radio navigation, details of lighthouses and beacons, administrative information, maps of harbours and nautical instructions. In case of difficulties at sea, contact **CROSS** (Centre Régional Opérationnel de Surveillance et de Sauvetage), a coastguard and sea-rescue organization.

DIRECTORY

SAILING

Formules Nautiques Bretagne
1 Rue de Kerbriant, BP 39, 29281 Brest cedex.
Tel (02) 98 02 49 67.
www.nautisme-bretagne.fr

Nautisme en Ille et Vilaine
Maison Départementale des Sports,
13B Avenue de Cucillé
35065 Rennes cedex.
Tel (02) 99 54 67 69.
Fax (02) 23 46 28 02.

Nautisme en Finistère
11 Rue Théodore le Hars,
BP 1334,
29103 Quimper cedex.
Tel (02) 98 76 21 31.
Fax (02) 98 53 37 30.
www.nautisme-finistere.com

Nautisme en Morbihan
Centre Nautique de Kerguélen, 56260 Larmor Plage. *Tel* (02) 97 33 77 78.

SURFING

ESB & WSA (École de Surf de Bretagne & West Surf Association)
Galerie Marchande,
56520 Guidel-Plages.
Tel (02) 97 32 70 37.
www.ecole-surf-bretagne.com

Ligue de Bretagne de Surf
Centre Nautique,
56520 Guidel Plages.
Tel (02) 97 65 32 85.

Fédération Française de Surf
6 Rue de l'Ocan,

56400 Plouharnel.
Tel (02) 97 52 41 18.
www.surfingfrance.com

DIVING

Comité Inter-Régional de Plongée de Bretagne et des Pays de la Loire
39 Rue de Villeneuve,
56100 Lorient.
Tel (02) 97 37 51 51.
www.ffessm-cibpl.asso.fr

CANOEING

Comité Régional de Bretagne
Base Nautique, Plaine de Baud,35 Rue Jean-Marie-Huchet, 35000 Rennes.
Tel (02) 23 20 30 14.
www.crck.org

Comité Régional Pays de la Loire
75 Avenue du Lac-de-Maine, 49000 Angers.
Tel (02) 41 73 86 10.

SAND YACHTING

Ligue de Char à Voile de Bretagne
22 Place de l'Église,
35100 Cherrueix.
Tel (02) 99 48 83 47.
www.charavoilebzh.info

USEFUL NUMBERS

CROSS Corsen (northern coast)
Tel (02) 98 89 31 31.

CROSS Étel (southern coast)
Tel (02) 97 55 35 35.

Œuvre du Marin Breton (publisher of *Almanach du Marin Breton*)
Tel (02) 98 44 06 00.

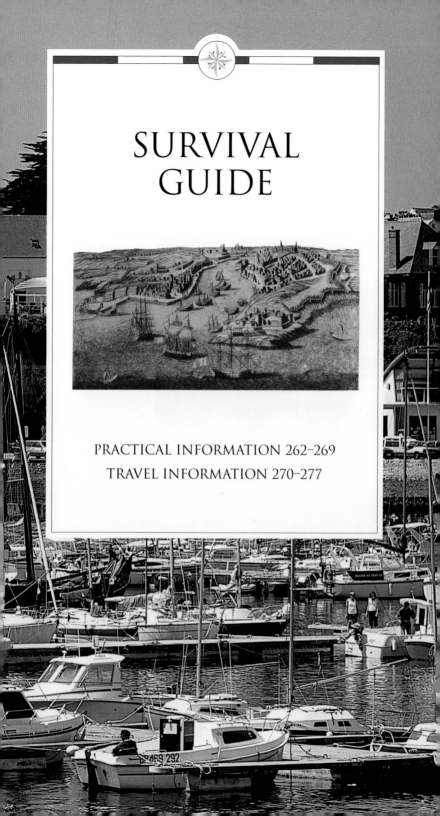

SURVIVAL
GUIDE

PRACTICAL INFORMATION

A prime tourist destination, Brittany attracts large numbers of visitors during the summer. At the height of the holiday season, which runs from 14 July to 15 August, the population of Brittany's coastal resorts can triple or even quadruple. This does not detract from its appeal, as Brittany has much to offer, especially a wide range of watersports, and is well geared to

Breton headdress

the needs of visitors. However, those who choose to visit at quieter times of the year will experience more intimate aspect of the region. Out of season, Brittany's beaches are almost deserted; its prehistoric monuments seem even more mysterious; and the region's towns and cities, with their fine architecture and strong historical associations, can more easily be appreciated.

The tourist office in La Turballe

WHEN TO GO

Outside French school holidays, Brittany is reasonably quiet. The best times to come are just before the summer holiday season, and just after. These times are in June, when the season is just starting to get under way, and September, by which time many holidaymakers have gone home.

September is, in fact, the best time to come to Brittany. By then, Bretons have more time to welcome visitors, historic monuments and other places of interest are no longer crowded, and the long autumn tides create sights of unforgettable beauty.

Nevertheless, Brittany in the summer offers all the pleasures of the beach, as well as walking and cycling through lush countryside. Restaurants, bars, nightclubs and festivals are then also in full swing.

brittany tourism. **com**
Brittany's official tourism website

VISAS

There are no visa requirements for EU nationals, or for visitors from the United States, Canada, Australia or New Zealand who plan to stay in France for less than three months. For trips of over three months, visas should be obtained prior to departutre from the French consulate in your own country.

Visitors from most other countries require a tourist visa. Anyone planning to study or work in France should apply to their local French consulate several months in advance.

TOURIST INFORMATION

Most towns and even some villages in Brittany have some kind of tourist information bureau. *Offices de tourisme* (tourist offices in larger towns), *syndicats*

d'initiative (tourist information centres in smaller towns and villages, often located in the *mairie*) and tourist spots pool information and dispense leaflets listing local attractions and outlining sightseeing tours as well as town maps, calendars of events and information on all types of accommodation. Of course, greater tourist information facilities will be found in the coastal resorts than in small villages in the interior of Brittany. Some tourist offices can also book hotel rooms for visitors.

It is also perfectly acceptable to ask passers-by for information. Bretons are obliging and are keen to help visitors appreciate the attractions of their region. The addresses and telephone numbers of tourists offices are given at the start of each entry throughout this guide.

ANIMALS

Visitors may bring their pets into France as long as the animal is not younger than three months old, that it has been microchipped, and that it has been vaccinated against rabies. You may be required to show your pet's vaccination certificate. It is advisable to obtain up-to-date information from a veterinary practice in your own country before leaving.

TAX-FREE GOODS

Visitors resident outside the EU can reclaim the sales tax TVA, or VAT, on French goods if more than 175€ is spent in one shop in one day. Obtain

The Plage de l'Anse sur Suscinio at Sarzeau, in the Golfe du Morbihan

a *détaxe* receipt and take the goods (unopened) out of the country within three months. The form should be presented to customs when leaving the country. The reimbursement will be sent on to you.

Exceptions for *détaxe* rebate are food and drink, medicines, tobacco, cars and motorbikes, although tax can be reimbursed for bicyles. More information and advice are available from the **Centre des Renseignements des Douanes** *(see p264)*.

DUTY-PAID AND DUTY-FREE GOODS

There are no longer any restrictions on the quantities of duty-paid and VAT-paid goods you can take from one EU country to another, as long as they are for your own use and not for resale. You may be asked to prove the goods are for your own use if they exceed the EU suggested quantites. If you cannot do so, the entire amount of the goods (not just the deemed excess) may be confiscated and destroyed. The suggested limits are very generous: 10 litres of spirits, 90 litres of wine, 110 litres of beer and 800 cigarettes. Visitors under the age of 17 are not allowed to import duty-paid tobacco or alcohol.

WEBSITES

Wide-ranging information on Brittany, whether from a cultural, tourist or practical

TV Breizh, focused on Breton culture

point of view is available on the internet. There are general websites on Brittany *(www. tourismebretagne.com)*, and others describing each region of Brittany, such as *www. centrebretagne.com*. Still others suggest tours of the region *(www.bretagne-evasion.com)* and gives lists of accommodation *(www. hotels-bretagne.com)*. For more websites, see the Directory.

The website of the local daily newspaper *Ouest France* also gives comprehensive information on tourism in Brittany *(www.france-ouest.com)*.

ADMISSION CHARGES

For museums and historic monuments, admission charges range from €1.5 to €6. Concessions are offered to students (bearing a valid student card), to people under the age of 26 (bearing an international youth card), and to people over the age of 65. There is sometimes no admission charge for children. Full details of youth and student reductions are available from youth information centres.

Ouest France and Le Télégramme, two local newspapers

OPENING HOURS

Most municipal museums are closed on Mondays, and most national museums on Tuesdays. In the high season, many of them are open every day and do not close for lunch. It is, however, always best to telephone in advance to check a museum's opening times.

Some country churches are kept locked. By inquiring at local information centres or even by asking passers-by, you can usually find out who holds the key. Admission is usually free, except for church treasuries, crypts and cloisters.

Bretagne Magazine and ArMen, two local magazines

Most shops have longer opening hours during the summer. Outside the high season, shop opening times are usually 9am–noon and 3–7pm, Tuesday to Saturday.

MEDIA

The main national French dailies are, from right to left on the political spectrum, *Le Figaro, France Soir, Le Monde, Libération* and *L'Humanité*. Like every region of France, Brittany also has good local newspapers. The daily *Ouest France* has the largest circulation. Regional magazines include the monthly *Ar Men* and the quarterly *Bretagne Magazine*. Both contain information on cultural events in Brittany.

The major nationwide TV channels are *TF1* and France 2. *TV Breizh* concentrates on Breton culture. News bulletins broadcast by *France 3* (at noon and 7pm) cover local events. For English-language media, *see p269*.

TRAVELLING WITH CHILDREN

Although children are welcome in most hotels and restaurants, it is best to check in advance that facilities are available. Hotels offering facilities for children, such as cots and baby-sitting services, are indicated in the hotels listing on pp218–31. Many restaurants provide highchairs and offer children's menus or smaller portions for children.

Family tickets on public transport and for admission to museums, chateaux and other attractions are also available. Most activities for children are organized in school holidays.

As in other countries, children in cars are legally required to travel in child car seats.

DISABLED TRAVELLERS

Unfortunately, few hotels, restaurants and tourist sites in Brittany have adequate provision for disabled visitors. However, several organizations offer assistance to disabled travellers in Brittany and can arrange holidays especially adapted to people with disabilities (see p217 and Directory, below) .

SMOKING

In France, smoking is forbidden on public transport and in all public places such as museums, historic monuments and cinemas. Since January 2008 smoking has been banned in restaurants, bars and cafés, although it is allowed on outside terraces.

ELECTRICITY

The current in France is 220v-AC with two-pin, round-pronged plugs. While some hotels provide adaptors on request, it is best to take some with you to be on the safe side, especially if you are staying in self-catering accommodation.

FRENCH TIME

France is one hour ahead of Greenwich Mean Time (GMT) in winter, and two hours in summer. The French use the 24-hour clock; for example, 7pm is expressed as 19:00.

DIRECTORY

TOURIST INFORMATION

CIDJ (Centre d'Information et de Documentation pour la Jeunesse)
101 Quai Branly, 75015 Paris.
Tel 0825 09 06 30.
www.cidj.com

CIJB (Centre Information Jeunesse Bretagne)
Maison du Champ-de-Mars,
6 Cours des Alliés,
35043 Rennes Cedex.
Tel (02) 99 31 47 48.
www.crij-bretagne.com

CRIJ (Centre Régional Information Jeunesse)
28 Rue Calvaire, 44000 Nantes.
Tel (02) 51 72 94 50.
www.infojeunesse-pays-de-la-loire.net

Customs (Douane)
(general information)
Tel 0820 024 444.

Ministère de l'Éducation Nationale
www.education.gouv.fr

Comité Régional du Tourisme de Bretagne
1 Rue Raoul-Ponchon,
35000 Rennes.
Tel (02) 99 36 15 15.
www.tourismebretagne.com

Comité Régional du Tourisme des Pays de la Loire
2 Rue Loire, 44200 Nantes.
Tel (02) 40 48 24 20.
www.enpaysdelaloire.com

Maison de la Bretagne
203 Boulevard St-Germain,
75007 Paris.
Tel (01) 53 63 11 50.

Secrétariat d'État au Tourisme
www.tourisme.gouv.fr

WEBSITES

www.tourismebretagne.com
www.region-bretagne.fr (culture, current affairs, tourism)
www.bretagne-evasion.com
www.ouest-france.com
www.centrebretagne.com
www.pays-de-dol.com
www.morbihan.com
www.westernloire.com

COMITÉS DÉPARTEMENTAUX DU TOURISME

Finistère
4 Rue du 19 Mars 1962,
29000 Quimper.
Tel (02) 98 76 20 70.
www.finisteretourisme.com

Ille-et-Vilaine
4 Rue Jean Jaures, 35000 Rennes.
Tel (02) 99 78 47 46.
www.bretagne35.com

Loire-Atlantique
11 Rue du Château de l'Eraudière,
CS 40698, 44306 Nantes Cedex 3.
Tel (02) 51 72 95 40.

Morbihan
P.I.B.S. Kerino, Alée Nicolas-Le-Blanc, 56000 Vannes.
Tel 0825 13 56 56.

DISABLED TRAVELLERS

Association des Paralysés de France
17 Boulevard Auguste-Blanqui,
75013 Paris.
Tel (01) 40 78 69 00.
www.apf.asso.fr

CNRH (Comité National pour la Réadaptation des handicapés)
236 bis Rue de Tolbiac,
75013 Paris.
Tel (01) 53 80 66 66.

EPAL
11 Rue d'Ouessant, BP 2,
29801 Brest.
Tel (02) 98 41 84 09.
www.epal.asso.fr

MDLF Canada
H3A 2W9 Montréal.
Tel (00) 154 288 2026

Voyages ASAH
4 Rue Charcot, 75013 Paris
Tel (01) 42 03 61 67

Personal Security and Health

With competent local authorities and efficient public services, Brittany is a safe as well as a pleasant place to visit. However, to guard against petty crime, take a few simple precautions: do not flaunt valuable possessions and never leave them in full view in a parked car; also take care in crowds, where there may be pickpockets.

PERSONAL SECURITY

Like the rest of France, Brittany is not an area where violent crime is a problem, although you should take the precautions that you would at home.

If you are the victim of theft or assault, report this to the police immediately or, in small towns or villages, go to the *mairie* (town hall). If you are involved in a car accident, avoid confrontation. In potentially difficult situations, try to stay calm and speak French if you can, as this may help to defuse the situation.

EMERGENCIES

If you are involved in, or witness, an emergency at sea, call CROSS (Centre Régional Opérationnel de Surveillance et de Sauvetage), an organization that coordinates sea rescue in Brittany. **CROSS Corsen** covers the north coasts of Brittany, and **CROSS Étel** the south coasts. These centres in turn call on the services of the French Navy or of SNSM (Société Nationale de Sauvetage en Mer), a voluntary lifeboat organization.

In the case of an accident or emergency on land, call **SAMU** (Service d'Aide Médicale d'Urgence) by dialling 15, or the **Sapeurs Pompiers** (fire brigade) by dialling 18.

Military lifeboatmen answering an emergency call

MEDICAL TREATMENT

All European Union nationals are entitled to French social security coverage. However, medical treatment must be paid for and hospital rates vary widely. The European Health Insurance Card, which is available from the UK Department of Health or from a main post office, covers emergencies only; private medical insurance is needed for all other types of treatment. Non-EU nationals are obliged to carry medical insurance, taken out before they arrive.

For minor health problems, go to a pharmacy (identifiable by a green cross), where the staff will give appropriate medication, or will refer you to a doctor. A card in the window will give details of the nearest duty pharmacy *(pharmacie de guarde)* for night openings.

In the case of serious illness or injury, go to the casualty department *(services des urgences)* of the nearest hospital. Your consulate should also be able to recommend an English-speaking doctor.

BY THE SEA

Many of Brittany's beaches are patrolled by lifeguards, and most are marked with flags indicating whether it is safe to swim. A green flag indicates that swimming is safe, orange that it is dangerous, and red that it is forbidden. It is absolutely crucial to respect these indications, and also to be aware of weather forecasts. Most accidents are caused by ignorance of the power of winds, currents and tides.

As elsewhere in the European Union, a blue flag indicates that the beach and the water are clean.

Banking and Local Currency

You may bring any amount of currency into France, but anything over 7,500 euros (in cash or cheques) must be declared on arrival. The same applies when you leave. Travellers' cheques are the safest way to carry money abroad, but credit and debit cards, both of which can be used to withdraw local currency, are by far the most convenient. Bureaux de change are located at airports, large railway stations, and ferry ports, and can also be found in some hotels and shops.

USING BANKS

Bear in mind that most banks in rural areas do not have bureaux de change. They do, however, have ATMs (automatic teller machines) outside, or in an indoor area that is open 24 hours a day. ATMs accept credit cards in the Visa/Carte Bleue or MasterCard groups, and debit cards (Switch, Maestro,Delta and Cirrus).

This is the quickest and easiest way of obtaining money in local currency, although a small charge will be deducted from your account for this service. Also bear in mind that ATMs may quickly run out of notes over public holidays and also before the end of ordinary weekends.

If there is no ATM, you can withdraw up to €300 per day on a Visa card at the foreign exchange counter of a bank showing the Visa sign. The bank may need to obtain telephone authorization for such withdrawals.

BUREAUX DE CHANGE

As in other areas of France except Paris, independent bureaux de change are rare. Those that exist are usually located in airports, central city railway stations and ferry ports. In Brittany, even in areas with a high density of tourists, bureaux de change are difficult to find. They may also not offer rates as favourable as those obtained from the banks.

TRAVELLERS' CHEQUES AND CREDIT CARDS

Travellers' cheques can be obtained from **American Express** and **Travelex**, or from your bank. If you know that you will spend most of them, it is best to have the cheques issued in euros. American Express cheques are widely accepted in France. If cheques are exchanged at an Amex office, no commission is charged. In the case of theft, cheques are replaced at once.

Because of the high commissions charged, many French businesses do not accept the American Express credit card. The most widely used credit card is Carte Bleue/Visa. Eurocard/MasterCard is also widely accepted.

Credit cards issued in France are now "smart cards", which means that, instead of having a magnetic strip on the back, they have a *puce* (a microchip capable of storing data). Many retailers have machines designed to read both smart cards and magnetic strips. Conventional non-French cards cannot be read in the smart card slot. Persuade the cashier to swipe the card through the magnetic reader (*bande magnétique*). You may also be asked to tap in your PIN code (*code confidentiel*) and press the green key (*validez*) on a small keypad by the cash desk. Retailers accept payment by credit cards only for amounts above a certain figure.

Machine for reading credit cards

DIRECTORY

BUREAUX DE CHANGE

CÔTES D'ARMOR

La Poste
Place de la Liberté,
22021 St-Brieuc.
Tel (02) 96 62 68 89.

FINISTÈRE

La Poste
19 Rue Gambetta,
29680 Roscoff.
Tel (02) 98 69 71 28.

ILLE-ET-VILAINE

Brittany Ferries
Gare Maritime du Naye,
35400 St-Malo.
Tel (02) 99 40 64 41.

LOIRE-ATLANTIQUE

Change Graslin
17 Rue Jean-Jacques-Rousseau,
44000 Nantes.
Tel (02) 40 69 24 64.

MORBIHAN

Banque Populaire
Place Maurice-Marchais,
56000 Vannes.
Tel 0821 08 40 28.

LOST CARDS AND TRAVELLERS' CHEQUES

American Express
Tel (01) 47 77 70 00 (cards).
Tel 0800 83 28 20 (travellers' cheques).

Mastercard
Tel 0800 90 13 87.

Travelex/ Mastercard Services
Tel 0800 90 83 30.

Visa/Carte Bleue
Tel 0892 70 57 05.

BANKING HOURS

Most banks in France are open for business from 8.30 or 9am to 5pm, Tuesday to Saturday, closing for lunch from noon to 2pm. Banks usually close at noon on the day before public holidays (*see p31*).

THE EURO

The Euro (€), the single European currency, is now operational in 16 countries of the European Union – namely, Austria, Belgium, Cyprus, Eire, Finland, France, Germany, Greece, Italy, Luxembourg, Malta, the Netherlands, Portugal, Slovakia, Slovenia and Spain. Of the 16 countries in the European Union, only the United Kingdom, Denmark and Sweden have retained their respective currencies, with an option to review their decision in the future. Euro notes are identical across all 16 countries. Euro coins have one side identical (the value side), and one side unique to each country. Both notes and coins are valid and inter-changeable within each of the 16 countries using the euro.

Banknotes

Euro banknotes have seven denominations. The 5€ note (which is grey) is the smallest, followed by the 10€ (red), 20€ (blue), 50€ (orange), 100€ (green), 200€ (yellow) and 500€ (purple). All notes shows the stars of the European Union.

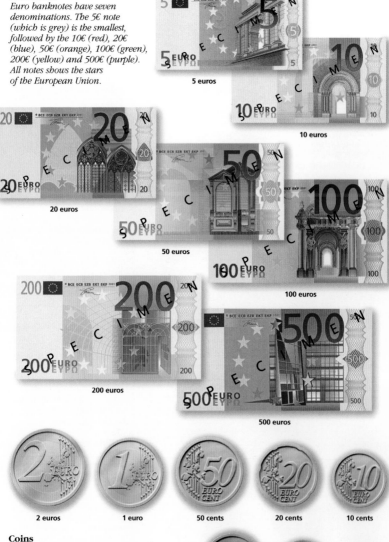

5 euros

10 euros

20 euros

50 euros

100 euros

200 euros

500 euros

2 euros 1 euro 50 cents 20 cents 10 cents

Coins

Euro coins have eight denominations: 1€ and 2€; and 50 cents, 20 cents, 10 cents, 5 cents, 2 cents and 1 cent. The 1€ and 2€ coins are silver and gold. The 50-cent, 20-cent and 10-cents coins are gold. The 5-cent, 2-cent and 1-cent coins are bronze.

5 cents 2 cents 1 cent

Communications

French telecommunications, run by France Télécom, are reliable and efficient. Public telephones are located in most public places – frequently in the central squares of towns and villages – and post offices *(bureaux de poste)* are identified by the blue-on-yellow La Poste sign. La Poste used to be called PTT *(postes, télégraphes, téléphones)*, so road signs often still indicate "PTT".

Foreign-language newspapers are available in most large towns and major resorts in Brittany. Some national television channels and radio stations broadcast foreign-language programmes.

A distinctive yellow French mailbox

TELEPHONING IN FRANCE

To use a payphone *(cabine)*, you usually need a phonecard *(télécarte)*, which is sold in newsagents *(maisons de la presse)* and tobacconists *(tabacs)*. These phonecards are available in 50 or 120 telephone units, and are simple to use. For local calls, a unit lasts up to six minutes. Many public telephones now also accept credit cards (with a PIN number). It is uncommon to find a payphone that take coins anymore.

Cheap rates, giving 50 per cent lower call charges, operate from 7pm to 8am Monday to Friday, from midnight to 8am and from noon to midnight on Saturday, and all day Sunday.

Some post offices have telephone booths *(cabines)* where you make the call first then pay afterwards at the counter. Long-distance calls made in this way are much cheaper than from hotels, where hefty surcharges are often added.

The Home Direct, or *pays directe*, calling service allows you to book a call through an operator in your own country, and to pay by credit card or by reversing the charges (collect call). Sometimes, you can also call a third country by this method.

All French telephone numbers have 10 digits. The first two digits indicate the region: 01 indicates Paris and the Île de France; 02 the northwest (Brittany falls into this region); 03, the northeast; 04, the southeast (including Corsica); and 05, the southwest. Remember that when you are phoning from outside France, you do not dial the initial zero.

MOBILE PHONES

Most new mobile phones brought in from another European or Mediterranean country can be used in France exactly as at home. However, US-based mobiles (cell phones) need to be "triple band" to be usable in France. Mobile phones are also readily available for hire in France.

Remember that making or receiving international calls via a mobile phone is very expensive for both parties.

USING A PHONECARD TELEPHONE

1 Lift the receiver and wait for the dialling tone.

2 Insert the *télécarte*, arrow side up.

3 The display will show how many units are stored on the card and will then tell you to dial.

4 Key in the number and wait to be connected.

5 If you want to make another call, do not replace the receiver; simply press the green follow-on call button.

6 When you have finished the call, replace the receiver. The card will emerge from the slot.

FRANCE TELECOM
600 AGENCES
PARTOUT
EN FRANCE

TELECARTE 50

FRANCE TELECOM

USING LA POSTE

The postal service in France is fast and reliable. However, it is not cheap, especially for sending parcels abroad, since all surface-mail services have been discontinued.

At La Poste, postage stamps *(timbres)* are sold singly or in books *(carnets)* of ten. Stamps for ordinary letters within the EU are also sold in newsagents and tobacconists. Letters are posted in yellow mail boxes, which often have separate slots for the town you are in, the *département* and other destinations *(autres destinations)*.

For a small collection fee, post offices also provide a mail-holding service *(poste restante)*, so that you can receive mail care of post offices anywhere in France.

Post offices are usually open from 8am to 7pm Monday to Friday, often closing at lunchtime, and 8am to noon on Saturdays.

Some of the larger post offices also have ATMs from which cash can be withdrawn with a banker's card *(see p266)*.

USING MINITEL

Minitel, use of which is free in post offices, provides a variety of services through a screen and keyboard connected to the

An automatic teller machine at a post office

A cybercafé, one of a growing number in Brittany's larger towns

telephone line. To use Minitel, press the telephone symbol and enter the Minitel number and code. For directory information, press the telephone symbol and key in 3611. When beeping starts, press Connexion/Fin. Specify the service or name of the supplier required. Enter the town or area. Press Envoi to search. To disconnect, press Veille or Connexion/Fin.

INTERNET ACCESS

As elsewhere in France, the internet is widely accessible in Brittany, in Internet cafés, libraries and in many hotels. The French modem socket is incompatible with US and UK plugs. Although adaptors are available, it is cheaper to buy a French modem lead.

NEWSPAPERS

In resorts and large cities, many British newspapers are available on the day of publication. Some, like *Financial Times Europe* and *Guardian Europe,* are European editions. Others may arrive slightly later. English-language publications include *The Weekly Telegraph, Guardian International, USA Today, Economist, Newsweek* and *International Herald Tribune.* For details of French newspapers, *see p263.*

TV AND RADIO

The popular subscription and satellite channels in France (collectively known as TPS, or *télévision par satellite)* include English-language *MTV, CNN,*

Sky and *BBC World.* English-language films on French television are generally subtitled when they are first shown; dubbed versions appear some time later.

UK radio stations can be picked up in France, including *Radio 4* during the day (648 AM or 198 Long Wave). On the same wavelength, *BBC World Service* broadcasts through the night. *Voice of America* can be found at 90.5, 98.8 and 102.4 FM. *Radio France International* (738 AM) gives daily news in English from 3 to 4pm. For details of French television, *see p263.*

TRAVEL INFORMATION

Brittany can easily be reached by air or, via the Channel Tunnel, by train, car or coach. There are flights from London direct to Brittany's three international airports, Brest, Rennes and Nantes. An alternative, with more frequent services, is to fly to Paris and catch a connecting

A Brit'Air plane, from a fleet serving Brittany

flight or train to a choice of destinations in Brittany. The whole region is served by fast rail connections from Paris, and, linked by the Autoroute de l'Ouest, it is no more than three hours' drive from the French capital. There are also regular ferry services direct to Brittany from the UK.

Passengers in the check-in hall at Nantes-Atlantique airport

ARRIVING BY AIR

Brittany has three international airports – Brest, Nantes and Rennes – and six domestic airports, including an aerodrome. From the UK, there are flights direct to Rennes, Nantes, Brest and Dinard, and flights to Paris with onward connections to Nantes, Rennes, Dinard, Brest, Quimper, Lannion, St-Brieuc, Morlaix and Lorient.

Ryanair has daily flights to Dinard and Nantes from

AIRPORT	ℹ INFORMATION	DISTANCE FROM CITY	TAXI TO CITY
CÔTES D'ARMOR			
Lannion	(02) 96 05 82 22	12 km (7 miles)	8€ to Lannion
FINISTÈRE			
Brest-Guipavas	(02) 98 32 01 00	5 km (3 miles)	15€ to Brest
Morlaix-Ploujean	(02) 98 62 16 09	3 km (2 miles)	9€ (weekdays), 12€ (weekends) to Morlaix
Quimper-Cornouailles	(02) 98 94 30 30	7 km (4 miles)	15€ to Quimper
ILLE-ET-VILAINE			
Dinard-Pleurtuit-St-Malo	(02) 99 46 18 46	10 km (6 miles) from Dinard 15 km (9 miles) from St-Malo	11€ (weekdays), 14€ (weekends) to Dinard 15€ (weekdays), 23€ weekends to St-Malo
Rennes	(02) 99 29 60 00	8 km (5 miles)	11–12€ (weekdays), 15€ (weekends)
LOIRE-ATLANTIQUE			
Nantes-Atlantique	(02) 40 84 80 00	12 km (7 miles)	25–30€ to Nantes
MORBIHAN			
Aérodrome de Belle-Île-en-Mer	(02) 97 31 83 09	5 km (3 miles)	9–14€ to Le Palais
Lorient-Lan-Bihoué	(02) 97 87 21 50	10 km (6 miles)	12–14€ (weekdays), 20€ (weekends) to Lorient

London Stansted, and to Brest from Luton airport. **EasyJet** has flights from Nantes to Gatwick and from Paris to Luton airport.

Many direct flights from London to Paris are provided by British Airways, **British Midland** and **Air France**.

From the US, there are flights direct to Paris from about 20 cities, mainly with **American, Delta**, United, Northwest, Continental, Virgin and British Airways. From Canada, Air France and Air Canada fly direct to Paris. During the summer, **Air Transat** also operates flights from Toronto and Montreal to Nantes. **Qantas** provides connecting flights from Australia and New Zealand.

CONNECTIONS FROM PARIS

From Paris-Orly and Paris-Roissy-Charles-de-Gaulle, there are several flights a day to Brest, Lorient, Quimper, Lannion, Rennes, St-Brieuc and Nantes. They are operated by **Air France** via **Brit'Air** and **Regional** (the parent company that runs Regional Air Lines, Flandre Air and Proteus). **Finist'Air** flies from Brest to the Île d'Ouessant.

From Brussels, it is also possible to travel to Nantes on a combined Air France-Thalys (flight and high speed-train) ticket called TGVAir.

Brittany is also served by rail links from Paris, including a TGV (high-speed-train) service to Rennes and Nantes (see pp272–3).

AIR FARES

Whether they are provided by the no-frills budget airlines or the classic, full-service major airlines, flights to France are usually more expensive during school holidays and at half-terms, especially in the summer months. However, APEX (Advance Purchase) fares give substantial savings. APEX fares can be ideal for a vacation if your dates are fixed, as they require you to pre-book outward and return flights that cannot be changed or cancelled.

Competition between airlines has resulted in other advantageous reductions. Airline companies usually give reductions to families, to people under the age of 25, to students under the age of 27, to retired people over the age of 60, and to groups of at least six people.

Through its range of *Tempo* fares, Air France offers four levels of reduction: the further ahead you are able to book (up to 15 days before departure), the greater the reduction offered. Children under the age of two travel free on domestic flights, although they are not allocated a seat of their own, and fares for children under 12 are also subject to a 50 per cent reduction.

AIRPORT CONNECTIONS

None of Brittany's airports are further than 15 km (9 miles) from the centre of the city that they serve, and

DIRECTORY

AIRLINES

Air France (Brit'Air and Regional)
Tel 3654. www.airfrance.fr
www.britair.com
www.regional.com

Air Transat
Tel 0825 32 58 25.
www.airtransat.ca

American Airlines
Tel 0155 17 43 41.

British Airways
Tel 0845 779 9977 in UK.
Tel 0825 82 54 00 in France.
www.ba.com

British Midland
Tel 0870 607 0555 in UK.
www.flybmi.com

Delta Air Lines
Tel 0811 64 00 05.
www.delta.com

easyJet
Tel 0870 6000 000 in UK.
Tel 0899 65 00 11 in France.
www.easyjet.com

Finist'Air
Tel 0298 80 54 87.
www.finistair.fr

Qantas
Tel 0811 98 00 02.
www.qantas.com

Ryanair
Tel 0892 23 23 75.
www.ryanair.com

most are much nearer than that. All the aiports are connected to the city centre by regular bus services.

It is also possible to travel from the airport by taxi. The table opposite gives distances between the airports and town centres, as well as average taxi fares.

AIRPORT CAR HIRE

Avis, Budget, Europcar, Hertz and other major international car hire companies all have offices either in Brittany's airports themselves, or in the nearest town. The central-booking contact details of car hire companies operating in Brittany are given on p275.

Terminal at Rennes-St-Jacques airport

Travelling by Train

It is easy and enjoyable to travel in France by train, and this is also one of the best ways both of reaching and of travelling around Brittany. While both Nantes and Rennes are served by TGVs (high-speed trains) from Paris, *trains corail* (intercity trains) link Brittany's main towns, and TER (local express trains) provide connections to smaller towns and villages in the region. Areas of Brittany without a rail service can be reached by bus (SNCF runs a fleet of modern buses, which are free to rail-pass holders) and sometimes by boat.

Automatic ticket machine

ARRIVING BY TRAIN

For travellers arriving from Britain, **Eurostar** gives access to the entire French rail network. At Lille, two hours by Eurostar from London, passengers can change to onward TGVs (high-speed trains), which bypass Paris and continue southwest to Brittany.

Two hours fifteen minutes from London St Pancras, Eurostar arrives at Paris Gare du Nord. This is also the terminus for high-speed Thalys trains from Brussels, Amsterdam and Cologne.

Trains for Brittany leave from Gare Montparnasse, in the southwest of Paris.

HIGH-SPEED TRAINS

Trains running on new high-speed lines are the pride of the SNCF (the national rail company). Note that in some towns, the new TGV station is separate from the main station, and can be out of the town centre.

Journey times by high-speed train from Paris are as follows: 2 hours to Rennes or Nantes, 2 hours 35 minutes to St-Nazaire, 2 hours 50 minutes to St-Brieuc, 3 hours to Vannes, 3 hours 30 minutes to Lorient, and 4 hours 10 minutes to Brest or Quimper. The journey time from Paris to St-Malo by ordinary train is 3 hours. Other direct TGV links are Lille–Rennes (3 hours 50 minutes), Lille–Nantes (3 hours 50 minutes) and Lyon–Nantes (4 hours 30 minutes).

Advance booking is compulsory on TGV trains, and is available up to five minutes before departure time. The inspector will then allocate you a seat.

Special family coaches (*Espace Famille*), located in second-class, consist of four facing seats with a table in the middle, separated off by half-doors. The nursery nearby is equipped with a changing mat and facilities for heating babies' bottles.

BOOKING WITHIN FRANCE

Automatic ticket and reservation machines (*billeterie automatique*) are found at main stations. They take credit cards or coins. You can also check train times and fares and make reservations by phoning **SNCF** or via the SNCF website (*see p273*). Tickets may be purchased by credit card, then collected at the station.

As with all travel by TGV, reservations are compulsory for all train journeys on public holidays, and for a *couchette or siège inclinable* (reclinable seat). Remember that both reservation and rail tickets must be validated in a *composteur* machine before boarding the train and that failure to do so can result in a fine.

BOOKING OUTSIDE FRANCE

Tickets and passes for rail travel (including Motorail) in France can be booked and paid for in advance direct from SNCF. Book online on their website (allow 7 days for ticket delivery), or by phone on 00 33 892 353 539, a special **SNCF** bookings line for English speakers (7am to 10pm daily). You can pay for your tickets by credit card. Online booking is also possible on the **Eurostar** website.

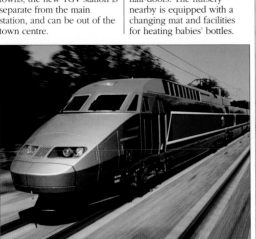

A TGV train, providing swift and comfortable passenger transport

Foreign rail travel agents like **Rail Europe** can take bookings by post, by phone, online, or in person at their London shop. Rail Europe bookings must be made between 14 and 60 days in advance, and a small charge is made for credit card bookings. Note that reservations made in another country may be difficult or impossible to change in France; any alterations to your booking should be made by the original issuing company.

Pontrieux railway station, served by a steam train during the summer

TICKETS AND PASSES

There is a basic fare for each rail journey, but numerous discounts are available on French trains. These reduced fares and travel passes are for certain categories of passengers and should be booked in advance. Substantial fare discounts are offered to people over 60 (*Découverte Senior*), to those under 26 (*Découverte 12–25*), for up to four adults travelling with a child under 12 (*Découverte Enfant Plus*), or anyone booking more than 30 days or more than 8 days in advance (*Découverte J30 or J8*).

Rail passes give even larger fare reductions. Strictly for non-residents, the France Railpass can only be bought outside France. It gives un-limited travel for 3 days within a month. If you are planning to travel in other countries too, choose One Country Pass for individual countries, allowing travel between 3 and 8 days, or Interail Global pass, which allows travel for a continuous period of 22 days to one month. When purchasing a rail ticket – whether in France or abroad – it is also possible to pre-book a car (*Train + Auto*) or bike (*Train + Vélo*)

to await you at your destination, or even a hotel (*Train + Hôtel*).

Discounts and passes are not valid on certain dates and at certain times. The SNCF *Calendrier Voyageurs* (Travellers' Calendar), available at all stations, shows blue and white periods. Almost all fare reductions are valid only in blue periods. The white period is normally only Monday 5–10am and Friday and Sunday 3–8pm.

For 10€ the Pass Bretagne allows unlimited travel in Brittany on TER trains and SNCF buses on Saturdays, mid-June to mid-September.

TIMETABLES

French railway timetables change twice a year, in May and September. Stations sell

Passengers in the ticket hall at Rennes railway station

the SNCF's *Ville-à-Ville* timetable, which details main-line routes nationwide. SNCF also provides regional time-tables and issues free leaflets giving information on travel-ling with children, reduced fares, train travel for disabled people and the TGV network.

DIRECTORY

Eurostar
London St Pancras International
Tel 08705 186 186 (from the UK). **www**.eurostar.com

Rail Europe
1 Regent St, London SW1
Tel 0844 848 4064.
www.raileurope.co.uk

Rail Europe Group
Westchester One, 44 South Broadway, White Plains, New York, NY 10601.
Tel 888 438 7245 (freephone from the US).
www.raileurope.com

SNCF France
Tel (00 33) 0892 353 539 (English). **www**.voyages-sncf.com

The railway station at Brest

Brittany by Road

Brittany has an excellent road network. Roads linking its major towns and cities consist both of motorways, which are toll-free, and of fast dual carriageways. By following Brittany's major roads and more especially its minor roads, visitors will discover picturesque villages and remote places of interest. Many of the coast roads command spectacular views.

Road sign for a roundabout

A minor road in Brittany with a magnificent view of the sea

GETTING TO FRANCE BY CAR OR COACH

There is a good choice of car-ferry services from various destinatons in the UK (*see pp276–7*). You can profit from discount fares for short breaks, a flat rate for a car with up to five passengers. You can take your car on the **Eurotunnel** shuttle through the Channel Tunnel. **Eurolines** provides a coach service to Brittany direct from the UK or via Paris.

THE CHANNEL TUNNEL

The Channel Tunnel is a 52-km (31-mile) rail tunnel that runs beneath the English Channel between Britain and France. Its English terminal is at Folkestone, in Kent, and the French terminal is at Sangatte, 3 km (2 miles) from Calais. The terminal leads directly onto motorways – the M20 in England and the A16 in France.

MOTORING IN BRITTANY

Motorways (*autoroutes*) lead directly into Brittany from Caen, in the north, Rennes in the east and Nantes in the south. The main route into Brittany from Paris is the A11 motorway to Le Mans, followed by the A81 motorway, then the M157 to Rennes (see road map on inside back cover).

Once off the motorways, drivers can use the efficient network of major roads (*routes nationales*), which link Brittany's major towns, as well as the more scenic minor roads (*routes départementales*). Roads from Paris can become congested at weekends and at the beginning and end of the summer holidays. The worst times are from mid-July to the end of August. In Brittany itself, congestion on the roads is rare. However, traffic can sometimes build up in coastal resorts towards the end of the day, when people start to leave the beaches and when offices close.

Road signs in French and Breton

WHAT TO TAKE

Many motor insurers now offer a green card (which gives full cover abroad) as a free extension with fully comprehensive policies. The AA, RAC and Europ Assistance also have special policies providing a rescue and recovery service.

It is compulsory to take the original registration document for the car, a current insurance certificate, or green card, and a valid driving licence. You should also carry a passport or National ID card. A sticker showing the car's country of registration must be displayed near the rear number plate. The headlights of right-hand-drive cars must be adjusted for left-hand driving or have deflectors fitted (kits are available at most ports). You must carry spare headlight bulbs, a red warning triangle and a fluorescent jacket if your car does not have hazard warning lights.

RULES OF THE ROAD

Unless road signs indicate otherwise, *priorité a droite* means that you must give way to vehicles joining the road from the right, except on roundabouts or from private property. Most major roads outside built-up areas have the right of way indicated by a *passage protégé* sign.

Contrary to convention in the UK, flashing headlights in France means that the driver is claiming the right of way.

Other French motoring rules include the compulsory wearing of seat belts, the use

One of several fast dual carriageways in Brittany

of booster seats for children under 10, and the obligation to carry a valid driving licence or identification papers at all times. For further details, consult the **RAC** website.

SPEED LIMITS AND FINES

Speed limits in France are as follows:

On *autoroutes*: 130 km/h (80 mph); 110 km/h (70 mph) when it rains.

On dual carriageways: 110 km/h (70 mph); 90–100 km/h (55–60 mph) when it rains.

On other roads: 90 km/h (55 mph); 80 km/h (50 mph) when it rains.

In towns: 50 km/h (30 mph), unless marked otherwise. In some places it may be lower. Normal limits may not always be indicated.

On-the-spot fines of around 150€ are summarily levied for not stopping at a Stop sign, for overtaking where forbidden, or other driving offences. Drink-driving can lead to confiscation of the vehicle or even imprisonment.

BUYING PETROL

Diesel fuel *(gazole or gasoil)* is comparatively cheap in France and is sold almost everywhere. Unleaded petrol *(sans plomb)* is a more expensive option. A cheaper alternative is to visit the larger supermarkets that sell all of them at a discount. Filling up the tank is known as *faire le plein*. Petrol stations in many rural areas will often be closed on Sundays.

Logos of three major car hire companies

AUTOROUTE TOLLS

When you join an *autoroute à péage* (tolled motorway), collect a ticket from the machine as you pass through the toll point. This identifies your starting point on the *autoroute*. You do not pay until you reach an exit toll. You are charged according to the distance travelled and the type of vehicle. While at least two booths per toll point are

A pay-and-display ticket machine, widely used in town car parks

always manned by attendants, automatic machines can also be used. These take coins, and will give change, and also accept credit cards.

CAR HIRE

All the main international car-hire companies operate in France. They have offices either in Brittany's main airports or in the centre of major towns.

It is worth ringing round before you leave for France as there are many special offers for rentals booked and prepaid in the UK or USA.

For car hire booked in combination with flights, your travel agent can usually organize a good deal. SNCF (the French state railway) offers combined train and car-hire fares. Phone **Rail Europe** for information *(see p273).*

For non-EU residents planning to drive in France for a minimum of three weeks, the best option is the short-term tax-free purchase-and-buy-back service (TT leasing) offered by Citröen, Peugeot and Renault.

PARKING

Finding a parking space in coastal towns in Brittany during the summer can be difficult. However, almost all large towns have car parks with a pay-and-display system *(horodateur).* Villages have free, usually very central, parking areas.

DIRECTORY

ROAD CONDITIONS

RAC
Great Park Road, Bradley, Stoke, Bristol BS32 4QN. *Tel 09064 701 740.* **www**.rac.co.uk

Autoroute information
Tel 0892 681 077.

CriCr western France (Centre Régional d'Information et de Coordination Routière de l'Ouest)
Tel 0826 022 022.

COACH COMPANY

Eurolines
Tel 0892 899 091.
www.eurolines.com

CHANNEL TUNNEL

Eurotunnel
Tel 0810 630 304.
Tel 08705 35 35 35 in UK.
www.eurotunnel.com

TT LEASING

Citroën
25 Rue de Constantinople, 75008 Paris *Tel (01) 53 04 34 80.*
www.citroentt.com

Peugeot Open Europe
115 Avenue de l'Arche, 92400 Courbevoie
Tel (01) 49 04 81 81 (Paris)

Renault Eurodrive
Renault Ventes Spéciales Exportation,
186 Avenue Jean-Jaurès, 75019 Paris.
Tel 0825 101 112 (Paris).

CAR-HIRE COMPANIES

Avis
Tel 0820 050 505.
www.avis.fr

Budget
Tel 0825 003 564.
www.budget.com

Europcar
Tel 0825 358 358.
www.europcar.com

Hertz
Tel 0825 861 861.
www.hertz.fr

Rent-a-car
Tel 0891 700 200.
www.rentacar.fr

Brittany by Boat

Breton motorboat

With frequent ferry crossings from the UK to Roscoff, St-Malo and Cherbourg, as well to destinations further north along the French coast, Brittany is easy to reach by sea. As with the rail shuttle through the Channel Tunnel, travelling by ferry allows you the convenience of bringing your own car.

With Belle-Île, the Île d'Ouessant and the Golfe du Morbihan among its most picturesque attractions, Brittany also invites exploration by boat. A wide range of boat trips are on offer. There are regular sea links to Brittany's many islands, and trips out to sea in old sailing ships. Sailing along Brittany's rivers and canals, which are now reserved for pleasure boats, is a particularly pleasant way of experiencing the riches and variety of Brittany's cultural heritage.

Motorboat approaching the landing stage at Roscoff

CHANNEL FERRIES

In addition to the Eurotunnel vehicle-carrying rail shuttles (*see p272*), there are several ship or catamaran crossings between the UK and Continental ports.

P&O Ferries now no longer run from Portsmouth and only run from Dover to Calais. **Brittany Ferries**, however, runs high-speed services from Portsmouth to Caen (6 hrs), Cherbourg (3 hours), St-Malo (11 hrs) and a service from Plymouth to Roscoff (6–8 hrs) and Poole to Cherbourg (3 hrs). Also, from Poole to Cherbourg, **Condor** Ferries has a conventional ship (4 hrs 30 mins), and a fast ferry, the

Passengers disembarking on the Île de Sein

DIRECTORY

LINKS TO THE ISLANDS

Compagnie Navix (Arz)
Tel 0825 16 21 00. **www**.navix.fr.

Compagnie Océane
(Belle-Île, Île de Groix, Houat, de Hoedic) *Tel* 0820 056 156.
www.compagnie-oceane.fr

Vedettes de Bréhat
(Bréhat)
Tel (02) 96 55 73 47.
www.vendettesdebrehat.com

Armein (Batz)
Tel (02) 98 61 77 75.
www.armein.fr

Golfe du Morbihan
(Île de Houat)
Tel 0825 134 110.
www.compagniedesiles.com

Penn-Ar-Bed Brest
(Molène, Ouessant, Sein)
Tel (02) 98 80 80 80.
www.pennarbed.fr

Vedette Biniou-II (Sein)
Tel (02) 98 70 21 15.
www.vendette-biniou.fr

Navix
(Belle-Île, Le Golfe, Île de Houat)
Tel 0825 132 100.

La Morbihannaise
(Belle-Île, Île de Groix) *Tel* 0820 056 000. **www**.smn-navigation.fr

Vedettes de l'Odet
(Îles de Glénan)
Tel (02) 98 57 00 58.

Izenah Croisière
(Île aux Moines)
Tel (02) 97 26 31 45.

CANAL & RIVER TRIPS

CÔTES D'ARMOR

Vedettes de Guerlédan
22530 Caurel.
Tel (02) 96 28 52 64.

Vedette Jaman 4
22108 Dinan.
Tel (02) 96 39 28 41.

FINISTÈRE

Aulne Loisirs-Plaisance
29520 Châteauneuf-du-Faou.
Tel (02) 98 73 28 63.

ILLE-ET-VILAINE

Cotre Corsaire Le Renard
35408 St-Malo.
Tel (02) 99 40 53 10.

LOIRE-ATLANTIQUE

Bateaux Nantais
44000 Nantes.
Tel (02) 40 14 51 14.

MORBIHAN

L'Étoile du Blavet
56930 Plumeliau.
Tel (02) 97 51 83 09.

FERRIES

Brittany Ferries
Tel 0825 828 828.
www.brittany-ferries.com

Condor Ferries
Tel 0825 13 51 35.
www.condorferries.com

LD Lines
Tel 0825 30 43 04. **www**.ldlines.fr

P&O Ferries
www.poferries.com

Condor Vitesse (2 hrs 15 mins).
LD Lines runs a service from
Newhaven to Le Havre and
Irish Ferries sail from Rosslare
to Cherbourg (16 hours) and
to Roscoff (15 hours).

BOAT AND CANAL TRIPS

There are many opportu-
nities for visitors to take
boats trips out to sea, usually
in an old restored sailing
boat and usually lasting
either a full day or half a day.
Cotre Corsaire Le Renard
organizes trips in the Baie de
St-Malo of one or several
days. Various suggestions for
boat trips out to sea appear at
the head of the relevant

entries in this guide.
Information on other boat
trips and cruises is available
from tourist offices.

Brittany has 600 km (375
miles) of canals and navigable
rivers. There are several
major routes. One, an 85-km
(53-mile) trip along the
Ille-et-Rance canal and the
Vilaine river, goes from St-
Malo, in the north, to La
Roche-Bernard, in the
south. Others are the
Nantes–Brest canal (360
km/225 miles long), which
joins the Erdre, Oust and
Aulne rivers, the Blavet
valley (Lorient to Pontivy),
and St-Nazaire to Nantes,
along the Loire.

The small harbour at Dinan,
on the Rance river

SEA LINKS TO THE ISLANDS

Brittany's largest islands all have sea links
with the nearest harbour on the mainland.
The routes are: Vannes–Île d'Arz (15 mins);
Pointe de l'Arcouest–Île de Bréhat (15 mins);
St-Quay-Portrieux–Île de Bréhat (1 hr 15
mins); Roscoff–Île de Batz (15 mins); Le
Conquet/Brest–Île d'Ouessant (1 hr/ 2 hrs 30

mins); Le Conquet/Brest–Île Molène (30
mins/1 hr 45 mins); Crozon/Audierne–Île de
Sein (1 hr); Lorient–Belle-Île (1 hr 30 mins);
Quiberon–Belle-Île (45 mins); Lorient–Groix
(45 mins); Concarneau–Îles de Glénan (1 hr);
Bénodet/Loctudy–Îles de Glénan (1 hr
30 mins); Quiberon–Houat (45 mins)
Quiberon–Hoëdic (1 hr 10 mins/ 1 hr 25 mins);
Port-Blanc–Île aux Moines (5 mins).

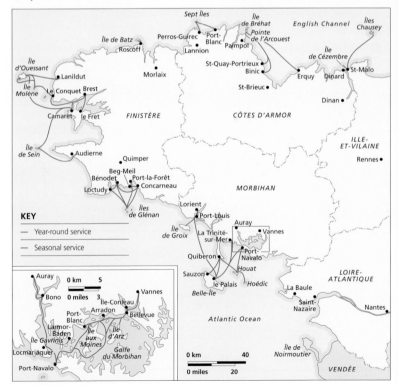

General Index

Acknowledgments

Dorling Kindersley would like to thank the following people and institutions whose contributions and assistance have made the preparation of this book possible.

Main Contributors

Gaëtan du Chatenet
Entomologist, ornitholist, corresponding member of the Muséum National d'Histoire Naturelle de Paris, draughtsman and miniature painter, Gaëtan du Chatenet is the author of many works published by Delachaux & Niestlé and Gallimard.

Jean-Philippe Follet
Jean-Philippe Follet, who was born and brought up in the Morlaix area, studied at the Faculté de Celtique in Rennes and at the Centre de Recherches Bretonnes et Celtiques in Brest. He works as a writer and translator.

Jean-Yves Gendillard
The son of Breton parents, Jean-Yves Gendillard is a teacher. He has a special interest in Brittany and in religious art. He has spent a considerable amount of time in southern Finistère, and has a particular knowledge of the chapels and calvaries of that area.

Éric Gibory
Born in St-Malo, Éric Gibory spent his childhood and adolescence there. He has helped to organize cultural events, is the author of four *Guides Bleus* published by Hachette and has contributed to several travel magazines.

Renée Grimaud
A specialist in tourism, Renée Grimaud has contributed to many travel guides and has edited several illustrated books on the regions of France, notably on the Loire and its chateaux. A native of the Vendée, she has a detailed knowledge of the Loire region and of Brittany, which she visits regularly.

Georges Minois
A senior history teacher at the Lycée Renan in St-Brieuc and the holder of a doctorate, George Minois is also the author of 30 books, including several on Brittany, such as *Nouvelle Histoire de la Bretagne*, *Anne de Bretagne* and *Du Guesclin*, published by Fayard.

Other Contributors
Sophie Berger, Vanessa Besnard, Isabelle De Jaham, Marie-Christine Degos, Mathilde Huyghes-Despointes, Lyn Parry, Sonia Rocton, Sarah Thurin and Sébastien Tomasi.

Photography
Philippe Giraud.

Studio Photography and Additional Photography
Max Alexander, Anne Chopin, Andrew Holligan, Ian O'Leary.

Picture Research
Marie-Christine Petit.

Cartography
Fabrice Le Goff.

Additional Cartography
Quadrature Créations.

Illustrations

François Brosse
Architectural drawings, Street-by-Street maps and drawings pp56–7, 78–9, 108—9, 116–17, 158–9, 166–7, 184–5, 186–7.

Anne Delaunay-Vernhes
Architectural drawings pp60–1, 104–5, 122–3, 162–3, 192–3, 208–9.

Éric Geoffroy
Illustrations on "Exploring" and "At a Glance" maps, on small town plans and tour maps pp50–1, 54–5, 59, 76, 81, 88–9, 98, 103, 114–15, 126–7, 133, 140–1, 144–5, 161, 172–3, 182–3, 189, 198–9, 202–3, 205.

Emmanuel Guillon
Façades, perspectives and artwork pp18–19, 20–21, 104–5, 122–3, 151, 192–3, 208–9.

Guénola de Sandol
Artwork pp60–1, 162–3.

Proofreaders
Cate Casey, Emily Hatchwell.

Index
Lucilla Watson

Special Assistance
M. Alexandre and M. Tournaire at Service Départemental de l'Architecture et du Patrimoine du Finistère; Mme Delmotte, M. Charles-Tanguy Leroux and M. Christian Gerardot of DRAC de Bretagne; Marie Godicheau of the Service Météorologique de Rennes; M. Guillet, Château des Ducs de Bretagne; M. Job an Irien of Éditions Minihi-Levenez; M. le Curé Louis Le Bras and M. Paul Nemar of the church at Crozon; Henri Le Roux (butter toffees, Quiberon); Philippe Le Stum, curator at the Musée Départemental Breton in Quimper; Mathieu Lefèvre of the festival *Étonnants Voyageurs*, St-Malo; the mayor of St-Malo; Florent Patron of Éditions Coop Breizh; M. Alain-Charles Perrot (Parlement de Bretagne); Mme Marie-Suzanne de Ponthaud (head architect, Cathédrale St-Tugdual, Tréguier); Océanopolis, Brest; public relations department, Banque de France; information service, *Bretagne Magazine*; public relations department, La Poste; public relations department of the city of St-Malo for the *Quai des Bulles* festival; press office, Air France; press office, *Transmusicales*, Rennes; ADA; Musée des Vieux Outils, Tinténiac; Musée des Terre-Neuvas, Fécamp. Armor Lux (clothing, Quimper); Saint-James (clothing, Saint-James); Phytomer (beauty products, St-Malo); Thalado (beauty products, Roscoff); Verreries de Bréhat; the shop Quimper-Faïence de Paris; Fisselier (traditionally made liqueurs, Chantepie).

Design and Editorial Assistance
Claire Baranowski, Sonal Bhatt, Simon Davis, Rhiannon Furbear, Amanda Hodgkinson, Carly Madden, Sangita Patel, Pollyanna Poulter, Ellen Root, Dora Whitaker.

Photography Permissions
The publisher would like to thank those individuals who gave permission to photograph on their premises:

Mme Martine Abgrall, for the alignments at Carnac; Mme Martine Becus, at the Château des Rochers Sévigné in Vitré; Florence and Marc Benoît, at the Hôtel La Reine Hortense in Dinard; Mme Burnot, curator at the Musée du Château de Dinan; M. de Calbiac, at the Manoir de Kerazan; Mme Caprini and Lan Mafart, at the Librairie Caplan in Guimaec; Mme Gaillot, at the Musée de la Pêche in Concarneau; M. and Mme Gautier, in Plouezoc'h; M. Bernard Guillet and Christelle Goldet, at the Château des Ducs de Bretagne in Nantes; M. Hommel, of the Musée de l'Automobile in Lohéac; M. Patrick Jourdan, curator at the Musée des Jacobins in Morlaix; M. Le Goff, of the Musée du Léon in Lesneven; M. Bernard Lefloc'h, of the Musée Bigouden in Pont-L'Abbé; Mme Lilia Millier, at the Hôtel Castel Marie Louise in La Baule; Mme Françoise Louis, for the Château de Suscinio; M. Mézin, curator at the Musée de la Compagnie des Indes in Port-Louis; Mme Quintin, at the Musée de la Fraise in Plougastel-Daoulas; Mme Riskine, curator at the Musée de la Préhistoire in Carnac; Mme de Rohan, at the Château de Josselin; Mme de Sagazan, at the Manoir de Traonjoly in Cléder; Mme Michèle Sallé, at the Château de la Hunaudaye; M. Sanchez, at the Parlement de Bretagne in Rennes; M. Jacques Thorel, at the Auberge Bretonne in Roche-Bernard; M. Bernard Verlingue, curator at the Musée de la Faïence in Quimper; Faïencerie H. B. Henriot in Quimper. The staff at the Château de Kerjean; the staff at the brasserie La Cigale in Nantes; the director at the Parc Animalier de Menez-Meur; Camac Harps in Mouzeil; the staff at the Maison de la Mariée on the Île de Fédrun; the owner of the Château de Goulaine; the shop L'Épée de Bois in Paris. The publisher would also like to thank all those who gave permission to photograph at various other shops, restaurants, cafés, hotels, churches and publics places too numerous to mention individually.

Picture Credits

Every effort has been made to trace the copyright holders and we apologize in advance for any unintentional omissions. We would be pleased to insert the appropriate acknowledgments in any subsequent edition of this publication.

t = top; tl = top left; tlc = top left centre; tc = top centre; trc = top right centre; tr = top right; cra = centre right above; cl = centre left; c = centre; cr = centre right; clb = centre left below; cb = centre below; crb = centre right below; bl = below left; b = below; bc = below centre; bcl = below centre left; bcr = below centre right; br = below right.

The publisher would like to thank the following individuals, companies and picture libraries for permission to reproduce their photographs:

6–7: RMN/R.-G. Ojeda. *Port Breton*, Paul Bellanger-Adhémar. Château-Musée, Nemours. **7**: Hachette/drawing by F. Benoist et Sabatier. **8cla**: Alamy Images/Stockfolio. **8tc**: Alamy Images/Claude Thibault. **9cl**: Alamy Images/Jon Arnold Images/Walter Bibikow. **9br**: Corbis/Robert Estall. **9tr**: Chris Lisle. **13a**: Musée Départemental

Breton. *Souvenirs de la Bretagne*, Louis Caradec (1850). **14c**: Béghin-Say. **16tl**: Jacana/S. Chevalier. **16tr**: Jacana/S. Cordier. **16cl**: Jacana/C. Bahr. **16cr**: Jacana/M. and A. Boet. **16bcl**: Jacana/H. Brehm. **16bcr**: Jacana/M. and A. Boet. **16bl**: Jacana/S. Cordier. **16br**: Jacana/W. Wisniewski. **17a**: Jacana/G. Ziesler. **17cl**: Jacana/B. Coster. **17cml**: Jacana/P. Prigent. **17cmr**: Jacana/C. Nardin. **17cr**: Jacana/S. Cordier. **17bl**: Jacana/P. Prigent. **17br**: Jacana/P. Prigent. **22tr**: R. Viollet. **22bl**: M. Thersiquel. **22br**: R. Viollet/Viollet Collection. **23t**: Darnis. **23c**: Darnis. **23b**: Andia Presse/Betermin. **24al**: A. Chopin. **24tr**: Éditions Minihi Levenez/ Y. Le Berre, B. Tanguy, Y. P. Castel. **24c**: Éditions Coop. Breizh. **24b**: Keystone Illustration. **25tl**: Corbis/Sygma/S. Bassouls. **25tr**: Scope/B. Galeron. **25c**: J. L. Charmet. *La Revue Illustrée*. Bibliothèque des Arts Décoratifs, Paris. **25b**: Rue des Archives. **26–7c**: M. Thersiquel. Fête des Brodeuses, Pont-l'Abbé. **26tr**: G. Dagli Orti. *Femmes de Plougastel au Pardon de Ste-Anne*, C. Cottet. Musée des Beaux-Arts, Rennes. **26cl**: Michael Thersiquel, brooch by P. Toulhoat. **26cr**: R. Viollet. **26bl**: M. Thersiquel. **26bc**: Éditions Jos Le Doaré. **26br**: Éditions Jos Le Doaré. **27al**: Gernot. Brest. **27 tr**: Éditions Jos Le Doaré. **27c**: Musée Départemental Breton, Quimper. **27bl, bc, br**: Éditions Jos Le Doaré. **28b**: Étonnants Voyageurs festival, Rennes. *Whales in the Ice in the Arctic*, William Bradford, Brandywine, Calgary, Canada. **29t**: A.-L. Gac. **30b**: G. Cazade, public relations, St-Malo. **31b**: A.-L. Gac. **32tr**: Scope/B. Galeron. **32tl**: R. Viollet. **32c**: Hachette/ C. Boulanger. **32bl**: Scope/B. Galeron. **32br**: Andia Presse/Le Coz. **33ar**: Scope/B. Galeron. **33br**: Y. Boëlle. **34**: AKG Paris. *Chronique de Bretagne*, Pierre Le Beau. Bibliothèque Nationale, Paris. **37t**: Leemage/L. de Selva. Morlaix church. **37c**: Archbishopric of Rennes. Cartulaire de Redon No. 9, 11th century. **38t**: *Josse. Capture of Dinan and Rendering the Keys*. Musée de la Tapisserie, Bayeux. **38c**: Josse, BN, Paris. **38b**: Hachette. **39a**: Leemage/L. de Selva. **39c**: AKG Paris/J. P. Dumontier. Église St-Yves, La Roche Meurice. **39b**: RMN/J.G. Berizzi. Musée des Traditions Populaires, Paris. **40t & 40c**: AKG Paris. *Chronique de Bretagne*, Pierre Le Beau. Bibliothèque Nationale, Paris. **41t**: G. Dagli Orti. *Chronique en Prose de Bertrand Du Guesclin*. Bibliothèque Municipale, Rouen. **41c**: Josse. *Procès de Gilles de Rais*. Bibliothèque Nationale, Paris. **41bl**: G. Dagli Orti. Detail of Dance of Death fresco. La Ferté Loupière church. **41bl**: Hachette. **42tl**: RMN. Miniature of Anne of Brittany (1499). Musée de la Renaissance, Écouen. **42tr**: Leemage/ L. de Selva. Coat of arms of Anne of Brittany (1514). Bibliothèque Municipale, Rennes. **42–3c**: G. Dagli Orti. *Marriage of Charles VIII and Anne of Brittany*, St-Èvre. Château de Versailles. **42cl**: *Chroniques et Histoires de Bretons*, Pierre Le Beau, Bibliothèque Nationale, Paris. **43tl**: Josse. *Louis XII and Anne of Brittany*. Musée Condé, Chantilly. **43tr**: G. Dagli Orti. *Vie des Femmes Célèbres*, A. du Four. Musée Dobrée, Nantes. **43c**: Bridgeman/Giraudon. *Claude de France*. Pushkin Museum, Moscow. **43bl**: G. Dagli Orti. Biblioteca Marciana, Venice. **43br**: Charles Hémon. Gold reliquary with the heart of Anne of Brittany. Musée Dobrée, Nantes. **44tl**: Marine Nationale, Service Historique de la Marine, Brest. *Carte Britanniae*. **44c**: RMN/F. Raux. *François d'Argouges* (1669), J. Frosne. Château de Versailles and Trianon. **44bl**: Hachette. Engraving by the Rouargues brothers. **45t**: AKG Paris/

S. Domingie. *Campaign of the Holy League in Brittany.* Uffizi, Florence. **45c**: G. Dagli Orti. Lollain, private collection, Paris. **45b**: Hachette. **46a**: AKG Paris. *Jean Cottereau*, A.F. Carrière. Bibliothèque Nationale, Paris. **46c**: G. Dagli Orti. Musée Dobrée, Nantes. **46bl**: Hachette. Engraving by Berthault after Swebach-Desfontaines. **46br**: Hachette. Lithograph by Bernard-Romain Julien. **47t**: RMN/Arnaudet. Opening of the railway line from Paris to Brest. Musée de la Voiture, Château de Compiègne **47b**: A. Chopin. **49**: Hachette. Engraving by Y. M. Le Gouaz. Bibliothèque Nationale, Paris. **51bl**: Andia Presse/Diathem. **57b**: Robien Collection. *Head of an Angel*, Botticelli. Musée des Beaux-Arts, Rennes. **58b**: RMN. *Effet de Vagues*, Georges Lacombe. Musée des Beaux-Arts, Rennes. **61c**: Inventaire Général-ADAGP/C. Arthur/Lambart, 1998. *La Félicité Publique.* Centre de Documentation du Patrimoine, Rennes. **63t**: G. Dagli Orti. *The Romance of Tristan* (11th century). Musée Condé, Chantilly. **63cl**: AKG Paris. *Histoire de Merlin*, R. de Boron. Bibliothèque Nationale, Paris. **63cr**: Hachette. *The Holy Grail Appears before the Knights of the Round Table.* Bibliothèque Nationale, Paris. **63bl**: J. L. Charmet. *King Arthur and the Knights of the Round Table*, fresco by Viollet-Le-Duc. Bibliothèque des Arts Décoratifs, Paris. **63br**: J. L. Charmet. *Merlin and Vivien*, Gustave Doré. Bibliothèque des Arts Décoratifs, Paris. **67b**: Hachette. **68c**: D. Provost. clogs, 1928. Musée de l'Outil et des Métiers, Tinténiac. **69b**: Hachette. Lithograph by Lardereau. **72**: Dorling Kindersley except **72b**: Hachette/Musée de Bayeux. **73–5**: Dorling Kindersley. **77t**: Jacana/M. Willemeit. **82a**: Lee Miller. **94br**: Gaulish village, Pleumeur Bodou. **95b**: Jacana/J. T. Guillots. **97b**: Bertrand Brelivet Collection/carte-postale.com. **99br**: RMN/ P. Bernard. *Rue à Bréhat*, Henri Dabadie. Musée des Beaux-Arts, Lille. **101a**: G. Dagli Orti. Engraving from *Petit Journal.* **102bl**: Alain Grenier, private collection. **104b**: Quintin town hall. Musée-Atelier des Toiles de Lin. **105c**: Musée Mathurin Méheut, Lamballe. **117cr**: Musée de Morlaix. **119t**: P. Seitz/Caplan and Co. café-bookshop, Morlaix. **121t**: Office Municipal de Tourisme, Roscoff. Musée des Johnnies. **127t**: Musée Départemental Breton/P. Sicard. *Le Miroir du Monde*, Michel le Nobletz. See of Quimper. **127br**: Écomusée des Goémoniers et de l'Algue/ S. Allançon, Plouguerneau. **129c**: Jacana/B. Coster. **133t**: RMN/J. de la Baume. *La Mer Jaune*, Georges Lacombe. Musée des Beaux-Arts, Brest. **135tl**: Georges Perrot, Brest. **135tr**: Océanopolis/ T. Joyeux. **147b**: Abbaye de Landevennec. Frontispiece of the Évangéliaire de Landevennec

(c. 870). **148–9**: Louis Le Bras, parish priest at Crozon. **153b**: SCOPE/B. Galeron. **155t**: Keystone. **158tr**: Musée Départemental Breton, Quimper. **158tl**: Musée Départemental Breton, Quimper. **161t**: RMN/M. Bellot. *Le Génie à la Guirlande*, Charles Filiger. **164cl, cr, c**: Musée Départemental Breton, Quimper. **167br**: Josse. Musée du Château, Versailles. **168b**: Le Gonidec canning factory. **169b**: Josse. *La Belle Angèle*, P. Gauguin. Musée d'Orsay, Paris. **177t**: Keystone Illustration. **181tl**: Gamma/T. Rannou. **194b**: Pontivy town hall. **199br**: Chateau Clisson. **205t**: RMN/ M. Bellot. *Louis XII and Anne of Brittany at Prayer.* Musée Dobrée, Nantes. **206tl**: Musée du Château des Ducs de Bretagne. **206b**: G. Dagli Orti. Musée Dobrée, Nantes. **207al**: ADAGP, Paris 2002/RMN/C. Jean. *Le Gaulage des Pommes*, Émile Bernard. Musée des Beaux-Arts, Nantes. **207ar**: Hachette. Musée de Chantilly. *Duc de Mercoeur.* **211b**: Josse/Anonyme. *D'Elbée Libérant les Prisonniers Bleus*, Cholet. **213**: J.L. Charmet. *L'Hôtel de France à St-Malo.* Musée Carnavalet, Paris. **214bl**: La Villa Kerasy. **217t**: Logis de France. **217tl**: Fédération Unie des Auberges de Jeunesse – www.fuaj.org. **232t**: Coreff. Brasserie des Deux Rivières, Morlaix. **233bc**: Hemispheres Images: Philippe Renault. **233cr**: Alamy Images/Stockfolio. **235c**: Alamy Images/AA World Travel Library. **235tl**: Authors Image/Christine Pinhera. **250a**: Conserverie Le Gonidec. **250cl**: CRTB/ J.P.Gratien. **251t**: CRTB/Martin Schulte-Kellinghaus. **251b**: G. Fisher. **252**: A. Chopin except *Almanach du MarinBreton*: œuvre du Marin Breton, and nautilus shells: Verreries de Bréhat. **253**: A. Chopin. **254t**: A.-L. Gac. **254b**: G. Saliou. **261**:Hachette. View of Brest harbour. **262cb**: Brittany Tourism. **262cla**: Francois Le Divenah. **263cl**: TV Breizh. **263cr**: *Armen; Bretagne Magazine.* **263b**: A. Chopin. **266c**: Dorling Kindersley/ M. Alexander. **267**: Banque de France. **268**: Dorling Kindersley/M. Alexander. **269t**: Andia Presse/Bigot. **270t**: Brit Air. **270c**: Dorling Kindersley/P. Kenward. **272t**: Dorling Kindersley/M. Alexander. **272b**: SNCF-CAV/Fabro & Levêque. **274tl**: Dorling Kindersley/M. Alexander. **275**: Dorling Kindersley/M. Alexander.

Jacket: Front – Getty Images: Stone/Peter Cadec main; NHPA: John Shaw clb. Back – DK Images: Philippe Giraud cla, bl; John Heseltine clb; Roger Hilton tl. Spine – DK Images: Ann Chopin b; Getty Images: Stone/Peter Cadec t.

SPECIAL EDITIONS OF DK TRAVEL GUIDES

DK Travel Guides can be purchased in bulk quantities at discounted prices for use in promotions or as premiums. We are also able to offer special editions and personalized jackets, corporate imprints, and excerpts from all of our books, tailored specifically to meet your own needs.

To find out more, please contact:
(in the United States) **SpecialSales@dk.com**
(in the UK) **travelspecialsales@uk.dk.com**
(in Canada) DK Special Sales at **general@tourmaline.ca**
(in Australia)
business.development@pearson.com.au

Phrase Book

In Emergency

Help!	Au secours!	oh sekoor
Stop!	Arrêtez!	aret-ay
Call a doctor!	Appelez un médecin!	apuh-lay uñ medsañ
Call an ambulance!	Appelez une ambulance!	apuh-lay oon oñboo-loñs
Call the police!	Appelez la police!	apuh-lay lah poh-lees
Call the fire department!	Appelez les pompiers!	apuh-lay leh poñ-peeyay
Where is the nearest telephone?	Où est le téléphone le plus proche	oo ay luh tehlehfon luh ploo prosh
Where is the nearest hospital?	Où est l'hôpital le plus proche?	oo ay luh opeetal luh ploo prosh

Communication Essentials

Yes	Oui	wee
No	Non	noñ
Please	S'il vous plaît	seel voo play
Thank you	Merci	mer-see
Excuse me	Excusez-moi	exkoo-zay mwah
Hello	Bonjour	boñzhoor
Goodbye	Au revoir	oh ruh-vvwar
Good night	Bonsoir	boñ-swar
Morning	Le matin	matañ
Afternoon	L'après-midi	l'apreh-meedee
Evening	Le soir	swar
Yesterday	Hier	eeyehr
Today	Aujourd'hui	oh-zhoor-dwee
Tomorrow	Demain	duhmañ
Here	Ici	ee-see
There	Là	lah
What?	Quel, quelle?	kel, kel
When?	Quand?	koñ
Why?	Pourquoi?	poor-kwah
Where?	Où?	oo

Useful Phrases

How are you?	Comment allez-vous?	kom-moñ talay voo
Very well, thank you.	Très bien, merci.	treh byañ, mer-see
Pleased to meet you.	Enchanté de faire votre connaissance.	oñshoñ-tay duh fehr votr kon-ay-sans
See you soon.	A bientôt.	byañ-toh
That's fine.	Voilà qui est parfait	vwalah kee ay parfay
Where is/are...?	Où est/sont...?	oo ay/soñ
How far is it to...?	Combien de kilomètres d'ici à...?	kom-byañ duh keelo-metr d'ee-see ah
Which way to...?	Quelle est la direction pour...?	kel ay lah deer-ek-syoñ poor
Do you speak English?	Parlez-vous anglais?	par-lay voo oñg-lay
I don't understand.	Je ne comprends pas.	zhuh nuh kom-proñ pah
Could you speak slowly please?	Pouvez-vous parler moins vite s'il vous plaît?	poo-vay voo par-lay mwañ veet seel voo play
I'm sorry.	Excusez-moi.	exkoo-zay mwah

Useful Words

big	grand	groñ
small	petit	puh-tee
hot	chaud	show
cold	froid	frwah
good	bon	boñ
bad	mauvais	moh-veh
enough	assez	assay
well	bien	byañ
open	ouvert	oo-ver
closed	fermé	fer-meh
left	gauche	gohsh
right	droit	drwah
straight ahead	tout droit	too drwah
near	près	preh
far	loin	lwañ
up	en haut	oñ oh
down	en bas	oñ bah
early	de bonne heure	duh bon urr
late	en retard	oñ ruh-tar
entrance	l'entrée	l'on-tray
exit	la sortie	sor-tee
toilet	les toilettes, les WC	twah-let, vay-see
free, unoccupied	libre	leebr
free, no charge	gratuit	grah-twee

Making a Telephone Call

I'd like to place a long-distance call.	Je voudrais faire un interurbain.	zhuh voo-dreh fehr uñ añter-oorbañ
I'd like to make a collect call.	Je voudrais faire une communication PCV.	zhuh voodreh fehr oon komoonikah-syoñ peh-seh-veh
I'll try again later.	Je rappelerai plus tard.	zhuh rapel-eray ploo tar
Can I leave a message?	Est-ce que je peux laisser un message?	es-keh zhuh puh leh-say uñ mehsazh
Hold on.	Ne quittez pas, s'il vous plaît.	nuh kee-tay pah seel voo play
Could you speak up a little please?	Pouvez-vous parler un peu plus fort?	poo-vay voo par-lay uñ puh ploo for
local call	la communication locale	komoonikah-syoñ low-kal

Shopping

How much does this cost?	C'est combien s'il vous plaît?	say kom-byañ seel voo play
I would like ...	je voudrais...	zhuh voo-dray
Do you have?	Est-ce que vous avez?	es-kuh voo zavay
I'm just looking.	Je regarde seulement.	zhuh ruhgar suhlmoñ
Do you take credit cards?	Est-ce que vous acceptez les cartes de crédit?	es-kuh voo zaksept-ay leh kart duh kreh-dee
Do you take traveler's checks?	Est-ce que vous acceptez les chèques de voyage?	es-kuh voo zaksept-ay leh shek duh vwayazh
What time do you open?	A quelle heure vous êtes ouvert?	ah kel urr voo zet oo-ver
What time do you close?	A quelle heure vous êtes fermé?	ah kel urr voo zet fer-may
This one.	Celui-ci.	suhl-wee-see
That one.	Celui-là.	suhl-wee-lah
expensive	cher	shehr
cheap	pas cher, bon marché	pah shehr, boñ mar-shay
size, clothes	la taille	tye
size, shoes	la pointure	pwañ-tur
white	blanc	bloñ
black	noir	nwahr
red	rouge	roozh
yellow	jaune	zhohwn
green	vert	vehr
blue	bleu	bluh

Types of Shops

antiques shop	le magasin d'antiquités	maga-zañ d'oñteekee-tay
bakery	la boulangerie	booloñ-zhuree
bank	la banque	boñk
book store	la librairie	lee-brehree
butcher	la boucherie	boo-shehree
cake shop	la pâtisserie	patee-sree
cheese shop	la fromagerie	fromazh-ree
dairy	la crémerie	krem-ree
department store	le grand magasin	groñ maga-zañ
delicatessen	la charcuterie	sharkoot-ree
drugstore	la pharmacie	farmah-see
fish seller	la poissonnerie	pwasson-ree
gift shop	le magasin de cadeaux	maga-zañ duh kadoh
greengrocer	le marchand de légumes	mar-shoñ duh lay-goom
grocery	l'alimentation	alee-moñta-syoñ
hairdresser	le coiffeur	kwafuhr
market	le marché	marsh-ay
newsstand	le magasin de journaux	maga-zañ duh zhoor-no
post office	la poste, le bureau de poste, le PTT	pohst, booroh duh pohst, peh-teh-teh
shoe store	le magasin de chaussures	maga-zañ duh show-soor
supermarket	le supermarché	soo pehr-marshay
tobacconist	le tabac	tabah
travel agent	l'agence de voyages	l'azhoñs duh vwayazh

Sightseeing

abbey	l'abbaye	l'abay-ee
art gallery	la galerie d'art	galer-ree dart
bus station	la gare routière	gahr roo-tee-yehr

cathedral	la cathédrale	katay-**dral**
church	l'église	l'ay**gleez**
garden	le jardin	zhar-**dañ**
library	la bibliothèque	beeblee**o**-tek
museum	le musée	moo-**zay**
tourist	les renseignements	roñsayn-**moñ** too-
information	touristiques, le	rees-**teek**, sandee-
office	syndicat d'initiative	ka d'eenee-sya**teev**
town hall	l'hôtel de ville	l'oh**tel** duh veel
train station	la gare (SNCF)	gahr (es-en-say-ef)
private mansion	l'hôtel particulier	l'oh**tel** partikoo-**lyay**
closed for	fermeture	fehrmeh-**tur**
public holiday	jour férié	zhoor fehree-ay

Staying in a Hotel

Do you have a	Est-ce que vous	es-kuh voo-**zavay**
vacant room?	avez une chambre?	oon shambr
double room,	la chambre à deux	shambr ah duh
with double bed	personnes, avec	pehr-**son** avek un
	un grand lit	gronñ lee
twin room	la chambre à	shambr ah
	deux lits	duh lee
single room	la chambre à	shambr ah
	une personne	oon pehr-**son**
room with a	la chambre avec	shambr avek
bath, shower	salle de bains,	sal duh bañ,
	une douche	oon doosh
porter	le garçon	gar-**soñ**
key	la clef	klay
I have a	J'ai fait une	zhay fay oon
reservation.	réservation.	rayzehrva-**syoñ**

Eating Out

Have you	Avez-vous une	avay-**voo** oon
got a table?	table libre?	tahbl leebr
I want to	Je voudrais	zhuh voo-**dray**
reserve	réserver	rayzehr-**vay**
a table.	une table.	oon tahbl
The check	L'addition s'il	l'adee-**syoñ** seel
please.	vous plaît.	voo play
I am a	Je suis	zhuh swee
vegetarien.	végétarian.	vezhay-**tehryañ**
Waitress/	Madame,	mah-**dam**,
waiter	Mademoiselle/	mah-demwah**zel**/
	Monsieur	muh-**syuh**
menu	le menu, la carte	men-**oo**, kart
fixed-price	le menu à	men-**oo** ah
menu	prix fixe	pree feeks
cover charge	le couvert	koo-**vehr**
wine list	la carte des vins	**kart**-deh vañ
glass	le verre	vehr
bottle	la bouteille	boo-**tay**
knife	le couteau	koo-**toh**
fork	la fourchette	for-**shet**
spoon	la cuillère	kwee-**yehr**
breakfast	le petit	puh-**tee**
	déjeuner	deh-**zhuh-nay**
lunch	le déjeuner	deh-**zhuh-nay**
dinner	le dîner	dee-**nay**
main course	le plat principal	plah prañsee-**pal**
appetizer, first	l'entrée, le hors	l'oñ-**tray**, or-
course	d'oeuvre	duhvr
dish of the day	le plat du jour	plah doo zhoor
wine bar	le bar à vin	bar ah vañ
café	le café	ka-**fay**
rare	saignant	say-**noñ**
medium	à point	ah **pwañ**
well-done	bien cuit	byañ **kwee**

Menu Decoder

l'agneau	l'anyoh	lamb
l'ail	l'eye	garlic
la banane	banan	banana
le beurre	burr	butter
la bière, bière	bee-**yehr**, bee-yehr	beer, draft
à la pression	ah lah pres-**syoñ**	beer
le bifteck, le steack	beef-**tek**, stek	steak
le boeuf	buhf	beef
bouilli	boo-**yee**	boiled
le café	kah-**fay**	coffee
le canard	kanar	duck
le chocolat	shoko-**lah**	chocolate
le citron	see-**troñ**	lemon
le citron pressé	see-**troñ** press-**eh**	fresh lemon juice
les crevettes	kruh-**vet**	prawns
les crustacés	kroos-ta-**say**	shellfish
cuit au four	kweet oh foor	baked
le dessert	deh-**ser**	dessert

l'eau minérale	l'oh **meeney**-ral	mineral water
les escargots	leh zes-kar-**goh**	snails
les frites	freet	chips
le fromage	from-**azh**	cheese
le fruit frais	frwee freh	fresh fruit
les fruits de mer	frwee duh mer	seafood
le gâteau	gah-**toh**	cake
la glace	glas	ice, ice cream
grillé	gree-**yay**	grilled
le homard	omahr	lobster
l'huile	l'weel	oil
le jambon	zhoñ-**boñ**	ham
le lait	leh	milk
les légumes	lay-**goom**	vegetables
la moutarde	moo-**tard**	mustard
l'oeuf	l'uf	egg
les oignons	leh zon**yoñ**	onions
les olives	leh zo**leev**	olives
l'orange	l'oroñzh	orange
l'orange pressée	l'oroñzh press-**eh**	fresh orange juice
le pain	pan	bread
le petit pain	puh-**tee** pañ	roll
poché	posh-**ay**	poached
le poisson	pwah-**ssoñ**	fish
le poivre	pwavr	pepper
la pomme	pom	apple
les pommes de terre	pom-duh **tehr**	potatoes
le porc	por	pork
le potage	poh-**tazh**	soup
le poulet	poo-**lay**	chicken
le riz	ree	rice
rôti	row-**tee**	roast
la sauce	sohs	sauce
la saucisse	soh**sees**	sausage, fresh
sec	sek	dry
le sel	sel	salt
la soupe	soop	soup
le sucre	sookr	sugar
le thé	tay	tea
le toast	toast	toast
la viande	vee-**yand**	meat
le vin blanc	vañ **bloñ**	white wine
le vin rouge	vañ **roozh**	red wine
le vinaigre	vee**naygr**	vinegar

Numbers

0	zéro	zeh-**roh**
1	un, une	uñ, oon
2	deux	duh
3	trois	trwah
4	quatre	katr
5	cinq	sañk
6	six	sees
7	sept	set
8	huit	weet
9	neuf	nerf
10	dix	dees
11	onze	oñz
12	douze	dooz
13	treize	trehz
14	quatorze	ka**torz**
15	quinze	kañz
16	seize	sehz
17	dix-sept	dees-**set**
18	dix-huit	dees-**weet**
19	dix-neuf	dees-**nerf**
20	vingt	vañ
30	trente	tront
40	quarante	ka**roñt**
50	cinquante	sañk**oñt**
60	soixante	swas**oñt**
70	soixante-dix	swasoñt-**dees**
80	quatre-vingts	katr-**vañ**
90	quatre-vingt-dix	katr-vañ-**dees**
100	cent	soñ
1,000	mille	meel

Time

one minute	une minute	oon mee-**noot**
one hour	une heure	oon urr
half an hour	une demi-heure	oon **duh-mee** urr
Monday	lundi	luñ-**dee**
Tuesday	mardi	mar-**dee**
Wednesday	mercredi	mehrkruh-**dee**
Thursday	jeudi	zhuh-**dee**
Friday	vendredi	voñdruh-**dee**
Saturday	samedi	sam-dee
Sunday	dimanche	dee-**moñsh**